Birds in Place

A Habitat-based Field Guide
to the Birds of the Northern Rockies

BY

Radd Icenoggle

To Melinda for your loving patience,
Dad for all the encouraging words,
Mom for always being there,
Grandma and Auntie Margie for
all the books and National Geographics

ISBN: 1-56037-241-9
Library of Congress Control Number: 2003100445

For more information on our books write:
Farcountry Press, P.O. Box 5630
Helena, MT 50604 or call: (800) 654-1105
or visit www.farcountrypress.com

Created, produced, and designed in the United States. Printed in Korea.

Table of Contents

Thinking Habitat First

Slipping through cattails and bulrushes, an American Bittern blends effortlessly with its environment. The streaked coloration of its body mimics the streaks of shadows and light within the vegetation. This bird lives only within large expanses of wetland vegetation; it is linked to the marsh habitat

type. The elongated shape, defensive posture and plumage are all reflections of the relationship between bird and habitat. If you learn to recognize that characteristics of the wetland habitat, the *"pump-ler-lunk"* call of the Bittern can be easily identifiable to the birder or nature enthusiast.

Habitat can be thought as the platform on which all species stand. Habitat provides a bird with all of the elements that it requires for survival: food, water, and cover. This place, this platform, is essential to the survival of the species. Habitat dictates how birds function in the community and the pattern of occurrence for the species across the broader landscape. Most bird species tend to display a preference for one type of habitat over others. That is not to say that most are obligates to a specific habitat type, rather relatively few bird species could be considered as obligates. I acknowledge that most birds occur in multiple habitats; however, most species show a preference among the habitats in which they are present. There are a few exceptions to this rule, notably American Robin and Great Horned Owl. These habitat preference patterns make it possible to organize the birds of the Northern Rockies by habitats. In this field guide, I have grouped the birds of the Northern Rocky Mountains by 21

types of habitats. The methods by which they were organized were a combination of scientific literature review, observations of others, my own observations, and trends that I have observed.

I concentrated on the Northern Rockies of the United States and Canada, so the habitats could be more easily defined and the bird associations with those particular

1

habitats are clearer. The Rocky Mountains extend 3,100 miles from Canada to New Mexico. The elevations range from about 2,000 feet in the western valleys to 13,800 feet in the Wind River Range, and the widths range from 75 to 405 miles. The Northern Rockies began their existence when they were uplifted in the late Cretaceous period (140 million to 65 million years ago). This is relatively young in terms of geology, and the jagged nature of the Rockies is due to the lack of long-term effects of erosion and recent glaciation. A complex of igneous and metamorphic rock make up these great mountains, although sedimentary rocks are present in northwest Montana and in the Overthrust belt that runs from the Bob

Marshall into Canada. The Rocky Mountains have been glaciated now and again from the Pleistocene Epoch (1.8 million to 70,000 years ago) to fewer than 11,000 years ago. To put the degree of glaciation in context, think about the immensity of Yellowstone National Park at 2.2 million acres and consider that some 15,000 to 20,000 years ago it was 90% covered by glaciers.

The habitats covered in this field guide reach from where the Great Plains touches the Front Range to the wind-swept alpine regions atop the peaks. Habitat and vegetation patterns in the Rockies are determined mainly by elevation, aspect, and precipitation. However, the complexities of environmental gradients such as temperature, solar heat, light, wind, soils, and hydrology play an important role in the establishment of habitats in localized situations.

Habitat is not stagnant, nor is it eternal; it is constantly changing through a variety of processes. Among the events that alter habitat, there are some that are relatively slow and others that happen in the blink of an eye.

Succession is the gradual and continuous process by which one habitat is replaced by another, and it includes living and non-living components. This process is ongoing even though the habitat may appear the same year after year to the observer. Succession comes in two varieties, primary and secondary. Primary succession occurs on bare areas not previously supporting vegetation. Examples include areas of water, sand, or rock. Primary succession begins with soil developed by colonizing plants reacting with the rock over long periods of time and the freeze-thaw action of water to eventually provide bits of soil that, in time, will support larger vegetation. With the accumulation of soil, new plants germinate, grow, and reproduce to begin the stages of a new succession. Secondary succession occurs after a large habitat-altering event such as a catastrophic forest fire, flood, or clear-cutting.

The most stable phase of succession is the climax community, which is also constantly undergoing changes. The communities that come before the climax are known as the seral stages of habitat succession.

As the habitat changes, the community of birds that live within that location will change accordingly.

A great example of succession in action and how the avian community changes over time is the transition of a beaver pond to a mature climax Douglas-fir forest.

When the beavers first build their dam, the newly formed pond floods the surrounding forest and kills the trees that were present. The habitat transforms into the pond habitat, and wetland and riparian habitats on the margins. The birds that can utilize these habitats are Canada Goose and Ring-necked Duck on the pond itself, and Spotted Sandpiper and Lincoln's Sparrow on the margins of the pond. The snags provide nesting for cavity nesters.

As the water-loving plants in the beaver pond complete their lives and die, their organic matter begins to accumulate on the pond's bottom along with incoming sedient, causing the pond to become progressively shallower.
Along the edges, small shrubs and trees have begun to colonize, as well as cattails in the extremely swallow portions of the pond. At this stage of succession, Red-naped Sapsuckers and Wilson's Warblers have moved into the new habitat.

As the beaver pond continues to dry out, sedges colonize the margins of the pond, and water-loving grasses establish a meadow habitat, which draws in the Broad-tailed Hummingbird. Either aspen or cottonwood will gradually replace the shrubs along the outside. Tree Swallows and Downy Woodpeckers simply thrive within this deciduous forest habitat type. The Downy Woodpeckers feed on mostly larval insects in the trees, and the Tree Swallows live in cavities in the forest and feed on the wing over the pond where aquatic larvae hatch into flying insects.

Gradually, pioneering species of conifers begin to fill in the rest of what was once the pond. The process winds up with the climax community becoming established — which community depends on the altitude, latitude and other aspects. If the climax community is moist Douglas-fir, for example, Pileated Woodpeckers and Cassin's Vireo will live in the now mature, climax forest.

The natural world is always in a state of flux. Habitat is never destroyed; it simply changes into another form. The birds that live within these changing habitats also change over time. Habitat and birds have a mutually dependent relationship — habitat governs which birds live within it and birds help to shape habitat.

Explanation of Species Accounts and Organization

The organization of this field guide makes it unique and friendlier for the actual field user. The Habitat-First Method organizes the bird species of the Northern Rocky Mountains into 21 groups of habitat associations. These associations are the result of an extensive review of the literature, the observations of the trends by experienced field birders, and my own personal observations through my experience of birding in the region.

Each habitat section begins with a short explanation of the habitat, its structure and characteristics, and its benefits to the birds that reside within it. The images that accompany these summaries depict typical views of the habitat through the seasons of the year.

Each species account is organized in a way that communicates information more quickly and easily to the reader than most traditional field guides. The first thing you see at the top of each account is the information box. Within this box, you can quickly gather the habitat association, species name (both common and Latin), its yearly abundance pattern in the Northern Rockies, the occurrence status, feeding behavior, and food preference. This is an example of an information box for a hypothetical species.

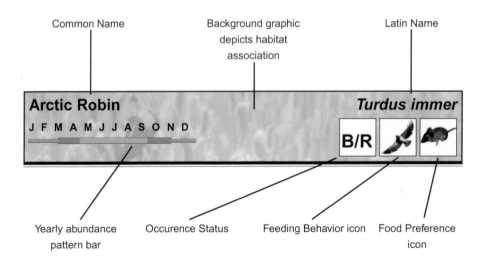

Common Name

Background graphic depicts habitat association

Latin Name

Arctic Robin   *Turdus immer*

J F M A M J J A S O N D   B/R

Yearly abundance pattern bar

Occurence Status

Feeding Behavior icon

Food Preference icon

The yearly abundance pattern bar is a graphical representation of the average pattern of occurrence of the species over the entire region. The thickness of the bar gives an indication of the likelihood of encountering the species. Thick translates to very common, medium thickness indicates somewhat common to relatively uncommon, and a thin bar means very uncommon to rare. Also communicated in this graphic is the timing of breeding, migration/altitudinal movement, and wintering, which is based on the color of bar. These colors also correspond to those on the range map (to be discussed later). Here is an example of the yearly abundance pattern bar and explanation of its components.

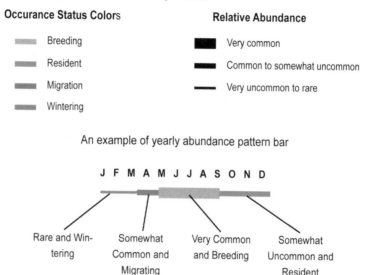

Occurance Status Colors

- Breeding
- Resident
- Migration
- Wintering

Relative Abundance

- Very common
- Common to somewhat uncommon
- Very uncommon to rare

An example of yearly abundance pattern bar

J F M A M J J A S O N D

Rare and Wintering

Somewhat Common and Migrating

Very Common and Breeding

Somewhat Uncommon and Resident

On the right hand side of the information box there is a group of three icons. The first of these icons is the occurrence status icon, which tells you the bird's status during its time in the Northern Rockies. **B** stands for breeding, **R** stand for resident, **M** stands for migrant, and **W** stands for wintering. Some species have a split personality, meaning that they may be a yearlong resident in the southern portion of the Northern Rockies and only breeding in the remainder of the covered region. For these incidences, the occurrence status will have a split such as **B/R**.

The second icon is the feeding behavior icon, which represents the most common feeding tactic employed by the bird. These are the icons and their meanings.

Aerial Diver	Aerial Gleaner
Dipper	Surface Diver
Hoverer	Patroler
Pursuit	Sallies

Bark Gleaner	Dabbler
Gleaner	Ground Forager
Pouncer	Prober
Stalker	Swooper

The third and last icon is the food preference icon, which represents the food item category that is most often consumed by the bird when it is present in the Northern Rockies. The following table summarizes the icon and their meanings.

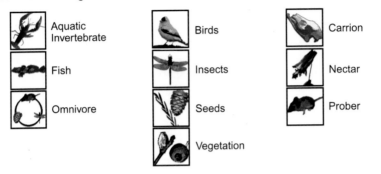

The background image of each information box depicts the habitat section. The image is used on each account and the habitat introduction.

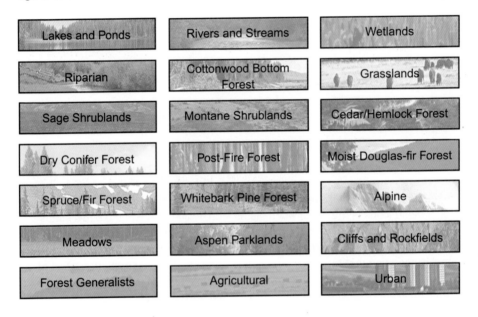

The next section of the species account is the account text, species image, and species range map. The species image is a photograph that is selected for how accurately it represents a typical specimen of the bird in both plumage and behavior. When a species is sexually dimorphic (males and females possessing different plumages), there will be two smaller images depicting the male and female. Species images will show the species in breeding plumage except for those that are migrants, which will be shown in the plumage that is typical when they are present.

The species text is arranged into sub-sections that related various aspects of the bird and its lifestyle. The **Description** sub-section contains identification information and visual clues that may help you pin down your identification. Various plumages, nonbreeding, juvenile, and immature (birds that are adult in form, but not plumage) are included when the species account warrants such information.

The **Feeding** sub-section describes how the bird feeds and what it consumes.

The **Habits** sub-section contains those habits that are unique to the bird and when it engages in these behaviors.

The **Nest** sub-section has the particular species' breeding behavior and timing, the structure of the nest, parental care of the nest and young, the number eggs laid and their characteristics, and the behavior of young after hatching.

Each bird has a unique voice; the **Voice** sub-section has a description of the song and/or call given by the species. These vocalizations are either the most common heard or those that truly separate it from the other species. The vocalizations are spelled phonetically.

The **Primary Habitat Characteristics** sub-section provides characteristics of the primary habitat association, which are the key factors to finding the bird in the field.

Other Habitats are those habitats where the species can also be found. These secondary habitats are sometimes other breeding habitats, and, at other times, those habitats utilized during the winter and migration.

The **Conservation** sub-section discusses the present population status of the species and the threats to its security.

A **Range map** is included in each species account. This map is graphical representation of the resident, breeding and wintering ranges, and migration routes of the species within the Northern Rocky Mountains. Given that a species range can change over time and even from year to year, these maps are generalizations based on current geographical information about the species. The colors used the ranges and routes are the same as those used on the yearly abundance pattern bar. The example bottom is for a hypothetical species.

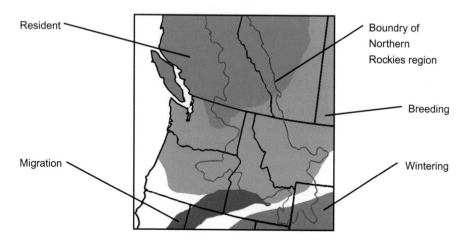

Resident

Boundry of
Northern
Rockies region

Breeding

Migration

Wintering

Lakes and Ponds

A lake is the landscape's most beautiful and expressive feature. It is earth's eye; looking into which the beholder measures the depth of his own nature.

–HENRY DAVID THOREAU

Lakes and ponds provide birds with food, water, and protection from predators. In the West, water can be in scarce supply, so lakes and ponds provide much-needed oases. The shoreline is a sharp and distinct break from the surrounding habitats. This provides edge for birds to utilize. Edge is defined the abrupt interface between two habitats. The Belted Kingfisher is a master of using edge to its advantage. Where forest meets lake, limbs hang over the water. The Belted Kingfisher uses these limbs as observation perches from where it will spy small fish. The bird will fly from this perch and dive into the water to capture its prey. The hunting tactic of the Belted Kingfisher is dependent on the edge created at the shore of a lake surrounded by forest.

Lakes are defined as bodies of water large enough to have more than one thermal layer and deep enough that rooted vegetation is not present across the entire bottom of the body of water. Ponds are bodies of water that have but one thermal layer, and rooted vegetation can be present across the entire bottom. Many ponds are seasonal, while most lakes are permanent. Some lakes and ponds are man-made; these include livestock watering ponds and reservoirs.

Lakes and ponds are generally plentiful in food sources. Life in the water is regulated by water temperature, oxygen saturation, light penetration, and nutrients. The density of rooted and aquatic vegetation, insect and invertebrate life, and fish in the water attract a wide of birds. To understand the value of lakes and ponds take Freezeout Lake for an example. Freezeout Lake is located in the Front Range of the Rockies near Choteau, Montana, and the complex of lakes, ponds, and wetlands is a little over 11,000 acres in size. Each spring, during their migration, up to three-quarters of a million Snow and Ross's Geese and hundreds of thousands of other waterfowl species descend on the lake complex. Clouds of swirling white cover the sky with loud calls and the whistling of wings. Here they gorge themselves with enough food to fuel the remainder of their journey northward. Imagine this amount biomass sustained by this small amount of lake/pond complex. This illustrates how productive lakes and ponds can be.

Geological, biological, and meteorological processes create lakes and ponds. These processes can occur in either catastrophic or gradual events. An example of a catastrophic lake-forming event is Earthquake Lake in southwest Montana. On an August night in 1959, a massive earthquake rocked the Yellowstone region. High above the Madison River, about 30 million cubic meters of the mountain began crashing earthward. Slamming into the river, the debris covered the Rock Creek Campground, killing 28 people. This material dammed the river and created a new lake that is, at the maximum, 53 meters deep. Today, this recently formed lake is used by American White Pelican, grebes, and various waterfowl species.

An example of a pond created with a gradual geologic process is the pothole pond. Pothole ponds are found along the Front Range and in some of the larger intermountain valleys such as the Mission Valley in northwest Montana. At the height of the last Ice Age, these areas were covered with a thick layer of ice. As the glaciers retreated, they left behind large chunks of themselves that were covered with soil and rocks. With the slow melting of the insulated ice, a pothole pond was left behind in the depression that was created. These ponds are surrounded by rolling hills that were created by the scouring action of the glaciers. The pothole ponds are extremely important to waterfowl production, not only for the Northern Rockies but for the entire continent. The pothole region produces up to 50% of the total waterfowl in North America, but the potholes' surface area accounts for only 10% of the available waterfowl habitat. The pothole also provides breeding habitat for species like the Pied-billed Grebe and migrating shorebirds. Many potholes have been drained for agricultural purposes, so the remaining ponds are extremely valuable and important.

One more type of lake or pond is the reservoir. Reservoirs are man-made retainments of water, which are created when dams block streams or rivers. Water backs up behind the dam to form a new lake or pond. This new body of water, in general, provides the same opportunities as natural lakes and ponds to the birds that use them. However, many reservoirs are somewhat less productive than natural lakes or ponds. Larger reservoirs are normally associated with power generation and drinking water supplies. The smaller ones are used for irrigation and limited flood control. The main issue with large reservoirs and their associated dams is that they radically alter the rivers that they block. Very few of the historic salmon and steelhead runs that coursed up the rivers to the west of the Continental Divide have continued to exist since dams blocked their paths. The bird species (Bald Eagles preyed and scavenged on the dead and spawning fish, and Spotted Sandpipers that feasted on the eggs) that used the runs as an important food source have had to find other sources.

One other creature that builds dams and creates habitat is the American Beaver, found throughout the Northern Rockies. The beavers use their incredible incisors to gnaw down trees and limbs to block a stream in several spots. They are constantly repairing these dams and building new ones. Why build dams? The ponds create

security for the beaver. They place a dome-shaped lodge in the midst of new pond. Within the beaver pond, they submerge leafy branches that provide forage throughout the cold months of winter. The fish in these ponds often grow larger than those in the adjacent stream. These fish attract birds such as the Hooded Merganser. The beaver pond also creates riparian habitat around itself.

The vegetation surrounding lakes and ponds varies greatly. It can be anything from alpine tundra to cattail marsh. The vegetation that surrounds the body of water is usually a thin circling band of riparian vegetation. Marshes may develop on the edges of lakes and ponds where the water is shallow. As the water levels drop during the summer, mudflats may become exposed. The islands in the midst of the lake may be covered with conifer forest. The lake can be viewed as a matrix of habitats. In this book, these shoreline marshes and other habitats found in and around are treated as separate habitats.

Why do birds concentrate in or around lakes and ponds? Well, it comes down to two things; aquatic animals and aquatic plants. Within the lake or pond, a great variety of aquatic invertebrates live and die in the water, on the bottom, and in the muddy shallows. These invertebrates include water boatman, dragonfly larvae, worms, small crustaceans, and many others. The birds that feed in these species can be lumped into three groups. The probing feeders walk about on the mudflats and in the shallows using their long, thin bills to probe deep into the muck to find their invertebrate prey. The sensitive tips of their bills feel the food and the bill snaps shut to capture it. Such birds include Black-necked Stilts and other shorebirds. Shorter-billed shorebirds, the plovers, use their vision to find prey. What about aquatic invertebrates that are located in deeper water? The divers submerge to the depths with their torpedo-shaped bodies. They swiftly pursue their prey and snap them up with their adapted bills. In addition to aquatic invertebrates, the divers also pursue another form of prey, fish. In many lakes and ponds, fish such minnows, trout, and other species are plentiful. The divers can be broken

down further into two subgroups, the surface divers and the aerial divers. The surface divers submerge from the surface of the water, and they include the Common Loon and grebes. The terns (notably the Common and Caspian) are the aerial divers, and they make spectacular dives from heights of 5 to 30 feet after they have spotted a fish that is unaware. They plunge head first into the water and the pointed bill snares the fish.

On occasion, species associated with wetlands will come out onto the lake itself. Great Blue Herons will stand in the shallows and hunt for fish. The mudflats of late summer and autumn are a magnet for resident and migratory shorebirds.

The vegetarians feed on plants such duckweed and emergent aquatic plants. The waterfowl species make up of the bulk of the plant-eaters on the lake/pond. They can be grouped into the divers and the dabblers. The dabbling ducks swim atop the pond and pick plant items from the surface. The divers like the Redhead go to the bottom of lake to gather their food. After they have brought the plant material to surface, thieves, notably the American Wigeon, confront the divers. This species makes it a habit to steal the work of others, thereby avoiding the expenditure of energy in diving for its own meal.

One more group of birds benefits from the production of the lakes and ponds. The aerial insect foragers are often seen flying low over the surface of the water. When an aquatic insect larva morphs into an adult, it will take flight from the water's surface. Many species of these insects "hatch" in coordination, coming out in large swarms. The aerial foragers exploit these concentrations of prey. Swallows and swifts are the two groups of these birds most often associated with the hatch.

Throughout the moonlit April night as I lay in the sleeping bag, the cacophony of tens of thousands of Snow Geese drowned out any notion of slumber. With the first milky light, I opened the zippered tent door to find the white wings twenty feet above the yellow dome. Walking out to Pond 6 of the Freezeout Lake Wildlife Management Area, I gazed out on a sight few people ever see. The surface of the pond was more bird than water. The geese were so thick that it appeared that I could walk across their backs to the other side. On the periphery, American Wigeons and Tundra Swans fed upon aquatic weeds. Ice still covered about a quarter of the pond. Every

so often, the entire flock burst into a swirling cloud; the occasional blue-morph was spotted. They would fly for less than minute before returning to the pond and continue feeding. This shallow, partially ice-covered pond is one of the focal points of Snow Goose migration in the West.

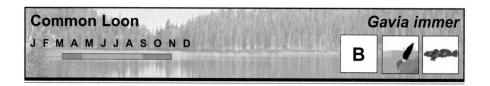

Description: The Common Loon is large (28-35") with a wide wingspan (58"). The low-profile body has a black head with a heavy, sharp black bill. A white necklace and checkers adorn its black top. The underside is whitish. Winter plumage adults, seen during migration, have white extending up to the head and the black fades to a dark gray. The head is normally held horizontal to the water.

Common Loon in the late afternoon sun

Feeding: A surface diver, the Common Loon feeds upon small fishes, aquatic invertebrates, and the occasional amphibian. They may partially submerge the head, including the eyes, and peer down in search of prey. The large, webbed feet propel the loon to depths of 250 feet, and each dive averages about 40 seconds.

Habits: May dive for as long as 3 minutes when threatened. Due to their adaptations for a life on the water, Common Loons are quite awkward on land.

Nest: The yodeling-call claims the nesting territory. Common Loons may first breed at 5-10 years of age. Built close to the water, the nest is a mat of wet aquatic vegetation. Sometimes, it is a simple ground scrape. 1-2 black-spotted olive-brown eggs are laid. The downy chicks ride on the backs of both parents early in life.

Voice: The Common Loon has four types of calls associated with breeding. The loon's laughter is the most heard, the yodel of the early dawn and dusk, a haunting wail, and a host of single note "talking" calls.

Primary Habitat Characteristics: The Common Loon is usually found on lakes with little or no disturbance. The water must be deep enough for escape from enemies by diving, and large enough so that the bird can take flight, which can take up to $1/4$ mile.

Other Habitats: Slow rivers with coniferous forest margins.

Conservation: Disturbed by water recreation, which results in nesting loss. Can be affected by lead poisoning through ingesting lead sinkers.

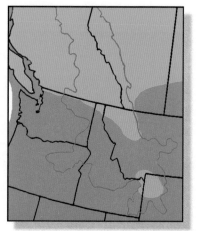

Description: The Pied-billed Grebe is short and compact (14"). Adults are mostly drab brown with a blackish crown and a thin, white eye-ring. The bill is noticeably short and thick with the black ring circling the whitish bill. The throat is black during the breeding plumage. The young are uniquely striped black and white. The underparts are white.

Adult Pied-billed Grebe

Feeding: A surface diver and dabbler that feeds on aquatic invertebrates (particularly crayfish), fishes, and aquatic insects. It will eat some soft vegetation parts, snails, and tadpoles.

Habits: When entering breeding territories, rival males display by tilting heads and calling. The white rear feathers are sometimes flashed when alarmed. This species is the most solitary of the North American grebes. Quite adept at using emergent vegetation for cover during the breeding season.

Nest: Courtship involves a great deal of duet calling. A solitary nester with normally one pair per pond. A floating platform of aquatic vegetation is built by both sexes. It is attached to emergent vegetation with open water on at least one side. The open water allows for approach to the nest underwater, thereby affording the nest site a somewhat decreased chance of detection by predators. There are 4-7 white eggs.

Voice: The calls are generally a series of *"cow cow cow"* with intersperse clucking sounds. These frequent calls are heard mainly during the breeding season.

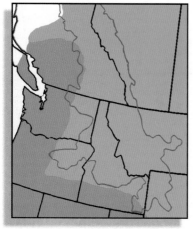

Primary Habitat Characteristics: The breeding habitat is usually moderately vegetated with emergent plants (cattails and bulrushes), less than 20 acres in total size, and generally 15-25 inches deep.

Other Habitats: Wetlands and sluggish rivers.

Conservation: Somewhat adaptable to human activity; however, populations are decreasing. As with the other grebes, the Pied-billed Grebe is susceptible to poisoning by PCB and organochlorine compounds.

Adult Horned Grebe

Description: The Horned Grebe (13½") has a rufous neck, breast, and flanks that contrast with the dark back. The conspicuous golden ear tufts resemble horns, hence the name. The short, straight bill is black with a white tip. The nape is black and narrows to a thin stripe as it descends. The winter plumage is a white breast and foreneck contrasting with a dark crown and back. There is a pale spot present on the lores in the winter plumage. Juveniles are similar to the winter plumage.

Feeding: Like most grebes, the Horned Grebe is a surface diver that preys on fish and aquatic invertebrates. It will occasionally take food items from the water's surface. Normally seen singly while feeding.

Habits: The Horned Grebe engages in feather swallowing like most grebes. It may lower its body while swimming so that only the head is above the surface. Tends to leap forward as it prepares to dive. It is not gregarious.

Nest: A common courtship display is a rising up with head feathers extended and rapidly turning heads. A usually solitary floating nest is built of plants anchored to reeds, cattails, or bulrushes near the shore. It is constructed by both sexes. The 4 whitish eggs are incubated for 22-25 days, and young can swim almost immediately after hatching. They are often seen riding atop their parents' backs. Only one pair will normally be found on a pond/lake.

Voice: Silent most of the year except during the breeding season, when it utters series of croaks, chatters, and shrieks.

Primary Habitat Characteristics: The Horned Grebe requires emergent vegetation for nesting and shallow open water for feeding. Usually found on ponds of less than 20 acres.

Other Habitats: Wetlands and large rivers.

Conservation: Horned Grebes seem to be decreasing. Oil spills can affect wintering areas.

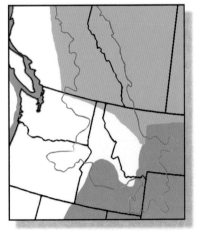

Description: With off-white cheek patches and a rusty red neck, the Red-necked Grebe is distinctive. The body is drab colored. They are short bodied (20") and long necked. The head is broad and the neck is thick. The yellow bill is long and tapered, and it is nearly equal length to the head. The juveniles possess a drably colored body and a striped head.

Red-necked Grebe at its nest

Feeding: Dives from the surface to feed on or near the lake bottom. Catches mostly small fish and some aquatic insects such as water boatmen. Will also eat a small amount of vegetation. One uncommon feeding strategy is to pluck prey from vegetation above the water. As with other grebes, the Red-necked Grebe will eat its own feathers.

Habits: Dives when alarmed, sometimes with young clinging to the adult's back. Red-necked Grebes spend much of the daylight hours sleeping. They are rather noisy during the breeding season. Very rarely seen in flight.

Nest: During courtship there are a wide variety of behaviors including: crest raising, loud braying calls, a weed dance, and a chest-to-chest head wagging ritual. Each pair of solitary nesters requires 10 acres of pond or lake to build their floating nest of grass, reeds, and bulrushes in water 2-3 feet in depth. One clutch of 4-5 white eggs with a blue tint is incubated for about 22 days. The young are percocious. They are swimming and feeding soon after hatching.

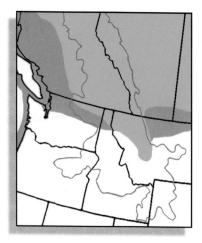

Voice: Long wails, short vibrating wails, and trills are heard during the breeding season.

Primary Habitat Characteristics: The margins of lake habitat must have cattails, reeds, or sedges. These shallow lakes are normally surrounded by unbroken habitat, whether it is grassland or forest.

Other Habitats: Marshes adjacent to the larger bodies of water. Winters primarily on the ocean.

Conservation: Sensitive to pesticides, which cause eggshell thinning.

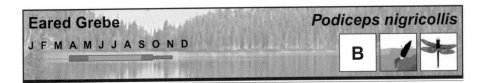

Eared Grebe on its nest

Description: The Eared Grebe (12$\frac{1}{2}$") has a striking plumage with a black head, upperparts, and throat with rufous flanks. The dark head is crested and contrasted by golden tufts that spread out from behind the eyes. The bill is slender and sharp. The eyes are an intense scarlet. The nonbreeding plumage is bicolored with dark above and white below from the chin to the belly.

Feeding: The Eared Grebe dives from the surface for aquatic insects and their larvae. It also consumes some fish and other invertebrates. Most prey items are taken in underwater foot-propelled dives; however, they will occasionnally take food from the water's surface.

Habits: The Eared Grebe is highly gregarious, breeding in huge, noisy colonies. These large concentrations of birds in small areas make the species susceptible to environmental change. It migrates and winters in flocks.

Nest: One courtship display is side-by-side swimming with both the male and female calling loudly. Then, the pair may race atop the water, somewhat similar to the Western/Clark's Grebe display. The females build the nests in colonies on shallow water. It is poorly constructed platform of cattail stalks and rushes. Eared Grebes build more than one nest, but use only one. Eared Grebes normally lay 3-4 white eggs that are incubated for about 20 days. Siblings of the brood are hatched in a sequential order.

Voice: The *"pu-weep"* call is froggy and rhythmic. It also emits shrill calls at times.

Primary Habitat Characteristics: The dense colonies require shallow water for feeding. Normally there is a marsh/wetland component to their habitat. They winter both on the coast and on inland lakes near the coastline.

Other Habitats: Wetlands.

Conservation: Eared Grebe populations recovered from past declines, which were possibly caused by collecting and habitat loss.

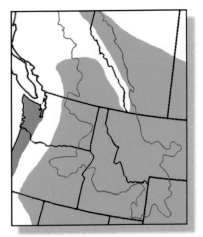

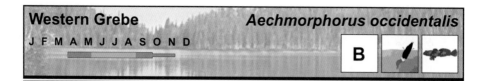

Western Grebe

Aechmorphorus occidentalis

J F M A M J J A S O N D

B

Description: A grebe trying to become an elegant swan describes the Western Grebe (25"). With its long neck, fiery red eyes, and offsetting grayish-black above and white below plumage, the Western Grebe is impressive. The black cap covers the eyes and the long bill is a greenish-yellow. The non-breeding plumage is very similar to the breeding plumage with a lightening around the eyes and flanks. The young are almost entirely white, with fluffy feathers and a short, white-tipped bill.

Western Grebe on Cottonwood Reservoir

© Ross Knapper

Feeding: Eats fish with occasional mollusks and other invertebrates that it captures underwater. Forages both by diving in pursuit of prey and dabbling on the surface. Uses its feet for underwater propulsion. The Western Grebe's long neck allows for a thrusting motion when capturing fish. Young are fed adult feathers.

Habits: Very gregarious and is often seen sleeping in huge rafts.

Nest: Courtship displays include water-running races in pairs, or more, which end with simultaneous dives and the presenting of vegetation to one another. Colonies of hundreds or thousands with nests closely spaced. The nest is a floating platform of fresh and decaying plant material. The nest may be placed out in the open or concealed in the tall vegetation. Lays 3-4 greenish white eggs that are incubated for 24 days. The newly hatched young promptly climb onto a parent's back. The nestlings have a bare yellow head patch that turns crimson when under stress.

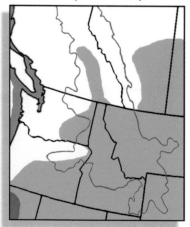

Voice: *"Creet-creet"* whistles that carry for great distances.

Primary Habitat Characteristics: Shallow water and emergent vegetation (prefers bulrush) are needed for nesting, and large expanses of open water for feeding.

Other Habitats: Wetlands. Spends the winter months on the coast in bays and coves.

Conservation: Populations increased after the end of the millinery trade around 1900.

© E.J. Peiker

Notice the position of the Clark's Grebe's eye

Description: Clark's Grebe (25") is very similar to the Western Grebe; differing slightly in plumage and voice. The facial pattern is the best separator of the two. The Clark's Grebe's eye is completely surrounded by white feathers.

Feeding: Eats mostly fish with mollusks and other invertebrates that it dives for. Forages both by diving in pursuit of prey and on the surface, although feeding on the surface is rather rare. Uses the same thrusting motion for capturing fish as the Western Grebe. Adults feed juveniles feathers.

Habits: Courtship displays include water-running races in pairs, or more, which end with simultaneous dives and the presenting of vegetation to one another. Very gregarious and is often seen sleeping in huge rafts.

Nest: The nesting behavior and nest structure are nearly identical to that of the Western Grebe. Colonies of hundreds or thousands with closely spaced nests on top of shallow water around one foot deep. The nest is a floating platform of fresh and decaying plant material. It may be placed out in the open or concealed in the tall vegetation. Lays 3-4 greenish white eggs that are incubated for 24 days. The newly hatched young promptly climb onto a parent's back. A patch of yellow skin on the head of young turns red when begging for food.

Voice: The Clark's Grebe's call is an ascending *"creek"*.

Primary Habitat Characteristics: Requires emergent vegetation for nesting and large expanses of open water (more than 20 acres) with abundant prey fish populations.

Other Habitats: Wetlands.

Conservation: Populations are increasing throughout its range, although it is less common than the Western Grebe. Considered conspecific with the Western Grebe until recently.

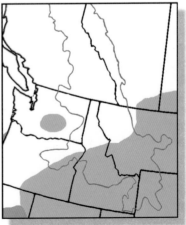

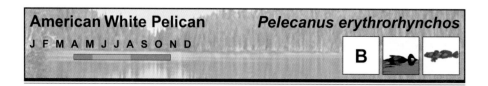

Description: A large white bird (62") with black wing primaries and the characteristic huge orange-yellow bill with the large throat pouch. The wingspan can be up 9 feet, which allows for easy soaring on thermals. During the breeding season, the upper mandible develops a horny "plate" and a dull yellow crest appears on the head. Following breeding, the chick-feeding adults develop a dark mottling on the top of the head. This coloration can be present along with bill "plate".

American White Pelican on the Yellowstone River

Feeding: Feeds while swimming by dipping its bill and head to net fish, usually those of little or no commercial or recreational value. Feeding is done in cooperative groups that cause panic among the fish, resulting in more captured prey.

Habits: Gregarious throughout the year, American White Pelican flocks fly in V or line formations. American White Pelicans are very buoyant, and not built for diving like their Brown cousins. They may travel many miles from the colony to feed.

Nest: A strutting display with bills pointed downward involving two or more individuals is seen during courtship. A bowing display with wings slightly raised can also be noted. Colonies of hundreds are located on flat islands with loose soil. Nests are simple ground scrapes or mounds of earth and debris. Both sexes incubate the two dull white eggs for 30-36 days. These eggs become nest stained.

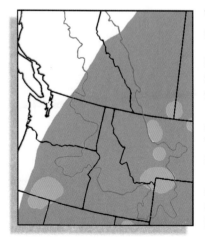

Voice: Normally silent with occasional pig-like grunts heard on the breeding grounds.

Primary Habitat Characteristics: Shallow water is preferred for feeding. Islands are needed for nesting and protection from nest predators.

Other Habitats: Large slow-moving rivers. These pelicans spend the winter along the southern coasts in sheltered bays.

Conservation: Populations are increasing; however, inland populations are vulnerable to draining of lakes for agricultural irrigation.

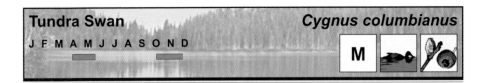

M

Tundra Swans at Freezout Lake

Description: A medium sized swan (47-58") that is entirely white except for the black bill, legs, and feet. There is a distinguishing yellow "tear drop" on the base of the bill, directly in front of the eye. This unique identifier can be absent in some rare individuals and abnormally large in others. The black facial skin comes to a point at the eye, and goes straight across the forehead. The head and neck are held erect when swimming or standing. Immature individuals are grayish and lack the yellow "tear drop".

Feeding: Feeds on mostly aquatic plants by plunging the head underwater. Will occasionally totally upend itself for deeper foraging. Also feeds on waste grain.

Habits: The Tundra Swan undertakes very long migrations in large flocks. It is strictly a migrant in the Rockies. Migrating flocks are composed of family groups.

Nest: During courtship, partners will face each other with spread wings and shake. Pair bonds are formed and maintained for extended periods of time. The nest is a mound of moss and grass 1-2' high. It is 2-3' in width. It is placed in varying distances from water. 4-5 cream-colored eggs are laid and, then, incubated by both parents. The young hatch in a little over thirty days (31-40 days is the range).

Voice: The high-pitched *"hoo-ho-hoo"* is heard during migration.

Primary Habitat Characteristics: The Tundra Swan will typically feed in shallow water where aquatic plants grow in abundance. It needs 15-20 feet of open water for take-off.

Other Habitats: Wetlands are important feeding areas for migrating Tundra Swans, and they nest on the tundra of the far north.

Conservation: Populations are increasing throughout its range. The draining of many southern wetlands has eliminated former wintering areas; however, the Tundra Swan has adapted to feeding on grain fields.

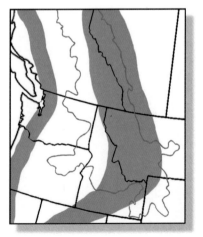

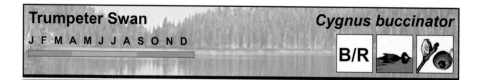

Trumpeter Swan

Cygnus buccinator

J F M A M J J A S O N D

B/R

Description: A larger swan than the similar Tundra Swan (58-72"), it is, in the fact, largest waterfowl in North America. It is entirely white with a solid black bill. The black facial skin comes to wide point at the eyes, and it forms a "V" on the forehead. The slope of the head is even with the straight bill. The Trumpeter Swan holds its head and neck in a slight curve when swimming. Immature swans are gray-brown until the spring.

Trumpeter Swan on the Madison River

Feeding: Feeds in shallow water for all parts of aquatic plants. In deeper water, it may tip up in dabbling duck fashion. The sensitive bill is used to feel for food under-water. The young will consume insects and other invertebrates.

Habits: Populations in the area are split into resident and migratory groups. Migrates in V-shaped flocks.

Nest: A nest up to 5 feet across is constructed of bulrushes, grasses, and reeds on a muskrat lodge, beaver lodge, or, rarely, on land. The same nest might be used for more than one year. Highly territorial, pairs usually nest at least half a mile from the nearest other pair. Pair bonds are long term, perhaps even lifelong. The swans will lay 5 to 6 creamy-white to dull-yellow eggs, which are incubated for 33-37 days.

Voice: A one-pitch, trumpet-like *"koo'hoo"*.

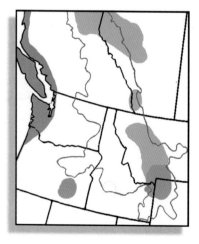

Primary Habitat Characteristics: An abundance of open water is needed for take-off and landing. Emergent and submerged vegetation is also characteristic.

Other Habitats: Large, slow rivers with ample aquatic vegetation.

Conservation: In a remarkable recovery from near extinction, the Trumpeter Swan is being re-introduced throughout much of its former range. Normally it is very sensitive to human distur-bance, although it can be become habituated in areas such as Yellowstone National Park.

Greater White-fronted Goose

Anser albifrons

J F M A M J J A S O N D

M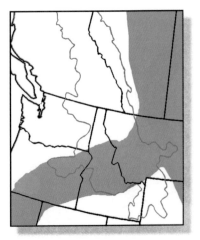

Grazing Greated White-fronted Geese

Description: Rarely seen in Northern Rockies, the Greater White-fronted Goose is an exciting find. The gray-brown adults have variable black barring on the lower breast and belly. The white front is a prominent band of white at the base of the bill, which is pink or orange with a white tip. The legs and feet are bright orange. The underwings are washed with a bluish-gray and a white U-shaped rump patch can be seen when the goose is in flight. The Greater White-fronted Goose (30" average) is quite variable in size, usually along subspecies and regional group lines.

Feeding: A grazer of wetland and agricultural grasses. Waste grains are a particular favorite. It will consume some insects and snails. You often see these geese walking along the ground with heads down and picking at the soil. When feeding in water, they will submerge their heads or completely upend themselves.

Habits: Huge flocks of thousands are possible during the migration. These flocks commonly contain Canada Geese as well. Migrate during both the day and night.

Nest: Fifteen to twenty pairs nest in colonies on the tundra with ground-depression nests in the tall grass surrounding lakes. The hollows are filled with grasses, moss, sticks, and down. The female incubates 3-6 cream-colored eggs for 22-27 days. Both parents tend for the young, which fledge in 43-48 days.

Voice: With two- to four-syllable calls that are high-pitched, they sound like barking dogs. A *"wah, wah, wah"* is also heard.

Other Habitats: Agricultural fields and wetlands.

Conservation: Populations are increasing throughout its range, except for the Pacific Flyway. Greater White-fronted Geese populations experience wide fluctuations in numbers.

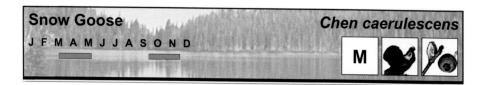

Description: Entirely white except for the black-tipped wings. The Snow Goose is large (29" average) with a longer neck and bill than those of the closely related Ross's Goose. The bill is pink with a large "grinning patch" on each side. The white head usually becomes rust-stained over the summer. The blue color morph has a white head and neck, a brown back; black wings, and white underparts. The blue morph is a rare sighting in the West. There are intermediates between the two color morphs. Juveniles resemble adults by their first spring. The wingbeats average fewer beats per second than those of the similar Ross's Goose.

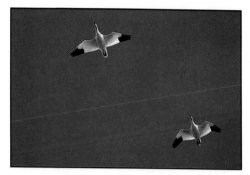

Migrating Snow Geese

Feeding: Normally feeds in flocks while walking in shallow water or on land. Browses agricultural fields during spring migration and consumes waste grains in the autumn journey. Snow Geese consume almost entirely plant material. This material includes the leaves, seeds and roots of grasses, sedges, bulrushes, and other plants. Young Snow Geese will consume insect larvae.

Habits: Snow Geese migrate in huge flocks that undulate across the sky in wavy lines. Over-abundant populations have a potential to destroy fragile tundra habitat.

Nest: Expansive colonies (up to 1200 pairs) in the north country. They build nests of ground depressions that are filled with moss, and lined with grasses and down by the female. The female incubates 3-5 white eggs that usually become nest-stained. The

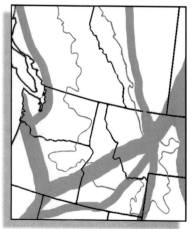

young leave the nest soon after hatching and feed themselves. Both parents tend the young until they fledge at 45 days.

Voice: Among the most vocal of waterfowl, it emits a high-pitched *"honk"*.

Other Habitats: Agricultural fields and marshes are extensively utilized during migration.

Conservation: Populations have increased so much that they are now destroying habitat in their tundra breeding grounds such as those around southern Hudson's Bay.

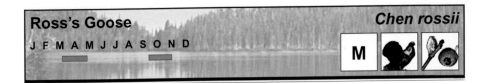

Ross's Goose

Chen rossii

J F M A M J J A S O N D

M

Notice the stubby bill of the Ross's Goose

Description: A smaller goose (24") than the closely related Snow Goose, which will hybridize with the Ross's Goose. Like the Snow Goose, it is all white with black wing tips. The neck is shorter; the shorter bill and the more rapid wingbeat distinguish it from the larger Snow Goose. Also, unlike the Snow Goose, its head rarely becomes rust-stained. There is a rare blue morph; however, it is extremely rare in the West and darker than the blue morph Snow Goose. Like its cousin the Snow Goose, the Ross's Goose can have intermediate morphs between the white and blue morphs.

Feeding: Consumes grasses and waste grains while grazing on land. Ross's Geese will also feed while walking in shallow water. Most commonly seen feeding along with Snow Geese during migration.

Habits: Smaller flocks than the Snow Goose, although it is more likely than not to be encountered along with Snow Geese.

Nest: First breeds at 2 or 3 years of age. Females dig depressions like that of Snow Geese and then mound them with twigs, moss, and lichens. These nests are normally located on islands that offer a degree of protection from tundra predators such the arctic fox. Their breeding grounds were not discovered until the 1930's. The female lays and incubates 4 white eggs for about 22 days. Both parents tend to the young after they are led to the water. The goslings fledge after 40 days or so.

Voice: The call is similar to the yelp of a small dog. A grunt *"kug"* and a weak *"kek, kek, kek"* are also heard.

Other Habitats: Agricultural fields and marshes are used in addition to shallow lakes during the migratory period.

Conservation: Populations are increasing. Until the 1860's, the Ross's Goose was thought to be just a small Snow Goose.

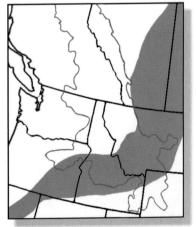

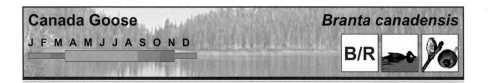

Description: Different races vary greatly in size (25-45"). A black head and neck with a white chinstrap. The body is gray-brown to dark brown in color. The bill, legs, and feet are black. The belly, flanks, and undertail coverts are whitish. During flight, the white undertail coverts and U-shaped rump patch show in contrast with the black under-wings. Juveniles attain a dusky adult-like plumage after several months.

Adult Canada Goose

Feeding: Surface-dips for aquatic vegetation and grazes on land for young grasses and sprouts. Enjoys waste grains in stubble fields. Feeding usually takes place in the early morning and late afternoon.

Habits: Flocks fly in the stereotypical V pattern, the spring and autumn image so familiar in our minds' eye. The family group, unlike most birds, remains intact through-out the first year. Yearlings separate upon arrival to breeding grounds. The goose has adapted well to civilization, nesting on golf courses and in city parks. Males defend territories with a hissing display with head lowered to the ground and the bill held open.

Nest: The Canada Goose may mate for life. A nest of sticks and grasses lined with down is placed at the water's edge or on rocks. The female incubates the 4-7 white eggs for 25-28 days. Both parents lead the young to water 1 or 2 days after hatching.

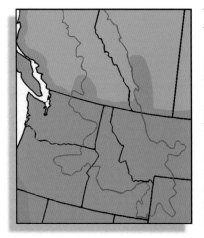

Voice: The male's *"ahonk"* is distinct from the female's *"hink"* call.

Primary Habitat Characteristics: Food supplies must be ample.

Other Habitats: Marshes, large rivers, and fields during the winter months.

Conservation: All populations are increasing, except the Aleutian Canada Goose, which is endangered. In fact, the Canada Goose has become a pest on golf courses and parks. It has been introduced into Great Britain.

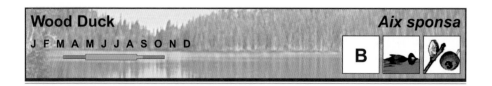

Male and female Wood Ducks

USFWS/Menke

Description: The male Wood Duck (18") is, perhaps, the most beautiful of the North American waterfowl. It has a distinct pattern and coloration of the head and body. The bill is multi-colored and there is a white chinstrap. The crest extends back from the head and nearly touches the back. A red eye is apparent. The eclipse plumage male is a drab version of the distinctive breeding plumage. The female is drab with teardrop eye-rings.

Feeding: The Wood Duck feeds on aquatic plants, the seeds of trees and shrubs, and the occasional invertebrate. Known to feed on land; however, most of the foraging takes place in the water. They will dabble the surface for food items, submerge the head just under water, and upend for feeding in deeper water.

Habits: Pair bonds form in the late winter. Wood Ducks will parasitize each other's nests. It is the only perching duck in the Northern Rockies.

Nest: The male uses a variety of postures that show off its plumage during courtship. Natural nests are typically large cavities, although occasionally Northern Flicker and Pileated Woodpecker holes are used, up to 65 feet above the ground. These cavities are lined with down. The Wood Duck readily uses nest boxes; in fact, these boxes have been instrumental in the species's recovery. The female incubates the 8-10 white eggs for 28-37 days. The morning after hatching, the young leap from the nest, bouncing off the ground upon impact. The female tends to the young.

Voice: The swimming male gives a soft, slurred whistle; and the female an *"oo-eek"* flight call.

Primary Habitat Characteristics: Surrounding forest of usually large deciduous trees.

Other Habitats: Wetlands and sloughs of larger, slower moving rivers.

Conservation: Thanks to a massive recovery effort, which prompted the installation of thousands of nest boxes around the country, Wood Ducks are increasing.

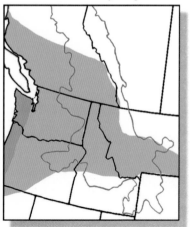

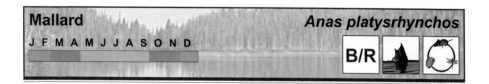

Description: Quite variable in size (20-28"), the Mallard is easily the most recognizable duck to many of us. Males have an iridescent green head and neck separated from a brown chest by a white ring. The wing undertail coverts contrast with the black rump and upturned tail feathers. The male's bill is yellow with a small black spot on the tip, and female's bill is orange with black marking in the middle of its length. A dark blue speculum is seen in flight. Females are mottled, drab-brown. Eclipse plumage males look rather similar to the female except but the bill is olive brown.

Male Mallard

Feeding: Quite omnivorous in feeding habits. Most of the diet is plant material (seeds, roots, and stems); the animal portion is made up of insects and aquatic invertebrates. Tips up in shallow water for whatever food items happen to enter its bill. Known to consume waste grains and scavenge salmon.

Habits: They form large rafts in the winter. Mallards can become habituated in certain circumstances (i.e., city parks).

Nest: The female incites by following her mate while flicking her bill up over one side of her body. A nest of reeds and grass lined with down is placed on the ground near water in tall vegetation. It is sometimes placed in a hollow log. The female incubates the 7-10 white eggs for approximately 28 days. Soon after hatching the young are led to the water by the female. They feed themselves; however, the female does tend to them for some time.

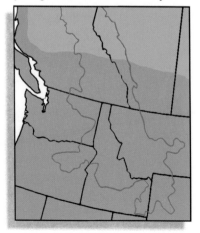

Voice: Highly vocal with females having the classic *"quack"* and males uttering *"raeb-raeb"* and a quiet *"kwek"*.

Primary Habitat Characteristics: Shallow water is needed for feeding.

Other Habitats: Urban areas (golf courses and parks) and marshes.

Conservation: By far, the most abundant duck in North America.

 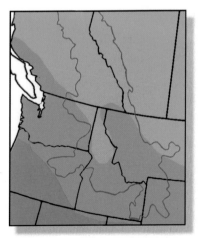

Description: The smallest of the puddle ducks (12-16"), the male Green-winged Teal has a white belly, dark underwings, and an iridescent green speculum. The head is rust colored with an iridescent green face patch. A vertical white stripe separates breast from sides. Females are drab gray-brown with a buff patch on the dark undertail coverts. The female's bill is slightly smaller.

Feeding: Dabbles the soft mud for aquatic plants (accounts for 90% of the diet), insects, and other invertebrates. Uses the bill to filter mud for food. Feeds on waste grains during the fall. It will also pick food from the water's surface and probe into the mud. Known to consume fish eggs on occasion.

Male Green-winged Teal

Habits: One of the earliest migrants to return in the spring, Green-winged Teals fly swiftly in moderately sized flocks that dive and turn in unison. These ducks are often seen perched on low branches over the water. The only teal that regularly over-winters in the Rockies region, although the wintering population is considerably smaller than the breeding season population.

Nest: Grass, weeds, and down are placed in a ground depression that is hidden within vegetation. It can be up to a mile from the water. Males abandon nest before incubation starts. Females cover the eggs with debris when leaving the nest. She incubates the 9-12 cream-colored eggs for 20-24 days. The newly hatched young leave the nest soon after hatching. They fledge in around 35 days.

Voice: The *"krick'et"* of the male and the high-pitched decrescendo of the female are commonly heard during the breeding season.

Primary Habitat Characteristics: Green-winged Teal habitat is usually densely vegetated with either emergent or riparian plants.

Other Habitats: Wetlands, either they are isolated or adjacent to other habitats, are also utilized.

Conservation: Populations are moderately increasing throughout their range.

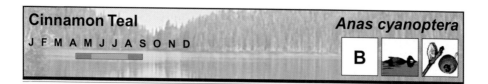
Description: A small duck (14") with males having an almost completely cinnamon-red head and body. Along the back there are striations of blue and black. Females are mottled brown with a green speculum; they look very much like the Blue-winged Teal female. The eye of the male is always red. The spatulate bill is longer than that of the Blue-winged Teal. The juvenile and eclipse plum-ages resemble the female's plumage.

Male (r) and female (l) Cinnamon Teal

Feeding: Almost identical to the Blue-winged Teal; however, Cinnamon Teal tend to favor more alkaline water conditions. This duck uses its bill to filter water and mud for food. It feeds mainly on seeds of pondweeds, sedges, and grass. It will consume a small amount of animal matter, particularly in the spring. Normally feeds with a partially submerged head. May feed in small groups that may include both other species of teal, and the group's combined movements may stir up additional food items.

Habits: The Cinnamon Teal is known to hybridize with the Blue-winged Teal. Up to 100 pairs may nest in a square mile. Females may utilize a broken-wing display to protect ducklings.

Nest: Multiple males will engage in courtship with a single female, performing ritual feeding and preening. Often on high ground, 100 feet or more from water, the concealed nest is made in a hollow and lined with grass and down. The female incubates the 8-12 whitish eggs for 21-25 days. The young are led to water by the female

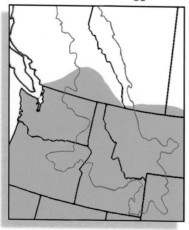

and they find their own food upon arrival at the pond. Fledging occurs in approximately 7 weeks.

Voice: Males have a rattling chatter and a series of *"chuk"* notes. Females sound rather similar to Blue-winged Teal females.

Primary Habitat Characteristics: Shallow lakes surrounded by grass for nesting.

Other Habitats: Marshes and river sloughs.

Conservation: Threatened by the draining of wetlands, the Cinnamon Teal is decreasing.

Anas discors

B

Male Blue-winged Teal

Description: The namesake blue wing patch seen during flight distinguishes the Blue-winged Teal (15") from other ducks. Males have a white facial crescent, white rear flank, and a gray-blue head. The breast is tan with brown spots. Both sexes have a green speculum and brown underparts. Females are uniform gray-brown with an indistinct white lore and dark eyestripe. The eclipse plumage male resembles the female.

Feeding: Rarely diving or upending, the Blue-winged Teal skims the surface or dips only the head for plant seeds, algae, and aquatic invertebrates. The spatulate bill is used to filter food items from the water and mud.

Habits: The representative duck of the prairie pothole, the Blue-winged Teal favors these small lakes of the grassland. The tight flocks appear very swift in flight. Will readily perch atop logs and rocks at the water's edge. Pair bonds form in late winter and continue during spring migration. It will hybridize with the Cinnamon Teal.

Nest: Courtship starts in late winter and continues during migration. During the courtship, the male gives a wide array of displays and behaviors. The most unique courtship display by the male is the submersion of his body with tail raised so that the feet are waved in the air. The nest in hidden in tall prairie grasses, constructed of grasses lined with down and feathers. The female incubates 8-12 white, olive tinted eggs for 24 days, after which she alone cares for the young for a few weeks. The young take flight in approximately 35-49 days.

Voice: The peeping *"tsse"* of males is accompanied by the females' high-pitched quacking.

Primary Habitat Characteristics: Tall, emergent vegetation is required for nest concealment and open water for feeding.

Other Habitats: Wetlands, sloughs, and oxbows of the larger rivers.

Conservation: Populations are stable; however, habitat loss is a concern.

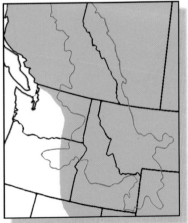

Description: The spatulate bill, which is longer than the head, is the key feature to identifying the Northern Shoveler (19"). The colorful drakes have dark green heads and necks with white breasts and rear flanks. The sides and belly are red and the tail is black with white outer tail feathers. The bill of the male is black. The drab mottled brown females have large, gray spatulate bills. Eclipse plumage males have a pale crescent that develops between the eyes and bill. Both sexes have blue forewing patches.

Female (l) and male (r) Northern Shovelers

Feeding: Feeds in small groups with feet stirring up mud and bills dabbling the surface. During feeding, the shovelers sweep their bills across the water's surface. Comb-like edges of the bill filter the water. As a result, the Northern Shoveler's diet is very broad. It seldom does the tip-up like some of its cousins, the *Anas* ducks.

Habits: Usually found in small flocks or pairs. During the breeding season, there is much aggression between males conveyed by displays. Pair formation starts in late winter and continues throughout the spring migration.

Nest: Courtship involves a unique display of short flights or swimming away. The female accepts the male when she follows him during one of these displays. Males of this duck species tend to stay with the females throughout the incubation period, although they do not incubate the eggs at any time. The nest is a ground depression, often far from water, lined with grasses and down from the female's breast. The female incubates 8-12 olive-buff to white eggs for 21-27 days. The juveniles fledge at about 55 days.

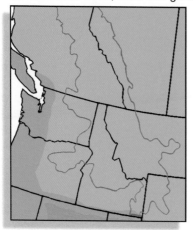

Voice: In courtship, males emit a *"took-a"* note and females give a decrescendo quacking call. Otherwise, they are silent for much of the year.

Primary Habitat Characteristics: Muddy, shallow water and emergent vegetation.

Other Habitats: Wetlands are also used.

Conservation: Population levels are steady.

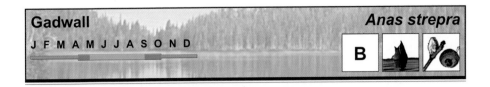

Male Gadwall

Description: The Gadwall is very nondescript, which can make field identification difficult at times. However, this characteristic can be used as an identifier. The males (18-22") are mottled gray-brown above with distinctive black tail coverts. The belly is white and the sides have a reddish-brown coloration. Females are uniform, mottled brown, and their foreheads are somewhat steeper than those of the males. The Gadwall is the only duck with a white speculum.

Feeding: Eats almost entirely vegetation, which is obtained by tipping. One of the few dabbling ducks that can, on occasion, dive for food. They eat more stems and leaves than other dabbling ducks. Invertebrates account for a small percentage of the diet, and fish an even smaller amount. The young start out feeding on aquatic insects and shift to a vegetarian diet as they grow.

Habits: Females engage in inciting displays. Males do a short grunt-whistle with their bills pointed down and backs raised. Gadwalls will feed far from shore.

Nest: Usually nests in small colonies on islands in lakes. Nesting occurs somewhat late in the summer, in comparison to other dabbling ducks. The nest is a ground hollow which is lined with plant material and down. The Gadwall has a higher nesting success than other dabbling ducks. The 8-12 cream to pale green eggs hatch in 24-27 days of incubation by the female alone. Two or more females may lay eggs in one nest. The juveniles take flight at 48-59 days.

Voice: Females quack and give a decrescendo that is higher-pitched than a Mallard's. Males whistle and emit a *"mepp"* call.

Primary Habitat Characteristics: Tall, surrounding vegetation is used in nesting. Habitat is not, normally, surrounded by forest.

Other Habitats: Wetlands.

Conservation: The Gadwall's range is expanding eastward.

American Wigeon
Anas americana

J F M A M J J A S O N D

B/R

Description: The white forehead and crown of the American Wigeon (21") is the male's most striking feature. A green band is located behind and below the white crown. His white, upperwing covert patch is visible in flight. The females have a grayish head with a dark eyespot. Both sexes have a bill that is blue tipped with black. The eclipse plumage is more drab than the breeding plumage.

Feeding: Dips for seeds, leaves, stems, and buds of aquatic plants both day and night. They are very fond of wild celery, which they take from diving species such as American Coots, Redheads, and Canvasbacks. American Wigeon also spends a great deal of time feeding on land; in fact, more often than the other dabbling ducks. They will eat a small amount of invertebrates.

Male American Wigeon

Habits: The American Wigeon is commonly seen in the vicinity of diving ducks. They have a bill that is adapted for their habit of "aquatic grazing." Females mimic injury when threatened. They form pair bonds while on their wintering grounds.

Nest: The displaying male reaches his head forward and lifts his wings to expose white patches. American Wigeons nest later than the other dabbling ducks, save for the Gadwall. Lined with grass, leaves, and down, the concealed nest is placed in rushes or sedges on dry ground of islands. The female incubates 8-11 white eggs for 21-25 days, after which she stays with the young until they fledge at around 50 days.

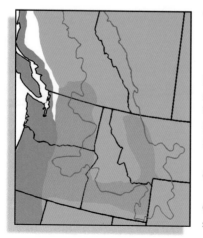

Voice: The drakes give a three-note whistle, *"whew, whew, whew"*. Females utter a weak *"quack"*.

Primary Habitat Characteristics: Exposed shoreline is a normal characteristic of American Wigeon habitat. It tends not to use small ponds has they may restrict feeding opportunities or increase risk of nest predation.

Other Habitats: Wetlands.

Conservation: Populations are remaining somewhat steady.

Male Canvasback

Description: A long bill that arises from a long, sloping forehead that characterizes the Canvasback (19-22"). Males have chestnut-red heads and necks, a black bill, and red eyes. The breast is black and the remainder of the body is white except for the black rump. Females have brown heads and dappled gray bodies. Eclipse plumage males closely resemble the females.

Feeding: Canvasbacks dive quickly and up to depths of 30 feet, although dives normally take place in much shallower water. It feeds upon roots, tubers, and other parts of bottom plants. The females and the young occasionally consume animal items, especially during the summer. They will stir up the mud in shallow water using the feet, which brings food out of the sediment, and then they dabble or upend as they feed. The bill is used to strain seeds.

Habits: Form huge rafts during the fall and winter in traditional areas. They migrate at high altitudes in V formations.

Nest: During courtship, the males will throw their heads back then forward, while giving clicking and cooing sounds. A bowl-shaped nest of reeds and sedges is lined with down. It is attached to surrounding plants or floating masses of plant material. The female incubates the 7-9 pale-green to olive-gray eggs. They hatch in 23-28 days, then she leads the young to water. The female remains with the young for several weeks; however, she departs before they fledge at 56-70 days. Redheads heavily parasitize Canvasback nests.

Voice: Drakes may coo during courtship and females give a purr, *"krr-krr"*.

Primary Habitat Characteristics: A border of emergent vegetation is needed for nesting.

Other Habitats: Prairie marshes, especially on prairies with matrices of pothole ponds.

Conservation: Draining of prairie potholes and wetlands have reduced breeding habitat. Populations have declined since 1996.

Redhead

B/R

Aythya americana

Description: The male Redhead (20") has, surprise, a bright red head. The lower neck and chest are black, as are the tail and tail coverts. The back is gray and the belly is white. The long, blue-gray bill is black tipped, and a white ring separates the blue-gray and black. Females are plain, warm brown with the black-tipped slate bill. The eclipse plumage male is very much like the female; however, the bill color is the identification marker to watch for in the late summer.

Redhead family

Feeding: In general, these ducks use a variety of feeding strategies. They dive to 10 feet for submerged leaves and stems, and enjoy occasional aquatic insects. May be seen dabbling on the surface from time to time. Redheads may also upend in water that is too shallow for diving.

Habits: Engages in nest parasitism of many other waterfowl species.

Nest: Built over the water by attaching the basket-like nest of cattails, reeds, and rushes to stems of living plants, such as cattails. However, the female Redhead often parasitizes the nests of other ducks. By dumping their eggs into the nests of other Redhead or Canvasbacks, the Redhead may avoid expending energy on building its own. However, the hatching success of these foreign eggs is low due to nest abandonment. Most ducks engage in this behavior; however, the Redhead takes it to the extreme. Due to the parasitic nesting behavior, it is difficult to determine much of the nesting behavior of Redheads.

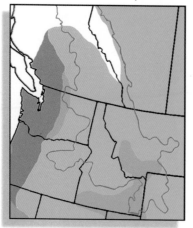

Voice: Very vocal during courtship. Males give a rattle-like call as well as a *"whee-ough"* calls. Females emit a soft growling sound.

Primary Habitat Characteristics: A border of emergent vegetation. The landscape around the body of water is usually grassland or intermountain valley.

Other Habitats: Wetlands and prairie sloughs.

Conservation: Redheads are increasing.

USFWS/Menke

Female Ringed-necked Duck

Description: In profile, the glossy purple-black head of Ring-necked Duck (16") appears pointed. The male's breast and back are black, and flanks are gray. A vertical, white mark on the breast separates the black breast from the gray sides. Females are grayish brown with white eye-rings. The ringed bill is the most unique feature of both sexes, although the male has a second ring around the base of the bill. The namesake neck ring is almost always hidden. The nonbreeding plumage males have drab gray sides and flanks and, for the most part, are less contrasty.

Feeding: Eighty percent of the diet is vegetation, which is obtained by diving. Animal items make up the remainder of the food budget. Normally feeds in water only a few feet in depth. They will also dabble the water's surface.

Habits: Gregarious throughout the year, sometimes forming single-sex flocks during the fall migration. They will, on occasion, associate with dabbling ducks during feeding on shallow water. Ring-necked Ducks can take to flight without the pattering run typical of most of the diving ducks.

Nest: Copulation is preceded by bill-dipping displays. Pairs bond in late winter. They build a bulky nest of grass and moss lined with down at the waters edge or just above it. The female incubates 6-12 green to olive-gray eggs for 25-29 days. The female tends to her brood usually in dense emergent vegetation for protection of the young. The female will remain with the young until they are 50-55 days old.

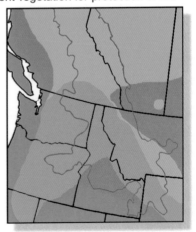

Voice: The low-pitched whistle of the male is heard during displays. Soft, purring growls belong to the female.

Primary Habitat Characteristics: The Ring-necked Duck needs dense emergent vegetation, in particular bulrushes, for nesting.

Other Habitats: Marshes and forested bogs.

Conservation: Breeding range has expanded.

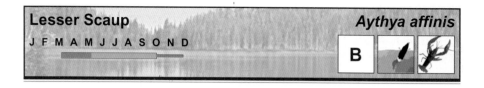

Description: The head appears to have a pointed crown. The male possesses a dark head that may appear iridescent purple and green under a bright sun. Along the side and flank of the male there is extensive white. The back is slightly mottled with white and black. The female is drab overall and has extensive white behind the bill. The bill of both sexes is blue with a black tip. Both sexes have a yellowish eye that shines. They are smaller than the Greater Scaup at 17".

Male (r) and female (l) Lesser Scaup

Feeding: Dives rapidly using feet for propulsion and with wings closed. The depths reached are usually 5-6 feet, but they can dive to 20 feet. The Lesser Scaup's diet consists mainly of invertebrates (primarily insects and crustaceans). They will eat a small amount of vegetable matter, mainly stems, seeds, and leaves of pondweeds.

Habits: Lesser Scaup are late nesters, sometimes young do not hatch until late July. They also are late-fall migratory. Winter flocks can number in the thousands. During courtship, the males give a display that involves shaking the head, tossing it backward and returning upright quickly. Also, they engage in ritualized preening.

Nest: Well concealed in tall vegetation (bulrush seems to be preferred), 100-200 feet from open water, the nest is placed in a ground hollow and excessively lined with grass and feathers. The female incubates the 8-12 pale green to olive eggs for 21-27 days, and then she tends to the young until they fledge at 45-50 days.

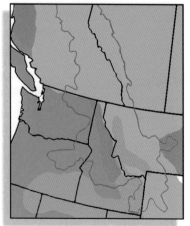

Voice: The courting male gives a *"whee-ooo"* and the females have a rattling purr.

Primary Habitat Characteristics: Lesser Scaups need dry, open areas, either grassland or very open forest, adjacent to the water.

Other Habitats: Wetlands, especially bulrush marshes.

Conservation: Lesser Scaup is decreasing their populations, although it is one of the most numerous species of North American waterfowl.

Common Goldeneye
Bucephala clangula

J F M A M J J A S O N D

R

Male (r) and female (l) Common Goldeneye

Description: The solidly built Common Goldeneye (18") male has a black and white body with a noticeable round, white patch in the lore region on its greenish black head. Bill color is matching to the head color, although the female's bill is tipped with yellow. The head is rather triangular in shape when compared to the Barrow's Goldeneye. The black wings have a white patch. Females are gray and black in the body and have a brown head. The eclipse plumage male is a drab version of the breeding plumage.

Feeding: Dives for insects, crustaceans, and pond vegetation. The dives can be to depths of 20 feet or more. A small amount of plant material is ingested during the fall.

Habits: The rapidly beating wings produce a whistle, giving the Common Goldeneye its local name, "Whistler". First breeds at 2 years of age.

Nest: The courtship display includes the male throwing his head back almost to his tail. When nesting sites are limited, Common Goldeneye females may resort to nest parasitism. The typical nest site is a large tree cavity, usually near water but can be upwards of one mile away. The cavity is 6-60 feet high and the nest proper is 5-15 feet below the 4" entrance. The nest is a depression of wood chips that is lined with white down. Six to eleven blue-green eggs hatch in 30 days and the young are led to the water by the female after a day or two, after they have made a leap from the nest.

Voice: Courting males give a harsh *"zee-zee"* and an *"rrrt"*. Females utter a low-pitched *"quack"*.

Primary Habitat Characteristics: It requires trees that are large enough for nest cavities to be close to clear, cold water.

Other Habitats: Marshes and rivers surrounded by suitable forest.

Conservation: Stable in the West. The Common Goldeneye is much more numerous than the Barrow's Goldeneye.

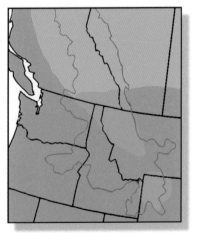

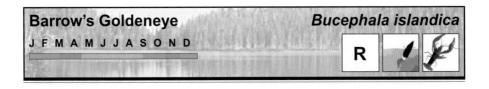
Description: The plumage is very similar to that of the Common Goldeneye. The white head patch of the male Barrow's Goldeneye (19") is crescent shaped and the head is purplish black. The nape feathers are elongated. Compared to the Common Goldeneye, the forehead is steeper, the bill is stubbier and more triangular, and the head is less triangular. Females are very similar to Common Goldeneye females with the exception being the yellow-orange bill and a slightly darker head.

Male (l) and female (r) Barrow's Goldeneye

Feeding: Dives for aquatic insects, crustaceans, and some water vegetation. Known to feed upon fish eggs and dead salmon after the spawn. The Barrow's Goldeneye will consume some plant material, especially during the summer and fall. They very rarely dabble the water's surface for food.

Habits: Wings whistle much like those of the Common Goldeneye. It will associate with Common Goldeneye and Bufflehead in mixed species flocks during the winter. Hybrids of Barrow's and Common Goldeneye are known to exist.

Nest: Courtship, which includes a head-pumping display, begins in late winter with pair bonds forming soon afterwards. A cavity in a natural opening or abandoned woodpecker nest is the most common situation. Barrow's Goldeneye will, in treeless areas, nest in rock cavities and stream banks. Nests may be reused for several years. The female incubates 8-14 bluish green eggs, and these hatch at 31-34 days. The young feed themselves, although the female tends them after until they fledge at 50-60 days.

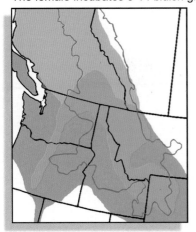

Voice: Females are mute. Males give grunts, meows, and clicking sounds during courtship.

Primary Habitat Characteristics: Bordered by trees that have suitable nesting cavities, and where the water tends to be clear and cold.

Other Habitats: Rivers with adjacent woods, especially those with beaver ponds.

Conservation: Increases have been observed.

39

B/R

The dimunitive Bufflehead

Description: The little Bufflehead (14") is a duck of contrasting black and white plumage. The large head is mostly black with a white wedge on the nape and hindcrown. This white wedge gives the Bufflehead or "buffalo head" its name. The back is black, and the flanks, breast and belly are white. Females are gray and brown with a white patch extending back from the eye. Eclipse and young males closely resemble females; however, the white on their heads is slightly more extensive.

Feeding: Dives in small groups with one or more remaining above as lookouts. Feeds mostly on aquatic insects, with snails, fishes, and plant material rounding out the diet.

Habits: Buffleheads are generally tame in their small flocks. Pair bonds are long term. Almost never seen in large flocks, usually seen in small flocks or in pairs.

Nest: Courtship can begin as early as January. Males engage in head bobbing and short flight displays during the courtship. Using old flicker holes or nest boxes, no more than 3 inches wide, females lay their eggs in the cavity. The cavity is between 5-20 feet above the ground and usually located within 200 yards of the water's edge. No additional nest materials are added. Eight to ten cream-colored eggs are incubated by the female alone. One to two days following hatching, the young are led to the water by the female.

Voice: Mostly silent with males having a squeaky whistle and females a harsh *"quack"*.

Primary Habitat Characteristics: Mixed conifer-deciduous forests near the water. May also key in on recently burned areas after primary excavators (i.e. woodpeckers) have moved in and created nesting sites.

Other Habitats: Wooded rivers that flow slowly.

Conservation: The number of Buffleheads are assuredly lower than historic levels.

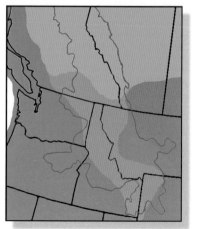

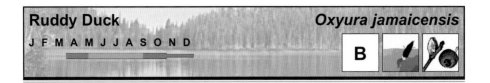
Description: Stocky is the best word to describe the Ruddy Duck's build (16"). The males have a broad, blue bill during the breeding season. The body is rusty brown with a white cheek patch and black cap. The tail of both the males and females is held upright and stiff. Females are brown with two-toned heads. The winter plumage of the male is quite dull, although the white cheek patch is still present. The winter female plumage is a drab edition of the breeding coloration.

Male Ruddy Duck

USFWS/Hollingswoth

Feeding: A diver that feeds on vegetation from the bottom. Seventy-five percent of the diet is plant material (seeds and roots of weeds, sedges, and grass), and the rest is aquatic insects, mollusks, and crustaceans. The bill strains and filters mud.

Habits: One of the most aquatic ducks, at times it seems unwilling to fly and quite ungainly on land. Will lay eggs in the nests of other duck species. Occasionally, it will feed in mixed species flocks with American Coots.

Nest: At the start of courtship, the male's tail begins cocking and his neck becomes enlarged. Males do a bill-slapping display on the water, smacking their bills against the water quite rapidly for several seconds. A concealed, basket-like nest is built among cattails and bulrushes, as much as 8 inches above the water.

Voice: A nasal sound is emitted during the breeding season.

Primary Habitat Characteristics: The Ruddy Duck prefers open water areas adjacent to emergent vegetation with passageways to allow for easy movement.

Other Habitats: Marshes in the breeding season. Ruddy Ducks may winter on ice-free portion of lakes and rivers.

Conservation: Ruddy Duck populations are inching upwards in the Northern Rockies.

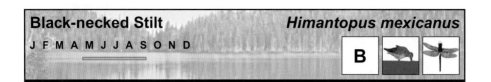

Black-necked Stilt — *Himantopus mexicanus*

J F M A M J J A S O N D

B

Alarmed Black-necked Stilt

Description: The graceful Black-necked Stilt (18") has a tuxedo-like appearance with black above and white below. The straight, thin bill is black. There is a small, white patch above the eyes. The long legs are reddish pink in color. The eyes are red. In flight, the white tail is evident. Females are slightly browner than the males. Juveniles are brown above, with less distinct edges.

Feeding: Walking along the shallows of lakes and marshes, the Black-necked Stilt uses its bill deftly to pick insects off the shore and the water's surface, and to probe the water for aquatic invertebrates. Some small fishes and seeds of marsh plants are also consumed. Black-necked Stilts seem to be keen on brine shrimp and brine flies.

Habits: In flight, the bill is held straight out as legs dangle behind. Colonies are defended vigorously. Although they are quite often observed with American Avocets, Marbled Godwits, and other shorebirds, this species tends towards water that is of a less alkaline nature. Nesting sites tend to change from year to year as shallow lakes dry up or become too flooded.

Nest: Ground-nesting colonies, often including American Avocets, near the shore in open areas that have very little or no vegetation. The nests are lined with stems, twigs, grasses, and, sometimes, fish bones. The 4 heavily blotched pale brown eggs are incubated by both sexes for 22-25 days. The young leave the nest soon after hatching, and they feed themselves. However, both parents tend to them.

Voice: A high-pitched *"yip-yip-yip"*.

Primary Habitat Characteristics: Lakes that tend to be shallow including those that are slightly alkaline. These lakes are normally situated in open country (i.e. grasslands and intermountain valleys).

Other Habitats: Marshes with some open water and interior open areas.

Conservation: Some increases have been recently noted.

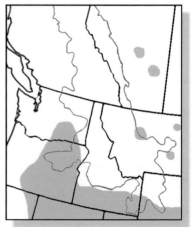

Recurvirostra americana

B

Description: The black and white wing and back plumage of the American Avocet (18") is visible from great distances. The head and neck are a rich cinnamon; this coloration changes to gray in the nonbreeding plumage. The long, thin black bill is strongly upturned with females having greater curvature than males. The coloration of the juveniles is an intermediate between the adult breeding and nonbreeding plumages.

Breeding American Avocet

Feeding: Feeds in shallow water while walking along with bills sweeping from side to side underwater. They feed upon a host of aquatic insects, crustaceans, and seeds. The sweeping action filters tiny food items and brings them to the mouth through capillary action. Often feeds in formations. May plunge head in deeper water.

Habits: Highly gregarious in noisy, aggressive colonies. Mobbing by multiple individuals is the first defensive action. When disturbed, the American Avocet may also engage in a distraction display. Prefers saline conditions in shallow lakes.

Nest: Bordering a shallow lake, a slight ground hollow is lined with a little grass. If the water rises, the pair will build up the nest with sticks and stems. Often nests in small colonies that contain Black-necked Stilts. Four black-spotted brown eggs are incubated by both adults, and these eggs hatch in 24-29 days. Both parents care for the young after they hatch, although the young feed themselves.

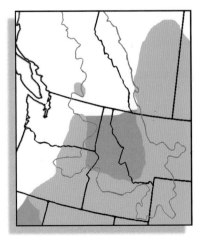

Voice: American Avocets explode with a loud, piercing *"kleet"* when alarmed.

Primary Habitat Characteristics: Lakes that are shallow, a water depth that allows for feeding. The lakes are also sparsely vegetation around their borders. Prefers lakes more alkaline than those favored by Black-necked Stilts.

Other Habitats: Wet meadows and pastures with some open water. Winters on coastal flats.

Conservation: American Avocet populations in the West are increasing.

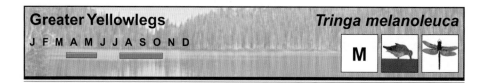

Adult Greater Yellowlegs

Description: A spring and autumn visitor to the Northern Rockies, the Greater Yellowlegs (14") is distinguished from its smaller cousin (Lesser Yellowlegs) by its bill size ($1\frac{1}{2}$ times longer than the head), bill shape, and plumage. The legs are an orange-yellow, and the slightly, upturned bill is black. It is possible to see three plumages in this region. The breeding plumage is heavily streaked on the throat and breast, and belly and sides are barred. The nonbreeding plumage is a faded version of the breeding coloration that has a two-toned effect, dark above and light below. The juvenile plumage is rather similar to that of the nonbreeding; however, the belly is lighter.

Feeding: These shorebirds depend heavily upon aquatic insects and their larvae. Other aquatic invertebrates as well as small fishes are taken to a lesser extent. The birds forage in shallow water and appear to be quite active.

Habits: Frequently seen in flocks with Lesser Yellowlegs. During migration concentrations of shorebirds, the Greater Yellowlegs often seems to be the sentinal. As the bird is approached it starts to bob up and down, and gives its loud alarm call.

Nest: Males perform a display that is a flight with alternating flutters and glides while giving a whistling call. The nest is a shallow depression on the ground lined with grass. This nest is normally placed near a stump, log, or other object near the water's edge. Both parents incubate the 4 purplish-spotted olive eggs for 23 days. Upon hatching, the young are tended by the parents, who give distraction displays if threatened.

Voice: Greater Yellowlegs have descending three-note call of *"whew-whew-whew"*.

Primary Habitat Characteristics: They are seen on lakes with extensive mudflats.

Other Habitats: They breed in marshes and muskeg, and they are seen during migration on the bars of larger, slow-moving rivers.

Conservation: Populations seem to be secure.

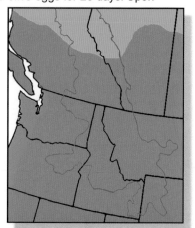

Description: More diminutive than the Greater Yellowlegs, the Lesser Yellowlegs (10½") is ⅔ the size. The straight, all-dark bill is equal in length to the head. Like the Greater Yellowlegs, the Lesser Yellowlegs appears in three different plumages. The breeding plumage is finely streaked on the breast and small bars on the sides and flanks. In the nonbreeding plumage, the upperparts become grayish and the belly appears lighter. The juvenile has plumage similar to the nonbreeding plumage, except for the back that is finely spotted, and the breast has very fine streaks that are barely visible.

Feeding Lesser Yellowlegs

Feeding: Insects, both terrestrial and aquatic, and their larvae make up the majority of the Lesser Yellowleg's diet. Other invertebrates and some fish are also consumed. Food items are picked from the water's surface or just below it. It is slightly less active feeder than the Greater Yellowlegs.

Habits: This bird can be very tame and allows close approaches before it flushes or simply strolls away. Frequently seen in flocks with Greater Yellowlegs.

Nest: Males perform a display of flight with alternating flutters and glides while giving a high-pitched, whistling call that is very similar to the one given by the Greater Yellowlegs. The nest is a shallow depression on the ground that is lined with leaves. This nest is often in the dry, open area, occasionally far from water. Both parents incubate the 4 brown-blotched buff eggs for 22 days. Upon hatching, the young are tended and protected by the parents, who give distraction displays if the young are threatened.

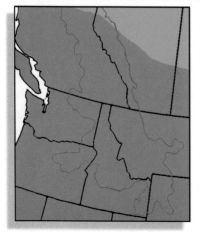

Voice: The call is a 1-3 note call of *"tew"*.

Primary Habitat Characteristics: Lesser Yellowlegs tend to use smaller ponds than the Greater Yellowlegs.

Other Habitats: They breed in large clearings near ponds. Winters on tidal flats.

Conservation: Lesser Yellowlegs appear to have stable populations.

45

Semipalmated Sandpiper — *Calidris pusilla*

J F M A M J J A S O N D

M

Juvenile Semipalmated Sandpiper refueling

Description: The Semipalmated Sandpiper (6¼") is the first of a group of diminutive sandpipers collectively called "peeps". In the breeding adult the back is grayish brown with very little black speckling and no red-brown coloration. The belly is white and a band of grayish brown crosses the breast. The fall-plumage adults are uniformly grayish brown on the back and only have the faintest of bands on the breast. Juveniles have a plumage much like that of the non-breeding adults except for a darker crown that lends the appearance of an eyebrow. The bill is of medium length and quite straight (no droop).

Feeding: Insects, mainly aquatic, and their larvae make up the majority of this sandpiper's diet. Other invertebrates (especially worms) are also consumed. Feeding is done by walking on exposed wet mud and picking items from the surface. They also probe the mud with their bills for worms.

Habits: This species will gather in huge flocks during its migration stopovers. Adults typically begin their southward migration about a month earlier than the juveniles. They can make very long non-stop flights, upwards of 2,000 miles.

Nest: During courtship, males will defend a territory with a display flight accompanied with a trill. This display attracts the females, who will engage in back-and-forth chases with the male. Both parents incubate the 4 eggs, which are variable in color, for 18-22 days. The juveniles are tended by the parents, although the females abandon them and the males after a few days.

Voice: The courtship call is a low *"cherk"* thrill.

Primary Habitat Characteristics: The Semipalmated Sandpiper is almost always seen on exposed mudflats next to very shallow water during migration stopovers.

Other Habitats: They breed in a large clearings near ponds on the tundra. Winter is spent on tidal flats.

Widespread Migrant

Western Sandpiper — *Calidris mauri*

J F M A M J J A S O N D

M

Description: Western Sandpipers (6½") are the second of the 3 "peeps". The adults, in breeding plumage, are distinguished from the other sandpipers by the arrow-shaped markings on the sides. The scapulars are washed with rufous-rust coloring. The crown and ear patch are a bright rufous. Adults in the nonbreeding plumage are very problematic to differentiate from the nonbreeding Semipalmated Sandpiper. The

Western Sandpiper — notice the drooping bill

juveniles can be separated from the juvenile Semipalmated Sandpiper by a less distinct eyebrow, a paler crown, and rufous back. The bill shape, which is tapered and droops at the end, is perhaps the best way to ensure proper identification.

Feeding: Consumes many insects (flies and beetles), spiders, and other invertebrates. Forages by walking along in shallow water or mud and picking items from the surface, or probing the mud with the bill.

Habits: Very closely related to the Semipalmated Sandpiper, though it differs in migration behavior. The Western Sandpiper migrates in a series of short to moderate length flights instead of the ultra-marathon treks of the Semipalmated Sandpiper.

Nest: Males engage in display flight over breeding territories, and perform courtship that has him displaying into front of the female with tail raised over the back while he emits a trill. The nest is a shallow depression lined with grass and other vegetation and placed near a bush or clump of grass. Both parents incubate the 4 brown-spotted white eggs for 20-22 days. The young are tended by both parents, although the male's share of the parenting duties may be greater.

Widespread Migrant

Voice: A high-pitched *"dzheet"* is a common call.

Primary Habitat Characteristics: Migrating Western Sandpipers tend to use exposed areas adjacent to shallow water.

Other Habitats: They breed on dry areas of the tundra. Winter on the coast near tidal flats.

Conservation: Quite abundant.

47

Least Sandpiper

Calidris minutilla

J F M A M J J A S O N D

M

A migrating adult Least Sandpiper at a stopover

Description: The smallest of the "peeps" seen in the Northern Rockies, the Least Sandpiper (6") in the breeding plumage is always darker above than the Western and Semipalmated Sandpipers. There are dark streaks along the sides that end at the upper breast, and the feathers on sides of the back have dark centers. The winter plumage is grayish-brown above, and the Least Sandpiper is still darker in this than the other two "peeps". Juveniles are very similar to the breeding adults, although the streaking in the sides is rather faint and washed with buff. The bill is thin and pointed. The leg color ranges from yellowish to greenish.

Feeding: Eats many forms of invertebrates, including insects, worms, amphipods, and isopods. They will consume a small amount of seeds as well. Forage on exposed areas of mud and pick items from the surface, or probe the mud with the bill, though not as frequently as the Western Sandpiper does.

Habits: Roosts in marsh vegetation. Disturbed flocks will take flight, wheel around in a tight circle, and then alight again. Joins mixed species flocks during migration.

Nest: Males will engage in display flights with alternating bouts of fluttering and glides. The nest is a shallow depression lined with grass and other vegetation, and placed in a bush or clump of grass near water. Both parents incubate the 4 eggs, which are green with pale brown and purple blotches, for 19-23 days. The newly juveniles are cared for by both parents.

Voice: A high-toned *"kreeet"* is the flight call.

Primary Habitat Characteristics: Migrating Least Sandpipers tend to use exposed mudflats adjacent to shallow water and bordered by marsh vegetation.

Other Habitats: They breed on tundra, sedge meadows and bogs. Winters on the coast on the edges of salt marsh and tidal creeks.

Conservation: Quite abundant.

Widespread Migrant

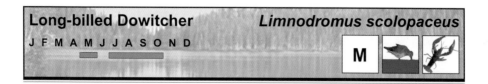

Long-billed Dowitcher   *Limnodromus scolopaceus*

J F M A M J J A S O N D

M

Description: The Long-billed Dowitcher (11½") is a migratory visitor to the Northern Rockies. The breeding adults are reddish below and their necks are heavily spotted, though these spots fade with wear. The sides are barred. This species can easily confused with the rarely seen Short-billed Dowitcher; however, the white scapular tips in the fresh breeding plumage are diagnostic. In the autumn migration, the juveniles

A lone Long-billed Dowitcher

are dark above and the breast is a light gray. The head of the juvenile is grayer than that of the adult.

Feeding: Seen wading up to their breasts in shallow water, small flocks of Long-billed Dowitchers probe deep into the mud for a wide variety of aquatic invertebrates. They can remain in one spot for quite some time or they may forage while walking rather slowly. Long-billed Dowitchers commonly associate with a variety of other shorebirds during migration.

Habits: Almost all dowitchers seen in the Rockies during fall are Long-billed Dowitchers. Juveniles begin the fall migration later than the adults.

Nest: The nest is a shallow depression lined with grass, placed under a bush or clump of grass near water, in fact so close that the bottom of the nest is often wet. Both parents incubate the 4 olive-colored eggs for 20 days, although the male does the majority of the incubating during the later stages. The newly-hatched juveniles are tended by the male (female abandons the brood after hatching) until they fledge.

Widespread Migrant

Voice: A series of *"keek"* calls is often given during flight.

Primary Habitat Characteristics: They need extensive mudflats for feeding.

Other Habitats: They breed on wet tundra. Winter on fresh water ponds.

Conservation: Quite numerous, and those numbers may be increasing.

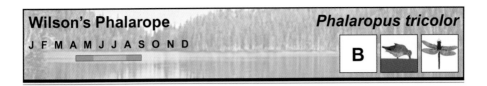

Wilson's Phalarope

Phalaropus tricolor

J F M A M J J A S O N D

B

Female Wilson's Phalaropes

Description: Wilson's Phalaropes (9¹/₄") are reverse sexually dimorphic; with the females being brightly colored and dominant, while the males are drab and submissive. The breeding males have a blackish crown, a black stripe that runs through the eye and down the neck, and some reddish wash on the neck. Breeding females have the eye stripe, more extensive reddish wash, a gray crown, and are more vividly colored. Nonbreeding adults molt into a plumage that is gray above and whitish below. Juveniles are similar to the nonbreeding adults, though they are browner above.

Feeding: Wilson's Phalaropes eat a variety of flies, aquatic bugs, and other insects. Other invertebrates and some plant material round out the diet. They have a unique feeding behavior, in which they spin in a tight circle while swimming, which brings small food items to the surface. This bird is known to actually catch flying insects.

Habits: Females are larger than males, and they may breed with multiple males.

Nest: Females establish and defend nesting territories and attract males to them. The nest is a shallow depression lined with grass placed a few inches above the water in marsh vegetation. After laying her eggs, the female abandons the brood to leave the male with all of the parenting duties. The male incubates the 4 black-blotched ivory eggs for 23 days. The newly hatched juveniles are tended by the male until they fledge. He will perform a broken-wing distraction display to protect the young.

Voice: A variety of soft grunts and *"wurk"* calls.

Primary Habitat Characteristics: They require areas of shallow water for feeding and emergent plants for nesting.

Other Habitats: They can be found in marshes. They winter on saline lakes in South America.

Conservation: Quite numerous, although they are susceptible to habitat loss through draining of wetlands.

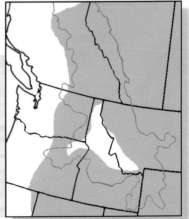

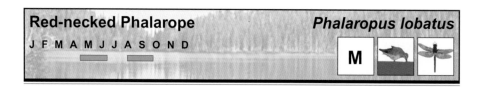

Description: The breeding female (7³/₄") is rufous on the sides and front of the neck, and this coloration is less prominent in the male. Both sexes have a dark back and the bill is very thin and pointed (it is shorter than that of the Wilson's Phalarope's). Winter adults are bluish-gray above, with white stripes and whitish below. The front of the crown is white and the black strip extends back from the eye. Juveniles resemble nonbreeding adults; however, they are darker above with buff stripes.

Feeding: The Red-necked Phalarope's diet is quite similar to that of the closely related Wilson's Phalarope. They eat a host of aquatic insects and other invertebrates. On occasion, they will consume small fish. They use the same spin-feeding tactic as their cousins.

Red-necked Phalaropes, male (foreground) and female

Habits: Females are larger than males. The female may breed with more than one male in a breeding season.

Nest: Females establish and defend nesting territories and attract males to them. The nest is a shallow depression lined with grass placed a few inches above the water in marsh vegetation. After laying her eggs the female abandons the brood to leave the male with all of the parenting duties. The male incubates the 4 brown-blotched olive-green eggs for 17-21 days. The newly hatched juveniles are tended to by the male until they fledge at 20 days. He will perform a broken-wing distraction display in the presence of potential predators of the young.

Widespread Migrant

Voice: A low-pitched *"tweak"* and a sharp *"kik"*.

Primary Habitat Characteristics: They require areas of shallow water for feeding and emergent plants for nesting.

Other Habitats: They breed on marshy areas of tundra. Winters on the open ocean.

Conservation: On their Arctic breeding grounds they are quite numerous, and those numbers may be increasing.

Adult American Coots

Description: With a slate black body, and a black head and neck, the American Coot (15-16") looks very much like a duck, although it is a rail. Its bill is white with a varying dark band near the tip. The forehead has a rusty brown shield that meets at the base of the bill above the eyes. The feet and legs are orange (in adults) or grayish (in immatures) with lobate feet. Immatures are pale versions of the adults.

Feeding: May tip up much like a dabbling duck or, more commonly, dive to depths of up to 25 feet propelled by its feet. It consumes all parts of a wide variety aquatic plants and may eat fish, snails, insects, and other animals. Will feed on land.

Habits: They bob their heads while swimming and run atop the water when gaining speed for flight. Parasitism of the nests of other American Coots has been noted.

Nest: During courtship males chase females while flapping wings. American Coots are very aggressive in the defense on their nesting territories. A floating nest of marsh plant stems attached to surrounding vegetation is built by both sexes, however, the nest used for brooding is usually built by the male. Both parents incubate the 6-9 brown-spotted pale buff eggs for 21-25 days. After hatching, the young are led to the water, where both of their parents feed them. Nests early enough for 2 broods in some areas.

Voice: American Coots possess a wide range of calls, including clucks, croaks, cackles, whistles, babbling, and grating *"kuk-kuk-kuk"*.

Primary Habitat Characteristics: Prefers emergent vegetation for nesting and hiding, and shallow water, 5 feet deep is the limit, is required for foraging.

Other Habitats: Winters are spent on lakes.

Conservation: Some birds may be permanent residents in areas that maintain enough ice-free water in the winter.

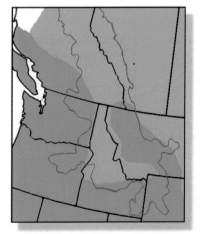

Description: The dark ring near the tip of the thin, yellow bill is the chief identifying characteristic. The legs are bright yellow. The wing tips are black with variable white spotting. A well-defined dark tail band that contrasts with the white tail base is seen when in flight. The eyes are pale. Adult (17$^1/_2$") plumage is reached in three years. Winter plumage adults have a mottling on the head. Juveniles have largely black, the back is gray, wings are brown, and there is brown mottling on the breast and belly.

Adult Ringed-bill Gull

Feeding: The diet of the Ring-billed Gull is highly varied. They consume rodents, eggs, nestlings, insects, fish, and carrion; basically anything that moves or has moved, the Ring-billed Gull will eat. They take advantage of any opportunity, and consequently, they employ a variety of feeding behaviors (wading, walking and swimming among others) to exploit these situations.

Habits: Usually associates with terns, other gulls, ducks, and cormorants in and around breeding colonies and feeding areas. Often seen at restaurant dumpsters. Flight is buoyant with swirling maneuvers. Migrates in flocks.

Nest: A colonial nester on the shores or peninsulas of lakes with low vegetation. These colonies can have other gull species as well. The nest is made up of weeds, pebbles, grass, and debris, and placed on the ground. Three brown- and black-marked olive eggs are incubated by both sexes for 21-28 days. On occasion, multiple females will lay eggs in the same nest and both sexes share incubation duties.

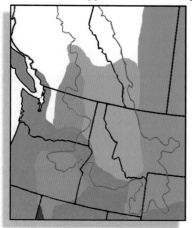

Voice: *"Kree, kree, kree"* and *"hyah hyah"*.

Primary Habitat Characteristics: Almost always found within close proximity to water.

Other Habitats: Dumps, agricultural fields, and urban areas. Winters on the coast and inland.

Conservation: Adaptation to humans and our garbage have led to increasing populations following persecution during the 19th century.

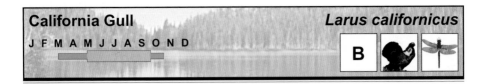

California Gull

Larus californicus

J F M A M J J A S O N D

B

Adult California Gulls

Description: Credited for saving the Mormons from the 1848 plague of grasshoppers, this gull (21") has a medium gray mantle that is darker than the Ring-billed Gull's. The legs are a greenish yellow. The yellow bill has a red and black spot on the lower mandible near the tip. The eyes are dark. Juveniles have an all-dark bill, except for first-year birds. The tail is dark brown with no banding.

Feeding: California Gulls will hunt as well as scavenge. During the summer, they eat mainly insects, and they round out their diet with other invertebrates, rodents, birds' eggs, and the young of other birds. Can be seen on adjacent farms feeding on insects and rodents. Like the Ring-billed Gull, they will utilize a plethora of foraging tactics including hovering and swimming.

Habits: Valuable to agriculture due to their habit of clearing fields of insects after plowing. Gatherings of up to 150,000 birds have been recorded around food concentrations. The California Gull attains adult plumage in four years.

Nest: In colonies, often mixed with Ring-billed Gulls, they build nests of sticks, debris, feathers, and plant material on the ground in shallow depressions. The 3 black-marked brownish eggs are incubated by both sexes for 23-27 days. Both parents rear the young until they fledge in 45 days.

Voice: Soft *"kow"* is called somewhat repetitively.

Primary Habitat Characteristics: Nesting colonies need open shorelines that are composed of sand or gravel with sparse, low vegetation. These colonies are normally located on barren, isolated islands.

Other Habitats: California Gulls will use agricultural fields for feeding, often seem to be following plows, and winter along the coast.

Conservation: Populations throughout the West are remaining somewhat steady, although this gull is not as common as the Ring-billed.

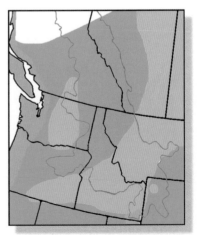

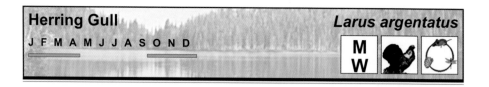

Herring Gull

J F M A M J J A S O N D

Larus argentatus

M
W

Description: Visiting mostly during the winter and late spring, the Herring Gull (25") is larger and more robust looking than the other gulls. The mantle is light gray. The tips of the wings are black, and the leading edges are white. The head is pure white in the breeding plumage, and brown streaked during the winter. The bill is yellow with a red spot on the lower mandible near the tip. The legs are pink. This species achieves adult plumage in four years.

© E.J. Peiker

Adult Herring Gull

Feeding: Typical of a gull, the Herring Gull is the ultimate omnivore. It will consume aquatic invertebrates, fish, birds' eggs, birds, small mammals, berries, garbage, and carrion. With such a varied diet, this species uses an incredible variety of feeding tactics at different times of the year.

Habits: An aggression display is done with head lowered and quickly raised. They are often in the company of Ring-billed Gulls.

Nest: The Herring Gull nests in colonies. The female adopts begging behavior during courtship. Both sexes line a ground depression with grass and feathers. They incubate the 2-3 black and brown-blotched olive eggs for 24-30 days. The nestlings fledge in 35-40 days.

Voice: The long call is *"ow ow ow keekeekee kyow kyow kyow"*. When alarmed, the Herring Gull gives a rapid *"ga ga ga ga"*.

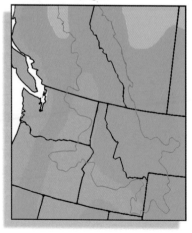

Primary Habitat Characteristics: It is often seen of the frozen edges of large lakes.

Other Habitats: Almost always found in association with large bodies of water. The Herring Gull's nesting sites must be free of terrestrial predators and within 25 miles of a reliable food source.

Conservation: Like many of the gull species, the Herring Gull is recovering from decimation during the 1800's.

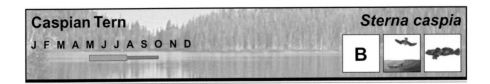

Caspian Tern cruising

© Peter LaTourrette

Description: The largest of the terns (21") in the Northern Rockies, the Caspian Tern has a crested, large head and generally thick body. The cap is black, and the bill is blood red with a black tip. The mantle is pearly gray, and the notched tail is white. The feet are black. In flight, wingbeats are slow and powerful, and there is extensive black on the tips of wings. Winter adults and juveniles have a dusky cap.

Feeding: Aerial diving for fish is the most-seen foraging method. The fish consumed are between 3 and 10 inches long. Caspian Terns also feed from the surface like gulls. They will steal fish caught by other birds.

Habits: When foraging, they fly low over water, otherwise the Caspian Tern flies high. A wide-ranging migrant that is present in the Northern Rockies for several months in numbers that vary from year to year. It has been confirmed to be breeding sparsely in the region. It is the most solitary of the terns in the Northern Rockies.

Nest: First breeds at 4-5 years of age. The nest is scraped out on a beach and lined with grass, in colonies or singly. The 2-3 black- and brown-spotted buff eggs are incubated by both sexes for 20-22 days. Both parents care for the young. Young will remain at the nest until they are able to fly, normally at 30-40 days.

Voice: The loud, harsh *"cahar"* and *"kwok"* are among the common calls.

Primary Habitat Characteristics: Open shorelines with sandy substrates, and little to no vegetation, are needed for nesting. These nesting sites are on large, open lakes.

Other Habitats: The Caspian Tern will occasionally be seen along larger rivers during the breeding season.

Conservation: The end of removal of eggs from colonies resulted in population increases.

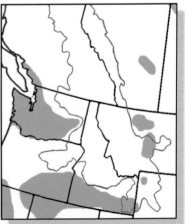

Description: The Common Tern (15") has gray underparts that contrast with the visible white tail coverts. The cap is black, and the bill is orange-red with a black tip. The back is gray, and legs and feet are red. The tail is white with black outer tail feathers. During flight, the black wedges on the underwings near the tips are visible. Winter adults have a white forehead. Juveniles have a white forehead and blackish nape and crown.

Common Tern above Freezeout Lake

The back is brownish. Winter adults and juveniles have a black shoulder stripe.

Feeding: An aerial diver that targets small fishes (less than 4"), Common Terns will hover for some time above schools of fish, and, then, plunge headfirst into the water. Common Terns will also consume some crustaceans, insects, and other invertebrates. They will occasionally flycatch insects.

Habits: May be seen feeding in groups. Common Terns dive bomb intruders into the colony. During migration, some birds may begin with a short northward movement before turning south for South America.

Nest: Courting males offer fish to females. Breeds first at 3 years of age. During courtship, groups and pairs engage in highflying forays. Colonies that may hold into the thousands of terns are located on islands. Both sexes scrape in the ground and then smooth the nest by turning their bodies in the depression. It is then lined with grass. Both parents incubate the 2-3 brown-blotched cream eggs for 21-25 days, after which both parents care for the nestlings.

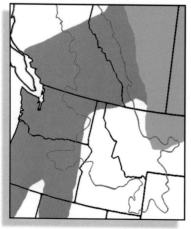

Voice: A short, high-pitched *"kip"* and the raspy, harsh *"kee-ar"* are the most often heard calls.

Primary Habitat Characteristics: Nests on shorelines that have sparse vegetation in locations that offer protection from predators.

Other Habitats: Winters on South American coasts.

Conservation: Populations have recovered from over-hunting for the millinery market.

57

Rivers and Streams

*Swift or smooth, broad as the Hudson or narrow enough
to scrape your gunwales, every river is a world of its own,
unique in pattern and personality. Each mile on a river will take
you further from home than a hundred miles on a road.*

−BOB MARSHALL

The hazy August sun slowly sinks down into the cleft of the Clark Fork River Valley, as caddisflies of a recent hatch dance among the rays and ripples. Ever-growing concentric circles follow the sound of a trout rising. As the fish snatches its meal from the surface, another creature eyes the trout from above. Through the binoculars, I see an Osprey hovering over the oblivious prey. With calculated decisiveness, the raptor drops into a dive. Hitting the water feet-first, it throws out a skirt of white spray that obscures the bird from my view for a brief moment. Two great strokes of the wings and the bird has regained the air accompanied by a captured cutthroat trout. Flying over the caddisflies and into the haze, the bird of prey takes its leave of the river to consume its meal in peace.

Each stream is unique, differing in flow speed, water temperature, oxygen saturation, nutrients, and the substrate composition of the bottom. Rivers and streams change as floods alter courses and sediment deposition widens channels.

The nature of a stream is influenced by internal factors as much as by the surrounding habitat. A stream in a spruce forest is entirely different from a slow-moving river on a valley floor. A stream's many features each help shape its characteristics and the creatures that live in it. Rapids and riffles scour the bottoms and bring particles and food in the current. The churning action of a riffle or rapid also dissolves life-sustaining oxygen into the water.

Another feature of rivers and streams is the thermal protection they offer. The air around streams stays cooler in the summer and warmer in the winter than that of the surrounding habitat. In general, larger rivers are warmer than mountain streams.

Those crystal-clear creeks are shaded by overhanging trees and shrubs that keep the water cool, whereas the larger rivers are heated by the sun.

The stream is an ever-changing habitat. In meandering streams, bends become cut off to form oxbow lakes and marshes. Streams on shallow to moderate slopes are more likely to be meandering as the water velocity is slower. Streams in steep gradients are more likely to experience violent floods that will move larger boulders and scour the surrounding riparian areas. Floods move sediment downstream and uproot vegetation. So, the actual location of the stream is in constant fluctuation over a long time period.

One factor has changed the nature of rivers and streams across the West like no other: dams. Dams have been placed across almost every large river in the Northern Rockies and many of the smaller ones. In fact, the Yellowstone River is the only large river to avoid the rash of damming in the last century. These dams were mostly for power generation and irrigation. The dams changed free-flowing wild rivers into series of stagnant lakes interspersed by sluggish rivers. They disrupted many natural processes, notably the migration of salmon and steelhead. The influx of this spawning, anadromous fish, their eggs, and fry were an important food source for many bird species. The great runs of salmon may return to the western Northern Rockies because conservationists are working to remove some of the

more outdated and less useful dams from the rivers of the West.

What does the river offer to the birds that make their livings there? Simply, a river provides edge, the interface between two habitats, and food. Edge can offer a bird the best of both worlds, land and water. Think of rivers and streams as snakes of productivity slithering through the surrounding habitat. Nesting sites, perches and security are provided by what is found upon the land, namely the riparian areas. Abundant food supply teems in the river. Think of the stream as a conveyer of food for the birds. In fact, all birds covered in this section eat primarily fish or aquatic invertebrates. Streams/rivers do not support the vast numbers of birds that more productive habitats such as lakes and

grasslands do, but they provide an environment for a select few that can effectively use the flowing water's nature.

Along almost every river in the Northern Rockies, you can spot stick platforms on top of snags and utility poles. The Ospreys create these structures as nests. The edge of the river creates a perfect nesting habitat for these large birds that is open landings on the nest. This species is specially adapted to capture large fish. Their feet have a fourth toe that can rotate back to form a configuration of two toes forward and two back. The talons are long and slender in order to slice into the flesh of a fish. On the pads of their feet there are spicules, tiny spikes that help to grab slimy prey. The eyes of the Osprey are adapted to account for the refraction of light at the water's surface. The Osprey is an example of a species that has evolved specific adaptations to take advantage of a particular habitat.

Unique among the songbirds, the American Dipper is an engima. This little slate gray songster will take to the water and swim under to find aquatic invertebrates. During the winter, it can be seen bopping atop an exposed rock in the midst of a set of riffles. As it bops, its white eyelids flash with each blink. This bird is very active and never seems to stay put for any length of time. It hops off the rocks and ice into the frigid water. Below the surface, the small bird "flies." The American Dipper "flies" underwater, or to be more precise, it uses its wings to propel itself to the bottom of the stream. The feet of this aquatic bird are not webbed, and they are almost useless for propulsion in the water. Once it reaches the bottom, it uses its bill to probe between the rocks for the larvae of aquatic insects and other invertebrates. The American Dipper is an evolutionary marvel, a songbird that is adapted to the rapid waters of Rocky Mountain rivers.

No matter where you are, there is a river or stream nearby. They act as corridors of oases in water-limited environments. They are intricate networks, not unlike the animal's cardiovascular system, providers of life. The major drainages in the Northern Rockies are the Columbia, Missouri, Fraser, and Saskatchewan.

The stream or river allows the dedicated birder a unique opportunity to wet a worm and still enjoy the beauty of the stream's bird-life.

Double-crested Cormorant   *Phalacrocorax auritus*

J F M A M J J A S O N D

B

Description: The gangly-appearing Double-crested Cormorant is large (26-32"), with a large head and long neck. Adults are all black with green and purple iridescence above, with an orange-yellow throat patch. The namesake double crest, which is formed by up-curled feathers on the crown of the head, is present only during the breeding season. The hooked bill is slender. The webbed feet are black. Immature have pale breasts and dark bellies. The neck is held slightly kinked during flight.

Adult Double-crested Cormorant over Ninepipe

Feeding: Surface dives in pursuit of small fishes, amphibians and, occasionally, mollusks and plant parts. The foot-propelled dives are normally 5-25 feet deep. The fish consumed are usually those of little or no commercial or recreational value. Occasionally feeds in groups, but more often than not, it is seen feeding singly.

Habits: The only cormorant regularly found inland north of Mexico. The feathers are not completely waterproof, so they are forced to dry out their wings in a half spread-eagle stance. Often swims with the neck and head above water.

Nest: Male courtship displays include water splashing, swimming in a zigzag fashion, and offering gifts of weeds to the female. They breed first at 3 years of age. Nests are built by both sexes in colonies and placed in a tree or on rocks. The nest, which may be used for up to 4 years, is composed of sticks and lined with grass, stems, and twigs. Both sexes incubate 3-4 bluish-white eggs for 25-30 days.

Voice: Gives a variety of croaks and grunts while at the nest; otherwise, it is silent.

Primary Habitat Characteristics: The Double-crested Cormorant needs large-diameter snags for nesting colonies and reliable food sources within 10 miles of the nesting colony.

Other Habitats: Lakes, wetlands, and coasts.

Conservation: Populations are recovering and expanding from decades of DDT-caused declines.

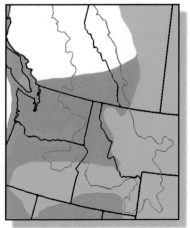

Osprey

Pandion haliatus

J F M A M J J A S O N D

B

Description: Ospreys (23") are brownish above and white below with buff to brown streaking on the breast. They have heads that are white with dark crowns and eye-stripes. The bills and long, curved talons are black. In flight, the wings are long and narrow with an obvious bend. The wrist and secondary feathers are dark, and the underside and coverts are white. Feet are gray.

Nesting Osprey

Feeding: Surveys the water from heights of 30-100 feet. When a fish is spotted, the Osprey will hover above, and then dive with feet and head forward. The fish is grasped with specialized feet and talons, and the Osprey takes off while turning the fish so that it is head first in flight. The diet is almost exclusively fish.

Habits: The only hawk-like raptor that can turn the outer toe backwards for a better grasp. Males bring females food during breeding and brooding. Migrating Ospreys travel alone and may be seen far away from water.

Nest: Pairs will circle one another during courtship. A platform nest of sticks is built atop a tree with a broken top, snag, telephone pole, or any other tall object (up to 60 feet tall) over or near the water that can support these massive structures. Nest locations tend to be open to the sky and free of obstructions. Nests are used perennially. Both adults incubate the 3 red-marked yellow eggs for 32-43 days. The nestlings fledge in 48-54 days ater care by both adults.

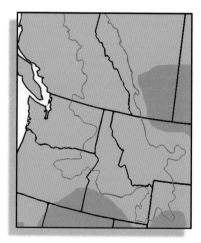

Voice: From the nest, the loud *"kip kip kiweek"* is heard. Whistles and chirps during courtship. Ospreys are relatively vocal raptors.

Primary Habitat Characteristics: Usually along those bodies of water that provide good habitat for larger fish species.

Other Habitats: Lakes and coastal areas.

Conservation: Populations on the rise since the 1972 ban of DDT and the advent of nesting platforms on utility poles, which has aided in preventing electrocutions.

63

Adult Bald Eagle

Description: The large Bald Eagle (30-43") has an impressive wingspan of up to 7'6" and a charismatic white head and tail. The body coloration is chocolate brown with a massive yellow bill. Adult plumage is attained at 3 or 4 years of age. Juveniles have variable plumages that are mottled. Flies with flat wings in the soar.

Feeding: Eats primarily fish, which are captured in an arching dive, snagged from the water by the bird's feet. Bald Eagles will also eat waterfowl, rodents, and other available prey. Consumes large amounts of carrion during the winter. They will also steal fish from Ospreys.

Habits: Congregations take place in the winter and early spring on prime feeding areas. Population has both resident and migratory factions. Territorial combatants may interlock talons mid-flight and plunge earthward in a spiral, only to release at the last second.

Nest: The largest of all pair-built nests, the platform of sticks atop an extremely tall tree can be 8' across and 12' deep. Moss, needles, grass, and feathers line the nest. New material is added to the nest every year, and pairs show a strong attachment to these nests. Two white eggs are normally laid, and both parents incubate them for 35 days.

Voice: Pairs give a reciprocating scream to one another, and a series of chatters and gull-like sounds are heard at the nest.

Primary Habitat Characteristics: Normally nests and hunts in close proximity to large bodies of water that have large trees for perching, and relatively little human disturbance.

Other Habitats: Large lakes and varied habitats, including grasslands and deserts, during migration.

Conservation: Populations are recovering from years of pesticide-related poisoning (mostly DDT), which cause thinning of the eggshells.

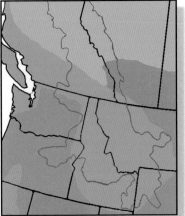

Description: The small (16") Harlequin Duck has a short bill and a striking appearance. Males possess a steely gray-blue body with a slate-blue head. The white crescent patch at the base of the bill, white ear patch, and white blaze along the neck adorn the head. The bill is short, and the rounded head has a steep forehead. The back is further emblazoned by white streaks. Females are brown with 3 less conspicuous white patches on the head. The tail is long and the under-wing is all dark.

Male Harlequin Duck

© Tom Ulrich

Feeding: A daytime feeder that dives for nymphs and larvae of aquatic insects. They dislodge these foods from the bottom gravels by using their bills. They may also occasional dabble in shallow water.

Habits: Unlike other diving ducks (except Hooded Merganser), the Harlequin Duck uses its wings as well as its feet to propel itself underwater. They may actually walk along the bottom of the swift stream much like an American Dipper. Flight is low and fast with twists and turns over the water. Migrants move inland following river courses bend for bend, avoiding overland flights.

Nest: The nest is a ground hollow, hollow log, or a cavity in rocks lined with grass and down. The nest is always concealed under brush or upturned roots. The average clutch size is 5-8 cream-colored eggs. The female incubates them for 28-30 days and cares for the young. Harlequin Ducks first breed at 2 years of age.

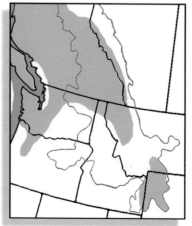

Voice: The high-pitched peeping whistles of the males are like a squeaking mouse. Females give smooth quacking and a nasal *"ekekekek"*.

Primary Habitat Characteristics: Streams that are clear and cool with many whitewater sections. Instream boulders are used for loafing. Forested surrounding habitat is beneficial to nesting.

Other Habitats: Rocky coasts in the winter.

Conservation: Oil spills are a concern.

Hooded Merganser · *Lophodytes cucallatus*

J F M A M J J A S O N D

B

Male Hooded Merganser

USFWS/McCabe

Description: The thin bill and head crest give the male Hooded Merganser (18") a unique look. Males have a black head with a rounded crest that has a prominent white patch. The hood can be expanded or relaxed, which varies the size of the white patch. The brownish-black back and rusty flanks are streaked with white blazes. There are 2 black spurs that alternate with white on the breast. Females are plain brown and have a rust orange crest. Both sexes have long tails.

Feeding: A consumer of fish, crayfish, mollusks, and aquatic insects that it expertly dives for. Eats less fish than the larger Common Merganser. The eyes are adapted to provide good vision underwater.

Habits: The swift, silent flight is just above the surface of the water. The wing-beats are very fast and shallow. May use wings to swim underwater.

Nest: Courtship displays may begin in mid-winter with males doing crest rising displays and females bobbing their heads. A tree cavity 10-50 feet above the ground is lined with down and grass. There is occasional parasitism of other Hooded Merganser nests as well as Wood Duck nests. Females are the sole incubators of 5-12 white eggs for 32-33 days. Hooded Merganser females may also use nest boxes that are normally intended for Wood Ducks.

Voice: In display, Hooded Merganser males give a froglike *"crrrooo"*. The hoarse *"gak"* is the female voice.

Primary Habitat Characteristics: Must have surrounding forest for nesting and sluggish water for feeding. Readily disturbed by human activity.

Other Habitats: Wooded lakes and ponds. May use nest boxes in marshier areas.

Conservation: Increasing numbers may be somewhat attributed to nest boxes.

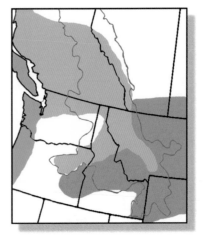

Description: Common Mergansers (25") have serrated, thin red bills that are tapered and hooked at the end. Males have glossy green-black heads, and the back is brownish-black. The breast, flanks, and belly are white. The females are generally gray with a white breast and chin, and a red crested head. Nonbreeding males look like females except for a white patch on the flanks. Juveniles also resemble females with more extensive white markings on the head.

Male (l) and female (r) Common Mergansers

Feeding: Dives to hunt for mostly fish, although crustaceans and mollusks are occasionally taken. Uses feet for propulsion, stroking both in unison. Apparently finds food by sight. The bill is a perfect adaptation to a diet of slimy, slippery fish.

Habits: Usuallly seen resting on exposed midstream rocks. Common Merganser takes a long, running takeoff.

Nest: Common Mergansers pursue each other fiercely on the water and in the air during courtship. They are known to even chase one other underneath the water's surface. The tree cavity nest, often near water, is lined with weeds and roots. They also use rock crevices and other natural or artificial cavities for nesting. The female incubates the 8-14 white to yellowish eggs alone for 28-34 days. Females will parasitize one another's nests. The nestlings fledge in 65-70 days.

Voice: Low rasping croaks are heard from both male and female.

Primary Habitat Characteristics: Forest adjacent to water is necessary for nesting. Streams are usually shallow and clear. The Common Merganser tends to live toward the headwaters of larger rivers and streams.

Other Habitats: Lakes surrounded by forests.

Conservation: Numbers have been stable in recent years; however, the birds are susceptible to streamside and stream disturbance.

USFWS/Menke

Migrating Red-breasted Merganser

Description: The double crest of the Red-breasted Merganser (23") gives this bird a regal appearance as it drifts along with the current. The male has a white collar and a streaked breast. Along the sides, it is patterned with black and white. The flanks are finely patterned. The head is all dark. A white patch that is interrupted by two black bars distinguishes the wing pattern. The female has a double crest and white throat patch, which distinguish it from the female Common Merganser.

Feeding: Feeds primarily on fish caught during underwater dives. Also eats fish eggs, frogs, nymphs, caddis flies, crustaceans, and mollusks. May feed in cooperative groups that dive in sequence in order to drive fish into shallower water.

Habits: The Red-breasted Merganser needs to have a long, running takeoff to achieve flight.

Nest: During courtship, the male stretches his neck forward, then plunges the front half of the body into the water. Nests on the ground under low, dense cover, preferably on islands. The female incubates the 7-10 olive eggs for a little more than 30 days. Red-breasted Mergansers are known to engage nest parasitism of each other's nests. The young fledge at 2 months of age.

Voice: *"Yaow-yaow"* is the call of the male Red-breasted Merganser. This vocalization is somewhat cat-like.

Primary Habitat Characteristics: Red-breasted Mergansers prefer to breed on small islands with low, dense vegetation or other natural features to cover the nest, and with open shores, gravel bars, or rocks to provide roosting and preening areas.

Other Habitats: Winters mainly in estuaries and sheltered bays, less frequently on inland freshwater.

Conservation: Populations are stable.

Widespread Migrant

68

Spotted Sandpiper

J F M A M J J A S O N D

Actitis macularia

B

Description: The small (7-8")
Spotted Sandpiper is uniformly gray-
brown above with contrasting light
underparts that are boldly spotted.
The long tail is rounded with white
outer feathers that have black bars.
The neck appears to be somewhat
short. A black line runs through the
eye with a white line above that. The
stubby wings have a short white
stripe above. Nonbreeders and
juveniles are plain brown above and
have a white unspotted breast.

Breeding Spotted Sandpiper

Feeding: Uses its bill to probe between rocks for insects, pluck prey from the
water's surface, or to catch some insects out of the air. Insects are the bulk of the
diet, with tiny fishes and crustaceans being consumed rarely.

Habits: The tail bobbing behavior is the most unique habit of the Spotted
Sandpiper. Flies with quick wingbeats with short glides low over the surface of the
water. It is usually seen alone outside of the breeding season, and, rarely, more
than pairs or family groups within the breeding season. Spotted Sandpipers like
to roost in plain view on rocks, logs, or stumps.

Nest: A depression, which is hidden, is lined with grass. The clutch size is normally
4 brown and gray-blotched buff eggs. The nest is normally close to the water and
may be located from sea level to 14,000 feet in the mountains. Females defend
breeding territories and may, on occasion, lay multiple clutches with several males.

Voice: The loud *"peet-weet"* is accompanied
by the tail bobbing.

Primary Habitat Characteristics: Somewhat
open vegetation along the shore is beneficial as
are elevated roosting sites such as stumps.

Other Habitats: Almost all habitats that border
water or that have open water within them.

Conservation: Populations are very stable.
Streamside and shoreline development can be
detrimental to Spotted Sandpiper nesting sites.

Perched Belted Kingfisher waiting for a meal

Description: With a blue-gray back and white underparts, the Belted Kingfisher (13") is a splash of color on the river. The bill is large and the slate-blue head has a double or shaggy crest. The throat is white with a blue band below it. Females have an additional rufous band below the blue band. The upperwing has a white patch followed by dark tips.

Feeding: From a perch or a midair hover 20-40 feet above the water, the Belted Kingfisher dives headfirst and uses its bill to capture small fish. It will actually totally submerge in the water, and return to a perch to consume captured fish. Will also eat amphibians, aquatic invertebrates, and young birds. Regurgitates bones and scales as pellets.

Habits: Often seen conspicuously perched over the water, the Belted Kingfisher is solitary except for the breeding season. Flight is irregularly timed with deep, rowing wingbeats. Migrants tend to follow stream courses. They will overwinter in areas where the water remains partially ice-free, mostly larger rivers in the Rockies.

Nest: The nest is a horizontal burrow that is dug by the pair into an exposed bank to a depth of 3 to 7 feet. The entrance is 3-4" wide. The nest chamber is lined with fish bones and scales. Territories usually encompass 500 yards of streamside. Both parents incubate the 6-8 white eggs for 22-24 days.

Voice: Gives a chattering rattle that can be heard above the rushing of the water. The rattle can be given in mid-flight or on the perch. This call is a territorial proclamation.

Primary Habitat Characteristics: Requires sufficient overhanging perches for fishing and soft dirt/clay banks for nesting. Clear water is beneficial for feeding.

Other Habitats: Lakes and ponds.

Conservation: Populations are decreasing throughout the West. The Belted Kingfisher is sensitive to disturbance during breeding and the loss of nesting banks to development.

American Dipper

Cinclus mexicanus

J F M A M J J A S O N D

R

Description: A generally silent, wren-like birds, American Dippers (7-8") have uniformly slate-gray bodies with thin, white eye-crescents above and below. The legs are long, and tail is short. When American Dippers blink, they expose a white eyelid. Also special clear eye membranes, that aid in keeping splashing water out of the eyes.

American Dippers are often atop midstream rocks

Feeding: Dives in flowing water, and swims or walks near or on the bottom, where it feeds upon aquatic insect larvae. Actually "flies" underwater, the wings used for propulsion. The larvae are picked from or underneath the rocks. They will consume fish eggs when available.

Habits: Tends to be a permanent resident in areas that remain ice-free, and they will move to ice-free streams at lower elevations during the winter. Usually seen bobbing up and down on rocks. Flies low over the water with a buzzing trill.

Nest: A round domed nest of grass and moss is built by the female and placed on a cliff ledge, behind a waterfall, on the exposed roots of an upturned tree, or under a bridge. The female alone incubates the 4-5 white eggs for 13-17 days.

Voice: The loud *"bzeet"* is heard when one flushes the American Dipper. A series of musical trills are the song, which is sung year round, and is loud enough to be heard over the rush of a mountain stream.

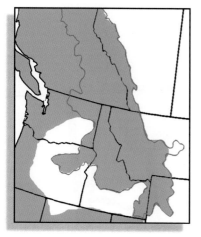

Primary Habitat Characteristics: Fast-moving, clear permanent streams with larger, rocky substrates. Also requires good water quality for successful feeding.

Conservation: Sensitive to pollutants, the American Dipper population is decreasing. They are considered good indicators of water quality as their food decreases with pollution. John Muir wrote of the American Dipper, "He is the mountain streams' own darling, the hummingbird of blooming water, loving rocky-ripple slopes and sheets of foam as a bee loves flowers, as a lark loves sunshine and meadows."

Wetlands

*Greater familiarity with marshes on the part of
more people could give man a truer and more
wholesome view of himself in relation to Nature.*

–ALDO LEOPOLD

The silhouette of a Yellow-headed Blackbird clinging to the top of a cattail is the morning introduction to the marsh. By far, the most ubiquitous wetland is the marsh. Marshes in the Northern Rockies are characterized by the tall emergent plants such as cattails and bulrushes. On the surface, duckweed and cow lilies float along with Northern Pintails. The water in marshes is usually moving very slowly and several feet deep. Many songbirds make their homes among the reeds, including the Marsh Wren and Common Yellowthroat. Marshes act as nature's water filters. As water passes slowly through the muck and spongy mosses, the sediments in the water are removed. Gross water in and clean water out. This effect is of unequaled importance to the health of an ecosystem. The odor (hydrogen sulfide) associated with marshes is a byproduct of decomposition of vegetation. When a cattail dies, it sinks down and becomes surrounded by mud and muck, which is an oxygen poor environment. The bacteria that break down the cattail are somewhat anaerobic in nature due to the environment. As a result, they release a host of gases, methane being a principle one.

Wetlands provide us opportunities to watch wildlife, fish, or simply go explore and catch frogs. Watching a child explore the marsh is a delight. There are snails, salamanders, and unique aquatic insects, all the creepy crawlies that fascinate me. The resonant *"pump-ker-lunk"* call of the American Bittern floats over the cattails. Muskrats collect dead reeds to build their damp lodges. Mud flats are patterned by the passing of deer, ducks, and dowitchers. Wetlands are present everywhere; no matter whether you are in town or the high country, a wetland is nearby. These wetlands are the primary habitat for many plants and animals.

Wetlands are areas where the water table is near, at, or above the level of the land. This definition is intentionally vague so as to to encompass all of the different types of wetlands. They are seasonal flood plains, meadows, marshes, ponds, wooded swamps, and bogs. They are found on the valley floor and up to the highest alpine tundra

Until the very recent past, wetlands were thought of as odorous, slimy snarls of thickets, unproductive waste lands. They were dredged for farmland and drained of water. This pattern of alteration destroyed habitat for hundreds of species restricted to wetlands. However, irrigation projects and livestock ponds also created some wetland areas.

The value of wetlands recently came to light. They act as giant stores of water that help to prevent drought. Some animals are resident to the wetland; others use wetlands for purposes ranging from watering to hiding cover. Wetlands create zones of vegetation that create edge effect, the distinct boundary between two habitats. The edges are among the most diverse areas as they attract large numbers of species.

Wetlands occur throughout out the Northern Rockies. Some form on the margins of lakes and ponds, while others are created in shallow depressions that hold a little water. Wetlands can be either ephemeral or permanent.

Each wetland is unique in both its structure and importance to the ecosystem.

Herbaceous wetlands are permenantly or temporarily flooded areas that are commonly associated with lake margins, prairie potholes, and river oxbows. The soils are normally saturated, and open water is usually present somewhere within the herbaceous wetland. This type of wetland is usually within the matrix of sur-rounding habitat, which can range from grassland to subalpine. The emergent

plants, such as cattails and bulrushes, are characteristic of herbaceous wetlands. Where the water is deeper, floating or rooted aquatic vegetation, such as water lilies, can be found. These plants rise in water a couple of inches to several feet deep. They provide cover and nesting opportunities for a great number of our birds. In general, forbs and shrubs are absent from the herbaceous wetland, although they can be found along the margins.

The draining of wetlands has dramatically reduced the total acreage of herbaceous wetland in the Northern Rockies. This loss of habitat has slowed of late, as laws governing the use and management of wetlands have taken effect.

Wetlands are used by a variety of birds at one time or another. Most waterfowl make use of them as stopovers during migration or as hiding cover during the eclipse plumage. When shorebirds are on the wetland, they can divided by their feeding behaviors and the depths at which they feed. Generally those with longer bills feed in deeper water, and those with shorter bills stay on the mudflats and shallow water. The birds discussed in this section are those that spend a majority of their lives in a wetland habitat.

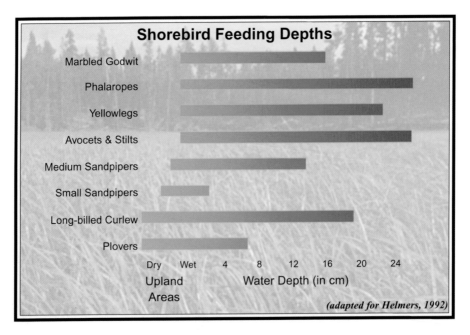

American Bittern

Botaurus lentiginosus

J F M A M J J A S O N D

B

The elusive American Bittern

Description: The American Bittern (23-25") is seldom seen. The brown streaked medium-sized bird blends into the cattails and reeds. The neck has black stripes along the sides. The legs are flat green, and the bill is a dark buff. In flight, the dark flight feathers are apparent, and neck is held crooked. Juveniles resemble the adults, but they are lacking the dark neck stripes.

Feeding: With bill held straight and body motionless, the American Bittern looks down into the water. A swift bill thrust captures its prey of fish, amphibians, snakes, and insects. Dragonflies and rodents are less frequent food items. They will hunt at any time; however, dawn and dusk are the most common feeding times.

Habits: Solitary outside of courtship. When threatened, the bird freezes with bill pointed up. The blotchy streaks of the neck plumage blend it into the tall, emergent vegetation of the marsh. Usually seen flying low over the wetland.

Nest: The booming calls of male advertise its relative health and defend the breeding territory. The male may attract and mate with up to three females. A solitary platform of cattails, reeds, and sedges is placed in the tall emergent vegetation just a few inches above the water. The female builds the nest alone as well as selects the nest site. The 3-5 pale brown eggs are incubated for 24-28 days after hatching. The female alone cares for the young and regurgitates partially digested food for them.

Voice: The repeated *"pump-ker-lunk"* is heard across the marsh during the breeding season . Forcing gulped air through a distended esophagus creates the call.

Primary Habitat Characteristics: Needs tall emergent vegetation for nesting and hiding.

Other Habitats: Winters are spent on ice-free wetlands of the South.

Conservation: Declining throughout its range due to the loss of marsh habitat.

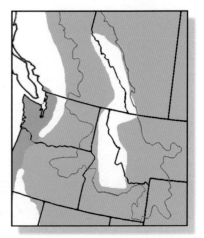

Great Blue Heron

Ardea herodias

J F M A M J J A S O N D

B/R

Description: The Great Blue Heron stands statue-like above many a wetland. A tall heron (50-54") with a white head that has a black crown and nape. Several short plumes project back from the head. A light gray neck with a vertical stripe fades into the blue-gray body. The foreneck is streaked with black, and the bill is yellow. The legs are dark green to brown. The juvenile has a black crown and no plumes are present.

Stalking Great Blue Heron

The standing posture has the head sunk back into the shoulders.

Feeding: A silent stalker with a long, sharp bill designed for spearing fish. It may strike from a perch, wading, or an occasional aerial dive. Great Blue Herons will also eat aquatic invertebrates, amphibians, snakes, and small rodents. They will feed on uplands as well, both day and night.

Habits: The largest of our herons, the Great Blue Heron is usually seen in a silent freeze waiting to strike. Males are seen on nests with their necks arched over the back and bills skyward.

Nest: The male selects the nest site, and, then, set forth to attract a mate. He displays with neck stretching out and the plumes held erect. In either colonies or singly, a flimsy platform of sticks lined with moss, twigs, reeds, and pine needles is placed on a ledge, in a treetop, or on the ground. The 3-5 pale greenish-blue eggs hatch in 25-30 days. Both sexes care for the young, feeding them by regurgitation.

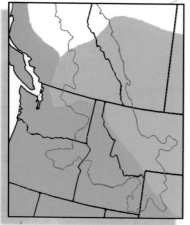

Voice: The normally silent Great Blue Heron gives a hoarse croak when flushed, and honks during flight.

Primary Habitat Characteristics: Wetlands with sufficient shallow water and aquatic life to provide hunting opportunities.

Other Habitats: Rivers, lakes, ponds, and other wetlands. Cottonwood bottom forests are common locations for colony sites.

Conservation: Numbers are increasing.

Great Egret

J F M A M J J A S O N D

Ardea alba

M

Description: The tallest of our three white egrets (39"), the Great Egret shows prominently when it is present on the marsh. The coloration includes an all-white plumage and a robust yellow bill. The legs and feet are black. During the breeding season, long white plumes emerge from back and extend well past the tail. Immature and non-breeding individuals lack the plumes.

Feeding: A consumer of mostly fish, the Great Egret will also eat crustaceans, amphibians, snakes, and aquatic insects. Feeds either by ambush or while slowly walking along in shallow water. Prey is captured with a sudden thrust of head from the coiled neck. On rare occasions, they will forage in agricultural fields with Cattle Egrets.

A rare Visiting Great Egret

Habits: Occasionally, it breeds far north of its normal breeding range. Will associate with other egrets, herons, and ibises. The Great Egret is very gregarious. They remain in communal roosts outside the breeding season. They will easily flush from the nest. They are sensitive to human disturbance, so great care must be taken to limit it.

Nest: Nests in colonies or sometimes in pairs. The colonies are often composed of mixed species including other egrets and ibises. The nest, which is a platform of sticks, is placed high in a tree. The nest can be up to 40 feet above the ground. The 3-4 pale blue-green eggs are incubated by both sexes, and they hatch in about 23-26 days. The young are fed by means of regurgitation by both parents.

Voice: The Great Egret gives a deep, rattle-like croak.

Primary Habitat Characteristics: The Great Egret needs extensive shallow, open water for foraging and nearby trees for nesting.

Other Habitats: Rivers, lakes, and ponds.

Conservation: Great Egret numbers recovered after the decimation of populations during the 19th century when the Great Egret was sought after by the feather trade.

Widespread Irregular Visitor

Snowy Egret

Egretta thula

J F M A M J J A S O N D

B

Description: The all white Snowy Egret (24") has a sharp, black bill. The lores are yellow and have no exposed feathers. In the breeding season, elegant, white plumes originate from the head, back, and the breast. The legs are black with yellow feet. During the height of breeding, the lores will turn red and feet an orange. Immature individuals have a yellow stripe extending up the back of the leg.

Snowy Egret at Yellowstone's Pelican Creek

Feeding: Fish, amphibians, reptiles, and aquatic invertebrates that are captured in a swift bill thrust are the bulk of the Snowy Egret's diet. Can be very active during feeding, running in the shallow water. They may also use ambush tactics for feeding. May use one foot to rake and stir the bottom and water in an attempt to flush prey. Aerial dives and active pursuit of fish are occasionally seen.

Habits: The yellow feet may actually be used as a lure for small fish. Nests are aggressively defended by calls, crest-raising displays, and fights. So social that they roost communally outside of the breeding season. Disperses widely after the breeding season.

Nest: After the male has selected a nest site, he engages a variety of displays; including skyward bill pointing, raising of plumes, and a display flight high over the col-ony that ends with a tumble earthward. Built on the ground to 30 feet in a tree, a platform nest of sticks is one of many in a colony of up to thousands.

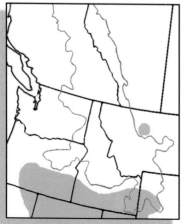

Voice: In the breeding colonies, a *"wah-wah-wah"* is often heard.

Primary Habitat Characteristics: Snowy Egret habitat normally has emergent vegetation and shallow, open water for foraging.

Other Habitats: River and lakeshores are also used as well as upland areas for feeding.

Conservation: Recovering from near extinction caused by hunting for its plumes, which were valuable to the feather trade.

79

Black-crowned Night-Heron   *Nycticorax nycticorax*

J F M A M J J A S O N D

B

Description: The stocky, elusive Black-crowned Night-heron (25") is normally seen during the day perched in motionless silence. The smoky black crown and back strongly contrast with the light gray body. The cheek is white. The plumes, which emerge from the back of the head, reach their maximum length during the breeding season. The neck is short and the feet barely extended beyond the tail in flight. Juveniles are streaked brown and buff in the front and dark brown with white markings. Adult plumage is attained in three years, so the second-year plumage resembles a brown version of the adult coloration without the head plumes.

Adult Black-crowned Night-Heron

USFWS/Farrell

Feeding: Black-crowned Night-herons consume mostly fish, although a wide variety of other items can be part of the diet (amphibians, crustaceans, insects and, even, carrion are among these). They normally forage by standing still on the water's edge utilizing an ambush technique. They occasionally can be seen foraging while walking slowly in shallow water. Most feeding happens at dusk and the early evening hours.

Habits: Regularly roosts in trees during the day. The height of activity occurs between dusk and dawn.

Nest: As is common among the wading birds, the male selects the nest site and displays to attract a mate. Neck stretching and a slow bow accompanied with a hissing are displays that he will utilize. Placed in an elevated location (10 to 40 feet above ground), the nest is usually among a colony of other night-herons or mixed species of other wading birds. Both sexes incubate the 3-5 greenish-blue eggs for 21-26 days.

Voice: The flight call, *"wok"*, is commonly heard.

Primary Habitat Characteristics: Stands of trees are usually nearby for nesting and roosting.

Other Habitats: A variety of aquatic habitats.

Conservation: Recovering from severe declines that can be linked to the use of DDT.

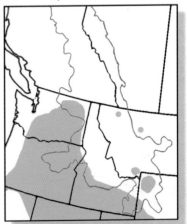

Description: The down-curved bill of the large (23") White-faced Ibis is accompanied with a chestnut-brown plumage. A white border of feathers is adjacent to the red facial skin from which the bill arises. The white border runs behind the red eyes and under the chin. The bill are dark gray and long. The legs are red.

White-faced Ibis moving at sundown

Feeding: Uses the bill to its advantage to capture and consume insects, aquatic invertebrates (in particular crayfish), amphibians, and fish. Its feeding tactics are to wade and probe soft mud with the bill or to pick prey or plant material from the water's surface.

Habits: White-faced Ibises tend to fly in circles in a line with flapping interrupted by gliding. They will take quick advantage of flooding or irrigation, which creates new feeding opportunities. The Western counterpart of the Glossy Ibis, it is the only ibis in the Northern Rockies.

Nest: The nest, a large bed of reeds and sticks, is attached to emergent vegetation several feet above the water or on a floating mat of dead plants built by both sexes. They nest in small colonies. Both parents incubate 3-4 variable blue to green eggs for 22 days. Feeding of young done through regurgitation by both sexes.

Voice: Some nasal grunting can be heard in flight, but the White-faced Ibis is normally silent.

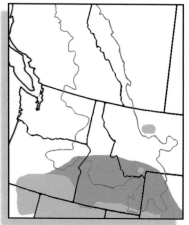

Primary Habitat Characteristics: The White-faced Ibis requires tall emergent plants for nesting, and very shallow water or exposed mudflats are necessary for feeding.

Other Habitats: Irrigated fields and damp meadows can present occasional feeding opportunities. Southern Pacific coast estuaries are visited in the winter.

Conservation: The loss of wetland habitat to draining and the use of pesticides pose threats to the White-faced Ibis.

Northern Pintail

Anas acuta

J F M A M J J A S O N D

B/R

Northern Pintail male

Description: The long, thin central tail feathers give the Northern Pintail (21-25") its name. The male's head is deep brown with a white stripe behind the eye, which extends from the white breast and long neck. The black patch separates the gray back and flanks. Females are a subdued, mottled brown with shorter tails than the males. The legs and feet are gray, and the bill is blue-gray. In flight, both sexes have a dark speculum bordered by white on the trailing edge of the wing, the "pintail" is readily evident, and the profile is narrow.

Feeding: A shallow-water feeder that tips up and gathers food underwater. 90% of the diet is plant material with aquatic invertebrates composing the remainder. The consumption of animal matter increases during the summer. When the water is frozen, the Northern Pintail resorts to feeding on waste grains in agricultural fields.

Habits: Pair selection begins in mid-winter. Head-pumping displays by both sexes precedes mating. They feed in deeper water than other dabbling ducks. Northern Pintails are extremely wary, so approach can difficult if not impossible.

Nest: Pairs form during the winter and migration, when flying chases are common. A concealed nest of sticks, grass, and leaves lined with down is placed at varying distances from water. The female alone incubates 6-10 cream to blue eggs. The young are led from the nest soon after hatching and the female cares for them.

Voice: The decrescendo quaking of the female is more hoarse than a Mallard female's. When courting, males give a fluty whistle.

Primary Habitat Characteristics: Marsh vegetation is usually present. Mudbanks or other exposed areas are good resting sites.

Other Habitats: Shallow lakes and ponds, and agricultural fields in winter.

Conservation: Populations are decreasing due to many factors.

Northern Harrier
Circus cyaneus

J F M A M J J A S O N D

B/R

Description: Flying buoyantly over the cattails, the Northern Harrier (17-20") holds its long wings in a shallow V (known as a dihedral). The tail is long and a rectangular white rump patch is visible at the base of the tail. Males are gray above, with variable reddish spotting below. Females are noticeably larger than males with brown above and white with brown streaking below. Juveniles closely resemble females with cinnamon below. On closer inspection, the face appears owl-like, being somewhat dish-shaped.

Male Northern Harrier

Feeding: Pursues and consumes mostly rodents and birds. They will also eat insects, amphibians and, occasionally, carrion. Prey is hunted with a low, undulating flight over the flats. Upon locating prey, the Northern Harrier hovers above dense vegetation. The facial disk may aid in hunting by sound, unique among *Falconidae*.

Habits: Males fly lower and faster than females when hunting. The only representative of the harriers present in North America. They can adopt a wide variety of flight techniques, including soaring with a shallow or deep dihedral with tail open or closed, gliding with straight wings, and a falcon-like glide with partially folded wings.

Nest: During courtship, the male does a roller-coaster flight pattern over the nesting territory. A platform of sticks, stems, and grass is built on the ground in vegetation that conceals. Nests are often in loose colonies with males breeding with multiple females. The female incubates the 4-6 bluish white eggs for 30 days. After hatching, the female remains with young while the male brings food.

Voice: The call is a rapid, nasal *"ke-ke-ke"*.

Primary Habitat Characteristics: Open terrain that contains areas of good cover where the nest can be hidden.

Other Habitats: Any kind of open habitat, particularly fields and prairies.

Conservation: Disappearing over much of its range in North America due to habitat loss.

83

Virginia Rail

Rallus limicola

J F M A M J J A S O N D

B

Description: Often heard, rarely seen aptly describes this denizen of the marsh. Nine inches long with a rusty breast that is faintly streaked black. The flanks have white and black barring, and the back is olive. The long, reddish bill is sandpiper-like. The legs are a reddish-brown. Males are slightly larger.

Juvenile Virginia Rail

© Peter LaTourrette

Feeding: Uses the bill to probe mud for a variety of invertebrates; however, it mostly consumes insects. It will eat duckweed, seeds, and other vegetation. The bill is stabbed forcefully in the pursuit of prey.

Habits: Courting males run in front of females with raised wings, they feed females, and both sexes do bobbing motions. Where Sora and Virginia Rail occur together, Virginia Rails tend to inhabit the drier areas of the marsh.

Nest: The male displays for the female by raising his wings and running in front of the female. Once a pair bond has been established, the pair will mutually feed and preen one another. The well-hidden nest is a loosely woven cup of grass, sedge, and rush; 7" high and 8" across is attached to vegetation, usually cattails or bulrush, about one foot above mud or water. It is constructed by both sexes. Both parents incubate 7-12 brown-spotted white eggs for 18-21 days. The care of the young is shared by the two parents for 25 days, at which time the juveniles fledge.

Voice: The *"ti-dick, ti-dick"* is emitted during courtship. A variety of other calls, including a *"wack-wack-wack"*, are also heard.

Primary Habitat Characteristics: Emergent vegetation is needed for proper nesting. Usually these stands of emergent vegetation are over shallow, standing water.

Other Habitats: Found almost exclusively in marshes.

Conservation: The loss of marsh habitat has led to some declines. There are pockets of Virginia Rails that overwinter in the Northern Rockies in places such as Ninepipes NWR.

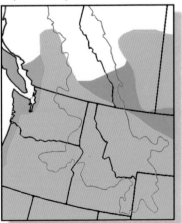

Porzana carolina

B

Description: The chicken–like Sora (9") possesses a short, yellow bill and a small, plump body. The upperparts and wings are for the most part brown, and the flanks are barred. A black face contrasts the yellow bill and gray head and neck.

Feeding: Feeds primarily on seeds and duckweed with mollusks and insects rounding out the diet. Food items are picked from the mud or water surface or the bill is used occasionally to probe the mud.

Juvenile Sora

Habits: A strong flier for a rail, the Sora may fly 3,000 miles during migration. Both sexes preen each other during courtship. They respond with alarm calls to loud noises such as clapping of hands. They spend most of their lives well concealed in vegetation.

Nest: During courtship, Sora pairs engage in mutual preening to reinforce the pair bond. A solid cup of cattails, grasses, and other vegetation is built by both sexes and lined with finer materials. It is placed just inches above the water and hidden by an arch of vegetation, especially sedges. Both the female and male incubate 8-12 chestnut-spotted olive eggs for 20 days. After parental care for about 25 days, the young fledge. Nesting territories are defended until the young fledge.

Voice: Plaintive whistles and whining pierce the stillness of the marsh. A rising, plaintive *"ker-wee"* is heard in the spring and the alarm call is a sharp *"keek"*.

Primary Habitat Characteristics: The Sora requires tall, dense emergent vegetation for nesting.

Other Habitats: Wet meadows with tall grass are sometimes used by the Sora. This bird will concentrate in areas of plentiful seed-producing grass or grain.

Conservation: Although widespread and common, the loss of wetlands has had a negative impact on the Sora. Flooding can destroy many nests.

Whooping Crane

J F M A M J J A S O N D

Grus americana

| M | 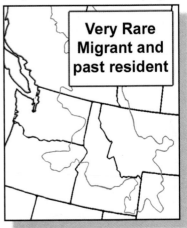 | |

The endangered Whooping Crane

Description: The tallest bird (60") in North America, the Whooping Crane is all white. The crown and chin are covered by red skin. The bill is orange, and legs and wing primaries are black. In flight, the long neck and legs are held extended.

Feeding: The summer diet of the omnivorous crane is not well known. It is assumed, however, to be relatively similar to that of the Sandhill Crane.

Habits: Whooping calls are heard in the courtship period, which includes dance, bowing displays, and the tossing of grass overhead.

Nest: Both sexes build a mound of grass, weeds, and mud on a marshy island.

Voice: The Whooping Crane's call is higher pitched and more constant than that of the Sandhill Crane. They engage in duet calling activity, as do Sandhill Cranes.

Primary Habitat Characteristics: Remote areas (Wood Buffalo National Park in Alberta) are being used now for nesting. These areas have numerous shallow, marshy potholes surrounded by aspen parklands and northern taiga forest.

Other Habitats: Formerly nested on prairie potholes.

Conservation: One of the rarest birds in North America, the Whooping Crane is staging a comeback from 15 birds in 1941. As of 1999, there were 183 Whooping Cranes in the wild, close to 100 in captivity, and 4 in the Rocky Mountain region. Until recently, 2 resided in the Rocky Mountains, 1 in Yellowstone National Park and another in the Centennial Valley of southwest Montana. The reasons for the near extinction of the Whooping Crane were loss of habitat, hunting, and decreased nesting success caused by egg collecting. Effort to restore the Whooping Crane has been monumental. A nonmigratory flock has been established in Florida, and the migratory flock that splits its time between the Texas coast and Wood Buffalo National Park has been stable for some time.

Very Rare Migrant and past resident

Sandhill Crane — *Grus canadensis*

J F M A M J J A S O N D

B

Description: The tall (50") Sandhill Crane has a uniformly gray body. Bare, red skin covers the crown, and the bill is green. The long legs are coal black. In the spring, they apply heavy amounts of oxidized iron-rich mud to their feathers. This turns the plumage reddish brown.

Sandhill Crane in wetlands habitat

Feeding: An omnivore that will eat vegetation, seeds, insects, amphibians, reptiles, rodents, and nestlings. They will consume the eggs of waterfowl and other species. They forage in flocks outside of the breeding season.

Habits: Sandhill Cranes are famed for their courtship dance where birds spread wings and leap into the air while calling. Females hold their bills horizontal while calling, and males hold theirs vertical during a call.

Nest: Sandhill Cranes are monogamous and form long-term pair bonds. In the shallow water of a marsh, a mound of plant material is built. The nest may be up to 5 feet across. Both parents incubate 2 brown-spotted olive-buff eggs for around one month. Sandhill Cranes will parasitize each other's nests. The young fledge after about 2 months of parental care by both sexes. Normally only one colt (crane chick) will survive to fledging.

Voice: Often carrying over one mile, the low, rattling *"garooooo"* call is common. Pairs perform a duet vocalization with males giving a low, long series of calls,

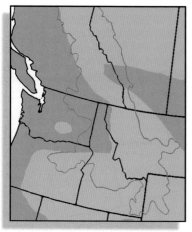

followed by three shrill notes from the female.

Primary Habitat Characteristics: Marsh vegetation is required for nesting and adjacent grasslands and agricultural fields for feeding.

Other Habitats: Grasslands near wetlands are used in the breeding season, and cranes may be in any open habitat outside that season.

Conservation: Populations have either stabilized or are increasing. Lead poisoning from spent shotgun pellets is a concern in marshes that see heavy waterfowl hunting use.

Solitary Sandpiper

J F M A M J J A S O N D

Tringa solitaria

B/M

Solitary Sandpiper in the Clark Fork Valley

Description: The Solitary Sandpiper (8¹/₂") is deep, dark brown on the wings and back. This brown is heavily covered with tiny white spots. The neck, breast and sides are thinly streaked with black. The belly is white. The white eye-ring truly stands out and is a good identification key. Closely related to the Lesser Yellowlegs, this sandpiper has olive legs that separate the two species. The tail pattern of dark central tail feathers and whitish outer tail feathers is quite unique.

Feeding: The bulk of the diet is made up of insects, which are captured from the water's surface while the bird wades through shallow water. It will also probe mud for various invertebrates. Possesses a unique feeding habit of using a foot to stir the mud and, thus, exposing potential prey items.

Habits: True to its name, the Solitary Sandpiper nests and migrates alone. It will bob its tail up and down when it senses a potential threat before it bursts into flight.

Nest: This has a nesting behavior unique among shorebirds. It uses the nests of songbirds (notably American Robin and Eastern Kingbird), either an old nest or one from which it evicts the current tenants, that are placed in spruce or other conifers. Nesting territories can be quite large, up to a square kilometer. Both parents incubate the 4 chestnut-speckled olive eggs for 24 days.

Voice: A sharp *"peet-weet-weet"* is the alarm call.

Primary Habitat Characteristics: In the Northern Rockies, it is normally seen during migration in wooded wetlands.

Other Habitats: The Solitary Sandpiper can occasionally be spotted along well-vegetated streams and lakes.

Conservation: Populations appear to be stable and secure in the Northern Rockies.

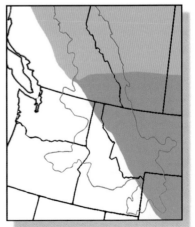

Description: A bird that sounds like its name, the Willet (15") has a stocky body that is prominently mottled on the back, wings and head. The belly is white. The bill is stout and rather straight. During flight, the boldly patterned black and white wings are easily seen. The legs are long and grayish. From late summer through fall, the plumage morphs into a medium-toned gray that subdues the mottling of the back.

Breeding Willet on Cottonwood Reservoir, Montana

Feeding: On its summer breeding wetlands, this species feeds largely upon aquatic insects and other invertebrates. These items are captured from the mud with a sensitive probing bill, or items are picked from the surface on occasion. Willets will consume a modest amount of plant matter and small fish.

Habits: Normally seen walking near the water's edge on mudflats probing the muck for prey. When disturbed, it readily takes off into a low flight with stiff wingbeats while giving its call.

Nest: The Willet nests in loose colonies, although this behavior is more pronounced on the East Coast. Males will fly high over a nesting site, while giving the *"willet"* call. The hidden nest is a shallow ground depression placed amid dense grass. Both sexes incubated the 4 brown and black-spotted greenish-buff eggs for about 25 days.

Voice: The *"pill-will-willet"* is the most often heard vocalization.

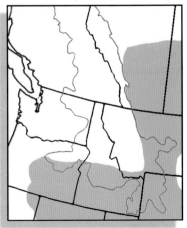

Primary Habitat Characteristics: Normally found on wetlands that are surrounded by native grasslands.

Other Habitats: Also present on wet agricultural fields and meadows.

Conservation: Willets can be affected by the loss of wetlands habitat. Once they were hunted for food.

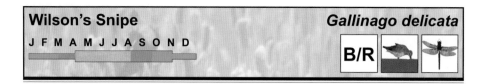

Wilson's Snipe

J F M A M J J A S O N D

Gallinago delicata

B/R

Description: A common resident of wetlands, the Wilson's Snipe (10½") is a plump shorebird with a long, narrow bill designed for probing. The head has alternating light and dark stripes. The flanks are heavily barred. The back is boldly striped white. The legs are rather short. During display flights, two stiff outer tail feathers are visible. These unique feathers produce the winnowing sound associated with snipes.

The recently renamed Wilson's Snipe

Feeding: The snipe uses its long bill to probe the mud to seek out a variety of insects, including the burrowing larvae of horseflies and other aquatic flies. They also consume a host of worm species.

Habits: Usually seen flushing inches from your feet with a rapid zigzagging flight that is accompanied with noisy calls. A lone Wilson's Snipe standing one legged atop a fence post is another common sight.

Nest: During courtship, the male Wilson's Snipe gives a spectacular aerial display of dives that produce the loud winnowing sound. A well-concealed shallow depression that is lined with grass, leaves and other vegetation serves as the nest. The female incubates the 4 brown and black-marked green eggs alone for approximately 20 days. Both parents care for the brood; however, they may split them into two groups. The young fledge in around 20 days.

Voice: Emits a rather harsh *"scaip"* notes when startled and *"wheet-wheet"* from perches near nesting sites.

Primary Habitat Characteristics: During the breeding season, they use wetlands with ample shallow, standing water.

Other Habitats: They also live in wet meadows, fields, and mudflats.

Conservation: It was recently split from its Old World counterpart, and the name changed from Common Snipe.

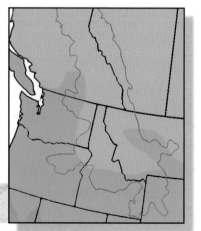

Description: A little gull (13-15")
with highly distinguishing white eye-
crescents that meet behind the eye
and are open in front. These crescents are rather thick. Breeding
adults have rosy breasts and black
heads. The center of the tail is gray.
The bill is dark red and short.
Franklin's Gull is a three-year gull.

Breeding Franklin's Gull

Feeding: The summer diet is almost
entirely insects. They are known to
follow plows for newly unearthed insects and worms. May catch some insects, such
as dragonflies, in midair.

Habits: Nesting colonies move unpredictably from year to year. Social feeders.

Nest: A colonial nester with nests built of grasses or dead marsh plants placed on
the ground or floating attached to emergent vegetation. Colonies can number up to
15,000-20,000 individuals. The precise location of the nesting colony can vary from
year to year as the water level flucuates. The 3 brown- and black-marked greenish-
brown eggs are incubated for 18-20 days. The young fledge in 25-30 days. The
family group remains together after fledging and stays intact until they begin the
migrate southward.

Voice: The most common call is a *"weea weea weea"*, however, other calls include
a soft *"krruk"* and a breeding season *"po-lee po-lee."*

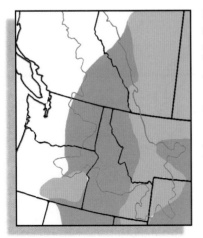

Primary Habitat Characteristics: Requires
sparse emergent vegetation (particularly cattails
and bulrushes) and shallow water (less than 6").
The Franklin's Gull prefers wetlands where the
vegetation is not very dense.

Other Habitats: Lakes and sloughs. The
Franklin's Gull winters on the coast of South
America, with some birds seen several miles
from shore.

Conservation: Range seems to be expanding
and populations increasing. Concern is warranted due to the limited colony sites.

Forster's Tern

Sterna forsteri

J F M A M J J A S O N D

B

Hovering Forster's Tern

Description: A medium sized tern (15"), the Forster's Tern has a black cap and black-tipped orange-red bill. The underparts are a paper white and the tail is gray with white edges. The forked tail extends farther than the folded wings — unlike the Common Tern, whose wings surpass its tail. The mantle and wings are gray. The wing primaries are also a silvery white in flight.

Feeding: Flying gracefully over the water and marsh, the Forster's Tern catches flying insects on the wing. They also pick dead and dying insects off the water. The plunge dive for fish is also a somewhat common feeding tactic. Fish are speared with the lower bill, then the upper closes over them.

Habits: The flight is like that of a swallow, with a snap in the shallow, rapid wingbeats. Known for aggressive colony defense like most terns. Nesting colonies are commonly associated with Yellow-headed Blackbirds.

Nest: Courtship displays are thought to be very similar to those of the Common Tern. A depression lined with grasses is placed near the water. The nest also may be placed on a mat of floating vegetation. They are known to use the abandoned nest of Pied-billed Grebes. Forster's Terns are loosely colonial in nesting behavior. Both parents incubate the 3 heavily dark-spotted olive eggs for 24 days, and care for the young for several weeks.

Voice: *"Zreep"*, *"kip"*, and a quick, high *"keer"* are known Forster's Tern calls.

Primary Habitat Characteristics: Marshy borders adjacent to open water are prime nesting sites. The Forster's Tern is primarily a bird of large wetland complexes.

Other Habitats: Southern coastlines in the winter months.

Conservation: Uses wetlands that also have agricultural value. Populations are decreasing. Warrants concern due to limited colony sites.

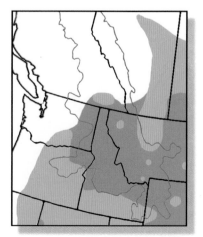

Black Tern

Chlidonias niger

B

Description: Buoyantly cruising over a cattail marsh, the Black Tern (9") is mostly black; I know you're shocked by this revelation. The mantle, wings and tail are slate gray. The wingtips are black. The bill is black. The undertail is white and the legs are bright red.

Black Tern cruising along Freezeout Lake

Feeding: Insects are the bulk of the diet, while aquatic invertebrates and small fish make up a much smaller portion of the diet. Flying insects are often caught on the wing in an aerial foraging fashion. The aquatic invertebrates and fish are plucked from the water's surface.

Habits: During the breeding season, Black Terns will form associations with Forster's Terns. Very gregarious throughout the year. Multiple individuals vigorously defend nesting territories with loud calls, and then dive-bomb intruders.

Nest: Reaches breeding maturity at 2 years of age. Males present small fish to the females as a courtship display. Black Terns show a measure of faithfulness to a particular nesting area year after year. The nest is a floating mat of decayed plants attached to dense emergent vegetation. Both sexes incubate the 3 dark-spotted brown eggs for 20 days. The young will remain with the parents for 4 weeks before they become independent.

Voice: The metallic *"kik"* is the most often heard call of the Black Tern.

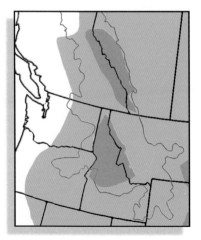

Primary Habitat Characteristics: Requires expanses of emergent vegetation and large areas of open water for feeding. The Black Tern favors wetlands with 25-75% vegetation density and that are larger than 20 hectares.

Other Habitats: Black Terns will frequent large and rivers with marshy margins, wet meadows, and other water-inundated habitats.

Conservation: Black Terns populations have been reduced in the past by the loss of habitat due to the draining of wetlands for agriculture and development.

Marsh Wren

Cistothorus palustris

J F M A M J J A S O N D

B/R

Marsh Wren atop a cattail stalk

Description: The small Marsh Wren (5") is brown above and whitish on the breast and belly. The flanks are buff colored. The head is darker brown with white superciliary stripe over the eye. The tail, which is almost always held cocked, has heavy black barring across it. The bill is thin and decurved, as with all wrens.

Feeding: Feeds heavily upon insects and snails that are gleaned from the surface of emergent plants. They will also, but rarely, capture insects in midair in flycatcher fashion. The eggs of other species are also consumed. These eggs are penetrated with the sharp bill, and contents are allowed to drip out.

Habits: They compete vigorously with other marsh-nesting birds, such as Red-winged Blackbirds. The Marsh Wren will destroy the unattended eggs and nestlings of these species. Will use nests outside of the nesting season for roosting sites.

Nest: A courting male will engage in a display that has him puffing up, cocking his tail over the back and flapping the wings for a prospective female. The male builds many dome-shaped nests of grass and reeds and attached to cattails or bulrushes. Only one or two of these nests are used for nesting. The females lines the selected nest with grass and feathers. She incubates the 4-5 purple- to gray-spotted brown eggs for 12-16 days. These young will fledge in around 15 days. Marsh Wrens regularly double brood.

Voice: The fluid rattle of the Marsh Wren can absolutely fill a cattail marsh with sound. A sharp *"tusk"* is given as an alarm call.

Primary Habitat Characteristics: Prefers larger wetlands with an abundance of tall emergent vegetation.

Other Habitats: The Marsh Wren will use slow rivers and lakes with marshy margins.

Conservation: Very abundant, in fact, found in almost very marsh in the Northern Rocky Mountains.

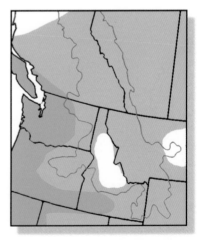

Description: The adult male Common Yellowthroat (5") is a masked desperado. A black mask wraps around the face from well behind each eye. A faint white border sits atop this mask. Bright yellow extends from the throat to the breast. The back is brown and the undertail coverts are yellow. The female is sans the black mask; however, she does have a whitish eye ring. Immatures resemble a dull brown female in overall plumage.

Male (l) and female (r) Common Yellowthroat

Feeding: Maneuvering skillfully in dense vegetation, the Common Yellowthroat takes a wide array of insects from the surfaces of plants. They will hover-glean occasionally, and on even more rare occasions, they will catch insects out of midair.

Habits: Often seen cocking its tail while it briefly perches. The only warbler in the Northern Rockies that will nest in open cattail marshes.

Nest: Males court the fairer sex with a display that involves the repeated flicking of the tail and wings. The open cup nest of grass, leaves, weeds and other plant material is built by the female low (under 3 feet) in a shrub or in cattails. The female incubates the 4 marked cream-colored for 12 days. The male feeds the female during the incubation period. Both parents care for the young and they fledge in 10 days. They normally have two broods per year.

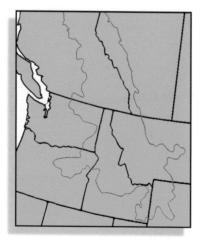

Voice: They will give a rolling *"wichity-wichity-wichity."* This song can be quite variable among individuals. A raspy *"chuck"* is a common call.

Primary Habitat Characteristics: The Common Yellowthroat favors a mixture of dense, low emergent growth and small shrubs/trees for nesting and foraging opportunities.

Other Habitats: Riparian habitat is used from time to time.

Conservation: As its name implies, the Common Yellowthroat is very common and secure.

Red-winged Blackbird

Agelaius phoeniceus

J F M A M J J A S O N D

B/R

Male (l) and female (r) Red-winged Blackbird

Description: The male Red-winged Blackbird (9") possesses a glossy black body. On the wings, a roughly rectangular red patch with an adjacent yellow bar below is clearly visible. The pointed bill and legs are black. The female is dark brown above and whitish below with heavy brown streaking. The bill and legs are a dull brown.

Feeding: These blackbirds consume dragonflies, damselflies, beetles, and other flying insects. These insects are captured from the ground, gleaning of plants, and flycatching in the air. A very small amount of seeds are also consumed during the breeding season and winter.

Habits: Extremely territorial with breeding pairs having several hundred square yards of exclusive territory. They also compete with Marsh Wrens and, like the wrens, they will destroy and consume their competitors' eggs and young. Red-winged Blackbirds give myriad displays and vocalizations; males have 12 displays and about twenty vocalizations, and the female has 9 displays and 6 vocalizations.

Nest: Up to 15 females will reside within a single male's territory. She builds a nest composed of reeds and grass and lined with rushes. For 12-14 days, the female incubates the 4 black- and purple-marked pale bluish eggs. After the eggs hatch, both parents feed the altricial young for 11 to 14 days. The young may be fed occasionally upon fledging. They may have two broods in a breeding season.

Voice: Both males and females give a multitude of calls and songs; however, the *"konk-la-reeeee"* song is the most common and the *"check"* is oft-heard alarm call.

Primary Habitat Characteristics: Red-winged Blackbirds tend to breed in marshes with trees within or nearby, and these marshes tend to have a good amount of edge.

Other Habitats: Will breed in wet agricultural fields on occasion.

Conservation: Very common and secure.

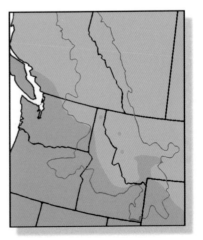

Description: The male Yellow-headed Blackbird (9") makes a striking impression. The black body contrasts the bright yellow head. Yellow extends to the chest. The bill is sharp and black, and this black extends back to the eye. A white wing patch is seen in flight. Females are a blackish-brown with rather pale yellow on the head. Juveniles males closely resemble the female except the head is brown and the wing coverts are tipped with white.

Feeding: The Yellow-headed Blackbird is a specialist consumer of primarily dragonflies and damselflies that are abundant within wetlands. Ground forages and gleans these insects from vegetation. They, from time to time, flycatch insects from midair. They also consume a small amount of seeds.

Male Yellow-headed Blackbird

Habits: They actively announce their presence with a head tossing call that comes from atop a cattail stalk.

Nest: This species is polygynous with each male having 1-6 females within his territory. The female builds a nest out of wet vegetation and lines this cup with fine grass. These nests are attached to emergent vegetation over the water. The female incubates the 4 brown-mottled pale blue eggs for 12 days. After she has cared for the young for 9 to 12 days, they will fledge and become increasingly independent.

Voice: Males gives a fluid song and another that is a buzzing *"kuk-koh-koh-koh waaaa."* Females will also sing an unmusical chatter.

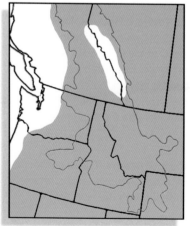

Primary Habitat Characteristics: The Yellow-headed Blackbird prefers tall emergent vegetation, such as cattails or bulrushes, over standing water. They will occasionally roost in willows within the wetland complex.

Other Habitats: They will use agricultural fields, in addition to wetlands, during the winter.

Conservation: Very common; however, they can be affected by blackbird control programs in the South, which intend to protect crops from the millions of wintering blackbirds.

Down from the Tundra: Shorebird Migration

A cold wind blows off the east slopes of the Bridger Range and sweeps across the Shields River Valley of southwestern Montana. It cuts through my clothing and leaves goose bumps across my skin. It is the beginning of August and already there is a whisper of autumn on the wind. At this medium-sized reservoir, the late summer's irrigation needs have started to draw down the water level, and the exposed mudflats have begun to bake and crack. Walking out to the water's edge, I find the mud progressively more hostile, grabbing at my shoes and ripping them off my feet. Several yards across the shallow water on a small exposed mud island stand a group of shorebirds, those wonderful creatures that possess both swift, agile flight and the ability to stalk about the mudflats. Marbled Godwits, Willets, and Killdeer, all of which breed in the

Northern Rockies, stand alongside a group of Western Sandpipers and a lone Semipalmated Plover. These latter species have flown down from the north, and they are using this small lake and its mudflats as an important stopover area. Here they will replenish the critical fat supplies and rest their weary muscles. Catching sight of me, they burst into whistling flight. The godwits and Willets take deep, slow wingbeats. The Western Sandpipers become one entity once they take flight. Each individual turns in unison with its neighbors, creating a wave effect as the white underwings catch the warm reflected light from the water's surface. These tiny birds are marvels of migratory prowess.

Shorebirds have two surges of migration through the Northern Rockies. The first wave of shorebirds comes in April and May, and the fall migration begins in late July and concludes by early September. Total distances of these travels can be measured in thousands of miles and many days. Some species, notably the Baird's Sandpiper, may cover as much as 15,000 miles round trip during the year. Shorebirds can achieve speeds upwards of fifty miles per hour and altitudes of well over 10,000 feet. They fly at night and alight upon stopovers as the sun creeps over the horizon.

The migration of shorebirds follow established corridors or flyways. These corridors are determined by landscape features and the all-important stopover areas, where food is dependable and plentiful. As shorebirds migrate through the Northern

Rockies, they do so as small groups that hop from one stopover to the next. Without the stopover areas, the shorebirds would not be able to put on enough fat to continue their migration. It is imperative that the stopovers be protected from degradation through draining and conversion to agricultural fields. As shorebirds migrate through

the Northern Rockies they follow the north-south intermountain valleys and the Front Range. Within the intermountain valleys, the important stopovers include areas such as Ninepipe National Wildlife Refuge and Grays Lake National Wildlife Refuge. The most important stopover along the Front Range is Freezeout Lake.

Migration is an endeavor that has many perils and challenges. Storms can prevent the birds from reaching their stopover or blow them far off-course. Exhaustion is a constant concern. Imagine that these small birds must put on sufficient fat at each stopover, in order to make the next. If the bird does not have enough stored energy, it can reached exhaustion and land in an inhospitable habitat. A new peril of migration for the shorebird is the placement of radio and utility towers. As the birds migrate at night, they have been known to fly directly into these structures, resulting in injury or death.

With such an expediture of energy, why migrate and take on the risks associated with this behavior. Contrary to popular belief that these migratory birds are fleeing the onset of cold weather, they actually are moving on to the areas where food is in abundance. Of course, the shorebirds' food supply and the weather are interrelated. During the spring, the Arctic is bathed in eternal light, which produces massive amounts of insect life. The shorebirds arrive in the North to take advantage of this food source and produce young. The end of the short-lived feast of the Arctic necessitates the return journey south. They must leave their breeding grounds before winter storms bring a halt to teeming masses of insects. As they descend, each stopover is teeming with food. Upon their arrival on the wintering grounds, the shorebirds find that food once again is in bountiful supply. The behavior of migration is all about maximizing the availability of food and avoiding climatic conditions that are adverse to insect life.

As the sun descends into the Bridger Mountains, long shadows are cast across the water and mudflats. I turn to walk back across the sagebrush flat, as the soft sound of little wings rises behind. In the fading light, the light colored bodies of little shorebirds reflect straw yellow. The flock flies with one mind, moving in unison. They are beginning their night flight for their next stopover. I know which direction they are heading, but I turn away to preserve the mystery of the migration.

I hear the whispering voice of spring,
the thrush's trill, the catbird's cry.

−OLIVER WENDELL HOLMES

The thick willow and red-oiser dogwood has all but hidden a secretive Gray Catbird. As I attempt to move around the small cluster of trees, the catbird simply moves to the opposite side, giving me just a glance of the red undertail coverts. This bird uses the notably dense vegetation to its advantage. From the top of a younger cottonwood, a Song Sparrow gives its song to the morning. I entered this riparian thicket at sunrise, some twenty minutes earlier. Within this brief time period, I have already spotted 22 species. Five warblers, three thrushes, catbird, and Cedar Waxwing are among the notables. This thicket extends only about 20 feet from either bank of the small East Gallatin River, and yet I have seen more species and greater diversity of birds in this limited area than in any other area in the valley. I think the importance of riparian corridors in the Northern Rockies can not be overstated, and yet they account for so little of the total landmass.

The riparian habitats of the Northern Rockies are most commonly along the banks of rivers and creeks. These streams can be either perennial or intermittent. They may also be present around some lakes/ponds and wetlands. They follow the courses of the streams in narrow bands that seldom exceed 200 feet in width. Due to their location, they have access to good amounts of water. Many of these riparian areas have dense canopies, and abundant grass and forbs in the understory. The dominant shrub species in riparian habitats of the moister regions of the Rockies are alder, willow, birch, and red-oiser dogwood. All of these species thrive in this environment where water is plentiful and spring flooding common. In the drier areas of the Northern Rockies, black hawthorn, serviceberry, and chokecherry are the dominant species. Ponderosa pine and Douglas-fir can also be found in the dry region riparian corridors. Wild rose, common snowberry, and other smaller shrubs species are usually found underneath the canopy shrubs. The habitats through which the riparian corridor slices through are all of the forest-type habitats, shrublands, and grasslands.

Fire, ice rafting, and damage caused by flooding are the major forces that drive stand structure and replacement. As they surround water needed by large grazing mammals, riparian areas can quickly become degraded by overgrazing and physical damage caused by these animals, particularly cattle.

What is the importance of riparian habitats to the birds of the Northern Rockies? Think about the fact that riparian vegetation accounts for less than 1% of the total landmass, yet about half of the breeding bird species will nest in this habitat. Many of the remaining species will visit riparian areas for watering and cover. Riparian habitats are essential to the survival of birds and other creatures across the West. Riparian corridors are the among the most biological diverse and productive habitats in the Northern Rockies. Dick Hutto, an ornithology professor at the University of Montana, summed up the importance of riparian areas to birds in a unique, elegant way. There are roughly 235 breeding birds in Montana. Of those 235, 90% use riparian areas at one time or another through the year. Half of that 90% or 45% of the total breeding birds are relatively restricted to riparian areas. Now here is the kicker, riparian areas only account for one half of one percent of the total landmass. So, nearly half of all Montana birds are present on $\frac{1}{2}$% of the land.

Riparian corridors are not only important to breeding birds, but also to migrating songbirds such warblers like the Blackpoll and Palm Warblers. These tiny songbirds follow the courses of riparian habitat rather than attempting a crossing of less hospitable habitats like extensive conifer forest and grasslands.

One of the birds that absolutely depends on riparian habitat is the Gray Catbird. This thrush-sized bird is gray overall with splashes of crimson on the head and the undertail coverts. This shade of gray has the unique ability to blend in with both the

shadows and sunlight. The bird expertly gleans insects from almost every surface found in the riparian habitat.

The most interesting thing about the Gray Catbird is its vocal abilities. It is a member of a family of song mimics. *Mimidae* is a family of birds that includes the thrashers, Northern Mockingbird, and the Gray Cat-

bird. Members of this family have evolved the ability to mimic the songs and calls of other birds that they encounter. One theory is that by learning many different songs, the bird appears to be more fit than one with a limited sample of songs. The appearence of fitness becomes important when a Gray Catbird is defending and maintaining its breeding territory and pair bond.

It is not exactly known how the Gray Catbird learns its songs and phrases. The snippets of vocalizations are, however, retained from year to year even as new phrases are added to the repertoire. They may even have learned songs of birds that they only encounter on the southern wintering grounds of Mexico and Central America.

The male begins to sing its incredibly complex song at the beginning of the breeding season, which commences upon arrival in the Northern Rockies. The singing seems to peak at dawn and dusk, although the Gray Catbird will sing at almost any time.

So just how much can an individual Gray Catbird learn? There is a record of a single male Gray Catbird having 170 different phrases included in a four and a half minute singing bout. How many songs can you remember in four minutes? This little fact gives insight into the ability of this mimic.

The Gray Catbird has one song that is all its own: the *"mew"* that gives this bird its name. The cat-like vocalization is the Gray Catbird's alarm call, and appears to be one of the few calls that belongs solely to it.

As the sun continues towards its point of maximum intensity, I break free of the willow thicket. Behind me the habitat that was earlier a cacophony of sounds, has fallen silent save for the occasional Yellow Warbler and *"mew"* of the Catbird. As summer begins to fade, most of the birds will follow the warmth of summer south to Mexico and Central America.

Black-chinned Hummingbird   *Archilochus alexandri*

J F M A M J J A S O N D

B

Male Black-chinned Hummingbird

Description: A small bird (3$\frac{1}{2}$"), the Black-chinned Hummingbird has a medium length bill that decurves slightly. The male is green above and a pale off-white below. The black chin comes from the iridescent black gorget that has a purple band along the bottom edge. The purple band is rather difficult to see. The female is a golden green above and pale gray below. The throat of the female is relatively unmarked.

Feeding: Feeds mainly on nectar from an array of flowers, including penstemons, paintbrush, and other nectar-producing flowers. Black-chinned Hummingbirds will consume insects, which are captured in flycatcher fashion or gleaned from vegetation. The sap from sapsucker wells appears to be a favorite treat.

Habits: While in a hovering flight, the tail is pumped in a constant rhythm. The bird is quite tolerant of human activities. Never overwinters in the Northern Rockies.

Nest: The male performs a series of U-shaped dives that produce a buzzing sound at the bottom of each repetition during the breeding season. The nest is placed on a branch several feet above the ground. Constructed by the female, it is made up of plant fibers held together with spider webs. The outside of the nest is encrusted with leaves and other vegetative parts. The female incubates the 2 white eggs for 13-16 days. She also cares for the nestlings for about 20 days until they fledge.

Voice: The warbling song is rarely heard; however, the soft *"tchew"* call is common.

Primary Habitat Characteristics: Black-chinned Hummingbirds almost always occur in habitats with a deciduous component and with low percentage of canopy cover. In the Northern Rockies this translates to riparian corridors.

Other Habitats: They can also be found feeding in shrublands.

Conservation: Widespread and common throughout the West.

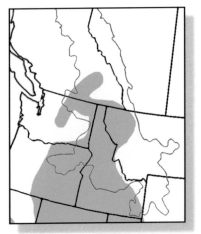

© Tom Ulrich

Description: The Rufous Hummingbird is very boisterous for its small size (4"). The male's back is a rufous color and the underparts are white. The gorget is a bright red with golden iridescence. The female has a copper penny-green back and white underparts. The flanks are rufous as are the undertail coverts.

USFWS/Biggins

Male Rufous Hummingbird

Feeding: This hummingbird tends to utilize flowers that have short to medium length petals. These include fireweed, larkspur, paintbrush, and columbines. Feeding is done while hovering. Early arrivals in the spring will consume insects until the flowers come into bloom.

Habits: A very aggressive hummingbird that will drive other hummers away from nectar sources. This species breeds farther north than any other hummingbird. Male Rufous Hummingbirds arrive first on the breeding grounds, and the females follow a couple of weeks later.

Nest: During courtship, the male will do a ritual U-shaped dive that is accompanied with a *"dit-dit-dit"* vocalization. The female builds the small cup of plant fibers and moss held together by spider silk. Lichens are attached to the exterior of the nest for camouflage. The nest is placed within the branches of a coniferous tree. The female incubates the 2 small, white eggs for 12-15 days. These young will then fledge in 3 weeks.

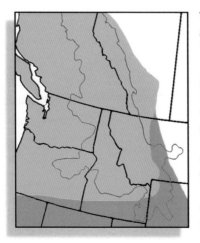

Voice: This hummingbird has no known song, although a variety of sharp calls, such as *"tchip"*, can be heard.

Primary Habitat Characteristics: The Rufous Hummingbird's habitat usually has a strong conifer component, which is required for nesting, along with willow/alder in the riparian corridor.

Other Habitats: Meadows surrounded by conifer forest are also used by this species.

Conservation: It is declining, and this decline may be due to habitat alteration.

© Peter LaTourrette

Willow Flycatcher in habitat

Description: The *Empidonax* flycatchers are the bane of many birders, and the Willow Flycatcher (5³/₄") is but one among this group of look-alikes. The bill of this flycatcher is relatively heavy and the eye ring is very subdued. The back is an olive-brown. The white throat transitions into an olive breast, which fades into a rather pale yellow belly. The wingbars are white and not prominent. Like all Empids, the Willow Flycatcher is best identified by its voice.

Feeding: The Willow Flycatcher will wait on a low perch, and, then, it suddenly flies out to snatch a flying insect from the air. The flycatcher will then return to its original perch. Flying insects are the bulk of its food and spiders make up the much smaller remainder.

Habits: Willow Flycatchers tend to migrate late in the spring and early in the fall.

Nest: It actively defends the nesting territory with singing. The female usually places the nest in a willow on a vertical branch. She builds a cup of woven grass, stems, plant fibers, and stripes of bark, which is lined with grass. The female incubates the 3-4 brown-spotted off-white eggs for 12-15 days. Both sexes care for the young after they hatch. The young fledge at 2 weeks.

Voice: The nasal *"fitz-bew"* of the song is unique to the Willow Flycatcher and a great identification key. A soft *"wit"* is commonly heard call.

Primary Habitat Characteristics: Strongly associated with willows in riparian habitats.

Other Habitats: Sometimes they can be seen in deciduous stands some distance from water.

Conservation: The Willow Flycatcher's dependence on riparian corridors causes it to be susceptible to habitat alteration from development. Once it was lumped with the Alder Flycatcher into the Traill's Flycatcher.

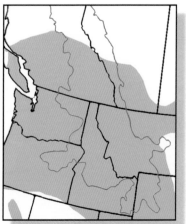

Cordillaran Flycatcher

J F M A M J J A S O N D

Empidonax occidentalis

B

Description: Another Empidonax flycatcher, the Cordillaran Flycatcher (5³/₄") is brownish above and yellowish below. There is a brown wash across the breast. The pale eye ring is teardrop-shaped with the portion behind the eye thicker than the remainder of the eye ring. This eye ring shape is unique among our Empidonax flycatchers.

Feeding: Flying insects comprise the majority of the Cordillaran Flycatcher's diet. They are captured midair as the bird bursts from its perch. These perches tend to be rather high in conifers. This species will also hover-glean insects and caterpillars from the surface of vegetation.

© Peter LaTourrette

The teardrop eye-ring of the Cordillaran Flycatcher

Habits: They will incorporate bits of string and paper into their nests. The Cordillaran Flycatcher tends to use lower perches than some other flycatchers.

Nest: The Cordillaran Flycatcher will build its nest in a variety of locations; the vertical branch of a shrub, the top of a stump, and under a bridge are some examples. The female builds an open cup of moss, grass, hair, and plant fibers lined with hair and feathers. She incubates the 3-4 red- and purple-spotted, brown-blotched white eggs for 14-15 days. Both sexes care for the young until they fledge in a little over 2 weeks.

Voice: The male's *"pit peet"* call is good identification differentiator between the Cordillarran and other Empidonax flycatchers.

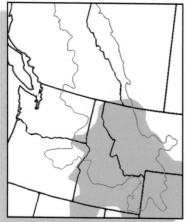

Primary Habitat Characteristics: It usually breeds in riparian habitats in the mountains with a surrounding conifer forest that contains standing snags.

Other Habitats: The Cordillaran Flycatcher can be found foraging in dry Douglas-fir forest and other semi-open habitats.

Conservation: Until recently the Cordillaran Flycatcher was considered the same species as the Pacific-slope Flycatcher under the name Western Flycatcher.

Northern Roungh-winged Swallow

Description: The most nondescript swallow in the Northern Rockies, the Northern Rough-winged Swallow (5") is often seen feeding with other swallows at the edges of the flock. They are generally brownish above, with gray-brown on the chin and throat that fades into white on the belly. When compared to the other swallows, this bird has longer wings and flies with slower, deeper wingbeats.

Feeding: Flying insects are the Northern Rough-wing's bread and butter. A solitary Northern Rough-winged Swallow captures most of these insects on the wing over a stream of lake.

Habits: Tends to more solitary than other swallows during the breeding season. Outside of this time, they form large feeding-flocks.

Nest: During courtship, the male will chase the female incessantly. The nest is a solitary burrow in a soft dirt bank near the water, although it can be located some distance from water. The swallows may create the tunnels or they can use an old Bank Swallow or kingfisher burrows. These tunnels go 1-6 feet into the bank and end with bulky nests of twigs, grass, and, stems lined with grass. The female incubates the 5-7 white eggs for 12-16 days. Both parents share the feeding and care of the young for 3 weeks, at which time the juveniles fledge.

Voice: When alarmed, a harsh *"breet"* call is given.

Primary Habitat Characteristics: The Northern Rough-winged Swallow depends on vertical dirt, clay, sand, or gravel banks for nesting. These banks are most often located on bends in rivers, resulting from erosion.

Other Habitats: Occasionally seen foraging over agricultural fields and in gravel pits.

Conservation: The use of human-created nest sites, namely gravel pits, may be leading to the increase of Northern Rough-winged Swallow populations.

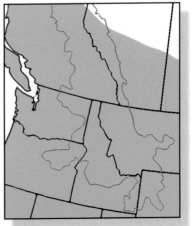

Description: At 4³/₄", the Bank Swallow is the smallest of our swallows. They are dark brown above and grayish white below. The brown chest band is idiosyncratic to the Bank Swallow. The tail is mildly forked. Can be confused with the Northern Rough-winged Swallow. The wing-strokes are much shallower and wingbeats are more rapid than the aforementioned cousin.

Perched Bank Swallow

Feeding: Like all swallows, the Bank Swallow aerial forages for a wide range of flying insects. Almost all feeding is done in flight. Tends to forage in large flocks that congregate over water. Feeding is done very low and close to the water. Bank Swallows will also feed over pastures and meadows that are close to water.

Habits: Very gregarious. The entire Bank Swallow colony will mob and harass an intruder until it is a safe distance away from the nests. The flocks that form after breeding may number in the thousands.

Nest: Nests in large colonies on vertical dirt banks. The burrow is dug to a depth up to 5 feet. Both adults excavate the burrow by digging with the bill and feet. The nest at the end of the burrow is made up of grass, rootlets, and stems lined with feathers. Both parents incubated the 4-5 white eggs for 14-16 days. The young leave the nest after a little more than 3 weeks of parental care.

Voice: When pairs meet, they emit a *"tchrrt tchrrt"* call.

Primary Habitat Characteristics: The vertical bank used for nesting is found in close proximity to water. Natural nest sites are typically eroded sand, gravel, or clay river banks.

Other Habitats: The Bank Swallow has adapted to use banks created by gravel quarries. The removal of gravel from these quarries can lead to the destruction of entire colonies, which will re-nest in the same gravel pit, possibly only to be razed again.

Conservation: Rather common and stable.

Barn Swallow — *Hirundo rustica*

J F M A M J J A S O N D

B

Adult Barn Swallow

Description: The most distinctive of our swallows, the Barn Swallow (6¾") has a deeply forked, long tail. The upperparts are a deep, iridescent blue-black, and the breast and belly are a warm cinnamon. The chin and throat are reddish-brown. Juveniles have a shorter tail and the underparts are pale gray.

Feeding: Feeds mostly on flying insects that are captured and eaten on the wing. Forages very low over water; in fact, the Barn Swallow may actually skim the water's surface in pursuit of newly emerging insects. They will occasionally consume berries and seeds.

Habits: Flies with graceful and fluid movements at low altitudes. The Barn Swallow has readily adapted to human activities. They are often seen bursting from under a bridge as we drive across it.

Nest: An aerial chase of females by the males is a common courtship behavior. Bonded pairs will engage in mutual preening. Natural sites for the nest are cliff crevices or caves; however, the Barn Swallow is more likely to use structures such as barns and bridges for nesting. Both sexes build a cup of mud pellets and grass lined with feathers under an overhang. The 4-5 brown- and purple-spotted white eggs hatch in 13-17 days of incubation by both parents. Both parents feed the young until they fledge in around 3 weeks.

Voice: A continuous twitter by both sexes.

Primary Habitat Characteristics: It is usually found near water surrounded by open land.

Other Habitats: Barn Swallows will feed over marshes, agricultural fields, and lakes. They are often associated with bridges and other structures built close to water.

Conservation: The use of buildings as nest sites is beneficial for the aptly named Barn Swallow, although overall numbers seem to be decreasing slightly.

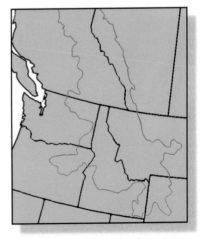

Description: The noisy song of the House Wren (4³/₄") is a hallmark of riparian habitats throughout the Rockies. This wren is overall brown above, and the back is unstreaked. The underside is grayish with a buff barring along the flanks. There is a faint, buff eyebrow. The tail is often held in a cocked position. The overall brown coloration of the House Wren is the most nondescript among wrens in the Northern Rockies.

House Wrens love insect larvae

Feeding: An insectivore in feeding behavior, the House Wren also consumes spiders, arthropods, and land snails and slugs. Normally seen foraging in the lower levels of the canopy where it gleans food items from the branches and leaves.

Habits: The House Wren is a very active bird, constantly flitting about the dense riparian vegetation. As it name implies, the House Wren can become quite accustomed to human activity. The House Wren is very aggressive towards other cavity-nesting species such as Black-capped Chickadees. They often destroy the eggs of these competitors.

Nest: The male sings his bubbly song during the courtship. He shows the female potential nest sites, at which he has already built a dummy nest. The female selects the nest site and finishes the nest by adding a lining of plant fibers, grass, hair, and feathers. The nest site can be any natural crevice or a birdhouse. The 6-8 red-mottled white eggs are incubated for 12-15 days. Both parents tend to the young for

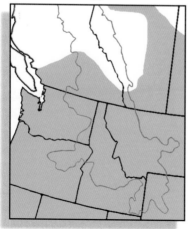

15-18 days. House Wrens may double brood in a year where conditions are favorable.

Voice: The House Wren's song is a series of bubbly whistled notes. A common call is a rattling *"churr"*.

Primary Habitat Characteristics: The House Wren tends to use areas that are semi-open.

Other Habitats: Winters in denser vegetation than that where it breeds and nests.

Conservation: Very widespread and common.

Swainson's Thrush

J F M A M J J A S O N D

Catharus ustulatus

B

A mellow Swainson's Thrush

Description: The joyful, ascending song of the Swainson's Thrush (7") slices through thick vegetation of the streamside. It is more often heard than seen. This brown thrush has a prominent buff eye-ring. The breast is spotted with small dark markings with a buff underwash. The sides are brownish.

Feeding: This thrush splits its diet between insects and fruits. The insect portion of the diet accounts for two-thirds of the total food consumed, and the types of insects eaten include flies, beetles, and almost every other species present. The fruits eaten, which are an important food source in the late summer, tend also to be along a broad spectrum.

Habits: The Swainson's Thrush is very elusive as it slips through dense riparian and deciduous understory vegetation.

Nest: Males establish breeding territories upon arrival in the spring. These territories are vigorously defended from other male Swainson's Thrushes with a threat display that has the territorial male pointing his bill upwards. Along the riparian corridor, the female selects a tree or shrub for a nest site. She places the nest on a branch up to 10 feet off the ground. The nest is a thick-walled open cup made of twigs, plant fibers, grass, and leaves. This nest is lined with finer materials. She incubates the 3-4 red- and purplish-blotched pale blue eggs for 2 weeks. Both parents care for the young until they fledge at 10-13 days.

Voice: An ascending spiral of whistles. The Swainson's Thrush has a *"whit"* call.

Primary Habitat Characteristics: The Swainson's Thrush depends on a deciduous component for nesting that is adjacent to water or in a damp site.

Other Habitats: Swainson's Thrushes can be found in coniferous forests that have deciduous undergrowth of Rocky Mountain maple and alder, for example.

Conservation: Very stable at the present time.

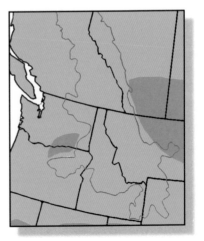

112

Gray Catbird
Dumetella carolinensis

J F M A M J J A S O N D

B

Description: The Gray Catbird's (8¹/₂") catlike meow betrays its presence within thick riparian vegetation. Gray overall with a black cap. The long black tail is held erect. The only splash of color for the Gray Catbird comes from the difficult to see reddish-brown undertail coverts.

Gray Catbird "mewing"

Feeding: This species splits its diet almost evenly between insects and vegetable matter. The insect portion comes from beetles, ants, and other bugs, which are taken in a ground foraging manner. Much like a thrasher, the catbird will flip over leaves and other debris in search of prey. As the summer lingers on, this species switches to a mostly vegetarian diet, and eats fruits and berries while it forages among the branches.

Habits: Very secretive and stays well within dense vegetation, only occasionally singing from an exposed perch. While in the open, the tail is pumped with vigor.

Nest: Upon establishing nesting territories, the males can be heard singing incessantly at dawn and dusk. During courtship, the male pursues the female and displays his chestnut undertail coverts to her. The female places the large nest of twigs, grass, stems, and leaves within a tangle of vegetation. The female alone incubates the oddly bluish green eggs for 2 weeks. The young fledge after a week and half of parental care by both sexes. It is one of few birds that deal well with Brown-headed Cowbird nest parasitism. The Gray Catbird will identify the foreign eggs, puncture them, and eject them.

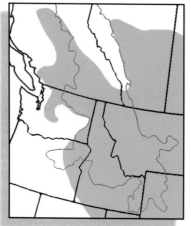

Voice: The Gray Catbird takes its name from the catlike *"mew"* call. Being a member of a family of mimics, this bird learns the songs and sounds of its surroundings, so it gives an eclectic blend of songs and a hodgepodge of other sounds as its sings.

Primary Habitat Characteristics: Dense deciduous growth is good Gray Catbird habitat.

Other Habitats: This bird, for nesting and feeding activities, can also use shrubby wetlands and hedgerows.

The rarely seen Brown Thrasher

© Tom Ulrich

Description: Among dense vegetation, the Brown Thrasher (11½") is generally aloof in temperament. Reddish-brown above, and a light breast and belly that are heavily streaked. The tail is long. The Brown Thrasher's bill is long and slightly decurved.

Feeding: The Brown Thrasher's diet consists of insects, fruits, and seeds. The insects consumed include grasshoppers, beetles, and other ground-dwelling insects. As summer fades into autumn, vegetable matter in the form of fruits, seeds, and nuts, becomes increasingly more important to the Brown Thrasher.

Habits: When disturbed, the Brown Thrasher will retreat into a thicket and give a series of cackling calls. Although typically a ground dweller, the male thrasher sings from atop a tree during the breeding season.

Nest: During the courtship phase, a Brown Thrasher pair will exchange twigs or leaves with each other. Also the male will sing very softly to the female. Within a dense tangle of vegetation, both sexes build the nest in a shrub or small tree 2-6 feet above the earth. Nests have been recorded up to 14 feet above the ground. The nest is a loosely constructed cup of twigs, leaves, grass, and plant fibers lined with grass. Both parents incubate the 4 chestnut-speckled white to pale blue eggs for 2 weeks. The parents continue their care of the young for 9-13 days.

Voice: The song is a repeating series of pieces of learned songs and sounds. The Brown Thrasher is an adept mimic, and it will incorporate many songs into its repertoire. The *"smuck"* is given when it is alarmed.

Primary Habitat Characteristics: The Brown Thrasher requires stands of dense, low deciduous cover for breeding and security.

Other Habitats: It will occur in dense deciduous stands under a conifer canopy.

Conservation: Declining across the West.

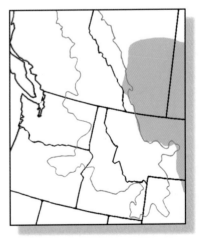

Cedar Waxwing
Bombycilla cedrorum

J F M A M J J A S O N D

B/R

Description: The muted trill of the Cedar Waxwing (7") is a common sound in the riparian thicket. The upperparts are warm brown. The wings have red-tipped secondary feathers. The crested head has a black mask and chin. The underparts are white. The undertail coverts are white. The rump is gray. The tail is tipped with a yellow terminal band.

Flycatching Cedar Waxwing

Feeding: During the summer, the Cedar Waxwing is often seen flycatching. The insects consumed are a variety of flying species. This species will also glean caterpillars and other insect larvae from the vegetative surfaces. As the chill of autumn approaches, the diet converts to the berries of many trees and shrubs, especially mountain ash.

Habits: Often seen in roving flocks, particularly during the winter. These flocks will concentrate around plentiful food sources.

Nest: The nest is a bulky cup of bark fibers, grass, stems, moss, and, occasionally, mud. The Cedar Waxwing will steal nest material from other species for its nest on a branch 5-50 feet above the ground. The female incubates the 3-5 black-speckled bluish gray eggs for a couple of weeks. She feeds the nestlings until they leave the nest after 2 weeks.

Voice: While in the flocks, the soft trill is given. The rarely heard song is a high-pitched hiss.

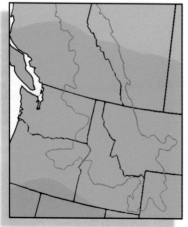

Primary Habitat Characteristics: The riparian areas that have bountiful berry-producing trees, especially mountain ash. They seem to prefer the edges of habitat.

Other Habitats: During the winter, the Cedar Waxwing will invade towns along with its cousin, the Bohemian Waxwing.

Conservation: The Cedar Waxwing is very common in the Northern Rockies. Edward H. Forbush wrote, "Who can describe the marvelous beauty and elegance of this bird?"

Orange-crowned Warbler near Red Rock Lake

© Peter LaTourrette

Description: The most distinguishing feature of Orange-crowned Warbler (4³/₄") is its lack of unique features. From the head down the backside, this species is olive-green. The underside is paler and very faintly streaked. The yellow underside coloration can vary in the intensity. The namesake orange crown is almost never in view.

Feeding: The Orange-crowned Warbler forages in the understory in a wren-like fashion. They pick and probe the vegetation for mostly insects; they will, however, occasionally consume a small amount of vegetable matter.

Habits: These quite vocal birds are normally solitary. They are extremely curious and will investigate most creatures that enter their territory. They are commonly seen with a variety of sparrow species during migration.

Nest: Upon arrival to the breeding grounds, the males establish territories through singing. These territories can be revisited by the same male in subsequent years. The female alone builds a cup of grasses, weeds, and feathers in a ground depression. She will incubate the 4-5 rufous-marked white eggs for 11-13 days. After hatching, she will continue to brood them; however, the male takes on the feeding duties. After about two weeks, the young will leave the nest, and the parents will continue to tend to them for several days afterward.

Voice: The Orange-crowned Warblers sing a rapid trill that falls off in volume and pitch toward the end of the vocalization.

Primary Habitat Characteristics: A variety of riparian habitats with moderate to dense shrub cover in canyons or gullies are used for nesting.

Other Habitats: They will breed in aspen stands at higher elevations.

Conservation: Orange-crowned Warbler numbers are stable.

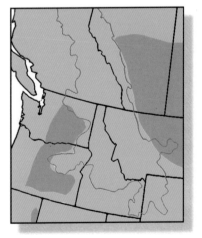

Description: A flash of sunshine in a dark, dense thicket, the Yellow Warbler (4³/₄") is the most abundant warbler in the Northern Rockies. This active warbler is yellow-green above, and a bright yellow explodes from the underparts. The male has reddish streaks on the breast, while the female lacks these colorations. There is a very indistinct eye-ring.

Yellow Warbler taking a drink

Feeding: Yellow Warbler feed by gleaning from low vegetation and up to treetops; however, there is a preference for the lower levels of the stand. Insect larvae are the preferred food with adult insects composing the rest of the diet. The Yellow Warbler hover-glean and sally.

Habits: Tail pumping is a common behavior for Yellow Warblers. The Yellow Warbler will respond to pishing.

Nest: The singing of the male is a pronouncement of territory. The easily found nest is located in a vertical fork of a branch. The female will build an open cup of grass and plant fibers, and line it with plant fibers and animal hair. For up to 12 days, the female incubates 4-5 brown-speckled greenish eggs. After hatching, both parents tend to the young. Yellow Warblers are a common Brown-headed Cowbird host; they have evolved, however, a unique strategy for dealing with the nest parasitism. They identify the foreign eggs and proceed to construct a new nest on top of the old one. They have been known to build up to 6 layers of new nests.

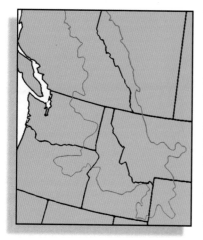

Voice: The classic *"sweet-sweet-I'm so sweet"* is the song of the Yellow Warbler.

Primary Habitat Characteristics: Dense, moist deciduous vegetation such as willow or alder is needed for foraging and nesting.

Other Habitats: Yellow Warblers will breed in higher elevation deciduous shrublands and young aspen stands.

Conservation: It cannot be overstated how common this bird is in the Rockies. It is one of the most common warblers.

117

Northern Waterthrush
Seiurus noveboracensis

J F M A M J J A S O N D

B

A bobbing Northern Waterthrush

© Tom Ulrich

Description: The Northern Waterthrush (5³/₄") is easily distinguished from other warblers in the Northern Rockies. It is brownish above and whitish with heavy streaking below. Above the eye there is a prominent buff supercilliary stripe. The cheeks are a streaky buff, which lends to the impression of a brown stripe going through the eye. The wings and tail are dark brown.

Feeding: A ground forager underneath the riparian vegetation, the Northern Waterthrush consumes mostly invertebrates. This bird will pick prey off of the vegetation, turn over leaves and duff to uncover food, or they will occasionally wade into shallow water to find aquatic invertebrates.

Habits: When startled, the Northern Waterthrush will fly up to a low perch and engage in bobbing.

Nest: The male sings constantly to attract a female and defend his territory from would-be interlopers. The female selects a nest site under a stump or an undercut bank where she constructs the cup-like nest out of leaves, moss, and other plant fibers. She lines this cup with very fine materials such as individual moss filaments. She incubates the 4-5 brown-spotted white eggs for 12 days. After the eggs have hatched, both parents care for the young for ten more days.

Voice: The Northern Waterthrush's song is a series of short, crisp notes that come at an irregular tempo toward the end. The metallic *"chink"* rings.

Primary Habitat Characteristics: The Northern Waterthrush prefers wet, shady deciduous growth like alders or willows with fallen trees surrounded by coniferous forest.

Other Habitats: It can be encountered in wetlands that have a prominent spruce-fir component.

Conservation: The Northern Waterthrush is common, though it is shy.

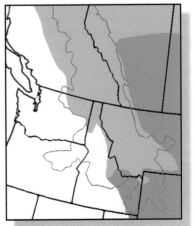

Wilson's Warbler

J F M A M J J A S O N D

Wilsonia pusilla

B

Description: A small (4³/₄") sprite that flits about the dense vegetation, the Wilson's Warbler is very common in the Northern Rockies, only the Yellow and Yellow-rumped Warblers having greater numbers. The general body coloration is a gradient from olive-yellow on the back to a bright, sunny yellow upon the breast. The only other marking of note is the black cap, which is solid in the males and variable in the females, which makes determining sex very difficult. The black bill is small, and the tail is long.

A Wilson's Warbler preparing for migration

© Peter LaTourrette

Feeding: The Wilson's Warbler is a rather active feeder that normally hunts within 10 feet of the ground. These birds will forage by gleaning, hover-gleaning, and sallying for insects. They will also consume berries in the late summer and fall.

Habits: Pishing will bring these inquisitive warblers in close for good views. The tail flips in a constant motion as the bird flies.

Nest: The nest is placed on the ground in a clump of moss or a patch of sedge at the base of a tree or shrub. The female alone builds the bulky cup of the nest, and it is composed of grass, leaves, and hair. She incubates the 4-6 chestnut-splotched cream-colored eggs for 10-13 days. After they hatch, both parents care for the young for somewhat less than 2 weeks, after which they leave the nest.

Voice: The slurred *"chip"* note is repeated in a rapid series. The distinctive *"chimp"* call can also be heard on a frequent basis.

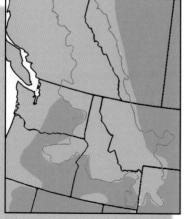

Primary Habitat Characteristics: Dense stands of willow or alder surrounded by open areas near a stream seem to be very vital to the Wilson's Warbler's success. These stands are often in an early successional stage.

Other Habitats: Alder and willow stands at or near the treeline as well as meadows with scattered deciduous shrubs or trees.

Conservation: One of the most common warblers in the West.

American Redstart
Selophaga ruticilla

J F M A M J J A S O N D

B

Male (l) and female (r) American Redstart

Description: The only black warbler (the male) in the Northern Rockies, the American Redstart (5") is unmistakable. The male is shiny black above with conspicuous orange patches on the wings, sides, and tail. His underside is white. The less colorful female is grayish-brown above and white on the underside. She has yellow patches in the same locations as the male.

Feeding: It is chiefly a consumer of insects, which are gleaned from the riparian vegetation. The American Redstart will quite often flycatch insects from midair, which it does much more often than any of the other Northern Rockies warblers. The males forage higher and make more flycatching attempts than the females, which tend to employ the gleaning technique.

Habits: The American Redstart is renowned as "the butterfly of the bird world." This title is well earned, as it is very active flitting about while feeding. It displays the orange or yellow patches by spreading the wings and wagging the tail.

Nest: The male American Redstart is known to mate with more than one female during the breeding season. The female builds the open cup nest of grass and plant materials lined with lichen and bark. It is placed in the fork of a tree 4-70 feet high. She incubates the 4 brown-blotched white eggs for 11-12 days. Both parents feed the young in the nest, and they fledge at 9 days. The American Redstart will commonly double-brood.

Voice: The variable song is composed of high-pitched, sharp notes ending with a down-slurred note.

Primary Habitat Characteristics: Open stands of willow and other deciduous trees are preferred.

Other Habitats: It can be found in deciduous stands some distance from water.

Conservation: This "butterfly" is still very common, although it is slightly declining.

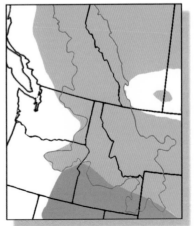

Yellow-breasted Chat
Icteria virens

J F M A M J J A S O N D

B

Description: Far and away the largest of our warblers at 7$^{1}/_{2}$", the Yellow-breasted Chat is definitely the black sheep of the warbler family. The upperparts are an olive-green and the breast is, well, yellow. They have the appearance of wearing glasses, with white eye-rings and a white marking above the dark lores. The lores are black in the males and a lighter gray in the females. The bill is very large and thick.

© Tom Ulrich

The largest Rocky Mountain warbler, the Yellow-breasted Chat

Feeding: A gleaner of insects from the foliage, the Yellow-breasted Chat only occasionally forages on the ground. The insects eaten represent a wide variety of the total species present. They will consume quite a bit of fruit and berries, which can comprise up to 50% of the total diet.

Habits: An extremely secretive skulker of the dense riparian areas. Even while singing, the males still tend to remain concealed.

Nest: The flight display has him singing on the way up, and then he slowly drops down with wings flapping and the legs dangling during the return to a perch. Perfectly concealed in a dense tangle of foliage, the large, open nest is built by the female. The nest is made of leaves, grass, and strips of bark. It is lined with finer plant fibers. The female alone incubates the 3-4 brown and gray-spotted cream eggs for 11 days. As in many warbler species, both sexes of the Yellow-breasted Chat care for the young. The juveniles fledge in as few as 8 days.

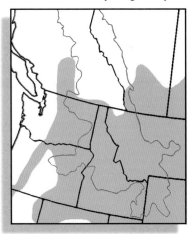

Voice: Its whistles, chatters and squawks make song identification easy. The song is the lowest-pitched of area warblers.

Primary Habitat Characteristics: Very dense stands of riparian associated shrubs with scattered young trees.

Other Habitats: Very rarely it can be found in dense thickets far away from any water.

Conservation: Yellow-breasted Chats have declined substantially over the past century.

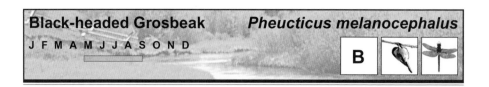

Male Black-headed Grosbeak

Description: The Black-headed Grosbeak (8¹/₄") is a robust songbird that sings proudly from the tops of trees along streams. The male possesses the black head, while the female has a striped head. The wings are black with white wingbars. The male's breast is a rich cinnamon. The female's underparts are a buff color. Both sexes show a yellow "armpit" during flight. The bill is large and triangular with the upper mandible darker than the lower.

Feeding: The robust bill of the Black-headed Grosbeak is well suited for a diverse diet of insects, seeds, and fruits. This bird spends much of its time gleaning insects from the foliage. The vegetable portion of the diet accounts for somewhat less than half of the total. With such a varied diet, the feeding behaviors of the Black-headed Grosbeak are accordingly diverse; they sally, hover-glean, and ground forage.

Habits: Readily hybridizes with the Rose-breasted Grosbeak where the two species meet on the Great Plains.

Nest: The male courts the female by flying with wings and tail fully spread over her while singing. The open cup nest is placed in a tree 4-25 feet above the ground. Mostly built by the female, the nest is a loose assemblage of twigs, weeds, and pine needles lined with finer plant fibers and hair. Both parents incubate the 3-5 brown and gray-spotted bluish green eggs for 2 weeks. The young will leave the nest in about 12 days; they continue to be fed for an additional 2 weeks.

Voice: The song is a rapid series of notes that resembles an American Robin in hyper-drive. The call is a low-pitched *"eek"*.

Primary Habitat Characteristics: The deciduous component of the habitat tends to be rather open.

Other Habitats: This bird also uses cottonwoods and, rarely, juniper shrublands.

Conservation: The Black-headed Grosbeak is common and populations are secure.

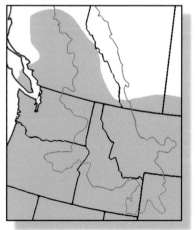

Description: Noisy scratching of the leaf litter usually betrays the location of the Fox Sparrow (7"). This particular sparrow is highly variable in plumages; although, most plumages in the Northern Rockies have a red rump patch, which extends to the base of the tail. The underparts are heavily spotted, and these spots merge into a central dot on the breast. The head and back are gray. The bill size can also be highly diverse throughout the region.

Fox Sparrow

USFWSLeupold

Feeding: During the summer, the Fox Sparrow consumes many different kinds of insects and other terrestrial invertebrates. These items are taken while the bird forages on the ground by scratching with both feet.

Habits: Almost always found on the ground when foraging, seldom in the lower canopy. Sings from an exposed perch with most of the singing bouts taking place during the morning and evening hours. The female Fox Sparrow will give a broken-wing distraction display around the nest.

Nest: Males aggressively defend their territories from interlopers, both other Fox Sparrows and other species. The female builds a nest of grass, stems, and moss lined with dry grass. The nest is located on the ground under a dense canopy of vegetation. The female incubates the 2-5 heavily reddish-blotched blue eggs for 12-14 days. Both parents care for the nestlings for 11 days.

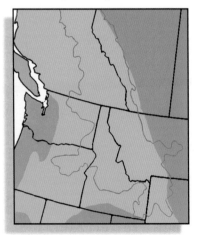

Voice: The song of the Fox Sparrow is a series of melodic whistles that begins with two or three syllables at different pitches.

Primary Habitat Characteristics: The Fox Sparrow prefers streamside thickets with mostly deciduous trees and shrubs.

Other Habitats: Fox Sparrows can occur in a variety of deciduous dominated habitats.

Conservation: The Fox Sparrow seems to be stable in the Northern Rockies.

123

Song Sparrow in a thicket

Description: One of the most familiar songbirds of riparian habitat, the Song Sparrow (5³/₄-7¹/₂") is quite variable in size. Across its range, the Song Sparrow has with many subspecies. The eyebrow is gray and the malar stripe is dark. The throat is white. The upperparts are normally streaked and the white underparts are streaked. The streaking normally converges into a central breast spot.

Feeding: During the summer, the Song Sparrow's diet consists mostly of a whole host of insects. The invertebrates are taken by ground foraging accompanied with scratching. As the warmth of summer fades into autumn and winter, the diet switches to mainly the seeds of grass and weeds.

Habits: When it flies from tree to tree, the tail is pumped throughout the flight. When foraging, this species can be quite retiring and it is difficult to locate a lone individual; however, the abundance of this bird makes it a common sight.

Nest: Males maintain and defend rather small territories, so densities can be quite high. The courting male will chase his intended, and display to her with a fluttering flight with head held high. She builds the open cup of the nest on the ground under a patch of grass or low shrub. The nest is made of weed stems, grass, and other plant material lined with grass and other fine plant fibers. The female incubates the 4 brown-spotted greenish eggs for 2 weeks. The young will fledge in 12 days, during which they are cared for by both adults.

Voice: The song is 3-4 short, sharp notes followed by a trill. Their call is a hollow *"chimp"*.

Primary Habitat Characteristics: Good Song Sparrow habitat has a pronounced deciduous component on a wet site near water.

Other Habitats: They also inhabit almost any habitat that is well vegetated with deciduous shrubs and trees.

Conservation: Very common and secure. It is the most common sparrow through the year.

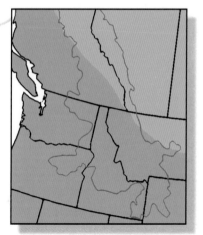

124

Description: The secretive Lincoln's Sparrow (5³/₄") can be difficult to spot within a dense riparian thicket. The upperparts are streaked brown. The crown is reddish-brown with a thin gray central stripe. The eyebrow is gray, and buff stripes come off of the bill. The chest and flanks are streaked with a buffy underwash. The remainder of the underparts is unmarked white.

A reclusive Lincoln's Sparrow

Feeding: The diet of the Lincoln's Sparrow's diet is very similar to that of the closely related Song Sparrow. The summer menu includes mostly insects, particularly those that are ground dwelling, for which the birds forage. They are often seen hopping about as they forage.

Habits: This species is generally secretive, except for singing males.

Nest: The female will give a repeating *"zee"* call that entices the male to dive at her. This behavior can lead up to mating. The female constructs a nest of grass lined with fine plant fibers. This fragile structure is placed on the ground under a protective clump of grass or a deciduous shrub. She incubates the 3-5 chestnut-spotted blue-green eggs for 10-14 days. Both adults are responsible for the care and feeding of the nestlings. The nestlings fledge at 9-12 days, and they remain with their parents for an additional 2-3 weeks.

Voice: The Lincoln's Sparrow's song is a rich assortment of trills and buzzing notes. The *"zee"* call is unique.

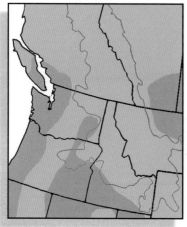

Primary Habitat Characteristics: The Lincoln's Sparrow prefers low, dense deciduous vegetation. These stands are usually located in very moist sites.

Other Habitats: They can also inhabit deciduous stands bordering wetlands, dense deciduous understories, and isolated damp shrub patches with coniferous forest.

Conservation: The Lincoln's Sparrow seems to have steady or increasing numbers.

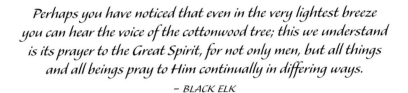

Cottonwood Bottom Forest

Perhaps you have noticed that even in the very lightest breeze
you can hear the voice of the cottonwood tree; this we understand
is its prayer to the Great Spirit, for not only men, but all things
and all beings pray to Him continually in differing ways.

— BLACK ELK

Under a canopy of newly sprouting leaf buds, the sweet smell of the still decaying fallen leaves fills my nostrils. Underfoot, this layer of rotten leaves both crunches and squishes. The alarm call of Downy Woodpecker slices through the veil of swaying branches and slow moving water. This small woodpecker spent the winter in an open deciduous stand. It picked and probed the trunks and branches for the larvae and pupae of insects, its long, barbed tongue snaring its prey and bringing it back. He concentrates most of his efforts of the dead and dying black cottonwoods. These trees have begun to bleach white in the sun as their bark sluffs off in shredded layers. From the feet of these giants, the next generation of cottonwoods is reaching skyward.

Along the floodplains of the rivers and streams of the Northern Rockies, cottonwood bottom forests grow in open structured stands. In the west and north, Black Cottonwood dominates, while narrowleaf cottonwood grows in abundance from the Greater Yellowstone ecosystem southward. These deciduous forests are found along almost every stretch of river and lower elevation stream across the West.

Cottonwood bottom forests generally occur in bands that correspond with stream channels and floodplains. The age-structure of these forests is directed by floods more than any other force. Periodic floods will remove some the mature and immature cottonwoods. As the flood recedes, fresh nutrients are left on the forest floor from which new cottonwood saplings spring toward the sun. The vegetation of the cottonwood bottom forest is constantly adjusting and changing a rapidly altering landscape. These forests are now subject to a new form of change, alteration of the floodplain. As humans build within the floodplain, we take measures to

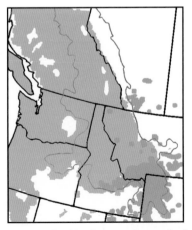

Combined ranges of narrowleaf and black cottonwood

ensure the viability of these structures. The stream is channelized, so that it cannot create new meanders and oxbows. Levees are built in order to control flooding. These practices affect the regeneration of the cottonwood forest.

Cottonwood bottom forests are among the most diverse habitats in the Northern Rockies. In their broad, leafy crowns, Yellow Warblers and Least Flycatchers nervously fly about while they glean insects from the surface of the yellow-green leaves. The large, standing snags are useful to primary excavators, such as Hairy Woodpeckers. The heartwood of the cottonwood quickly become soft, rotten; perfect for a nesting woodpecker. As the snags become riddled with cavities, the secondary cavity nesters move in. Black-capped Chickadees find the abandoned woodpecker nests to their liking. The proximity to water attracts Goldeneyes and Hooded Mergansers to the larger nesting cavities created by the Northern Flicker. The shrubby understory of red-osier dogwood, willow, and serviceberry draw in the typically riparian shrub nesting species.

The major draw to the cottonwood for the birds is the abundance of insects found within this habitat. Cottonwood forests have plenty of standing water within them. These pools of stagnant water are ideal breeding areas for numerous flying insects such as mosquitos and flies. The nearby streams and rivers are the scenes of massive hatches of caddis and salmon flies. These insects flood into the neighboring cottonwood forests. The flycatchers and gleaners come in numbers to take advantage of this mass of insect life. As cottonwood forest almost always have standing snags, the wood-boring insects thrive in these forests. The woodpeckers and nuthatches feed heavily on these insects and their larvae. The cottonwood bottom forests are the haven to the insectivorous bird.

The cottonwood bottom forest is a bird-rich habitat that is in constant flux. Amongst

these open stands, the sun filters down in greenish gold rays that warm the humid air. The haunting laughter of the White-breasted Nuthatch welcomes you as the *"chibek"* calls of a multitude of Least Flycatchers join the chorus. The cottonwood bottom forest is a place full of life and birds.

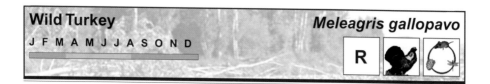

Wild Turkey

Meleagris gallopavo

J F M A M J J A S O N D

R

Description: Groups of Wild Turkey forage under the sparse canopy of a mature cottonwood forest. The Wild Turkey is strongly sexually dimorphic with males (46") being much larger than the females (37"). The male Wild Turkey has a dark body with irides- cent feathers. The bare skin of the head is blue with variable pink. The wattles are bright red. A black tuft extends from the breast. The legs have a long, heavy spur. The female

A gobbler looking for food

is dark brown and lacks the male's iridescence. She also lacks the red wattles, and bare facial skin is grayish.

Feeding: As the Wild Turkey forages on the ground, it consumes an omnivorous diet including seeds, grains, fruits, insects, and small vertebrates. It often scratches the earth to reveal hidden prey. Most foraging is done at morning and evening.

Habits: Spends much of its time on the ground; however, they are strong fliers. Will typically roost overnight in a tree.

Nest: The gobbling of the toms is a hallmark of spring. The male struts around with feathers puffed out and the spread tail is raised. The wattles on the face become inflamed, and he makes a low vibrating sound. He will attract and mate with several females. The ground scrape nest is located at the base of a tree, and it is lined with grass and leaves. They lay an incredible number of eggs, up to 15. The eggs are white with reddish-brown spots, which the female incubates for about 30 days. Very

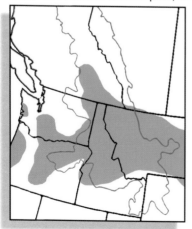

soon after hatching, the young leave the nest to feed themselves. However, they are tended to by the female for several weeks.

Voice: The gobbling of the male is common.

Primary Habitat Characteristics: The Wild Turkey prefers open forests with clearings.

Other Habitats: They also inhabit ponderosa pine and dry Douglas-fir forests.

Conservation: The Wild Turkey is locally com- mon where there is enough appropriate habitat.

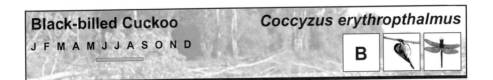

The shy Black-billed Cuckoo

© Caleb Putnam

Description: Elusive within dense tangles of foliage, the Black-billed Cuckoo (12") is counter-shaded with brown above and very pale gray on the undersides. The bill is black and decurved. The underside of the long tail has gray feathers with white tips. If one were to get a really good look at a Black-billed Cuckoo (this rarely happens), you would notice the red eye-ring.

Feeding: When the tent caterpillars become abundant, the Black-billed Cuckoo is in seventh heaven. They will eat many different kinds of insects, but caterpillars seem to be a particular favorite. They round out their diet with birds' eggs, other vertebrates, and some vegetable matter. This bird forages in the branches and leaves where it gleans prey from the foliage.

Habits: This species is very retiring, and it is almost always heard and not seen. They will, on occasion, parasitize the nests of other birds.

Nest: The male ritually feeds the female as part of the courtship. Both sexes build a platform nest of sticks lined with leaves, grass, and other plant materials in a tree or shrub 2-10 feet above the ground. They both incubate the 2-3 bluish-green eggs for 2 weeks. The parents continue to care for the nestlings for 3 weeks or so.

Voice: The soft voice of the Black-billed Cuckoo sounds reminiscent of *"cu-cu-cu"*.

Primary Habitat Characteristics: Almost all breeding and nesting of the Black-billed Cuckoo takes place in entirely deciduous thickets with shrubby understories.

Other Habitats: They can sometimes be found in other deciduous stands such as hedgerows and around certain wetlands.

Conservation: Local populations may be linked to the cyclic pattern of tent caterpillar abundance. The Black-billed Cuckoo is a bird of concern in the Northern Rockies due to its limited range and its need for riparian corridors.

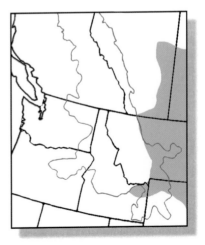

Description: This small owl is present where the Great Plains collides with the Rocky Mountains. It and the Western Screech-Owl are very similar, so great care has to be taken to ensure quality identification. The Eastern Screech-Owl (8¹/₂") is normally seen in the gray morph. The eyes shine with an intense yellow. The bill is gray with a pale tip and yellow base. The heavily streaked breast has widely spaced crossbars.

The fierce-looking Eastern Screech-Owl

USFWS

Feeding: Hunting at dawn and dusk, the Eastern Screech-Owl swoops down on its prey from a perch. This owl consumes an extremely varied range of prey, including insects, rodents, shrews, small songbirds, amphibians, reptiles, invertebrates, and even bats. As with most owls, this species hunts using its senses of hearing and sight.

Habits: This owl spends the day in a tree cavity roost. They often go unnoticed by people.

Nest: May mate for their short lives. During courtship, the males will feed the females. Together they will duet and mutually preen one another. The nest is a tree cavity, 10-30 feet off the ground. The female incubates the 4-5 white eggs for 21-36 days. The male feeds her during the incubation period. Both parents feed the young after they hatch. They will leave the nest in 4 weeks and the parents will continue to feed them for several weeks afterward.

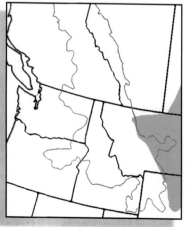

Voice: Its voice is an undulating whinny.

Primary Habitat Characteristics: This species prefers open areas near large cottonwoods that are suitable for nesting.

Other Habitats: They can be found in all habitats that contain a deciduous component, although in the Northern Rockies they seem to be restricted to riparian and cottonwood bottom forests.

Conservation: Widespread and common.

131

Western Screech-Owl

Otus kennicottii

J F M A M J J A S O N D

R

The small Western Screech-Owl

Description: During the darkest nights, only the call of the Western Screech-Owl (9") reveals its locations. Overall it is gray to brown. The whitish undersides are streaked with many fine black crossbars. The head has ear tufts, although they are commonly flat against the crown. The eyes are yellow and the bill is light-tipped. The facial disc is gray with dark streaking and a thick black border along the sides.

Feeding: This owl begins its hunting "day" about half an hour after sundown and continues to forage until roughly a half an hour before sunrise. Observing from a perch, it will swoop onto prey that includes insects, invertebrates, small mammals, and other birds. They are very opportunistic hunters, and tend to feed in the understory and the edges of the cottonwood bottom forest.

Habits: They roost in a natural cavities for the daylight hours.

Nest: The male feeds the female during courtship. They nest in an abandoned woodpecker hole 5-35 feet high. The female incubates the 2-5 white eggs for 26 days. The nestlings branch out at 4 weeks. Both parents continue their care of the juveniles for several more weeks.

Voice: The call of the Western Screech-Owl is a series of low-pitched whistles. The tempo of the series can be compared to that of a bouncing ball.

Primary Habitat Characteristics: Good Western Screech-Owl habitat provides both roosting sites and open areas for foraging. In the Northern Rockies, the Western Screech-Owl is most closely associated with black cottonwood.

Other Habitats: They will occur in a wide variety of forested environments with most observations coming from mixed-species conifer forests.

Conservation: The Western Screech-Owl is rather common, although it is often overlooked.

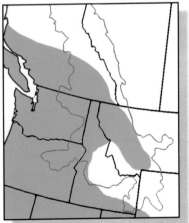

Red-headed Woodpecker   *Melanerpes erythrocephalus*

J F M A M J J A S O N D

B

Description: The conspicuous red head immediately draws the attention of the birder who sights the Red-headed Woodpecker (9¹/₄"). The red extends down to the bright white breast, and the back is black. The wings are black with white patches, which are seen in flight. They also have a white rump patch. The tail is fan-shaped.

Feeding: Most omnivorous of the Northern Rocky Mountain's woodpeckers, the Red-headed Woodpecker eats insects, invertebrates, fruits, nuts, birds' eggs, and, rarely, small vertebrates. Given its ample selection, this woodpecker employs a corresponding range of feeding tactics. It will flycatch, barkglean, and ground forage for its varied diet.

© Tom Ulrich

The Red-headed Woodpecker visits during the summer

Habits: This bird tends to stand out due to its brash nature and striking plumage.

Nest: The male's drumming and call proclaim territory and attract a female to it. The male excavates a cavity, which the female will either accept or reject. This cavity is usually in a large cottonwood snag. Both sexes incubate the 4-5 white eggs for almost 2 weeks. These attentive parents continue their care of the young for another 30 days in the nest.

Voice and Drumming: During the breeding season, the loud *"kweer"* call is commonly heard. The drumming pattern of the Red-headed Woodpecker is a series of short volleys of soft taps.

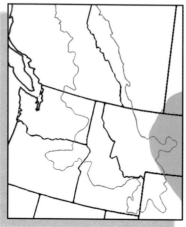

Primary Habitat Characteristics: This woodpecker seems to choose open, park-like forest with considerable openings.

Other Habitats: The Red-headed Woodpecker uses ponderosa pine savanna and prairie windbreaks.

Conservation: Loss of nest sites and increased competition with European Starlings for these limited nest sites have been fingered as possible reasons for the declines of Red-headed Woodpecker populations.

133

The common Downy Woodpecker

Description: The smallest woodpecker in the Northern Rockies, the Downy Woodpecker (6³/₄") is common. They look very similar to the closely related Hairy Woodpecker. The head is striped with white and black; the male has a noticeable red patch on the rear of the crown. The bill is diminutive and lends to the delicate appearance of the bird. The upperparts are black with a prominent white back patch. The wings have white spotting. The outer tail feathers are white with variable black bars or spots.

Feeding: A voracious consumer of all kinds of insects, the Downy Woodpecker takes most of its prey from the surface of trees. Due to its small size, this woodpecker can not only forage on the trunk, but also on the small branches and twigs.

Habits: Highly acrobatic, the Downy Woodpecker will hang upside down and dangle from fragile foliage.

Nest: Both the male and female begin drumming in the late winter and early spring. As spring comes into full bloom, they both excavate the nesting cavity, which is in the trunk or large limb of a snag. The entrance is normally 10-30 feet above the ground, and it is concealed with moss or lichen. For 12 days, they both incubate the 4-5 white eggs. After the young have hatched, the adults go out and return with bills filled with insects. They feed the nestlings in the nest for 25 days.

Voice and Drumming: The *"pik"* call is given year around. A whinny call and *"quack quack"* are given during the courtship phase. The drumming is a series of taps that is just slow enough so that one can count aloud with the individual percussions.

Primary Habitat Characteristics: It displays a preference for large deciduous trees.

Other Habitats: It will live in a variety of habitats that are forested.

Conservation: Very widespread and common.

Hairy Woodpecker

Picoides villosus

J F M A M J J A S O N D

R

Description: Larger than its cousin, the Downy Woodpecker, the Hairy Woodpecker (9³/₄") appears to be, in comparison, robust. The general plumage pattern is quite similar to that of the Downy Woodpecker. However, the outer tail feathers are completely white. The bill is much larger than the Downy Woodpecker's; its length almost equals that of the head.

Feeding: This woodpecker feeds mainly on insects, but concentrates on the larvae of wood-boring beetles. These tasty grubs are taken by peeling them from loose bark or excavating dead, rotten wood. The Hairy Woodpecker will also eat other insects, fruit, and the sap from sapsucker wells. They forage with much vigor and enthusiasm.

Foraging Hairy Woodpecker

Habits: This woodpecker is quite energetic, often calling as it works one tree after another. The Hairy Woodpecker requires larger trees than the Downy Woodpecker.

Nest: Much like the Downy Woodpecker, both sexes will drum in duet. Both sexes excavate the nest site in a large diameter snag 4-60 feet high. They share the incubation duties of the 4 white eggs for 2 weeks. They will feed the nestlings for close to a month.

Voice and Drumming: The *"pik"* call is similar to that of the Downy Woodpecker; however, it is lower-pitched. *"Wickiwicki"* is heard during courtship. When drumming, the beats are faster than those of its cousin.

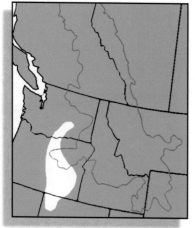

Primary Habitat Characteristics: The Hairy Woodpecker seems to require large diameter dead trees for nesting. It is more likely to be encountered near the edges of cottonwood stands.

Other Habitats: The Hairy Woodpecker occurs in ponderosa pine and Douglas-fir forests where there are large trees.

Conservation: Loss of nest sites to logging has caused declines in the past, currently population levels are increasing.

A cooperative Northern Flicker

Description: Foraging along the ground for ants, the Northern Flicker (12¹/₂") is unique among regional woodpeckers. The brown upperparts have black barring. The light gray breast and belly are spotted black. Across the chest, there is a quite visible black crescent-shaped bib. Once in flight, the white rump patch is seen. There are two different races; red-shafted and yellow-shafted, with most of the individuals seen in the Northern Rockies being of the red-shafted variety. The undertail is red and the males display a red mustache patch.

Feeding: Like most woodpeckers, it eats mostly insects, ants in particular. However, unlike most other woodpecker species, the Northern Flicker captures its six-legged meals on the ground and, to a lesser extent, the bark surface of trees. They are commonly seen hopping about and using their long bills to pick up prey.

Habits: When giving their loud call, they bob their heads up and down. This display serves a duel purpose, in that it cements pair bonds and announces territory to other pairs. Very strong flier with less undulating flight than other woodpeckers.

Nest: Males establish and defend nesting territories with calls, drumming, and the display of the tail's brightly colored underside. Their nest cavity is excavated by both sexes 6-20 feet above the ground in a large snag. The 5-8 white eggs are incubated both by parents for 11-16 days. They bring the young regurgitated meals.

Voice and Drumming: During the breeding season, *"woikawoikawoika"* is heard. The drumming pattern is a long, continuous roll.

Primary Habitat Characteristics: Tends to use broken forest that has large snags for nesting.

Other Habitats: It occurs in almost every forest that is not unbroken or dense.

Conservation: Competition with European Starlings has reduced overall Northern Flicker numbers.

Least Flycatcher

Empidonax minimus

J F M A M J J A S O N D

B

Description: The diminutive Least Flycatcher (5") is the smallest of the Northern Rockies' flycatchers. The small bill (the lower mandible is lighter than the upper) gives the head an inflated appearance. It has a bold white eye-ring and a white throat. The back is olive-brown and the belly is washed with yellow. The breast is a light gray. The conspicuous wingbars are yellow.

Feeding: Seen darting out from its perch, the Least Flycatcher captures flying insects on the wing. The location of its perch is usually in the lower portions of the canopy and adjacent to an open area within the cottonwood forest.

A couple of Least Flycatchers

Habits: Very territorial, the male Least Flycatcher chases other males from his area of 2-4 acres. They will also pressure some warbler species, notably American Redstart, from their territory as well.

Nest: In a small tree, such as mountain ash or willow, in the understory, the female builds a small cup nest of grass, sticks, and other plant fibers held together by spider webs. She incubates 4 cream-colored eggs for 13-15 days. After the young hatch, both parents care for them and bring them insect meals. Although they fledge in about two weeks, the Least Flycatcher parents may continue to feed them for another 3 weeks.

Voice: The *"chibek"* phrases of the song are great identifier of the Least Flycatcher. The call is a sharp, short *"wit"*.

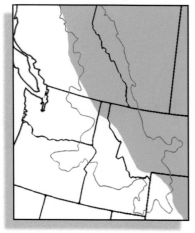

Primary Habitat Characteristics: The locations of feeding perches are normally on the edges of habitat or near openings within the cottonwood forest.

Other Habitats: The Least Flycatcher can be found in other deciduous forests and mixed deciduous-conifer habitats.

Conservation: A very common bird in the lowland and river-adjacent forests of the Northern Rockies.

Description: The Dusky Flycatcher (5³/₄") is almost indistinguishable from the closely related Hammond's Flycatcher. Habitat preference is the primary method for differentiating the two *Empids*. It is grayish brown above and a washed yellow on the underparts. It has a thin white eye-ring. The bill is light at the base and tipped with black. The tail appears long due the short wing projection.

Feeding: Like all of the flycatchers, the great majority of the Dusky Flycatcher's diet is flying insects. They will fly out from a perch to capture their prey, and then return to that perch for another feeding bout.

The Dusky Flycatcher is difficult to identify

Habits: Defends a territory from other Dusky Flycatchers.

Nest: The male proclaims his territory from a perch. The nest is built by the female in a short shrub (3-8 feet high) in a vertical fork of a branch. The cup is made of grass, other plants, and plant fibers and lined with feathers and hair. The 3-4 white to cream eggs are incubated by the female alone. Both parents feed the newly hatched young and continue this care for almost 3 weeks after fledging, which takes place in 15-20 days.

Voice: The Dusky Flycatcher gives *"chip greep swee"* as a song with the last note being high-pitched. The call note is *"whit"*.

Primary Habitat Characteristics: This bird needs a deciduous shrub component for nesting and seems to prefer more open locales. A small amount of interspersed conifers is a beneficial characteristic.

Other Habitats: Montane shrublands, dry Douglas-fir forests, and ponderosa pine forests are also places one is likely encounter the Dusky Flycatcher. The Dusky Flycatcher prefers drier sites than the Hammond's Flycatcher.

Conservation: The Dusky Flycatcher appears to be stable and widespread.

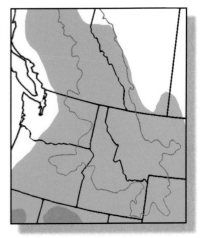

Blue Jay

Cyanocitta cristata

J F M A M J J A S O N D

R

Description: Becoming increasingly more common in the Northern Rockies as it expands its range, the Blue Jay (11") has been spreading westward recently. The blue color of the upperparts is barred with black and white along the back to the tail. The blue wings have white wing patches. The head has an obvious crest. A black necklace crosses the white breast.

USFWS/Menke

The invading Blue Jay

Feeding: This bird will eat practically anything that it can fit in its mouth. The Blue Jay's diet is mostly vegetable matter, which includes nuts, grains, and fruits. The animal portion of the diet includes such items as insects, spiders, eggs, garbage, and small vertebrates. Most of the feeding is done by gleaning, either in the treetops or on the ground.

Habits: Where Blue Jays and Stellar's Jays meet on the interface with the Great Plains, they are known to hybridize. This bird is quickly adapted to the mountainous West.

Nest: During courtship, the male Blue Jay will chase the female. The nest of sticks, grass, moss, and other plant materials is placed in a tree. Both parents incubate the 4-5 brown spotted buff eggs for 17 days. Both parents feed the nestlings for 17-22 days.

Voice: *"Jay jay jay"* announces the presence of the alarmed Blue Jay. A *"tooltoo"* is also quite common. These *Corvids* (members of the Crow family) are imitators of hawk cries.

May move westward in the winter

Primary Habitat Characteristics: The Blue Jay prefers to breed in deciduous forest, which in the Northern Rockies means primarily cottonwood bottom forest.

Other Habitats: Blue Jays will occur in cities and towns that have plenty of planted trees lining the streets and parks.

Conservation: Expanding their range throughout the West and reports have increased.

Tree Swallow

Tachycineta bicolor

J F M A M J J A S O N D

B

Resting Tree Swallow

Description: Flying swiftly just over the tops of the trees, the Tree Swallow (5³/₄") is one of the region's most common swallow species. The head through to the back is an iridescent, dark blue and the underparts are gleaming white. Note that the white does not extend up to behind the eye as in the Violet-green Swallow. Juveniles are similar to the adults except the grayish-brown upperparts.

Feeding: The sight of the Tree Swallow cruising back and forth overhead is an indication of their food preference and feeding behavior. An aerial forager of all sorts of flying insects, the Tree Swallow will even pick them off the surface of water. Up to one-fifth of its diet can be berries and seeds.

Habits: This swallow has readily taken to using birdhouses. Swarms of Tree Swallows can coincide with insect hatches.

Nest: The males arrive earlier in the spring than the females, and they establish territories. Once the female arrives, the male will show her potential nesting sites. After she selects a cavity, she places a cup of grass, moss, needles, and other plant materials into it. She lines it with feathers. The female incubates the 4-6 white eggs for two weeks. The male joins her in parental duties when the eggs hatch. They continue their care of the young for about 20 days after that.

Voice: Three descending notes followed by a faint warble is the song of the male Tree Swallow. The alarm call is a *"cheedeep"*.

Primary Habitat Characteristics: They require habitat that is open and has plenty of nest sites. This means cottonwood forests with snags previously excavated by woodpeckers.

Other Habitats: Tree Swallows can be found in almost any open habitat. They, through their ability to use nest boxes, have come into towns and agricultural areas.

Conservation: Very common and increasing due to nesting success associated with boxes.

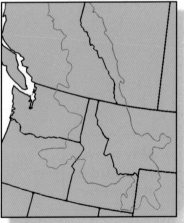

140

Violet-green Swallow

Tachycineta thalassina

J F M A M J J A S O N D

B

Description: Averaging slightly smaller than the Tree Swallow, the Violet-green Swallow (5¹/₂") makes a striking impression. The upperparts are almost metallic green and the underside is white. The white flanks extend up to meet the white rump patch. White extends from the neck and wraps behind of the eyes. The juvenile Violet-green Swallow is grayish brown above and the white behind the eyes is very indistinct.

Feeding: An aerial forager like swallows, the Violet-green Swallow is chiefly a consumer of insects, including flies, bees, male ants, and moths. The Violet-green Swallow tends to forage higher than the Tree Swallow.

Violet-green Swallow

Habits: Very similar in habits to the closely related Tree Swallow. It is known to associate with White-throated Swifts in mixed-species feeding flocks.

Nest: A cavity nester, the Violet-green Swallow will normally use an old woodpecker hole; however, the advent of nesting boxes has afforded the bird increased nesting opportunities. Within the cavity, both sexes build a cup of grass, twigs, and roots, which is lined with feathers. The female will incubate the 4-5 white eggs for 13-18 days. Once the eggs have hatched, the parents share of job of feeding and tending to the young. They tend to them for 24 days, when the juveniles will fledge.

Voice: Near the nest, the sharp *"chee chee"* is heard.

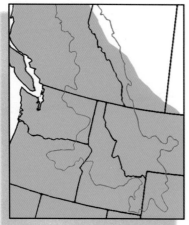

Primary Habitat Characteristics: Prefers habitats that are somewhat open for feeding and snags for nesting.

Other Habitats: Aspen stands, dry conifer forest, and rock walls are known nesting habitats for the Violet-green Swallow. The use of nest boxes has drawn the Violet-green Swallow into towns and farms.

Conservation: Populations are apparently stable due in part to the abundance of nesting boxes in urban and rural areas.

Black-capped Chickadee

Parus atricapilla

J F M A M J J A S O N D

R

A bold Black-capped Chickadee

Description: No bird seems as tame as the Black-capped Chickadee (5³/₄") while it lets you approach to within feet. The cap is black as is the bib, which can appear ragged along the bottom edge. The throat is white. The back is grayish and the flanks are washed with a buff color.

Feeding: A consumer of mostly insects, the vegetable portion of the Black-capped Chickadee's diet varies with the seasons. During the winter, about half of the diet is vegetative matter. The Black-capped Chickadee forages while hopping from one branch to another and picking food from the surface, often hanging upside down from the end of the limb. They will occasionally feed in the ground. In the winter when food is scarce, this bird is rather fond of the fat from carcasses and, due to people, suet feeders.

Habits: They are very tame and allow close approach, especially while pishing. They winter flocks with up to 10 chickadees, and these flocks maintain feeding territories of up to 20 acres.

Nest: Pair bonds form in the late autumn and these pairs remain together until the spring. Together they will excavate a cavity in rotten wood, although old Downy Woodpecker nest holes are used also. The female will place a nest of soft plant material lined with hair in the cavity. The female incubates the 6-8 red-spotted white eggs for 12 days. Both parents share in the parenting duties for about 2 weeks.

Voice: The territorial song of the Black-capped Chickadee is a two-note phrase. The call is the familiar *"chick-a-dee-dee"*.

Primary Habitat Characteristics: The Black-capped Chickadee prefers to use open areas near denser stands. The nesting trees are usually greater than 4 inches in diameter.

Other Habitats: They can be found in riparian thickets, mixed deciduous-conifer woods, and in towns where they use nest boxes.

Conservation: Always very common.

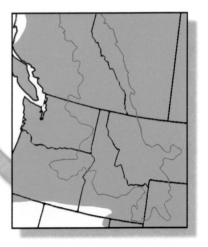

142

Description: Crawling up and down the trunk of a tree while it probes the crevices and furrows for insects, the White-breasted Nuthatch (5³/₄") is energetic, to say the least. The face and breast are white, and the belly is washed with rust. The cap is black. The back is bluish gray. The bill is black and thin.

A White-breasted Nuthatch feeding

© Peter LaTourrette

Feeding: The diet of the White-breasted Nuthatch is most similar to that of the Black-capped Chickadee. During the summer, the diet is almost entirely insects and other invertebrates that are found while gleaning the bark. With the on-set of winter, they switch their diet to a majority of seeds.

Habits: White-breasted Nuthatches will store seeds in cracks in the bark for later use. They have ability to crawl both up and down the trunks of trees. It is possible to find this bird in the company of the Red-breasted and Pygmy Nuthatches.

Nest: White-breasted Nuthatch pairs remain together throughout the year in their nesting territories. The male courts the female by bowing deeply with dropped wings and a raised head. In a cavity or woodpecker hole, the female constructs a cup of grass, weeds, bark stripes, and hair. The female incubates the 5-9 red- and gray-spotted white eggs, while the male returns to the nest frequently to feed her. The young fledge after 3 or so weeks of parenting by both sexes.

Voice: The song of the White-breasted Nuthatch is a *"werwerwer"*. This bird gives a variety of call including *"ip"* and *"ank-ank"*.

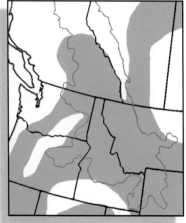

Primary Habitat Characteristics: The White-breasted Nuthatch prefers more open cotton-wood stands with nesting trees at least 12 inches in diameter.

Other Habitats: The White-breasted Nuthatch occurs in a variety of deciduous and mixed de-ciduous-conifer habitats, including riparian, montane shrublands, and dry conifer forests (especially ponderosa pine).

Conservation: May be slightly increasing.

© Mike Danzenbaker

A sun-loving Veery

Description: Secretively stalking about the shadows under a dense canopy, the Veery (7") is oft heard and seldom seen. The upperparts are reddish-brown and the underparts are white. The face and flanks are grayish. They have a very faint gray eye-ring. It is the plainest of the *Catharus* thrushes (Swainson's and Hermit Thrushes are the other two) in the Northern Rockies.

Feeding: All sorts of ground-bound (beetles and ants) and flying (flies and bees) insects make up most of the diet of the Veery. They will also eat other small invertebrates. As summer ends, they will begin to consume more berries and fruit.

Habits: Very secretive as it hops about through the leaf litter and lower branches. It is rather difficult to observe in the field, so one has to be patient and attentive.

Nest: Singing particularily at dusk from a low perch, the male establishes a nesting territory. During courtship, the male will harass and chase the female through trees. The female builds a cup-like nest of twigs, weeds, and other plant material on the ground. She lines it with fine plant fibers from bark or roots. She will lay and incubate the 4 greenish-blue eggs for 10-14 days. Once the nestlings emerge, both parents care for them for another 10-12 days.

Voice: The spiraling flute-like notes of the Veery's song are heard especially at dusk. The call is *"veer"*, which gives this bird its name.

Primary Habitat Characteristics: The Veery shows a preference for damp deciduous stands with an ample leaf litter layer on the ground and an understory of small trees and shrubs. They also located with close proximity to water.

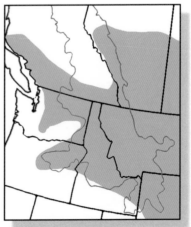

Other Habitats: They can be found in riparian thickets and, on occasion, in moist deciduous-conifer mixed forests.

Conservation: Brown-headed Cowbird parasitism is one element has caused overall population decreases.

Description: Moving amongst the leafy branches, the Warbling Vireo (5¹/₂") is a rather plain bird in plumage and exciting in behavior. It is grayish above and the underside is white with a variable amount of yellow washing. The wings are an unmarked brown. The eyebrow and lores are white.

Feeding: A gleaner of insects off the leafy foliage, the Warbling Vireo consumes many aphids, beetles, leafhoppers, flies, and caterpillars. They will occasionally hover-glean from the undersides of leaves. Like many of the songbirds found within the cottonwood bottom forest, it eats many berries in the late summer.

Warbler or Vireo?

Habits: The Warbling Vireo will sing throughout the day and the twilight hours well hidden amid the foliage.

Nest: The male performs a courtship dance for the female where he hops in front of her while spreading his wings and tail. In a deciduous tree, the Warbling Vireo builds a deep cup of grass, leaves, and plant fibers that is suspended between the fork of a branch. Both parents incubate 4 sparsely brown-spotted white eggs for two weeks. They continue their care of the young for another two weeks. The Warbling Vireo is a common Brown-headed Cowbird host.

Voice: Living up to its name, the Warbling Vireo's song is a long series of slurred, warbled notes.

Primary Habitat Characteristics: It thrives in open stands (low to moderate canopy cover) with scattered, mature trees.

Other Habitats: The Warbling Vireo will nest in aspen stands, riparian thickets, and other deciduous cover types. When it is present in mixed deciduous-conifer forests, the Warbling Vireo is associated with the deciduous trees.

Conservation: The Warbling Vireo is a common sight in the cottonwood forest and will continue to be a plentiful species for some time.

The treetop dwelling Red-eyed Vireo

© E.J. Peiker

Description: Singing from the tree-tops, the Red-eyed Vireo (6") is more often heard than seen. The white eyebrow is contrasted by a dark eye-stripe below it. The cap is bluish-gray and the back is olive. The underparts are white. The wings are olive and unmarked by wingbars. The bill is dark and slightly hooked. The name-sake red eye is only visible when you are close to a cooperative bird.

Feeding: Like other vireos, the Red-eyed Vireo eats mostly insects (moths, cater-pillars, ants, true bugs, aphids, beetles, and other small invertebrates), which are gleaned from the surfaces and undersides of the foliage. They will hover-glean more than the Warbling Vireo. In late summer, they begin to rely more heavily upon berries and other fruits.

Habits: This species tends to stay high in the canopy at the treetop level.

Nest: The male displays to the female by swaying his head back and forth during courtship. The female alone constructs the nest of weeds, grass, bark, other plant material, and spider silk, which is slung in the fork of a branch. The nest placed 5-30 feet above the ground. She incubates the 4 sparsely brown-spotted white eggs for 14 days. After hatching, the young are cared for by both parents for 12 days.

Voice: The Red-eyed Vireo will sing throughout the day, delivering a series of short whistled phrases. The call resembles *"nyaah"*.

Primary Habitat Characteristics: The Red-eyed Vireo likes to have a substantial under-story layer of young deciduous trees and shrubs below an open canopy.

Other Habitats: They will use other deciduous and mixed deciduous-conifer forests, but they avoid unbroken or pure conifer forest. They will also use the edge created by forest fires.

Conservation: The Red-eyed Vireo has declined in the past due to loss of habitat.

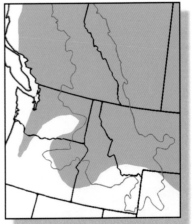

Ovenbird

Seiurus aurocapillus

J F M A M J J A S O N D

B

The ground-dwelling Ovenbird

Description: Walking along the forest floor, the Ovenbird (6") is strikingly patterned. The head has an orange crown that is bordered by dark brown on either side of it. The eyering is bold and white. The upperparts are olive-brown. The underparts are white with heavy black spots. The legs are pink, if you get a close look. The tail is most often held cocked.

Feeding: A connoisseur of insects, the Ovenbird eats beetles, caterpillars, ants, bugs, and other invertebrates (spiders in particular). The feeding usually takes place on the ground or in the low branches.

Habits: The Ovenbird walks on the ground, rather than hopping about like most other warblers. It will teeter forward as if losing its balance when perched.

Nest: The Ovenbird male actively defends his territory from other males by a tail tilting display. He will wildly chase the female while singing vigorously. The female builds a domed nest of leaves, grass, and twigs on the ground where vegetation cover is lacking. This nest is lined with hair. The 4-5 white eggs are spotted with gray and brown dots. The female incubates the eggs for around two weeks. Both parents care for the young for 20 days. Brown-headed Cowbirds heavily parasitize Ovenbird nests.

Voice: The Ovenbird's song is a metallic series, *"teacher teacher teacher"*. The voice seems to be thrown like a ventriloquist. The call note is a pointed *"chip"*.

Primary Habitat Characteristics: The Ovenbird is most common in mature cottonwood bottom forests that have a closed canopy and, therefore, little understory vegetation. They also prefer fallen logs in the understory.

Other Habitats: They will occur in damp riparian thickets and other types of forests that have a closed canopies.

Conservation: Brown-headed Cowbird parasitism has undoubtedly reduced Ovenbird populations.

Male Bullock's Oriole

Description: The brightly colored Bullock's Oriole (8") graces the drabness of the cottonwood bottom forest. The male has an orange face and underparts. The cap is black, and a black stripe extends back from the bill through the eye. The back is black. The black wings have prominent white wing patches. The female is drab brown above and has an orange-yellow head and breast. The belly is white. The immature Bullock's Oriole strongly resembles the female, except the cap is more drab.

Feeding: The summer diet of the Bullock's Oriole is mainly insects and other invertebrates with berries and fruits rounding out the food consumed. They will eat caterpillar species avoided by most other birds. Most of the feeding is done by gleaning from the foliage. They will sally for flying insects. They are known to take nectar when available.

Habits: Both the male and female sing during the breeding season. They use sugar-water feeders intended for hummingbirds.

Nest: During courtship, the male bows low to the female while raising the wings and spreading the tail. The female builds the pendulum nest of woven grass and other plant fibers in a tall deciduous tree 20-30 feet above the ground. The nest is lined with finer vegetative materials and hair. She incubates the 4-5 black- and purple-scrawled grayish eggs for a period of 14 days. Both sexes feed the young for 12-14 days, after which they leave the nest and fledge.

Voice: The song of the Bullock's Oriole is a 4-8 phrase series of whistles and harsh notes. The call is a 2-note *"teetoo"*.

Primary Habitat Characteristics: More open stands or the edges of forests seem to be favored by the Bullock's Oriole.

Other Habitats: Other deciduous stands.

Conservation: Once considered the same species as the Baltimore Oriole. They can and do interbreed where their ranges overlap.

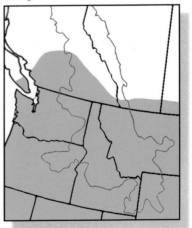

The Nightlife – Birding for Owls and Nightjars

Having just closed the car door, my eyes had not adjusted the inky indigo darkness of a February night. There is just enough of a sliver of moon to illuminate the snow with an odd bluish glow. Quickly, the cold weaves its way through my jacket, and slams hard against my skin, sending a shudder from head to toe. Turning on the headlamp, I send a tunnel of light boring its way through the darkness. Within a couple of minutes, the resonant hoots of a Great Horned Owl glide in the night air.

Owling is an entirely different kind of birding. It is mostly an auditory activity. You will rarely see an owl, but you will hear it. The first step in owling is to become familiar with the owl calls of the region. There are many products that feature the calls and songs of the birds of the West and Northern Rockies. Just sit down with the CD or tape, close your eyes, and concentrate on the patterning of the call. It might also be helpful to write down the call phonetically as a study aid. Another useful method is to learn how to produce the call yourself.

As most owls in the Northern Rockies begin their courtship in late winter or early spring, it is important that you dress appropriately for the cold conditions. When you are owling, you stand still for periods of time and this results in very cold toes and fingers. Wear boots that are rated for extreme cold and use gloves that have a modular system with both a liner and shell. Long underwear is a must for owling, and it is very helpful to layer your clothing. Since we lose a good deal of heat through our heads, it is important to wear a hat to adequately insulate your head.

Other equipment needed for owling includes a good headlamp or flashlight. I prefer a headlamp because the beam of light is always where your eyes are focusing. You will use the light source mostly to find your way around and to occasionally catch the eyeshine of an owl. If you are comfortable with the dark and there is some moonlight, it is often a good idea to go without an artificial light source. When you start out, let

your eyes adjust to the night for several minutes or so. Many owlers carry a tape player with them, in order to play tapes of owls calling. This will causes the owls to respond in kind.

The most important piece of equipment that you will bring with you for an evening of owling is your ears. The calls of owls can be rather soft and muted, and they do not carry over distances that well. It is often helpful to cup your hands around your ears like a radar dish. This focuses more of the sound into the your ears, acting as a low-tech amplifier.

It is sometimes difficult to pinpoint the location of the owl from its call. So, you can triangulate the call by listening at one spot and, then, move over several yards to listen again. From these two locations, you determine the location of the owl.

Once you have found the owl, you give the appropriate call or mimic a rodent/rabbit distress call. The owl will usually either respond or, perhaps, approach much closer to investigate. If you are lucky enough to see the owl, there several key identification points you should note:

- Notice the owl's habitat.
- Ear tufts or not.
- The eye and bill color.
- The plumage and other markings.
- The size of the owl.

One of best ways to see the well-camouflaged owl is shine your light toward the general direction of where you think the owl is located. The light will cause an eye shine if it hits the owl's eyes.

The best time to begin owling is usually just several minutes after sundown. This period of activity lasts for a couple of hours.

Due to their nocturnal nature and large, wise-looking eyes, owls have always held a special place in the hearts and minds of humankind.

Owls have also had a place in the mythology of people throughout the ages. The ancient Greeks believe that the goddess of wisdom, Athene, had favored the owl over all other feathered creatures. Many

The Calls of the Owls of the Northern Rockies

Barn Owl
Drawn-out raspy screech

Flammulated Owl
Soft single or double *"boot"*

Western Screech-Owl
Muted trill *"hoo-hoo-hoo"*

Eastern Screech-Owl
Eerie, mellow trill

Great Horned Owl
Resonant *"hoo-hoo hoooooo hoo"*

Barred Owl
"Who, cooks, for-you? Who, cooks, for-you, all?"

Great Gray Owl
Low *"whooo-ooo-ooo"*

Northern Pygmy Owl
Whistled *"too-too-too-too"*

Boreal Owl
Snipe-like winnow

Northern Saw-whet Owl
Monotonous, whistled *"hoop"*

Long-eared Owl
Low *"hoo, hoo, hoo, hoo"*

Short-eared Owl
Pulsing *"voo-hoo-hoo"*

Northern Hawk-Owl
Whistlelike *"ulululululu"*

Native American tribes assigned special values of wisdom and prophecy to the owl. The Apache believed that the owl was an indication of an impending death. The Hidatsa thought that the Burrowing Owl was a protective spirit for the warriors of the tribe.

The owls of many nursery rhymes and fables are embodiments of wisdom. The owl instructs the main characters on the proper path to take.

Another group of birds that are out at night are the nightjars, and, notably in the Northern Rockies, the Common Nighthawk and Common Poorwill. Both of these flying predators are voracious consumers of insects. They have wide, gaping mouths surrounded by bristles, which may help funnel insects into the open mouth. They come out with setting sun, and they can be seen and heard high above.

The Common Nighthawk gives an incredibly booming sound when courting. It is often seen during the daylight hours, especially when the weather is heavily overcast.

The Common Poorwill is very elusive; in fact, very few people ever see them. The most usual way to see this nightjar is to see the red eyeshine of the flying Common Poorwill in front of your headlights.

Out in the inky night, owls and nightjars rule the skies, along with bats. They are objects of fascination as they thrive at a time of day that terrifies the human being. If we overcome your fears and venture out into the darkness, we can be rewarded with seeing the most elusive of birds in the Northern Rockies.

Grasslands

The prairie, in all its expressions, is a massive, subtle place,
with a long history of contradiction and misunderstanding.
But it is worth the effort at comprehension. It is, after all,
at the center of our national identity.
–WILLIAM LEAST HEAT MOON

Walking across the swaying, verdant carpet, the morning's dew soaks through my pants and chills the skin of my legs. The rising sun's rays sweep across the prairie at parallel angles. Peering back into the early dawn glow, the vast grassland reaches endlessly to the east. Turning to face the west, I see the towering ramparts of the Rocky Mountain Front gleam green and blue. Above my head the first Horned Lark of the morning sings from an aerial perch a couple of hundred feet high. This place is special, the place where the Great Plains slams into the Rocky Mountains. In a matter of mere miles, the rolling grassland transitions into ragged peaks. In this place, birds of the grasslands are present in the Northern Rockies. As you stand silent in this place, the wind whistles softly in your ears as it carries the dawn chorus over the distances.

Front Range and Intermountain Grasslands

Within the region covered by this book, these grasslands stretch north to south along the eastern flanks of the Rockies and spread across the broad valleys between mountain ranges. The summers here are hot and dry, while the winters have moderate temperatures with frequent snow-melting Chinook winds.

Along the Front Range, the vegetation is dominated by a variety of grass species such as fescues and wheatgrasses. Many different forms of forbs grow in and amongst the grass. Shrubby cinquefoil is one of the more common shrub species. Trees like cottonwoods and willows dominate along the riparian corridors. Within the matrix of the sea of grass there are islands of pothole ponds. Grasses give way to areas of sage shrubland in the valleys of southwestern Montana.

With its moderate temperatures and the diversity in the matrix of habitats, the grassland can boast of having upwards of 150 breeding species and 50 migrating visitors. Most of the songbirds, which breed in this habitat, have a general streaked brown coloration on the upperparts. This scheme is excellent for concealing these birds as they feed and nest in the grass. Some of these birds nest directly on the ground, others in the scatter shrubs and trees, and one, the burrowing owl, in tunnels created by prairie dogs.

A particular area of the Front Range holds a special distinction as being one of the few places where the grizzly bear still descends

out of the mountains and onto the grasslands each spring. The Pine Butte Swamp Preserve, run by the Nature Conservancy, lies to the east of the Bob Marshall Wilderness. It contains the largest wetland complex on the Front Range and vast protected areas of grassland.

In the past, grazing by bison and periodic fires were major factors in the structure of the grasslands. Today, about 75% of the original grasslands have been transformed into agricultural and urban areas. The remaining patches are at risk of subdivision as people continue to increase in the Northern Rockies. With the arrival of Europeans, their weeds and grasses soon followed. These plant invaders have had a deleterious effect on the native plant communities through replacement and crowding.

Palouse Prairie

A unique type of grassland found within the Northern Rockies is the Palouse prairie.

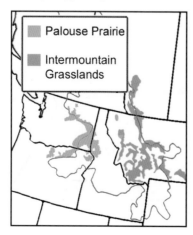

Palouse Prairie

Intermountain Grasslands

The word comes the French word "pelouse", which translates to "lawn" in English. This grassland is located primarily at the western fringes of the Rockies in western Idaho and eastern Washington and to a limited extent the Mission and Tobacco Plains valleys in northwestern Montana. Hot, dry summers and comparatively warm, wet winters characterize the climate of these grasslands.

The plant community of the Palouse prairie is a canvas of grass with splashes of shrubs and trees. Native perennial grasses such, as bluebunch wheatgrass and Idaho fescue are the

dominant plant species. These grasses grow in clumps, and they are adapted for dry conditions. On the wetter, north-facing slopes, shrubs like common snowberry, black hawthorn, and wild rose grow in the draws. Along the streams, cottonwoods, willows, and aspen flourish with the abundant water. Ponderosa pine and dry Douglas-fir forests can be located adjacent to these grasslands.

Elk and mule deer characterize the wildlife found in the Palouse prairie. The birds found within this habitat are those that also inhabit the intermountain and shortgrass prairie grasslands to the east of the Palouse prairie. The Columbian Sharp-tailed Grouse has disappeared from much of the Palouse prairie through loss of habitat. These grouse were once found in most of the intermountain valleys and Palouse in the Northern Rockies region. Now they exist in small pockets of a few hardy survivors. This species needs thousands of acres to be self-sustaining.

Most of the native Palouse prairie has been converted into agricultural fields, particularly of wheat and other grains, with the arrival of European-style farming. In fact, a little more than one percent remains intact. The remaining Palouse prairie occurs in scattered patches.

Two processes create and maintain grasslands in the West: fire and climate. The vegetation that thrives on the grassland has growing parts that are below the soil

Grazing Intensity

Overhead	Heavy	Medium	Light	None

Mountain Plover

McCown's Longspur

Ferruginous Hawk

Long-billed Curlew

Lark Bunting

Chestnut-collared Longspur

Spargue's Pipit

Baird's Sparrow

Bare ——— Short——— Medium——— Tall

Vegetation Height

Grassland bird distribution and grazing pressure (adapted from Knopf)

surface. This allows the plants to quickly regenerate following a sweeping grassland fire. The fires actually help to improve the productivity of the prairie.

The climate of the grassland is characterized by frequent droughts and drier conditions than in forests. These dry conditions are created by localized and regional rain shadows. A rain shadow is created when moisture passes over mountains. As the clouds rise up the windward side, they are relieved of much of their precipitation. The leeward side, where grasslands are typically located, has less moisture available to it.

The grazing mammals that live on the grasslands also have a marked effect on the structure of the habitat. In the past, massive bison herds nomadically roamed over the vast prairies. As they moved through an area, the grasses would be grazed on the soil surface. Following the grazing, the vegetation would regenerate anew.

Grasslands generally do not have uniform vegetation height. These differences in height create microhabitats that birds can use to their benefit.

What does the grassland offer to the birds that live there? It is all the food. On the grassland, seeds and insects are exposed and, therefore, readily available to the foraging bird.

In general, the birds associated with grasslands have been declining. The primary reason for these decreased numbers has been the conversion of the native prairie to agriculture. Another reason for the decline of grasslands bird numbers is the removal of large grazing mammals and prairie dogs. These creatures created shorter vegetation on the grasslands, which benefitted several birds greatly. Birds like the

not-aptly named Mountain Plover required the short vegetative structure created by these creatures.

Across the plains, a lone Horned Lark flies toward the sun. Somewhere on the ground, its shadow sweeps over tall grass in the warm light of the prairie dawn.

Turkey Vulture

Cathartes aura

J F M A M J J A S O N D

B

Turkey Vulture scanning for a meal

Description: Soaring high on the invisible cushion of a thermal, the Turkey Vulture (24-32") flies with its wings held in a shallow dihedral. With its nearly 6 foot wingspan, it is generally dark brown overall. The wings, when seen in flight, are two-toned with a dark leading edge and a silvery trailing edge. When observed at close distances, the red, bald head is evident. Immature vultures have gray heads. The flight seems to be unstable with frequent tilting.

Feeding: As it soars over vast reaches of open country, the Turkey Vulture uses its keen eyesight and sense of smell to locate carcasses. Its bald head is an adaption to feeding on decaying flesh. May key in on other scavengers present at a dead body.

Habits: They migrate in large flocks as far south as northern South America. When alarmed, the Turkey Vulture will regurgitate the rotten contents of its stomach.

Nest: During the courtship, several Turkey Vultures will gather in a circle with wings spread and hop around the ring. It nests in a protected spot such as cave, ledge, building rafter, or some other kind of hollow. Parents incubate the 2 brown-blotched white eggs for 34-41 days. Both parents feed the young by regurgitation. The young fully fledge at 9-10 weeks of age.

Voice: Generally silent, it will give a loud hiss when alarmed at the nest site or when competing for food.

Primary Habitat Characteristics: The Turkey Vulture prefers open country that is close to cliffs or some other nesting site.

Other Habitats: The abundant carcasses found near highways have drawn Turkey Vultures to the roadside.

Conservation: Populations are stable or increasing in the West.

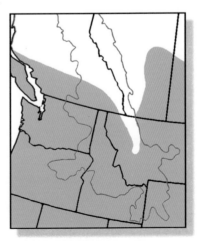

Swainson's Hawk

Buteo swainsoni

J F M A M J J A S O N D

B

Description: Often seen roosting atop a utility pole, the Swainson's Hawk (19") was once a common sight over the grasslands of the West. In line with many of its cousins, this hawk is quite variable in overall color. The dark morph is dark brown overall with white undertail coverts. The light morph is brown above and white below with a dark bib. There are many intermediate morphs between the two extremes. The wings are long and pointed.

The insect-eating Swainson's Hawk

Feeding: This medium-sized hawk consumes mostly insects throughout the year. When rearing young, its diet reflects a more typical raptor diet of small mammals and birds. This represents the majority of its diet when present in the Northern Rockies. It will also eat reptiles and carrion. Most of its hunting is done while soaring over its open habitat. When eating insects, hunting is done on the ground.

Habits: The long distance champion of the Northern Rockies *Buteos*, the Swainson's Hawk winters on the plains of southern South American.

Nest: Like many hawk species, this raptor engages in circular display flights and dives. They build a platform of sticks in a tree, usually 15-30 feet above ground, surrounded by foliage. The female incubates the 2-3 brown-spotted off-white eggs for 28-35 days. The adults bring the young food for a little over 30 days. The fledged juveniles may remain with their parents through their first fall.

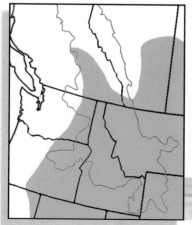

Voice: This raptor gives a long, thin whistle. It will give a cry when disturbed.

Primary Habitat Characteristics: The Swainson's Hawk favors grasslands that have scattered trees.

Other Habitats: They also be found in aspen parklands and agricultural areas.

Conservation: Dramatic population decreases in the recent past have been linked to the spraying of insecticides in South America.

B/R

The adaptable Red-tailed Hawk

Description: The most common raptor in the Northern Rockies, the Red-tailed Hawk (22") has many color morphs. Most birds in the west are the light morph where the head and upperparts are dark brown. The underside is light with a reddish wash and a wide belly band. The "wrists" on the underside of the wings are dark. These are known as patagial markings. Of course, the upperside of the tail is red. The dark morph is entirely dark with the red tail. The rufous morph is reddish-brown below and dark brown above. The hawk flies with the wings held in a shallow V or dihedral.

Feeding: Because it is a soaring hunter of rodents, the sight of Red-tailed Hawk swooping down into a field is common. The rest of its diet has an incredible range, and it includes birds, reptiles, amphibians, bats, insects, and carrion.

Habits: This species is an adapter on every level: plumage, diet, and habitat. Birds from the more northern portion of the Rockies are migratory. They are most often seen soaring in large wings that are held in a shallow dihedral.

Nest: The circling flight by the male and female is seen during courtship. The nest is a shallow bowl of sticks that is placed in a tree, on a cliff ledge, or on a utility pole. They will occasionally repair and add material to an existing nest. The 2-3 brown-blotched white eggs are incubated by both sexes for 4-5 weeks. Both parents feed the young until they fledge at 6-7 weeks.

Voice: The scream of the Red-tailed Hawk is commonly heard at the nests. A sharp *"chwirk"* call is given during courtship flights.

Primary Habitat Characteristics: Strongly associated with open country.

Other Habitats: It will occur in agricultural area, shrublands, and very open forests.

Conservation: The Red-tailed Hawk is very common. It appears to be somewhat tolerant of human activities.

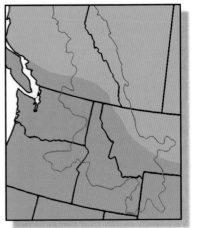

B

Description: The largest of the region's hawks, the Ferruginous Hawk (22$\frac{1}{2}$"-25") seems more like an eagle than a *Buteo*. Like all our *Buteos*, it has two general color morphs with intermediates between. The more common light morph has a rusty back and shoulders. The tail is white with a red wash at the tip. The head is paler and lightly streaked. The underside is white. The legs are rust-colored, and appear to form a V when seen in flight. The rare dark morph is dark brown over the entire body.

Light-morph Ferruginious Hawk

MTFWP

Feeding: Hawks scan the ground from soaring heights in search of their favorite prey: ground squirrels and prairie dogs. They will also consume other rodents, rabbits, birds, reptiles, amphibians, and insects. They will hunt on the ground, and this unlikely method seems to be the most successful for capturing rodents.

Habits: They are easily disturbed during the nesting season, abandoning nests.

Nest: Most nests are built on the ground, or rarely in small trees. The male collects the large sticks and roots for the nest, and the female arranges them. Both parents incubate the 3-4 brown-blotched white eggs for 28-34 days. The entire brood fledges in 38-50 days. The males fledge up to 10 days earlier than the females. They will remain close to their parents for another 10-40 days.

Voice: When alarmed, the Ferruginous Hawk gives a harsh *"kraa-ah"* cry.

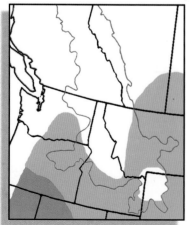

Primary Habitat Characteristics: Ferruginous Hawks tend to favor rolling terrain that is relatively unbroken in semiarid grasslands.

Other Habitats: They can also occur in a variety of shrublands and agricultural habitats, especially those with lower vegetation height.

Conservation: The population is at lower than historic levels. One possible explanation for the decreases is the elimination of prairie dogs from much of their historic range and the reduction of ground squirrel numbers.

159

Rough-legged Hawk

Buteo lagopus

J F M A M J J A S O N D

W

A different kind of snowbird

Description: A winter visitor from the arctic north, the Rough-legged Hawk (19-24") is common across the Northern Rockies every winter. This *Buteo* comes in two color morphs. The light morph is generally white overall with buff head, chest, and legs. There is normally a dark belly band. The underside of the wing has a dark wrist patch. The dark morph is dark brown overall with white tail feathers that have a dark band. The females have a single terminal tail band, while males have several black bands. The legs are fully feathered or "rough".

Feeding: They will hunt using a variety of methods, including perches, low patrols, aerial pounce, and ground stalking. They eat mainly small mammals along with a variety of vertebrates and carrion.

Habits: They flap their wings with a steadier rhythm than that of other *Buteo* hawks. The Rough-legged Hawk is quite trusting and will allow close approach.

Nest: The nest is built on the protected ledge of a cliff, or, occasionally, in a small tree. It is a platform of sticks lined with grass, feathers, and hair. The 3-7 heavily-marked eggs are incubated mostly by the female for about 30 days. The nestlings are cared for by both parents and leave the nest at 39-43 days. Males tend to fledge in about 4 days, earlier than the slightly larger females.

Voice: This hawk is generally silent, although, when alarmed they give cat-like "*kee-eer*".

Primary Habitat Characteristics: It prefers areas that have little in way of trees or other obstructions to visibility; however, it likes very scattered elevated perches for hunting.

Other Habitats: The Rough-legged Hawk will forage on agricultural areas and roost in isolated conifer groves during the winter.

Conservation: Rough-legged Hawk numbers fluctuate and are associated with the population cycles of lemmings and other small mammals.

Golden Eagle — *Aquila chrysaetos*

J F M A M J J A S O N D

R

Description: With its fearsome beak and golden crown, the Golden Eagle (30-40") is truly the king of the raptors in the Northern Rockies. Females are larger than males. The body is generally dark brown with the nape and crown washed with gold. The wingspan can reach an incredible 7 feet. The legs are fully feathered. It takes this eagle several years to mature into adult plumage. The juveniles have a white tail patch and a distinctive black terminal tail band. They also a large white patch on the underside of each wing.

Golden Eagle surveying for prey

Feeding: Often seen soaring on thermals, the Golden Eagle is chiefly a consumer of small mammals and birds. The mammals are anywhere from 70 to 97% of the total food. Carrion is an important component of the diet, especially during the winter when prey can become scarce.

Habits: The territories are very large.

Nest: During courtship, the Golden Eagle will gather in high circling groups in which they mock-attack and chase one another. The nest of sticks is built on the ledge of a cliff, or more rarely in a large tree. The nest is repaired and added to each year and can reach widths of 8 feet. All sorts of materials have been noted as lining the nest, including grass, forbs, feathers, bones, burlap, and garbage. The female incubates the 2-3 brown-blotched cream eggs for 41-45 days. The young fledge in 72-84 days, and their paternal care continues for 11 weeks afterward.

Voice: The scream of the Golden Eagle is the most often heard vocalization.

Primary Habitat Characteristics: It favors open country that has broken terrain such as canyons, gullies, or rock outcrops.

Other Habitats: During migration, it is seen high in the mountains. Uses cliffs for nesting.

Conservation: The Golden Eagle has been blamed for many livestock depredations, although that is a very rare occurrence.

Gyrfalcon

Falco rusticolus

J F M A M J J A S O N D

W

The powerful Gyrfalcon

Description: Slicing through the frozen winter air, the Gyrfalcon (20-25") is the largest falcon that visits the Northern Rockies. The overall coloration ranges from almost white to very dark. There are many intermediates between the two extremes. The cere and eye-ring are orange-yellow. The wings are broader and heavier than those of other falcons. The tapered tail extends past the wing primaries when the Gyrfalcon is perched. Females are considerably larger (up to 40%) than the males.

Feeding: Upon locating prey from a perch or in flight, the Gyrfalcon pursues it with a fast flight that may cover a good distance. It chiefly consumes birds, up to the size of a goose. They also eat mammals (rodents and rabbits, in particular).

Habits: Irruptions of Gyrfalcons occur every several years and coincide with prey population cycles.

Nest: The male will feed the female during the courtship phase. The nest site is a cliff ledge where no additional nesting is added. The 3-4 red-spotted white eggs are incubated by both parents for 5 weeks. The young fledge at 49-56 days.

Voice: When alarmed, the Gyrfalcon gives a harsh *"ki-ki-ki-ki"*.

Primary Habitat Characteristics: The Gyrfalcon seems to prefer open country that has vast vistas and great sweeps of flat to rolling terrian for hunting.

Other Habitats: On its Arctic breeding grounds, the Gyrfalcon hunts on the tundra and nests on cliffs. The Gyrfalcon can also be found near concentrations of migrating waterfowl during the spring on prairie lakes.

Conservation: The Gyrfalcon seems to have avoided the problems associated with DDT and other insecticides that have decimated the Peregrine Falcon. They are commonly used by falconers.

Irruptive Winter Visitor

162

Description: Sweeping over the plains at high speeds, the Prairie Falcon (16-20") has evolved to take full advantage of its habitat. The upperparts are drab brown and the underside is white with spotting on the breasts and streaking on the flanks. The head has a thin mustache stripe with a white stripe behind the "mustache" and has large eyes. When in flight, the black "armpits" and long, pointed wings are evident. They fly with quick wingbeats and soar with flat wings.

A hunting Prairie Falcon

Feeding: Birds and small mammals are the primary prey for the Prairie Falcon. Mammals probably make up a slightly greater portion of the diet throughout the year, especially in the spring and summer. Most of these prey items are taken in pursuits that follow their flushing by a high patrolling flight. Insects and reptiles are among the secondary prey for this opportunistic predator.

Habits: They are highly aggressive toward other raptors. Migrate locally.

Nest: The aerie or nest site is a ledge on the cliff face and no nest is built. The 4-5 fine-spotted off-white eggs are incubated for 29-33 days. The young fledge after 36-41 days in the nest.

Voice: The *"kik kik kik"* is very similar to that of the Peregrine Falcon, although the call of the Prairie Falcon is slightly higher pitched.

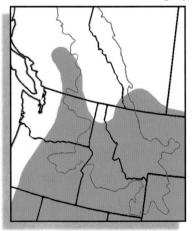

Primary Habitat Characteristics: The Prairie Falcon prefers very open country that have sporadic elevated perches (snags, cliffs, or utility poles).

Other Habitats: They will occur in agricultural areas and sparse shrublands. They use cliffs during nesting.

Conservation: Like other large predatory birds, the Prairie Falcon seems to be recovering from population declines caused by the use of organochlorine insecticides.

163

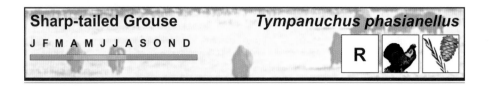

Sharp-tailed Grouse   *Tympanuchus phasianellus*

J F M A M J J A S O N D

R

Dancing Sharp-tailed Grouse

Description: During the breeding season, the Sharp-tailed Grouse (18") becomes hard to miss. The light brown back is marked with dark spots. These spots continue onto the white undersides. The tail comes to a squared-off point. Above the eye there is a yellow eye-comb. When the male is courting, the purple neck sacs are inflated and visible.

Feeding: Foraging as they walk along, the Sharp-tailed Grouse consumes mostly seeds. It will eat berries in the late summer and fall.

Habits: During the coldest nights of the winter, it may burrow into snow for increased insulation.

Nest: Sharp-tailed Grouse assemble in large numbers on the lek during the early spring. The males gather in the middle where they perform a dance with spread wings and stomping feet. A male will also inflate his air sac and deflate it with a deep cooing sound. The female scrapes a shallow depression and lines it with grass and leaves. She incubates the 10-14 speckled olive to brown eggs for 23-24 days. After they hatch, the young are tended by their mother for several weeks.

Voice: The deep cooing of the males during the breeding season is one of the most remarkable sounds on the grassland.

Primary Habitat Characteristics: Most often it is associated with clumps of trees or shrubs on the grassland. The grass itself usually is medium to tall in height.

Other Habitats: During the winter, they move into groves of trees.

Conservation: The Sharp-tailed Grouse has declined over much of its former range. One subspecies, the Columbian Sharp-tailed Grouse, has been extirpated from most of its range by loss of habitat.

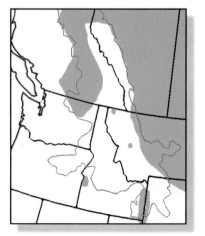

Killdeer

J F M A M J J A S O N D

Charadrius vociferus

B/R

Description: The most recognizable shorebird in the Northern Rockies, the Killdeer (10$\frac{1}{2}$") is often seen far from any shore. The most distinguishing feature of the Killdeer is its two chest bands. The upperparts are brown and the underside is white. There are white markings in front and behind the eye. The bill is black. During flight and courtship, a reddish rump patch is seen.

Killdeer

Feeding: The Killdeer is a voracious consumer of all kinds of insects. Other invertebrates and some seeds make up the rest of the diet. Most of the feeding is done by sight while walking. It uses its bill to pick up the food items from the ground, and to shallowly probe into mud.

Habits: Very bold, the Killdeer gives the *"kill-deer"* call when disturbed. It will perform a broken-wing display when a nest is threatened. The behavior helps to lead a predator away from the nest or nestlings.

Nest: The male will fly over its territory with a slow, fluttering flight while giving the *"kill-deer"* call. The nest is a ground scrape with low or no surrounding vegetation. It is sometimes lined with small debris. The 4 black-blotched buff eggs are incubated for 24-28 days. Both parents take on the incubation and nestling care duties. The young fledge about 25 days after hatching. The Killdeer often double broods.

Voice: Named for its call, *"kill-deer"*. It will give a suite of other calls and vocalizations.

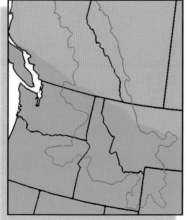

Primary Habitat Characteristics: Although it can be found far from water, the Killdeer reaches its maximum populations in association with shallow water.

Other Habitats: They will occur in agricultural areas, mudflats, wetlands, and the lawns and parks of suburban and urban areas.

Conservation: Very, very common, the Killdeer has spread to the lawns and golf courses of urban areas.

165

© Peter LaTourrette

Mountain Plovers are associated with prairie dogs

Description: The definite black sheep of the family, the Mountain Plover (8¹/₂") is a shorebird that rarely visits the shore nor is it common in the mountains. The upperparts are a light brown and underparts are white. This is the only plover in the Northern Rockies that has an unmarked breast during the breeding season. When it is on the breeding grounds, the forehead is white with a black patch above it. A dark line extends back from the bill and through the large dark eye.

Feeding: The known diet consists entirely of insects. The insects consumed include grasshoppers, beetles, and other ground-dwelling insects. It forages as it walks along the shortgrass prairie.

Habits: When disturbed, the Mountain Plover runs away rather than flies.

Nest: Much like the Killdeer, it flies over the nesting territory with slow wingbeats while calling. The female Mountain Plover may engage in sequential polygyny (mating with multiple males). The first clutch is left to the male, and the second clutch is incubated by her. The nest is a shallow depression that is lined with grass, small stones, and other debris. The 4 spotted olive eggs are incubated for 28-31 days. The young leave the nest soon after hatching and feed themselves. The parents simply tend to them. The young take their first flights at 33-34 days.

Voice: The call is a long, withering whistle.

Primary Habitat Characteristics: The Mountain Plover prefers areas very low vegetation, if not bare soil. It has a strong association with prairie dog towns as these rodents "mow" the grass around the town.

Other Habitats: It will occur on overgrazed agricultural pastures.

Conservation: Declined across the West as many shortgrass prairies were converted in agricultural lands.

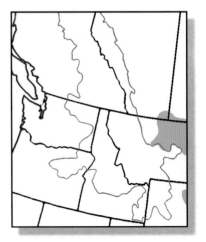

Upland Sandpiper   *Bartramia longicauda*

J F M A M J J A S O N D

B

Description: Often perched atop a fence post, the Upland Sandpiper (12") is yet another shorebird that can be found quite some distance from water. The upperparts are mottled brown. The head seems to be small in relation to the body. The eyes are large and the bill is short. The neck is long and streaked. The underparts are white. In flight, the underwings are seen to be heavily barred with white and brown.

Feeding: Much like a plover, it will feed while walking about the grassland. It is a consumer of chiefly insects and small amounts of grass seeds.

Habits: Upon landing on the ground, the Upland Sandpiper will raise its wings. They can be quite tame when perched on top of fence posts.

© Milo Burcham

Perched Upland Sandpiper

Nest: The display flight of the Upland Sandpiper has the male flying over the nesting territory with shallow wingbeats as he loudly calls. The nest is a shallow ground scrape within thick grass. It is usually lined with dried grass. Both sexes incubate the 4 red-spotted buff eggs for 22 to 27 days. The young feed themselves soon after hatching, although the both parents still watch over them. They take their first flight at around 30 days.

Voice: The wolf howl-like whistle of the Upland Sandpiper is reedy and haunting. During courtship flights, the *"pulip-pulip"* call is heard.

Primary Habitat Characteristics: The Upland Sandpiper prefers grasslands with taller grasses, which help conceal this species, and it feeds in grazed areas.

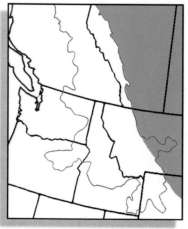

Other Habitats: During the late summer they will occasionally visit mudflats. They will stopover on lawns and some agricultural fields during the migration.

Conservation: The overall numbers of Upland Sandpipers are recovering from past overhunting. This sandpiper is so similar to a plover in both behavior and physical traits that at one time it was known as the Upland Plover.

167

© E.J. Peiker

The aptly named Long-billed Curlew

Description: With a bill that seems almost cartoonish, the Long-billed Curlew (23") is the largest shorebird in the Northern Rockies. The upperparts are mottled reddish-brown. The head is streaked with fine dark brown markings. The breast and belly are buff-colored. The females have much longer bills than the males. In flight, one can see the cinnamon underwings.

Feeding: The Long-billed Curlew often feeds in flocks that arrange themselves in line formations. They feed mainly on insects and other invertebrates. As they walk, the long bill is used to deftly pick up from the ground or, when on mudflats, they will shallowly probe for food.

Habits: These shorebirds are quite gregarious throughout the year. They will associate in mixed-species flocks with the Marbled Godwit. They will often perch on top of mounds, fence posts, or other elevated structures.

Nest: During courtship, the male does a roller coaster-like flight over the nesting territory. Near a rock, shrub, or some other prominent feature, the Long-billed Curlew scrapes out a shallow ground depression. Both parents incubate the 4 brown-spotted buff eggs for 27 to 30 days. The young feed themselves soon after hatching. Both parents continue their care of the young during the period until they fledge, usually in 32-45 days.

Voice: The Long-billed Curlew gives a rising *"cur-lew"* call.

Primary Habitat Characteristics: The Long-billed Curlew prefers to nest on grasslands with a damp hollow or wetland nearby.

Other Habitats: It will feed in pastures. During migration, it will be found in agricultural areas, wetlands, mudflats, and beaches.

Conservation: As the expanses of native grasslands have been tilled into fields, the Long-billed Curlew has decreased.

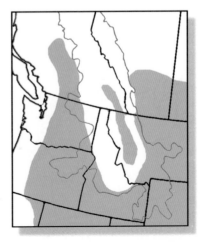

Description: Where the prairie meets the wetlands is where you will find the Marbled Godwit (18"). Brown overall, with backs heavily mottled with black. The underparts are heavily barred during the breeding season. The bill is long and slightly upturned, and it is pinkish-orange near the base and black near the tip. The area between the eyes and the base of the bill is dark. In flight, one can observe the cinnamon wing linings.

A lone Marbled Godwit on the prairie

Feeding: Grasshoppers are a particular favorite of the Marbled Godwit when it is on the prairie. The rest of the diet is composed of other insects, invertebrates, and a small amount of aquatic plants. It will use its long bill to pick up insects while walking or to probe the mud and muck of a mudflat or wetland.

Habits: The Marbled Godwit tends to stay in small groups, although they can occasionally be seen in the company of Long-billed Curlews and American Avocets.

Nest: The males engage in flight displays over the loose colonies of Marbled Godwits. The Marbled Godwit will nest in these colonies or in scattered pairs. The nest is a depression in the dry grass near to the water. Both parents incubate the 4 finely spotted olive eggs for 21-23 days. The young feed themselves almost immediately upon hatching. The adults protect for several weeks until they able to fly. They fully fledge in about 21 days after hatching.

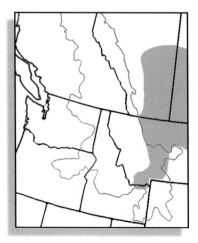

Voice: The Marbled Godwit gives a *"god-wit"* call.

Primary Habitat Characteristics: The Marbled Godwits favor the interface where grassland meets wetland, lake, or river.

Other Habitats: During the migration, they can be found on mudflats and marshes.

Conservation: As with many of the grassland shorebirds, the numbers of Marbled Godwit have been affected by the reduction in the amount of native grassland.

Baird's Sandpiper
Calidris bairdii

J F M A M J J A S O N D

M

Description: Every autumn great numbers of Baird's Sandpiper (7") pour across the grasslands of the West. They avoid the crowded mudflats other shorebirds have descended upon; the Baird's Sandpiper is a shorebird of the grasslands. The upperparts are patterned black on brown. The head is streaked with a buff underwash that extend downs to the chest. The belly is white. The wing primaries extend past the tail feathers. The legs are dark brown to black.

© Peter LaTourrette

Migrating Baird's Sandpiper

Feeding: Like many of the *Calidris* sandpipers, the Baird's Sandpiper uses its bill to pick and probe for insects on the upland areas and mudflats.

Habits: This particular sandpiper is often seen in small groups or alone. It will do a distraction display when the clutch or brood is threatened.

Nest: The nest site is on the ground in dry tundra. The male lines a shallow ground scrape with grass, moss, lichens, and leaves. Both sexes incubate the 4 brown-blotched olive eggs for 20-22 days. The nestlings are cared for by both adults for 16-20 days. The female abandons the brood before they fledge. The fledgings remain in the company of the father for some time.

Voice: The call is a low-pitched *"preer"*.

Primary Habitat Characteristics: When the Baird's Sandpiper arrives during migration, it chooses to feed in drier areas up from water. It is the only small sandpiper that will be found regularily in upland habitats.

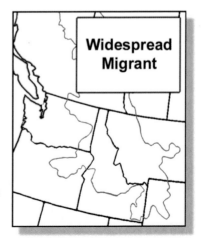

Widespread Migrant

Other Habitats: They breed on the tundra. During migration they will also feed on mudflats.

Conservation: This species is very numerous and these numbers seem to be stable. The Baird's Sandpiper is safe as long as its northern breeding grounds and southern wintering areas are protected from development.

Mourning Dove

Zenaida macroura

J F M A M J J A S O N D

B/R

Description: Often seen flushing from a fence post as you drive by, the Mourning Dove (12") is one of the more familiar birds on the grasslands. The overall plumage is gray-brown. The wings are marked with black spots. The long tail is pointed with white tips. The males have a lighter gray head and iridescent patches on the sides of the neck.

Graceful Mourning Dove

Feeding: Most feeding is done in the ground. Nearly 100% of the Mourning Dove's diet is seeds from grains, grass, and weeds.

Habits: The Mourning Dove will come to seed feeders for an easy meal.

Nest: The male gives his song while displaying in front of the female. During the display, he will puff out his chest and bow towards her. The female selects the nest site and builds a poorly constructed platform of twigs. The male brings the twigs to her and she places them. This nest is usually located in tree or bush. Both parents incubate the 2 white eggs for 2 weeks. The adults give the nestling a milk-like substance, which is produced in their digestive system and regurgitated. The young leave the nest after another 2 weeks; however, the parents will continue to tend them for 1-2 additional weeks. The Mourning Dove will have multiple broods each year, if conditions allow.

Voice: The mournful, throaty *"ooahoo oo oo oo"* of the Mourning Dove is familiar to almost everyone.

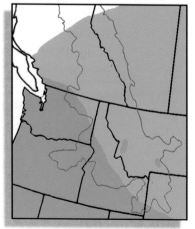

Primary Habitat Characteristics: The Mourning Dove prefers open country, but especially the edge where grassland meets scattered trees. It requires some bare areas within its habitat.

Other Habitats: These doves utilize towns and agricultural fields. They avoid dense forests.

Conservation: One of the most common non-songbirds present on the grassland. It is considered a gamebird in several states.

Snowy Owl

Nyctea scandiaca

J F M A M J J A S O N D

W

Heralded winter visitor, the Snowy Owl

© Milo Burcham

Description: An occasional winter visitor to most of the Northern Rockies, the Snowy Owl (20-27") creates a stir when it appears. Both the male and female are mostly white. The male is smaller and has an almost completely white body with some faint markings on the tail, back, and head. The larger female is much more heavily marked; only the face, center of the breast, and the back of the neck are completely white. The eyes are a bright lemon-yellow.

Feeding: From an elevated perch, it will visually and audibly scan below for its typically rodent prey. It will then swoop down for the kill. The owl occasionally hunts with a low patrolling flight. In the winter grounds, it consumes mostly rodents with birds making up the remainder of its diet.

Habits: The Snowy Owl irrupts far to the south of its usual winter range every 3-5 years. The reason for these invasions is the failure of lemming populations in the north. Unlike many owl species, the Snowy Owl is very much diurnal.

Nest: During courtship, the male circles the female in flight with deep wingbeats and he is usually carrying a rodent in his bill. The monogamous Snowy Owl nests on the ground atop raised mounds created by frost heaves. The 3-4 white eggs are incubated by the female for 31-34 days. The male feeds her throughout this time. Both parents will tend to the young for as long as 12 weeks.

Voice: The Snowy Owl is generally silent when it is present during the winter.

Primary Habitat Characteristics: Winters on grasslands and agricultural fields that have low growth and dense rodent populations.

Other Habitats: It nests on the tundra of the arctic North.

Conservation: The Snowy Owl is stable and common in the Arctic; however its presence in the Northern Rockies is cyclical.

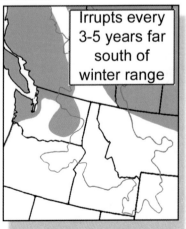

Irrupts every 3-5 years far south of winter range

Description: The early Western pioneers called it the howdy bird as it seemed to say hello from its burrow as they passed by. The Burrowing Owl (10") is a small owl with long legs. The head lacks ear tufts. The upperparts are brown with variable white spots. The underparts are white with brown barring. The white eyebrows extend back and to the base of the bill. The eyes are yellow.

Feeding: Using its feet to capture prey, the Burrowing Owl hunts mostly on the ground. It eats many small vertebrates (rodents, birds, reptiles, and amphibians) and many species of insects and invertebrates. Insects may make up a slightly greater portion of the diet. It tends to hunt insects during the day and mammals at night.

The "howdy bird"

Habits: It is strongly associated with prairie dogs and their towns. The prairie dogs create burrows that the owl uses for nesting and protection. The Burrowing Owl is often seen perched atop fence posts or some other prominent perch.

Nest: Mutually feeding and hovering display flights are among the courtship behaviors. Burrowing Owls nest in the abandoned burrow of a prairie dog or ground squirrel. They do not build any true nest within the burrow. The female alone incubates the 7-9 white eggs for 21-30 days. After hatching, both adults care for the young for approximately 6 weeks.

Voice: The alarm call is a loud chatter. The male coos during courtship.

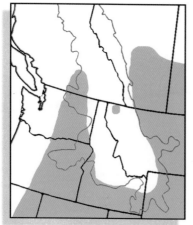

Primary Habitat Characteristics: Most often it is associated with prairie dog towns and other ground squirrel colonies. These mammals create the burrows that the Burrowing Owl uses for nesting. The vegetation height is low, and there are nearby perches.

Other Habitats: They will occasionally turn up within agricultural fields and along country roadsides.

Conservation: Very common, and populations seem to be steady.

173

Long-eared Owl
Asio otus

J F M A M J J A S O N D

B/R

Description: Looking somewhat like a small Great Horned Owl, the Long-eared Owl (13-16") retreats into thickets for daytime roosting. The overall coloring is very much reminiscent of the Great Horned Owl's. The ear tufts are conspicuous and set close together. The facial disc is orange with a black border. The eyes are yellow and encircled with black. Eyebrows and lores are white.

© Peter LaTourrette

Camoflauged Long-eared Owl

Feeding: The Long-eared Owl patrols low over its hunting grounds at night. It has acute hearing and is able to find prey in darkness through sound alone. Most of its food comes in the form of small rodents such as deer mice and voles. They will eat other small mammals and vertebrates as well.

Habits: During the winter, they will form communal roosts with 7-50 members.

Nest: The Long-eared Owl uses old, abandoned nests of American Crow and Black-billed Magpie. The female incubates the 5-7 eggs for 25-28 days; although the male may tend them for short periods. At 3 weeks the chicks leave the nest for the branches. They remain flightless until they are about 35 days old. The male and the female will feed the young while they are branching. The family may remain together until the winter.

Voice: The main vocalization of the Long-eared Owl is slow double *"hoo"*. They also give a call that is reminiscent of a bark.

Primary Habitat Characteristics: They need adjacent thickets or forest to the grasslands for nesting and roosting.

Other Habitats: Long-eared Owls can be found in agricultural fields and riparian thickets that have nearby roosting sites. They are often encountered as they roost and nest in thickets and forests.

Conservation: Long-eared Owl populations seem to be steady. They tend to be locally common in appropriate habitat.

Description: Flying in a unique moth-like fashion, the Short-eared Owl (15") is a common sight over grasslands. As the name implies, the ear tufts are very short. The facial disc is large and the yellow eyes are bordered by black. The bill is black. The upperparts are brown mottled with white. The underparts are off-white with brown to black streaks. In flight, the wings appear large in proportion to the body.

The bright yellow eyes of the Short-eared Owl

Feeding: A dawn and dusk predator, the Short-eared Owl will fly low over open country. As a hunter, it targets mostly voles and mice, but it will eat anything if the opportunity arises.

Habits: In ecological terms, it can be thought of as the nighttime counterpart of the Northern Harrier. During the winter, they will form communal roosts that are often located on the ground.

Nest: The Short-eared Owl nests on the ground where the female makes a scrape and lines it with grass and feathers. She will incubate the 5-7 eggs for 25-29 days. The young fledge in around 25 days; however, they do require some parental care for an additional 4 weeks.

Voice: Along with a variety of squeaks and barking vocalizations, the Short-eared Owl emits a long, low-pitched *"hoo"*.

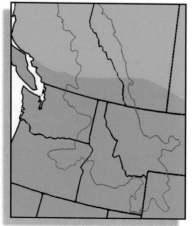

Primary Habitat Characteristics: It prefers large expanses of open country with ample rodent numbers for effective hunting. The terrian of this country is relatively flat to rolling.

Other Habitats: They occur in wetlands, a variety of open habitats, and agricultural fields in the process of returning to native vegetation. During the winter, the Short-eared Owl prefers areas with little or no snow.

Conservation: Loss of habitat has had a deleterious effect on Short-eared Owl numbers.

Resting Common Nighthawk

Description: With the conclusion of a warm day, the Common Nighthawk (10") appears above in the twilight sky. Mottled brown is the overall coloration. Most often seen in flight, the Common Nighthawk has long, pointed wings with a white bar across the wing. The tail is mildly forked. The underparts are barred white and black. The underside of the male's tail also has a white band.

Feeding: Flying insects are almost the entire diet of the Common Nighthawk. As the bird flies, it holds its wide mouth open and the prey is filtered from the air. Crepuscular by nature, the Common Nighthawk feeds mainly at dusk and dawn. They will feed on particularly overcast days.

Habits: It roosts on the ground, rooftops, or large branches. The Common Nighthawk is generally high flier, and most often feeds more than 40 feet high.

Nest: During the courtship, the male dives while he gives the booming sounds that are created by his wings. The female observes this performance from the ground. The nest is a simple ground scrape to which no material is added, in an open, flat area with little or no vegetation. The female incubates the 2 gray-spotted off-white eggs for 19 days. Both parents feed the nestlings regurgitated insects for their first 2 weeks of life outside the shell.

Voice: In addition to the booming call of the courting male, the nasal *"peent"* is very distinct over the night skies of the Northern Rockies.

Primary Habitat Characteristics: Open skies are essential for the feeding of the Common Nighthawk.

Other Habitats: The Common Nighthawk forages over meadows, forest openings, over large rivers and lakes, and above urban areas. Winters mainly in South America.

Conservation: Although numbers appear to be stable, insecticides are a potential threat.

Say's Phoebe — *Sayornis saya*

J F M A M J J A S O N D

B

Description: Often seen hovering for the grass-land, the Say's Phoebe (7¹/₂") makes a very brief appearance in the Northern Rockies. The upper-parts are brownish gray. The head, wings, and tail are darker than the back. The bill is dark. The throat and chest are gray, and the belly is cinnamon.

Feeding: Like the other flycatchers, the Say's Phoebe eats an almost exclusive diet of insects. It sallies out from the low perch, either a low shrub or rock. This species will also employ a hover-pounce tactic where it hovers over an insect and then pounces down into it. The indigestible exoskeletons of the consumed insects are regurgitated in pellets.

Habits: When perched, it bobs its tail incessantly. The Say's Phoebe will reuse a nest from the previous year.

© E.J. Peiker

Flycatching Say's Phoebe

Nest: The males are often seen singing over their territories on perches or in flight during the breeding season. The female builds a nest of grass, forbs, hair, spider webs, and other materials. This nest is placed into a crevice of some sort; between rocks, natural cavities, under eaves, and under bridges are examples. The female incubates the 4-5 occasionally red-spotted white eggs for 12-14 days. Both adults feed the nestlings in the nest for 14-16 days.

Voice: The Say's Phoebe's soft song is a series of *"pittseedar"*. The call is a high-pitched *"peeer"* that trails off.

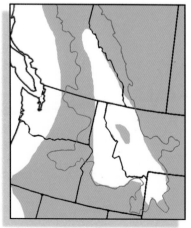

Primary Habitat Characteristics: The Say's Phoebe favors dry upland areas, often very far from water.

Other Habitats: They also inhabit agricultural areas, sage shrublands, and juniper/limber pine shrublands. It is nessecary that these habitats provide nesting sites such as buildings.

Conservation: With its ability to use buildings as nesting sites, the Say's Phoebe has dealt well with the conversion of grasslands into agricultural fields.

Western Kingbird

Tyrannus verticalis

J F M A M J J A S O N D

B

Yellow-breasted Western Kingbird

Description: Most ranchers in the Rocky Mountains know the Western Flycatcher (8³/₄") as it perches on their fencelines. The upperparts are very light brown. The tail is black with white outer tail feathers. The head, throat, and chest are light gray. On top of the head, there is a normally obscured orange-red crown patch. The short bill is black. The belly is a bright, sunny yellow.

Feeding: From a perch, the Western Kingbird darts out and captures insects mid-air. They use a hover-pounce tactic as well. They eat a small amount of berries in the late summer.

Habits: The Western Kingbird is aggressive around its nest, and typically expels other large birds from the area. When defending its territory, he displays the crown patch.

Nest: The male Western Kingbird gives an energetic display flight where he launches into the air and flutters while singing. Both sexes build a nest of grass, forbs, and other materials lined with hair and plant down. This cup can be placed in a variety of locations: on a branch, ledge, or atop an utility pole. The female incubates the 3-5 brown- and purple-blotched white eggs for 18-19 days. Both parents feed the nestlings. The young take their first flight at 16-17 days.

Voice: One of the Western Kingbird's more oft-heard calls is a sharp *"kit"*.

Primary Habitat Characteristics: The Western Kingbird prefers grasslands that have scattered trees or shrubs that can be both nesting sites and feeding perches.

Other Habitats: This species has readily adapted to ranching and farming and is seen with regularity in these habitats. The fenceposts and buildings of farms and ranches provide both perching and nesting sites.

Conservation: The Western Kingbird has been expanding its range eastward.

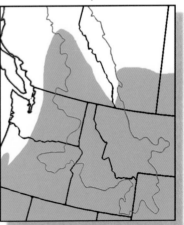

Eastern Kingbird — *Tyrannus tyrannus*

J F M A M J J A S O N D

B

Description: The Eastern Kingbird (8¹/₂") is found across most of the West. It is very dark gray above, and the head is black. The tail has a broad white terminal band. The underparts are white with a faded gray chest band. Like the Western Kingbird, it has a not-often-seen orange-red crown patch.

Feeding: The Eastern Kingbird waits on a perch for a nearby flying insect. Upon seeing the creature, it will sally out and capture the prey midair. The most common feeding perch is probably the fencepost. Driving along most gravel roads results in sighting Eastern Kingbirds.

Habits: It is a daytime migrant. Like other king-birds, the Eastern Kingbird is very aggressive around the nest. They will drive away other birds, predators, and the unwary birder.

White-breasted Eastern Kingbird

Nest: During courtship, the male will engage in acrobatic tumbling flights. He will show the female his orange crown and tail band. The nest is placed in a small tree or shrub 8-25 feet above the ground. The female constructs a cup of stems, grass, and twigs lined with grass and hair. She incubates the 3-4 brown and purple-blotched white eggs for 16-18 days. Both adults feed the young, which fledge at 16-18 days. It is a common Brown-headed Cowbird host; however, it usually ejects the parasite's eggs from the nest.

Voice: The Eastern Kingbird gives a variety of calls. The *"kitterkitterkitter"* is commonly heard on the nesting territory. A *"dzeet"* note is also emit in a rapid series.

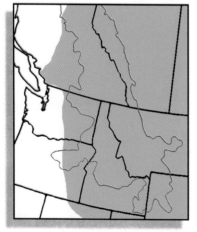

Primary Habitat Characteristics: The Eastern Kingbird prefers open country with scattered trees or some other kind of perch (utility poles or fence posts).

Other Habitats: They are often seen hunting from a dead branch overhanging a river or wetland. Agricultural lands are used frequently.

Conservation: The Eastern Kingbird is very common across its range.

Horned Lark
Eremophila alpestris

J F M A M J J A S O N D

B/R

Horned Lark in winter

Description: Driving along a gravel road during winter, often you see Horned Larks (7") hopping about looking for seeds in the gravel. The upperparts are variable hue of brown. The head is uniquely patterned. There are two "horns" erupting from the sides of the crown. A downward curved stripe extends back from the bill and under the eye. The forehead and chin are yellow. Across the chest, there is a black band. The underparts are whitish. Females are somewhat duller than the males.

Feeding: The Horned Lark consumes seeds and insects. The seeds that it eats come from grass and forbs. The insects are mainly ground-dwelling species such as beetles and ants. The larks forage mainly while on the ground and in flocks, except when they are nesting.

Habits: The Horned Lark forms large feeding-flocks during the winter.

Nest: During courtship, the male flies at great heights and sings while going in circles. Next to a clump of grass, the female builds a nest of grass, forbs, and other plant material lined with roots, grass, and plant down. She incubates the 3-4 black-marked greenish eggs for 10-12 days. Both adults feed the nestlings, which leave the nest in 9-12 days and take their first flights in another 6-7 days.

Voice: The song of the Horned Lark is a weak twittering given in flight or on the ground. The call is *"tsee-titi"*.

Primary Habitat Characteristics: The Horned Lark usually inhabits areas that have few or no trees, with other vegetation of low structure. They require bare ground for nesting.

Other Habitats: They are often found in agricultural fields, particularly during the winter.

Conservation: The Horned Lark has exploited the conversion of grasslands to fields and pastures, and it has increased its numbers over the last hundred years.

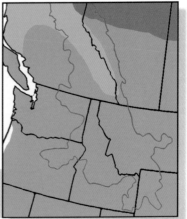

Black-billed Magpie

Pica pica

J F M A M J J A S O N D

R

Description: With an eloquently contrasting plumage, the Black-billed Magpie (19") is a common sight across the Northern Rockies. The upperparts are black. The iridescent wings have a white patch. The belly is white. The tail is very long. The bill is black and robust.

Feeding: Like many of its corvid cousins, the Black-billed Magpie is an omnivore. They will consume carrion, small vertebrates, birds' eggs and nestlings, berries, and nuts. However, this bird has a special affinity for insects and it consumes more of them than the other *Corvids*. They can become nuisances at camp grounds.

Iridescent Black-billed Magpie

Habits: The Black-billed Magpie has communal roosts throughout the year. It will mob raptors and gulls causing them to drop their food. They are gregarious throughout the year.

Nest: During courtship, the males will strut for and chase the females. Both sexes build the impressive bulky nest of sticks in a deciduous tree, particularly the black hawthorn in the Northern Rockies. The female incubates the 6-7 heavily brown-spotted greenish blue eggs for 16-21 days. The male feeds her throughout. Both adults feed the nestlings, which leave the nest after 25-29 days and stay in their parents' company for some time afterward.

Voice: This bird will give a rapid series of *"chak"* notes as an alarm call.

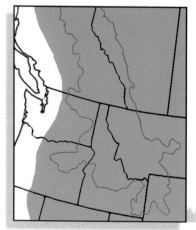

Primary Habitat Characteristics: The Black-billed Magpie favors grasslands, with scattered trees or riparian thickets.

Other Habitats: They also live in agricultural areas and towns.

Conservation: The Black-billed Magpie was poisoned and shot for many years as an agricultural pest; however, they have flourished.

The uncommon Sprague's Pipit

© Mike Danzenbaker

Description: Often heard and seen high over the prairie, the Sprague's Pipit (6$\frac{1}{2}$") is a cherished observation. The upperparts are light brown. The large dark eye stands out against the buff face. The underparts are generally white with a breast band of a buff underwash and fine streaking. The legs are pinkish-red. The outer tail feathers are white.

Feeding: The Sprague's Pipit skulks amongst thick grass where it gleans, most likely, insects. The dietary habits of the Sprague's Pipit are poorly documented.

Habits: The Sprague's Pipit is very secretive and usually seen alone or in pairs.

Nest: The male Sprague's Pipit performs a high aerial display in which he ascends and then spirals down while singing. The female selects a nest site in a grassy area, and she places a cup of woven grass into a shallow depression. The female incubates the 4-5 red-spotted white eggs. The females remain tight on the nest and are not prone to flushing. The young fledge in 10-11 days.

Voice: The song of the Sprague's Pipit is a descending *"sweep sweep"*.

Primary Habitat Characteristics: The Sprague's Pipit prefers extensive dry grasslands that have not been culivated, where grasses are medium height.

Other Habitats: This species is almost never found outside of native grasslands, although it has been observed on the alkaline flats and meadows surrounding alkaline lakes.

Conservation: As grasslands have been converted into agricultural fields, the Sprague's Pipit has declined. Theodore Rosevelt wrote of this bird, "The Missouri Skylark sings while soaring above the great plateaus so high in the air that it is impossible to see the bird; and this habit of singing while soaring it shares with some sparrow-like birds that are often found in company with it."

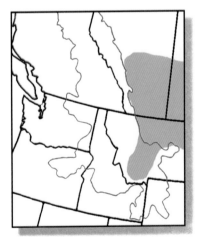

American Tree Sparrow

Spizella arborea

J F M A M J J A S O N D

Description: This little songbird visits the Northern Rockies each winter. The American Tree Sparrow (6¼") has an unmarked gray breast with a central dark spot. The upperparts are brown. The head and nape are gray with a rusty red crown. There is a thin rusty eye-stripe. The bill has a dark upper mandible and yellow lower mandible. The wings have 2 white wingbars. The underparts are light gray. The sides are washed with buff. The tail is long and notched.

The winter resident American Tree Sparrow

Feeding: In their feeding-flocks, the American Tree Sparrow is chiefly a consumer of all manner of seeds. It feeds while hopping about with much energy and vigor.

Habits: During the winter, the American Tree Sparrow gathers in feeding-flocks of 30-50 individuals that often break into smaller groups. These wintering flocks have a defined social heirarchy.

Nest: The female constructs a nest of twigs, grass, and moss lined with ptarmigan feathers and grass. The 4-6 brown-spotted bluish eggs are incubated by the female for 11-13 days. Both adults feed the nestlings, which fledge in 8-10 days.

Voice: The American Tree Sparrow gives a three-note *"teedle-eet"* during the winter. There is also a thin *"seet"* call.

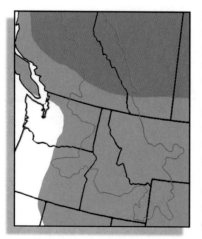

Primary Habitat Characteristics: During its winter stay in the Northern Rockies, the American Tree Sparrow thrives where open country meets isolated stands of trees or shrubs. Windbreaks are a good place to look for it.

Other Habitats: They breed on the shrubby areas of tundra. This species will also inhabit agricultural lands, riparian thickets, and wetland areas during the winter.

Conservation: The American Tree Sparrow is rather common during the winter, and its abundant numbers are stable.

183

B

Shrub-loving Clay-colored Sparrow

Description: From atop a shrub, the male Clay-colored Sparrow (5$\frac{1}{2}$") sings throughout the summer. The upperparts are brown. The crown is brown with fine black streaks and central white stripe. The eyebrow is whitish. There are a buff cheek patch and a faint whisker stripe. The breast is an unmarked light gray. The tail is long and notched. Juveniles keep an immature plumage, in which the eyebrow is buff and a buff breast band is present, through their first winter.

Feeding: During the breeding season, they eat many different kinds of insects, in particular those that dwell on the ground. They are very fond of caterpillars and other larval stage insects. In preparation for migrations, they feed in flocks on the ground where they consume the seeds of many plants.

Habits: The Clay-colored Sparrow is conspicuous when it is present. Before migration, they gather into flocks.

Nest: The males arrive first, followed shortly by the females. Males sing from exposed perches during the breeding season. The nest is placed low in a shrub or on the ground. The females constructs a cup of grass, twigs, and stems lined with grass and hair. She incubates the 3-4 brown- and purple-blotched blue-green eggs for 11-14 days. The young fledge at 8-12 days. It commonly double broods.

Voice: The song is a slow series of 3-5 buzzy notes.

Primary Habitat Characteristics: The Clay-colored Sparrow prefers isolated stands of shrubs and trees within the grassland matrix.

Other Habitats: It can be found in open, dry conifer forests, overgrown pastures, shelterbelts, and suburban areas.

Conservation: The range of the Clay-colored Sparrow has been expanding eastward during recent decades.

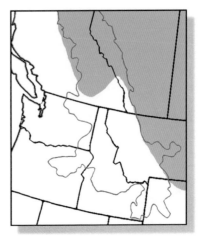

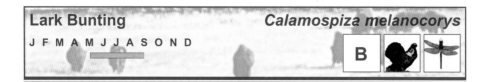
Description: Usually seen as a drab brown bird next to a sleek black and white one on a wire fench, the Lark Bunting (7") is strongly sexually dimorphic. The male is black overall with prominent white wing patches. The female is generally brown above with a brown streaked breast. She also has white wing patches on the brown wings. Both sexes have conical grayish blue bills. The general body shape of the Lark Bunting can be described as stocky.

Male Lark Bunting

© Tom Ulrich

Feeding: Running along the ground, the Lark Bunting flushes insects, grasshoppers in particular. It ground-gleans these creatures, or captures them in a short pursuit flight. They will ingest seeds; however, this food source is more important during the winter.

Habits: The Lark Bunting is very gregarious, except during the breeding season.

Nest: During courtship, the male gives a conspicious display flight accompanied by singing. The nest is placed under the overhanging grass. It is made of grass, stems, plant fibers lined with grass, plant down, and hair. The female incubates the 4-5 pale blue eggs for 11-12 days. Both adults feed the nestlings. The young leave the nest after 8-9 days.

Voice: The Lark Bunting's song is a rich mixture of whistles and trills. The whistled *"towhee"* is an often heard call.

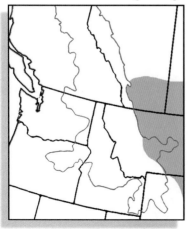

Primary Habitat Characteristics: The Lark Bunting prefers mixed-grass grasslands that have low vegetation height.

Other Habitats: They can also be encountered in taller grasslands, harvested fields, sage shrublands that have a suffecient grass understory, and grazed pastures.

Conservation: With the loss of grassland habitat to agricultural, the Lark Bunting has been declining.

Singing Savannah Sparrow

Description: From the fencepost perch, the Savannah Sparrow (5¹/₂") is commonly seen by drivers along country gravel roads in the Northern Rockies. The upperparts are typically streaked brown and black. Above the eye is a yellow eyebrow. The brown streaked crown has a thin white central stripe. The breast is streaked with brown. The tail is short and notched.

Feeding: The Savannah Sparrow consumes the two items that grasslands produce in abundance: insects and seeds. It feeds while walking on the ground in small flocks, except during the breeding season. In these small flocks there is much vocalization between members.

Habits: They often run along in a creeping fashion, and when they fly, it is just over the grass. They roost at night in small groups hidden within the grass. A distraction display is given when the brood is threatened.

Nest: During the courtship, the male will flutter his wings over his back while on the ground. He will also display in flight while giving a song. The male may have several females in his territory. On the ground within thick grass, the female constructs a nest that is all grass. She incubates the 2-6 brown-blotched white to green eggs for 10-13 days. Both adults feed the nestlings, which leave the nest after 8-11 days.

Voice: The Savannah Sparrow's song is a buzzy *"zit zit zit zeee zaaa"*. A thin *"seep"* call is given during flight.

Primary Habitat Characteristics: The Savannah Sparrow inhabits open, moist country with a few prominent perches, such as fenceposts and medium height vegetation.

Other Habitats: They are often found in agricultural fields, meadows, and, more rarely, the edge where grassland meets wetland.

Conservation: Populations are stable, and Savannah Sparrow has adapted well to agricultural conversion of grasslands. This is especially true if the field is irrigated.

Baird's Sparrow
Ammodramus bairdii

J F M A M J J A S O N D

B

Description: The Baird's Sparrow (5¹/₂") is almost never seen as it sneaks amid the tall grass. The overall plumage is buffy with brown streaking. The crown is streaked with black and there is a central orange stripe. The eyebrows are buff. The throat has 2 streaks on either side. Usually there is a necklace of fine streaks across the breast. The tail is short.

© Tom Ulrich

The Baird's Sparrow favors undisturbed grasslands

Feeding: When the Baird's Sparrow is present where the Great Plains meets the Northern Rockies, the bird forages for insects on the ground. They will also consume a small amount of seeds.

Habits: The Baird's Sparrow is very secretive. It rarely perches in the open and infrequently flushes. This species tends to be solitary, never forming large flocks.

Nest: The male walks slowly with tail spread and wings fluttering during the courtship. The female builds a nest of grass and forbs lined with grass, hair, and other materials in a shallow ground depression. She incubates the 4-5 chestnut-spotted light gray eggs for 11-12 days. As with many sparrow species, both parents feed the young. The nestlings leave the nest after 8-10 days. They remain with their parents for an additional 7-14 days.

Voice: The song of the Baird's Sparrow is several sharp, high-pitched notes followed by a musical trill.

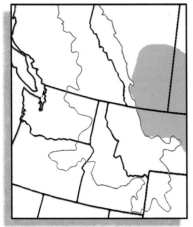

Primary Habitat Characteristics: The Baird's Sparrow favors native, undisturbed grasslands with tall grass and scattered shrubs. These grasslands are occasionally associated with wetlands.

Other Habitats: They can also be found in grain fields.

Conservation: This species has declined due to loss of habitat from the conversion of grasslands into agricultural fields. On the good side, the loss of habitat has slowed considerably.

Grasshopper Sparrow — *Ammodramus savannarum*

J F M A M J J A S O N D

B

Description: From atop a weed, the Grasshopper Sparow (5") gives its dry, grasshopper-like song. The upperparts are brown. The crown is brown with thin white central stripe. The eye-ring is white. There is normally an orange-yellow spot in the lore region. The head appears to be flat on top. The breast and sides are an unmarked buff. The tail is short, and the general body shape is stout.

© Peter LaTourrette

Named for its call, the Grasshopper Sparrow

Feeding: The Grasshopper Sparrow consumes mostly insects, in particular grasshoppers. They forage while walking or running on the ground. This bird also eats the seeds from various plants and grasses.

Habits: The female will give a distraction display if her brood is threatened. The Grasshopper Sparrow, like the Baird's Sparrow, does not form winter flocks. It uses the scattered shrubs in its territory as singing perches.

Nest: The male may chase the female while singing during courtship. He will do a low, fluttering flight as well. They may nest in loose colonies. At the base of a shrub or clump of grass, the female builds a nest of grass lined with finer materials. She incubates the 4-5 red- and gray-spotted cream eggs for 11-12 days. The young leave the nest after 9 days of parental care by both sexes.

Voice: The song of the Grasshopper Sparrow is a high-pitched buzz like *"tik-zzzzzzz"*.

Primary Habitat Characteristics: The Grasshopper Sparrow prefers native grasslands that have unbroken tall grass and scattered shrubs. These habitats normally have less than 35% shrub cover.

Other Habitats: They also live in fields that have tall growth, in particular those planted with orchardgrass and alfalfa.

Conservation: Like many grassland sparrows, the Grasshopper has declined following the advent of large-scale agricultural on the plains.

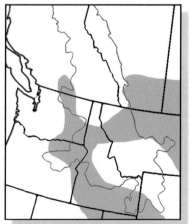

188

McCown's Longspur

Calcarius mccownii

J F M A M J J A S O N D

B

Description: The male McCown's Longspur (6") floats down onto the prairie while singing. The male's upperparts are streaked with buff and brown. The crown is black, and the face is white. A black malar stripe descends from the bill. There is a black bib on the breast. The sides are gray. The female is brownish overall, with dark streaking on the back and crown. Her bill is lighter than the male's. The tail of both is white with an inverted T-shaped marking at the end.

Male McCown's Longspur

© Tom Ulrich

Feeding: The McCown's Longspur splits its summertime diet between seeds and insects. They forage for the seeds and insects while walking or running about. They engage in short flycatching pursuit flights after flushed insects.

Habits: They form large flocks outside of the breeding season.

Nest: During courtship, the male flies up to 30 feet and descends on spread wings while he sings. The female places a grass nest lined with finer materials at the base of an isolated clump of grass. She incubates the 2-4 brown- and purple-marked olive eggs for 12 days. Both adults tend to the young, which leave the nest at 10 days. They remain in the company of their parents for an additional 3 weeks.

Voice: The McCown's Longspur's song is a series of fluid warbles. Their call is a *"chitup chitup"*.

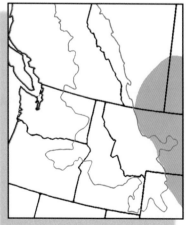

Primary Habitat Characteristics: This bird requires dry, open country with sparse, short vegetation.

Other Habitats: It is rarely found outside its primary habitat, although it has turned up in very open shrublands, grazed pastures, and cultivated fields on rare occasions.

Conservation: The initial conversion of grassland to agricultural use caused declines in the numbers of McCown's Longspurs. Their populations appear to be stable at the present time.

Lapland Longspur
Calcarius lapponicus

J F M A M J J A S O N D

M/W

USFWS/Leupold

Male Lapland Longspur

Description: One of our elusive wintertime visitors, the Lapland Longspur (6") is found in large flocks. The wintering male is brown overall with dark streaks on the back and crown. He has a streaked, chestnut collar. The female is a subdued version of the wintering male. Both sexes have white outer tail feathers.

Feeding: When Lapland Longspurs descend into the prairie, they feast upon the seeds of grasses and forbs. Their flocks methodically walk around and pick up the seeds from the ground. These flocks often have Horned Larks and Snow Buntings among their ranks.

Habits: The Lapland Longspur forms large feeding-flocks during the winter.

Nest: During courtship, the male Lapland Longspur flies and glides down while singing loudly. The female manufactures a nest of grass lined with dried grass and feathers, placed in a depression. She incubates the 4-6 brown- and black-marked greenish eggs for 12-13 days. Both adults care for the young, which fledge in as few as 8 days. They remain in the company of their parents for some time afterwards. The parents split caring for their brood evenly between themselves.

Voice: A luxurious warbling is given during the display flight. *"Tikerik tikerik"* is a common call, as is a fluid *"too"*.

Primary Habitat Characteristics: The Lapland Longspur favors open areas that have short vegetative growth during the winter. These areas include short grass prairie and harvested agricultural fields.

Other Habitats: They breed on the treeless tundra. They tend to avoid areas that are wet or damp unless there are elevated perches. While wintering, this species can also be located on overgrazed pastures and harvested fields.

Conservation: The Lapland Longspur is quite abundant and widespread.

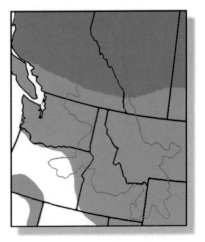

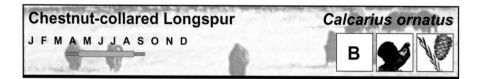
Description: The Chestnut-collared Longspur (6") is a prominent song-ster of the grasslands. The breeding male has upperparts that are black, brown, and buff. The collar is a rich chestnut. The head is patterned with black and white with a buff face. The breast and upper belly are black. The lower belly is white. The female is generally streaked brown overall. Both sexes have a triangular black patch on the end of the white tail.

Male Chestnut-collared Longspur

Feeding: The Chestnut-collared Longspur is chiefly a consumer of seeds and, dur-ing the summer, ground-dwelling insects. Other invertebrates, especially spiders, are ingested as well. Like the other longspurs, this species engages in short flycatching bouts for flushed insects.

Habits: This longspur will regularily visit watering holes. This bird is somewhat shy.

Nest: The male engages in a display flight in which he flies up, flutters his wings, and glides down. All the while he is singing. The female builds a nest of grass at the base of a clump of grass or some other plant. She incubates the 4-5 brown-, black-, and purple-spotted white eggs. The nestlings leave the nest after 10 days of paren-tal care by both adults, although they can hardly fly at this time.

Voice: The song of the Chestnut-collared Longspur can best be desrcibed as fluid, rapid twittering. One of the more frequently given calls is *"kittle kittle"*.

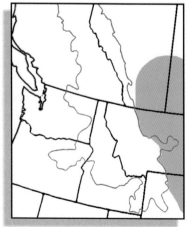

Primary Habitat Characteristics: The re-quired habitat is somewhat dense, short grass. The Chestnut-collared Longspur will use areas of taller vegetation than the other longspurs.

Other Habitats: It is rarely seen outside its primary grasslands habitat during the breeding season.

Conservation: In common with many of its nieghbors on the prairie, the Chestnut-collared Longspur has declined with the loss of much of its grasslands habitat.

191

J F M A M J J A S O N D

W

Snow Bunting

USFWS/Sowl

Description: The only wintertime songbird that is mostly white, the Snow Bunting's (6¾") large flocks are often seen on the snow-covered grasslands. Their coloration blends into the snow and exposed grass stalks. The wintering male is white overall with a buff, streaked back. His wings have black wingtips. He has a white rump patch. His bill is yellow-orange during the winter. The female is similar, except she is more brown and lacks the rump patch. The black and white tail is slightly notched.

Feeding: In flocks, the Snow Buntings forages upon the ground while walking or running in search of the seeds from grasses, forbs, and sedges. They occasionally glean seeds from the tops of grass.

Habits: The large winter flocks roost together on the ground in tight, huddling masses of birds. They shallowly burrow in the snow for insulation. They are often seen "bathing" in the snow.

Nest: The female places the nest in the crevice between rocks or some other natural cavity. She builds a nest of grass and moss lined with grass, plant down, hair, and feathers. She incubates the 4-7 brown- and black-marked blue-green eggs for 10-16 days. Both adults feed the nestlings, which fledge at 10-17 days.

Voice: The wintering flocks of Snow Buntings are alive with buzzy calls and whistled *"tew"* notes.

Primary Habitat Characteristics: The Snow Bunting prefers to winter on open grasslands that provide many seeds.

Other Habitats: They breed on the rocky areas with tundra vegetation. In the winter, they will also forage on agricultural fields.

Conservation: Snow Bunting populations are steady. They may have increased in the past due to the proliferation of agriculture, which provides many winter feeding opportunities.

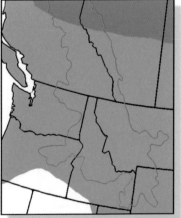

Bobolink

JFMAMJJASOND

Dolichonyx oryzivorus

B

Description: The male Bobolink (7") makes a striking inpression with its contrasting plumage. The male is black overall. He has a white rump patch and wing patches. The most identifiying feature is the straw-colored hindcrown. The female Bobolink is generally buff-colored overall. She is brown streaked on the upperparts and sides. Her head has heavy brown stripes. Both sexes have pointed individual tail feathers.

Male Bobolink

Feeding: The Bobolink forages for insects throughout the summer. They forage while walking about in loose flocks, except during the breeding season. This bird also eats a wide variety of available seeds from grasses and forbs.

Habits: This blackbird is commonly seen singing from a tall stalk of grass that bends under its weight.

Nest: During the courtship, the male Bobolink spreads his tail and sings softly to the female. The nest is a cup of grass and stems lined with grass. It is located within a dense tangle of tall grass and vegetation. The female incubates the 5-6 brown-and purple-blotched reddish eggs for 11-13 days. The young are fed by both adults. They leave the nest at 8-14 days, several days before they can fly.

Voice: The male gives a loud, bubbling *"bob-o-link"* song. In flight, they give a clear, sharp *"pink"* call.

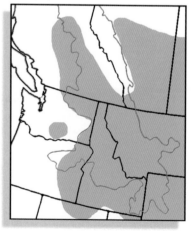

Primary Habitat Characteristics: Good Bobolink habitat has dense grass and weed cover with a few scattered shrubs.

Other Habitats: Though their native habitat is grasslands, the Bobolink is just as likely to be encountered in hayfields.

Conservation: The expansion of suburban areas has decreased available breeding habitat as it as been converted.

V-chested Western Meadowlark

Description: The first singing Western Meadowlark (9") of the spring is always a magical sound. The upperparts are mottled brown. The head is striped with black and white. There is some yellow coloration in the lore area. The dark bill is long and sharp. The underparts are bright, lemon yellow with a bold, black V across the breast. The outer tail feathers are white and are seen in flight.

Feeding: As the Western Meadowlark walks along the ground, it picks up many different species of insects and other invertebrates and seeds. The seed portion of the diet is of more importance during the autumn and winter.

Habits: When the Western Meadowlark flies it does so with rapid flutters followed by short glides. It readily hybridizes with the Eastern Meadowlark where their ranges overlap. They form large wintering flocks (up to 100 individuals) that forage and roost together. The male Western Meadowlark can have a repertoire of up to 12 song varations.

Nest: The female constructs a dome-shaped nest of grass that is woven into neighboring stems. The opening is on one side. She incubates 3-7 brown- and purple-spotted white eggs for 13-15 days. She does the majority of feeding of the young. They leave the nest at 10-13 days, and are able to fly within several days afterwards. The parental care continues for two weeks.

Voice: The song of this bird is a series of flutelike notes that speed up at the end. The common call is a low-pitched *"chuck"*.

Primary Habitat Characteristics: The Western Meadowlark favors open country with scattered perching sites such as isolated shrubs, dead trees, and, especially, fenceposts.

Other Habitats: They can also be found in agricultural areas.

Conservation: Populations are apparently declining, especially since the 1960's; although it is still an abundant species.

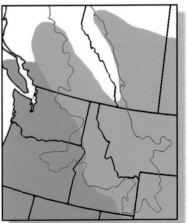

Brewer's Blackbird   *Euphagus cyanocephalus*

J F M A M J J A S O N D

B/R

Description: The Brewer's Blackbird (9") is the blackbird of the Northern Rockies region grasslands. The male is black overall with iridescence on the head and wings. This iridescence is greenish on the wings and purplish on the head. He has a yellow eye that stands out. The female is grayish brown overall, and her eye is dark. The tail is somewhat long in relation of the body.

Feeding: The Brewer's Blackbird eats mostly insects that are found on the ground. They will consume many different kinds of seeds as well. Most of the foraging takes place on the ground; however, they will occasionally flycatch and pick on mudflats.

Male Brewer's Blackbird

Habits: During the winter, the Brewer's Blackbird can be found in mixed-species flocks with European Starlings and other blackbirds. They will establish communal roosts that can number in the thousands.

Nest: The Brewer's Blackbird nests in small colonies. The nest can be placed in a variety of locations; however, 20-40 feet up a tree is the most typical. The female constructs the nest out of twigs, grass, stems, and conifer needles, lined with grass and hair. She incubates the 4-6 brown-spotted greenish gray eggs for 12-14 days. The male feeds her during the incubation period. The nestlings fledge in 13-14 days. Both parents care for them until they fledge.

Voice: The Brewer's Blackbird's song is a wheezy *"kasqueek"* and the call is a harsh *"chick"*.

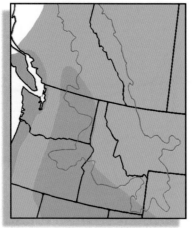

Primary Habitat Characteristics: The Brewer's Blackbird prefers moister open to semi-open habitats, often near water and human habitation. This species uses conifers or bulrushes for roosting sites.

Other Habitats: They also live in wetland areas, agricultural fields, suburban areas, aspen stands, and open riparian stands.

Conservation: Although very common, the Brewer's Blackbird is declining.

Common Grackle

Quiscalus quiscula

J F M A M J J A S O N D

B/R

Foraging Common Grackle

Description: Becoming a more and more common sight, the Common Grackle (12^1/$_2$") is a deliberate forager. Both males and females are generally black overall; however, the males have a purple iridescence on the head and back. The tail is long and keel-shaped. The female's tail is shorter than the male's. The eyes are a contrasting yellow.

Feeding: The Common Grackle has a *Corvid's* diet: it is an omnivore. As they walk on the ground, they will consume insects, invertebrates, seeds, berries, birds' eggs, and, on rare occasions, small mammals. They will occasionally steal from other birds such as American Robins.

Habits: During the winter, they will join communal roosts that often contain Red-winged Blackbirds. Several scattered individuals will overwinter in the Northern Rockies, particularly in urban areas where seed feeders are available to them.

Nest: The male displays to the female by fluffing his feathers and spreading his wings while singing. The female builds a nest of stems, grass, and twigs lined with grass, which is placed in the lower reaches of a deciduous tree. She incubates the 4-5 brown-blotched pale blue eggs for 12-14 days. The nestlings are fed insects by both adults. The young fledge in 16-20 days.

Voice: The Common Grackle's song is a short series of raspy notes like *"koguba-leek"*. The variety of calls include a *"chaah"*.

Primary Habitat Characteristics: It favors open habitats that have nearby stands of trees for roosting and nesting.

Other Habitats: The Common Grackle also lives in agricultural habitats, urban areas, cottonwood bottom forest, and some riparian stands. They can become voracious pests at feeders, crowding out other songbirds.

Conservation: The Common Grackle has remained common in the Northern Rockies over the last several decades.

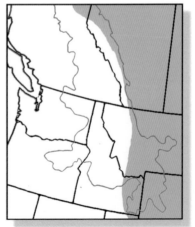

Description: The Common Redpoll (5¼"), along with the Hoary Redpoll, descends on seed feeders across the Northern Rockies. The upperparts are streaked brown. The forecrown is red, and the chin is black. There is streaking in the flanks and rump. The male has a rose wash on the breast, and the female's breast is unmarked. The Common Redpoll is more vividly colored than the Hoary Redpoll.

The irruptive Common Redpoll

© Peter LaTourrette

Feeding: The Common Redpoll feeds in flocks that forage on the ground and in the lower trees and shrubs. They consume mostly seeds, which can be stored in the crop for later eating.

Habits: This species is very irruptive, and shows up in large numbers during some winters. These flocks congregrate in and around areas with high seed production. They will also use seed feeders. They are often seen with the paler Hoary Redpoll.

Nest: During courtship, the male bows to the female while she crouches with dropped wings. The female conceals her nest of twigs, grass, and other plant materials lined with ptarmigan feathers in the low dense shrub or tree. She incubates the 4-5 purple-spotted green eggs for 10-11 days. The young fledge after 12 days.

Voice: The Common Redpoll's song is a mix of trills and buzzing notes. The calls include *"cit cit"* and *"sweet"*.

Irruptive Winter Visitor

Primary Habitat Characteristics: The Common Redpoll favors shrubby areas within the grasslands.

Other Habitats: During the winter, they can be seen foraging in forest clearings and in suburban areas where seed feeders have been put up. The Common Redpoll will visit the edge where grassland meets forest.

Conservation: Can be relatively common and incredibly abundant during irruptive years.

Hoary Redpoll
Carduelis hornemanni

J F M A M J J A S O N D

W

The uncommon Hoary Redpoll

Description: The Hoary Redpoll (5¼") is usually in the company of the Common Redpoll; you just have to pick the drabber Hoary out of thousands of Commons — no problem. The upperparts are finely brown streaked white. The forecrown is red, and the chin is black. There is no streaking in the flanks and rump. The male has a pale pink wash on the breast, and the female's breast is unmarked. The Hoary Redpoll is more subtly marked than its cousin, the Common Redpoll.

Feeding: The Hoary Redpoll feeds in flocks that forage on the ground and in the lower trees and shrubs. It consumes mostly seeds, which can be stored in the crop for later eating.

Habits: This species is irruptive, and shows up in increased numbers during some winters. Often seen in the company of the more abundant Common Redpoll.

Nest: During courtship, the male bows to the female while she crouches with dropped wings. The female conceals her nest of twigs, grass, and other plant materials lined with ptarmigan feathers in a low shrub or tree. She incubates the 4-5 reddish brown-spotted pale green eggs for 11 days. The young fledge in 9-14 days.

Voice: The Hoary Redpoll's song is a mix of trills and buzzing notes. The calls include *"cit cit"* and *"sweet"*.

Primary Habitat Characteristics: The Hoary Redpoll favors shrubby areas within the grasslands during their time in the Northern Rockies.

Other Habitats: During the winter, they can be seen foraging in forest clearings and in suburban areas where seed feeders have been put up. In general, the Hoary Redpoll prefers open areas during the winter.

Conservation: Always uncommon during the winter, and during irruptive years, it is present in somewhat greater numbers.

Irruptive Winter Visitor

Description: American Goldfinches (5") are often seen perched on roadside black-eyed susans as they feed on the flowers' seeds. The breeding male is bright yellow overall with black wings that have white wingbars. The crown is black. The black and white tail is slightly notched. The female is a dull version of the breeding male's plumage with the black crown. The nonbreeding male is generally brownish overall with black wings and tail.

Male American Goldfinch

© Ross Knapper

Feeding: The diet of the American Goldfinch is mostly seeds from a variety of sources, particularly members of the sunflower family. They feed mostly on the ground, although they are often seen dangling upside from a large flower.

Habits: This finch will form winter foraging-flocks with Pine Siskins and both Common and Hoary Redpolls. These flocks can number up to 300 birds.

Nest: The male will give a singing display flight during the courtship. During this flight, he gives the *"perchicoree"* call. The female builds her nest of forbs and stems lined with plant down and places it on a branch of a deciduous shrub or tree. She incubates the 4-6 pale blue eggs for 12-14 days. Nestlings fledge in 11-17 days.

Voice: The American Goldfinch is quite the songster with a couple of songs, one canary-like and another that is a short warble, and a variety of calls, *"sweeeet"*, *"beer-bee"*, and *"perchicoree"*.

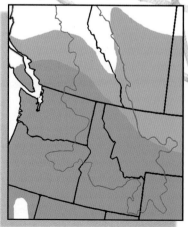

Primary Habitat Characteristics: They favor grasslands that have plenty of weeds and thistles, and scattered thickets or adjacent riparian areas for nesting.

Other Habitats: American Goldfiches are found along roadsides, riparian thickets (especially those with willows), and cottonwood bottom forest.

Conservation: The American Goldfinch is common, and its numbers are stable.

199

Sage Shrublands

*Now imagine dozens and dozens of males, all
swishing and plopping away like mad, and you'll begin to
understand why sage grouse courtship is considered one
of the great wildlife spectacles on the continent.*

−SCOTT WEIDENSAUL

Sage shrubland meets wetland and pond

The smell of sage hangs greasy in the air with each brush of one of the massive bushes. This sage is indeed big sagebrush, with trunks as thick as my leg and a slight bit taller than my six feet. This patch of sagebrush has grown taller and bigger as it is situated in a draw that carries more water than the rest of this bench in southwestern Montana. Looking up to the song of a Brewer's Sparrow, I see its form with bill open and pointed skyward. Back over my shoulder, a sea of sage sweeps over a series of rolling hills.

Sage shrublands occur in cold semi-deserts throughout the West and the southwest portion of the Northern Rockies physiographic region. The climate is characterized by long, cold winters and brief hot and dry summers. Winds are a constant element of the sage shrublands. There is little precipitation and evaporation rates are high, so the plants that take hold are extremely drought tolerant. There are several species of sage that dominate, and big sagebrush is the most common species among these shrubs. A few other species of shrubs grow along with the sagebrush. These include rubber rabbitbrush, antelope bitterbrush, and common sagebrush. In the understory, bunchgrasses are common, especially in the Intermountain sage shrublands. Bluebunch wheatgrass, Idaho fescue, and needle-and-thread grass are the most abundant species of grass in the sage shrubland. There are relatively few and scattered forbs such as various phlox species and fleabanes.

Sagebrush has several important adaptations that allow it to thrive in arid conditions. First, the root system is shallow and spreads out over a wide area (up to 90 feet in diameter). This allows the sagebrush to access more water during the brief periods of precipitation. A second important adaptation is that the sagebrush has two different forms of leaves, one for dry periods and another for more drought-like conditions.

The birds of the sage shrubland tend not to key in on the precise species composition of the stand, but on its physical characteristics. Sage stands can vary from 5-30% canopy closure, and within the stand there may be grassy openings. These openings can attract birds more closely associated with grassland habitats, which can be adjacent to the sage shrublands.

Relatively few birds make their permanent homes in sage shrublands when compared to the species that reside in the forest or on the grasslands of the West. However, many of these birds cannot be found anywhere other than the sage shrubland habitat type. These include obligates such as the Greater Sage Grouse, Sage Sparrow, and Sage Thrasher (aptly named, don't you think?) and near obligates like Brewer's Sparrow and Lark Sparrow.

The early morning crimson sunrise floods across the sage plains. It came up so suddenly that it hurts our eyes for a few brief moments. All morning we had heard clucking murmurs of the females and booms of the ornate males. The Greater Sage Grouse are now ramping up for full display of mating frenzy. Between scattered clumps of sagebrush, the drably colored females are milling around. The gathering of Greater Sage Grouse happens for just a scant few weeks each spring. In the center of the opening within this sea of sagebrush, several males are putting on an incredible show. They each inflate their air sacs to almost popping, and then they release a sound that is called "booming". Their yellow combs become readily visible. This behavior is known as lekking. A lek is a traditional displaying ground where generations of Greater Sage Grouse have done their courtship ritual. As males occupy themselves, the females are choosing their mates. The females select which males looks better to their discerning eyes.

The Greater Sage Grouse is a sagebrush obligate and it is not often found outside of sage shrubland habitat. Over the course of the year, they move from one sagebrush stand to another. During the spring, they are found in stands that average 20-40% canopy closure. The females build their nests in these stands. As summer scroches the landscape, they migrate into denser patches where they will remain throughout the winter.

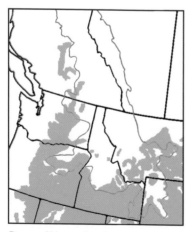

Range of big sagebrush

The Greater Sage Grouse is the ultimate sagebrush obiligate that takes advantage of the complete offerings of the sage shrubland. They use this habitat for thermal cover, a food source, a nesting location, and breeding territory. They depend on this habitat and much of it has disappeared as Greater Sage Grouse numbers have dropped.

Many of the birds that reside in the sage shrubland have declined in the past 30 years. In the Intermountain West, nearly 50% of the birds that utilize sage shrubland have declined. One reason for these decreases is the alteration and destruction of sage shrublands. Many sage shrublands have been converted to agriculture. The introduction of cattle grazing into the sage shrublands has eliminated many native bunch grasses from these habitats. The grazing cattle also damage the thin soils of shrublands as they move about.

Many non-native grasses and weeds have made their way into the sage shrubland community. These plants have crowded and out-competed the native vegetation. Cheatgrass is a major problem. This grass, introduced from Eurasia, will dominate the understory with a thick carpet of itself. This grass burns quite easily, which dramicatically changes the normal fire regime of the sage shrubland.

All is not lost, though. There is currently an ongoing management effort to restore many areas of sage shrublands. So, the outlook is upbeat; however, it will take time for the sage shrublands to recover naturally, especially in the more arid areas of the Northern Rockies.

Climbing out of the draw into a sage-covered bench, I see what once was a much more common sight. Three Greater Sage Grouse hens flushed up about twenty yards ahead of me. As they fly away with rapid wingbeats, they swing into the sun and disappear into the sagebrush sea.

	Tall, dense sagebrush	Open, patchy sagebrush	Grass cover for nests	Grassland	Short grass, bare ground	Seeps	Dry forest	Riparian
Sagebrush Obiligate Species								
Greater Sage Grouse	✓	✓	✓	✓	✓	✓		
Sage Thrasher	✓	✓	✓		✓			
Sage Sparrow	✓		✓		✓			
Brewer's Sparrow	✓	✓	✓		✓			
Shrubland Species								
Lark Sparrow		✓	✓	✓			✓	
Shrubland and Grassland Species								
Northern Shrike	✓	✓			✓		✓	✓
Loggerhead Shrike	✓	✓			✓		✓	✓
Vesper Sparrow	✓	✓	✓					

Habitat components used by sage shrubland birds (adapted from Paige & Ritter, 1999)

Greater Sage Grouse   *Centrocercus urophasianus*

J F M A M J J A S O N D

R

Male Greater Sage Grouse on the lek

Description: Each spring, the Greater Sage Grouse (28") gathers on traditional leks and puts on an incredible show. Both male and female are generally brown overall. The larger male has pointed tail feathers and yellow eye-combs. He possesses a black chin and throat, and a white breast. When he is displaying, the yellow air sacs on the breast are inflated. The female is smaller and has a brown breast. The belly is black.

Feeding: Not only is the Greater Sage Grouse found primarily in sage shrubland, it eats mostly sagebrush. It consumes the leaves and buds of the plant. During the summer, this grouse will eat the parts of other plants and a small amount of insects. All of its feeding is done while walking on the ground.

Habits: Well camouflaged, they flush with a loud wing noise.

Nest: The Greater Sage Grouse gathers in leks early in the morning where the males fan their tails and strut for a gathered crowd of females. The air sacs are inflated and deflated producing plopping sounds. These leks are traditional and used year after year. The female lines a depression with grass and sage leaves. She incubates the 7-9 brown-marked yellow-olive eggs for 25-27 days. The young feed themselves soon after hatching, and are tended by the female.

Voice: The male's air sacs produce a loud plopping sound. Feeding females make a variety of clucks.

Primary Habitat Characteristics: The Greater Sage Grouse will almost be always found in or around sagebrush.

Other Habitats: They are very rarely encountered in the absence of sagebrush.

Conservation: The removal of sagebrush is cause for concern, and this species should be watched carefully. It was recently split from the Gunnison's Sage Grouse of Colorado, which is now considered a separate species.

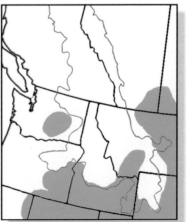

Singing Sage Thrasher

© Caleb Putnam

Description: The male Sage Thrasher (8¹/₂") will sing from atop a tall sagebrush. It is generally gray-ish-brown with a good deal of dark spotting on the light underside. The wings have apparent white bars. The tail is long with white corners. The eye is dull yellow. The Sage Thrasher looks rather like a thrush in coloration, without any rusty tones.

Feeding: It is chiefly an insectivore that gleans insects from, primarily, the ground and from the foliage. This bird eats grasshoppers, ants, and variety of other insects. It seems to be very fond of Mormon crickets. A small amount of berries and other fruits are also consumed.

Habits: It is almost never found away from sage shrublands. It will slip into dense sagebrush when disturbed. Pairs may mate for more than a single year.

Nest: The male will sing from conspicious perches, in addition to performing display flights, during the breeding season. The Sage Thrasher nests in the densest, tallest patches of sagebrush. The nest is placed in a large sagebrush or other shrub. They incubate the 3-5 brown-spotted greenish-blue eggs for 13-17 days. Both sexes feed and care for the young in the nest. The young leave the nest at 11-14 days. This species has been known to double brood.

Voice: The song is a long series of warbled notes that change in tempo.

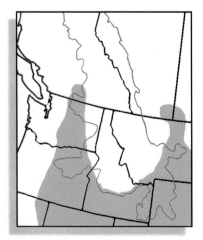

Primary Habitat Characteristics: It is considered a sagebrush obligate. They are very rarely found outside the sage shrubland habitat.

Other Habitats: It will rarely turn up in juniper-limber pine shrublands and mountain mahogany shrublands. These habitats tend to be adjacent of the sagebursh shrublands.

Conservation: It may be in decline like the other sagebrush obiligates, although the data seems to be inconclusive.

Loggerhead Shrike · *Lanius ludovicianus*

J F M A M J J A S O N D

B

© Ross Knapper

The Butcherbird, the Loggerhead Shrike

Description: The Loggerhead Shrike or Butcherbird (9") impales its prey on thorns. The crown and back are bluish-gray. A black mask extends from the bill through the eye. The black bill is stout and hooked. The underparts are white. In flight, the black wings show white patches. The tail is black with white corners. The white to gray rump is light. The pale juveniles have faint barring overall.

Feeding: The Loggerhead Shrike hunts where low vegetation is short or absent. It strikes out from its hunting perch. The prey items are mostly insects with the rest of the diet including small birds and mammals. The impaling behavior serves both as a sexual advertisement and a way to butcher the prey.

Habits: It impales prey on thorns and barbed wire fences.

Nest: During courtship, the male gives short display flights and feeds the female. They begin nesting quite early in the spring. The open cup nest of twigs and grass forbs lined with fine materials is placed in dense foliage of a thorny tree, especially Black hawthorn. The female incubates the 5-6 pale buff brown- and gray-spotted eggs for 16-17 days. The male feeds her throughout the incubation period. The young fledge at 3-4 weeks.

Voice: The song is a series of two syllable phrases that are repeated for a short duration.

Primary Habitat Characteristics: The Loggerhead Shrike prefers open country with low vegetation for hunting, and shrubs or small trees for perching and roosting. Hunting perches are crucial to the Loggerhead Shrike.

Other Habitats: This adaptable species can be found in montane shrublands, grasslands, and meadows.

Conservation: Its population has been reduced by loss of habitat through conversion to agriculture, urbanization, and overgrazing.

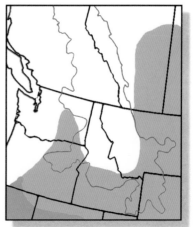

Northern Shrike

Lanius excubitor

J F M A M J J A S O N D

W

Description: The songbird-killing songbird, the Northern Shrike (10") arrives each autumn in the Northern Rockies. It has a pale gray crown and back. A narrow black mask extends from the base of the bill through the eye. The black bill is longer and more strongly hooked than the Loggerhead Shrike's. The underparts are white with very faint barring. The wings are black with white patches. The rump is white. The juvenile is generally more brown than the adults. Immature individuals are more gray and faded out than the adults.

The predatory songbird, the Northern Shrike

Feeding: The Northern Shrike strikes out from an exposed perch after its intended victim. During the winter, it hunts mainly smaller songbirds and some small rodents. These are captured with a specialized bill, and then impaled on a thorn or piece of barbed wire, where they are dismembered.

Habits: It often bobs its tail when perched. It is very solitary during the winter.

Nest: The male attracts a female by singing an amazingly complex song that includes portions of imitations of other birds' songs. The nest is placed in a shrub or small tree, and it is a cup of twigs, grass, and moss lined with finer materials. She incubates the 4-7 spotted gray eggs for 15-17 days. The young are fed by both parents. The young fledge in roughly 19-20 days.

Voice: The song is a series of phrases given with a fluid delivery.

Primary Habitat Characteristics: The Northern Shrike prefers open country with exposed perches for hunting.

Other Habitats: It can be seen on grasslands during the winter. It breeds on northern conifer forests and riparian areas.

Conservation: The Northern Shrike does not have a lot of population data associated with it; however, concern is warranted.

Perched Brewer's Sparrow

Description: Singing proudly from a twig of sagebrush, the Brewer's Sparrow (5") is found in almost every stand of sagebrush. The upperparts are dark streaked buff brown. The crown is brown with fine black streaking. The eyebrow is gray, and the ear patch is pale brown. The underparts are light and unmarked. The unmarked rump patch is lighter tan than the back.

Feeding: Actively feeding among the sagebrush, the Brewer's Sparrow descends to the ground where it feeds upon both insects and seeds from grasses and forbs. Occasionally, it will glean insects from the foliage. They feed in flocks outside the breeding season.

Habits: It sings from atop an elevated perch, often a tall sagebrush. Found in flocks as they prepare for migration.

Nest: During the breeding season, the male defends his territory by singing from an exposed perch. It builds an open cup nest of grass and weeds lined with hair and fine plant materials in the lower branches of a living sagebrush. The 3-4 brown-spotted blue-green eggs are incubated for 11-13 days. The young are fed by both parents for 8-9 days, when they leave the nest; however, they are not able to fly yet. The Brewer's Sparrow is capable of multiple broods.

Voice: The song is a long series of trills and buzzes that descends. The call is a high-pitched *"tsip"*.

Primary Habitat Characteristics: A near sagebrush obligate, the Brewer's Sparrow is closely associated with shrublands with scattered sagebrush and short grass.

Other Habitats: It will turn up in mountain mahogany shrublands, juniper-limber pine shrublands, and bunchgrass prairies as well.

Conservation: The alteration of sagebrush habitat has had a negative effect on the Brewer's Sparrow.

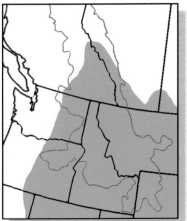

Description: The most common sparrow of the sage shrubland, the Vesper Sparrow (6") is very nondescript. The overall coloration is streaked grayish-brown. There is a distinct white eye-ring. The dark brown ear patch is bordered below by a white stripe, further bordered with a thin dark stripe. In flight, it shows white outer tail feathers.

Adult Vesper Sparrow

Feeding: Walking along the ground, the Vesper Sparrow is an active forager of insects and seeds that it finds upon the soil. The insects consumed include grasshoppers, caterpillars, and beetles. Outside the breeding season, it forages in small flocks.

Habits: The Vesper Sparrow is quite tame, and it will allow close approach. Along country dirt roads, it can be seen dust bathing in the ruts.

Nest: During courtship, the male will run around the female with his wings and tail spread. The nest is a cup of grass and weeds lined with finer materials that is placed in a depression next to clump grass. The female does most of the incubation of the 3-4 brown- and gray-blotched whitish eggs for 11-13 days. The young leave the nest after 9-10 days of parental care. The Vesper Sparrow will commonly double brood.

Voice: The song of the Vesper Sparrow is paired whistles that end with an accelerating trill. The call is a clear, sharp *"chip"*. The flight call is a buzzy *"seeet"*.

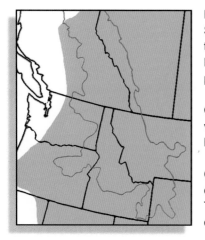

Primary Habitat Characteristics: The Vesper Sparrow favors areas that are a mix of low, scattered sagebrush in a matrix of short grass. Prominent shrubs are often used as singing perches.

Other Habitats: This species can be found in a variety of grassland, shrubland, and agricultural habitats.

Conservation: Overall, the Vesper Sparrow is common, and its numbers seem to be steady. The effects of grazing on this species seem to depend on the habitat utilized by the sparrow.

The striking Lark Sparrow

Description: The boldly patterned Lark Sparrow (6") is always a pleasant surprise in the Northern Rockies. The most unique feature of this species is the head pattern. The head is striped with white and rich chestnut. The ear patch is the same chestnut color. The upperparts are mottled brown. The underparts are light gray and unmarked, save for the dark central breast spot. In flight, the white corners of the dark tail are apparent. Juveniles strongly resemble the adults in pattern, although their colors are much duller.

Feeding: In small flocks, the Lark Sparrow forages on the ground for a variety of insects and the seeds of grasses and forbs.

Habits: It is often seen in the open, and almost seems to avoid cover. It flies high when moving, while giving a flight call.

Nest: When he is courting, the male displays his white tail corners to the female. The open cup nest of grass, twigs, weeds, and other materials is placed at the base of bunchgrass, shrub, or a small tree. This species will, on occasion, use the old nests of other birds. The female incubates the 3-6 brown- and black-spotted cream eggs for 11-12 days. The young fledge after 9-10 days of parental care.

Voice: The song is a slow mixture of rattling notes and trills.

Primary Habitat Characteristics: The Lark Sparrow is a bird that prefers a good mixture of grassland and sage shrubland. Prominent perch sites are needed for singing.

Other Habitats: It can be found in a variety of shrubland and grassland habitats. It is less frequently located in cottonwood and aspen stands.

Conservation: Populations have been declining for quite some time. These reductions may be linked to sage shrubland removal and alteration, and to grazing within sage shrublands.

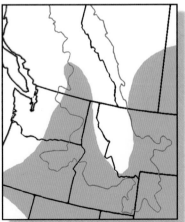

Description: The rarest of the sage shrubland sparrows found in the Northern Rockies, the Sage Sparrow's (6") name suits it well. The upperparts are streaked brownish buff, and the underparts are white with a dark central breast spot. There is a white eye-ring, and the lore regions are white. The white submoustachial stripe is bordered with a black malar stripe.

Feeding: The Sage Sparrow forages on the ground and lower portions of the sagebrush for mostly insects and some seeds. The insects consumed include many beetles, grasshoppers, ants, and other insects.

Habits: Males are often seen singing from atop a fence post or taller sagebrush. The sparrow often runs on the ground with its tail cocked up slightly.

© Caleb Putnam

Breeding Sage Sparrow in southwestern Montana

Nest: The male defends the nesting territory from an elevated perch. The Sage Sparrow builds an open cup nest of twigs lined with grass and weeds that is placed high in a sagebrush. The 3-4 brown, gray, and black-blotched pale blue eggs are incubated for 13-16 days. Both parents feed the young while they are in the nest. The young leave the nest in 9-11 days. It is an occasional Brown-headed Cowbird host and uses the same nesting territory year after year.

Voice: The song of the Sage Sparrow is a mumbled series of singsong-like notes.

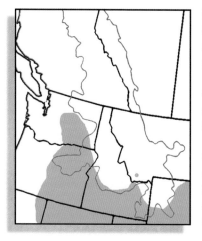

Primary Habitat Characteristics: The Sage Sparrow is a sagebrush obligate. it favors sage shrublands dominated by big sagebrush with perennial bunchgrasses in the understory.

Other Habitats: They will occasionally use areas of extensive rabbitbrush and antelope bitterbrush.

Conservation: This species' reliance on sage shrublands makes it especially vulnerable to habitat alteration. Fragmentation of sage shrublands has increased Brown-headed Cowbird parasitism.

Montane Shrubland

*If my Decomposing Carcass helps nourish the roots
of a juniper tree or the wings of a vulture - that is immortality
enough for me. And as much as anyone deserves.*

–EDWARD ABBEY

Under and between the bulbous forms of juniper, the soil is mostly gravel with sparse grass and forb cover. A misplaced step sends your foot backwards as if you were walking on a table of ball bearings. Although this shrubland is very dry, it does not have the feel of a desert or, even, a sage shrubland. It seems to be a mixture of stunted forest with dry grassland between the trees. Each juniper is covered with small blue berries. However, these are not berries in the botanical sense, they are actually small dense cone-like structures. The "berries" are unique in that they cannot germinate until the fleshy covering is removed by passing through the digestive system of a bird, such as the Townsend's Solitaire, or mammal, like a mule deer. The smell of juniper hangs in the air like an oil slick on top of water. The Native Americans sought this odor as a sacrament in religious ceremonies and medicine.

Montane shrublands covered in this field guide are divided into two basic categories: deciduous montane shrublands and juniper-limber pine shrublands, with a couple of less common shrubland types also occurring the Northern Rockies.

Deciduous montane shrublands are located over a wide range of elevations and slope aspects. Montane shrublands in wetter sites are composed of ninebark, serviceberry, Rocky Mountain maple, alder, and shiny-leaf ceanothus. Ceanothus is a plant of uncommon traits, an evergreen shrub. Ceanothus never loses it leaves, and it is an important winter food source for some ungulates. These shrublands may or may not be associated with riparian corridors. When a montane shrubland is near a riparian area, riparian associated birds can come into the shrubland and vice versa.

Deciduous montane shrublands provide important nesting habitat for many species

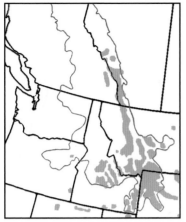
Range of limber pine

of songbirds. MacGillivray's Warbler and Spotted Towhee are among the songsters that particularly depend on deciduous montane shrublands.

Growing in thick stands on rocky slopes with each plant having gnarled branches from ungulate browsing, mountain mahogany shrubland occurs only in a small area from southwest Montana through to the Blue Mountains of Oregon and southward. Mountain mahogany grows on shallow, loose soils on steep, dry slopes. It is usually found in the transition between grassland and dry conifer forest.

This type of montane shrubland is found across a great elevation gradient and, generally, on southeast to southwest facing slopes.

The other major montane shrubland is the juniper-limber pine shrubland. This shrubland is found at lower elevations, and it is often associated the sagebrush and bunch grasses.

Covering the drier slopes of the foothills in the Northern Rockies, the Rocky Mountain juniper is one of the longest-lived plants in the Rockies, reaching ages upwards of 1,500 years. Most of this tree is toxic, save for the berries. Many Native American tribes ascribed healing powers to the aromatic smoke of the juniper.

Scattered among the junipers, an occasional limber pine takes hold in the rocky soil. The limber pine is appropriately named; you can take a branch of this tree and twist it without breaking the branch. This hardy pine is a close cousin of the whitebark pine, and it often grows in exposed sites that shaped the limber pine into contorted forms. limber pine is important to the Clark's Nutcracker, which consumes the fatty seeds of the five-needle pine. The nutcracker moves into these shrublands during the winter or when whitebark pine is otherwise unavailable.

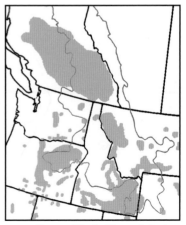
Range of Rocky Mountain juniper

Of the birds that live within the juniper-limber pine habitat type, one absolutely thrives. The Pinyon Jay is normally associated with the vast pinyon pine shrublands of the Great Basin; however, in the Northern Rockies, this colorful *Corvid* is found roaming amongst the junipers and pines of the foothills. This species is one of the most nomadic of the region's birds. The flocks of 20-100 individuals roam throughout large home ranges. In fact, it is almost unimaginable of find a lone Pinyon Jay that is not in the close company of its flock. The powder blue birds descend on a stand of juniper and limber pine and feed underneath the ancient trees. The nomadic wanderings of the Pinyon Jays are determined by the cyclical nature of cone crops. When the cone crop fails in one area of their home range, the jays will venture out to find another stand that has produced an adequate crop. To the observer, it appears that

the Pinyon Jay is a mirage. They are here in large, noisy flocks one day and gone the next.

Scattered across the Northern Rockies are isolated pockets of one very unique type of shrubland. Antelope bitterbrush shrublands are often found where intermountain and palouse grasslands graduate into the foothills. These shrublands occur in the Northern Rockies in southern British Columbia and scattered pockets in Montana and Washington. They prefer rather dry sites with glacially deposited soils. Most of the precipitation that quenches this habitat occurs during the cooler, wetter months of winter. The birds found within the antelope bitterbrush shrubland are a suite of

species that includes the several sparrow species that are more often associated with sage shrublands and those that are also found in the juniper-limber pine shrubland.

As the summer fades into autumn, Clark's Nutcrackers and Townsend's Solitaires invade the juniper-limber pine shrublands. The Townsend's Solitaire feeds greedily upon the juniper berries, while the nutcrackers concentrate on the seeds of the limber pine. Black-capped Chickadees flit about the junipers with the onset of winter. The winter in the montane shrubland is relatively quiet. The spring is when the montane sings with the songs of many Passerines. The juniper-limber pine and montane shrublands mark the transition from the lower elevation habitats and forests, and like many transition zones, they are remarkable for their abundance of birdlife.

215

American Kestrel

J F M A M J J A S O N D

Falco sparverius

B/R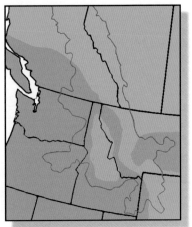

Hunting American Kestrel

Description: The colorful American Kestrel (9-10")
is the smallest falcon in North America. Their heads
have red and blue crowns with mustache stripes.
The upperparts are a colorful mix of cinnamon,
blue, and red. The smaller males have blue wings
and rust-colored tails. The male's breast is white
with black spots. The females are more cinnamon
overall with streaking, and the beast is tan with vertical streaks. The wings are typical of a falcon, long
(in relation to body size) and pointed.

Feeding: The most often utilized hunting methods
employed by the American Kestrel are the aerial
pounce and striking from an elevated perch. Insects
are the bulk of the summertime diet. Small mammals become increasingly important as winter begins. This small falcon will cache additional food.

Habits: The American Kestrel is the only falcon species in the Northern Rockies
that habitually hovers in place and aerial pounces its prey. It bobs its tail frequently,
especially when preparing for an attack.

Nest: During courtship, the male dives while giving a *"klee"*. Using old woodpecker
holes, natural cavities, or nest boxes, the American Kestrel does not build a nest
within these structures. Nest sites are usually on the edge of habitat. Both sexes
incubate the 3-7 fine brown-spotted cream eggs for 30 days. Both parents care for
the nestlings for 26-31 days. The juveniles gradually disperse from the nest for a
period of 2-4 weeks as hunting skills develop.

Voice: When agitated, it gives a rapid series
of *"klee-klee-klee"*.

Primary Habitat Characteristics: The American Kestrel prefers open areas with elevated
perches for hunting.

Other Habitats: American Kestrels are found
in grasslands, open forest, and urban areas
(especially near highways).

Conservation: Widespread and common.

Description: Often overlooked, as it tends to hide in thick brush, the Mountain Quail (11") is the largest quail in North America. They are grayish-brown above. The chin is rufous and the breast is a bluish-gray. The belly is chestnut with bold white barring along the sides. The most unique feature of this species is the two long plumes that erupt from atop the head.

The elusive Mountain Quail

Feeding: Scratching the ground and picking, the Mountain Quail consumes mostly seeds. They will also feed in the lower branches. The diet is rounded out by berries, other vegetative matter (bulbs and tubers), and insects.

Habits: They tend to sit motionless when approached or threatened, only to burst into flight at the last possible second. During the winter, they gather into coveys of up to 30 individuals. Throughout the year, they are altitudinal migrants, ascending in the spring and descending with the onset of autumn.

Nest: During the spring, the Mountain Quail male gives a wonderful call and display in front of the females by puffing out his feathers. A shallow depression lined with grass and leaves serves as the nest. The nest site is usually covered by a downed tree or thick shrub. The female does the bulk of incubating of the 9-10 buff eggs for 24 days. The young can feed themselves soon after hatching. The parents protect them and lead them to food sources.

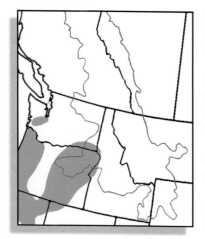

Voice: The male's mating call is a loud *"plu-ark"*. This vocalization can be heard for up to a mile away.

Primary Habitat Characteristics: The Mountain Quail requires dense vegetation for concealment. It is most often within one mile of water, especially during the breeding season.

Other Habitats: They are also found in riparian thickets and older post-fire forests.

Conservation: The overall numbers of Mountain Quail appear to be stable.

Calliope Hummingbird — *Stellula calliope*

J F M A M J J A S O N D

B

Male Calliope Hummingbird

Description: The most common hummingbird in the Northern Rockies, the Calliope Hummingbird (3") is the smallest breeding bird in North America. The male is bright green above and the underparts are creamy. The gorget is streaky purplish-red. The female is duller above and the underparts are creamy with a buff wash along sides and lower breast. Her subdued gorget is speckled with metallic spots. The bill of both sexes is black and of medium length (for a hummingbird).

Feeding: Primarily a nectar feeder, the Calliope Hummingbird hovers into the flower and inserts its bills into it. It will also flycatch some small flying insects.

Habits: While feeding, the tail is cocked upward. The male is very territorial and aggressive.

Nest: Like many hummingbirds, the Calliope Hummingbird engages in a dive display during courtship. He will fly back and forth in a U-shaped pattern, giving a *"tzing"* call at the bottom of the flight. The nest is a small cup of bark fibers and plant fine plant materials bonded by spider webs placed in a conifer with an overhanging branch above it. It is commonly coated with camouflaging bark and lichens. The female incubates the 2 white eggs for 14-16 days. She continues her complete care of the young by feeding them for about 3 weeks after hatching.

Voice: When defending its territory, the Calliope Hummingbird gives a weak *"tchip"*. The sound heard during the dive display is a ringing *"tzing"*.

Primary Habitat Characteristics: It favors areas near water.

Other Habitats: Often they can be seen in riparian thickets. Growth following forest fires is another often-used habitat.

Conservation: Our most common hummingbird, it has benefited from sugar feeders.

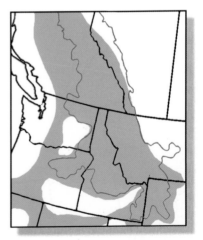

218

Common Poorwill

Phalaenoptilus nuttallii

J F M A M J J A S O N D

B

Description: Coming out at night, the Common Poorwill (7³/₄") is often overlooked by birders in the Northern Rockies. The overall coloration is a mottled gray and brown. The upper chest is banded with white and black. The wings are short and rounded, as is the tail. This arrangement gives the poorwill great maneuverability. If one gets a good look, rictal bristles surround the large, frog-like mouth. These bristles may aid in feeding by funnelling prey into the Common Poorwill's gaping mouth.

© Tom Ulrich

Ground-bound Common Poorwill

Feeding: From the ground or low branch, it flies upwards to snatch a flying insect. Unlike its cousin, the Common Nighthawk, the Common Poorwill will even feed on the ground. Moonlit nights are the best time to see the silhouette of this elusive bird.

Habits: During the cooler nights, the Common Poorwill will enter a state of torpor where its metabolic rate drops, as does its heart rate and body temperature. It is very nocturnal. It often roosts on the ground.

Nest: The *"poor-will"* is the male's territorial defense signal. The nest is nothing more than a ground scrape under the shade of a ponderosa pine, shrub, or rock ledge. No additional material is added to the nest. Both parents incubate the 2 white eggs for about 3 weeks. The young are fed regurgitated insects by the parents for 20-23 days. They may have a second brood if conditions allow for it.

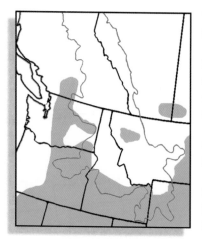

Voice: The *"poor-will"* call is emphasized on the *"will"*.

Primary Habitat Characteristics: The Common Poorwill is most often seen over the drier montane shrublands. These shrublands quite commonly have rocky areas within them.

Other Habitats: They occur over dry conifer forest and grasslands near rock outcrops.

Conservation: Somewhat common within its habitat across the West, although it was not described by science until 1844.

219

Pinyon Jay

Gymnorhinus cyanocephalus

J F M A M J J A S O N D

R

The roaming Pinyon Jay

Description: In flocks of grayish-blue, the Pinyon Jay (10¹/₂") calls harshly with each short flight from one feeding area to the next. The overall coloration is blue that is reminiscent of the Mountain Bluebird. The blue of the head and nape is darker than that of the rest of the body. The robust bill is long and black. It has the shortest tail of the Northern Rocky Mountains' *Corvids*. The throat is indistinctly streaked with white.

Feeding: The Pinyon Jay can be thought of as an omnivore, although it has special affinity for the seeds of pinyon and limber pines. Much like the Clark's Nutcracker, it caches pine nuts for later use during the winter. It forages mostly on the ground in flocks. It will also eat vegetative matter, fruits, grains, and insects.

Habits: Almost always seen in large flocks, with less than 100 individuals the norm. They stay in these flocks throughout the year. The Pinyon Jay is quite nomadic, typically roaming over about 15 square miles of feeding territory.

Nest: During courtship, several males will chase a female relentlessly. The Pinyon Jay nests in colonies. Both sexes build a nest of twigs lined with grass, pine needles, hair, and other plant material. The female incubates the 4-5 brown-spotted bluish eggs for 16-17 days. The young leave the nest after 21 days of parental care by both the male and female.

Voice: The Pinyon Jay gives two frequent calls, a series *"kway kwway kway"* and a loud flight call that is a somewhat catlike *"mew"*.

Primary Habitat Characteristics: The Pinyon Jay is most often seen within juniper and limber pine stands.

Other Habitats: Very rarely, they can be seen in riparian areas and ponderosa pine forest.

Conservation: The Pinyon Jay has a declining population. However, numbers rise and fall with abundance or failure of cone crops.

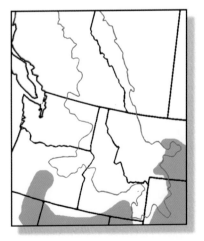

B

Description: Although it's named the Nashville Warbler (4¹/₂"), this active little bird spends more time in Montana than the Music City. The upperparts are an olive-brown. The head is gray with conspicuous white eye-rings. The underparts are dull lemon yellow. The area around the vent may be white. The rufous crown is usually hidden. The females are a little bit duller than the males.

USFWS/Reynolds

The Nashville Warbler prefers deciduous shrubs

Feeding: Gleaning from the lower reaches of its shrub habitat, the Nashville Warbler consumes insects of all types. They concentrate on caterpillars and other insect larvae to feed their young. They often feed toward the tips of branches.

Habits: The Nashville Warbler is often seen to bob its tail. When threatened or displaying, it will raise its crest and show its rufous crown.

Nest: During courtship, the male will give a singing display flight and sing from elevated, exposed perches. The nest is concealed within low, dense vegetation such as grass or ferns. The nest is a cup of grass, moss, and other plant matter. It is lined with grass and fur. The moss in the nest is usually around the rim. The female alone incubates the 4-5 rust-spotted white eggs for 11-12 days. The male will feed his partner while she is on the nest. The young mature quickly and leave the nest after only 11 days of feeding from mainly the female.

Voice: The song of the Nashville Warbler begins with a two-note phrase followed by a lower-pitched trill, *"see-bit see-bit si-si-si"*. The call is sharp *"pink"*.

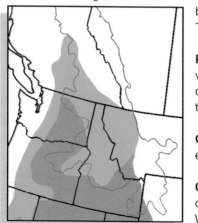

Primary Habitat Characteristics: The Nashville Warbler prefers shrubs in the understory or deciduous portions of mixed forest. These habitats are often regenerated after a fire.

Other Habitats: They will live in riparian thickets next to conifer forest.

Conservation: The Nashville Warbler is fairly common, and there are distinct Eastern and Western subspecies.

MacGillivray's Warblerr

J F M A M J J A S O N D

Oporonis tolmiei

B

Male MacGillivray's Warbler

Description: The very colorful MacGillivray's Warbler (5¹/₄") always seems to stay hidden within thick vegetation. The wings and upper-parts are olive-brown. The gray of the head forms a hood. The most unique features are the two white crescents around the eye, one above and one below. The underparts are yellow. Females are somewhat drabber than the males.

Feeding: Like most of its warbler kin, the MacGillivray's Warbler gleans the vegetation for mostly insects and other invertebrates. It feeds mostly in dense, moist vegetation among the lower branches, close to the ground.

Habits: Usually stays well within the thick vegetation, it hops while foraging. Responds well to pishing.

Nest: The male constantly during the breeding season and he switches perches frequently. The breeding pair's territory is exclusive of other MacGillivray's Warblers. The cup of twigs, grass, and other fine material is placed in an upright fork of a branch. The nest is lined with grass and fur. The nest site is often in a humid area. The female incubates the 4 chestnut-, gray-, and purple-spotted white eggs for 11-13 days. The young fledge quickly after only 8-9 days of care by both parents.

Voice: The song of this warbler comes in two pitches (first being higher), *"trree-trree-tree-tree, swit-swit"*. The call is sharp *"tsik"*.

Primary Habitat Characteristics: This species always breeds in low-growth deciduous shrublands. This habitats are normally near water and conifers. This type of stand is often created by avalanches. The MacGillivray's Warbler occurs from 4,500 to 8,000 feet.

Other Habitats: They may be found very rarely in riparian habitats in canyons.

Conservation: MacGillivray's Warbler numbers are steady, with local populations ranging from common to uncommon.

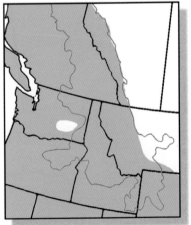

222

Lazuli Bunting

Passerina amoena

J F M A M J J A S O N D

B

Description: The male Lazuli Bunting (5^1/$_2$") is often seen singing from the top of a shrub. The male's upperparts and head are brilliant blue. The upper breast is washed with reddish-buff. The wings have two white wingbars. The female is drab brown above and white below. The female's upper breast is washed with buff. Her wingbars are fainter.

Feeding: When breeding in the Northern Rockies, the Lazuli Bunting is consuming mostly insects. The diet switches over to mainly seeds during the winter. Most foraging occurs on the ground and in the lower vegetation.

Habits: Sings out in the open from the top of a shrub or small tree. Known to hybridize with the closely related Indigo Bunting.

Male Lazuli Bunting

Nest: The male sings during the courtship, which establishes territorial limits. The female builds a nest of grass, leaves, and weeds lined with grass. This cup is attached to a vertical branch at 2-4 feet above the ground. The female incubates the 3-5 bluish eggs for 12 days. The young fledge at 10-15 days. The male may or may not be involved in feeding the nestlings.

Voice: The song of Lazuli Bunting is a rapid series of seemingly random notes. The male will "borrow" parts of a nearby male's songs and added them to his own. The call is a buzzy *"zzzzzzt"*.

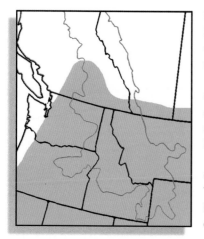

Primary Habitat Characteristics: The Lazuli Bunting favors shrublands that have grasslands or other open areas nearby. These shrublands are typically in the foothills.

Other Habitats: The more open riparian areas and regenerating post-fire deciduous shrub stands can also function as Lazuli Bunting habitat.

Conservation: Very widespread and common. The Lazuli Bunting can be heavily parasitized by the Brown-headed Cowbird, in fact to a level of concern to managers.

223

Green-tailed Towhee

© Peter LaTourrette

Description: The sound of a cat coming from a thick patch of juniper usually means that a Green-tailed Towhee (7¹/₂") is nearby, under the dense shrub canopy. As the name states, the tail is green, along with the wings. It is olive-brown above. The crown is rufous. The lores are white, and the throat is white bordered by a dark stripe and then white. The face is gray. The underparts are light gray.

Feeding: The Green-tailed Towhee's diet consists of slightly more insects than seeds. The insects eaten are those that dwell on the ground. The seeds consumed come from weeds and grasses. Most of the foraging occurs on the ground, with this bird scratching the litter.

Habits: Their distraction display is to run away from the nest with the tail raised high. They mimic certain phrases of other birds' songs.

Nest: The singing of the male defends the nesting territory. The nest of twigs, grass, and other plant material is lined with grass, rootlets, and hair. It is placed on the ground or in a shrub up to 3 feet off the ground. Common snowberry and wild rose are two often-used shrubs for nesting. The 3-4 brown- and gray-spotted white eggs are incubated for probably close to 2 weeks. Both parents feed the nestlings. The exact time of fledging is not accurately known.

Voice: The song of the Green-tailed Towhee is a 3-note phrase followed by a trill, *"weet-chrr-shee-churr"*. The call is a catlike *"meew"* that is somewhat similar to that of the Gray Catbird, though it is harsher.

Primary Habitat Characteristics: The Green-tailed Towhee favors open stands of juniper and limber pine that have low growth, such as common snowberry and wild rose, and scattered trees within them.

Other Habitats: They can be found in sage shrublands.

Conservation: Very stable at the present time.

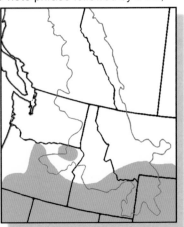

Spotted Towhee

Pipilo maculatus

J F M A M J J A S O N D

B

Description: Stalking within the thick growth, the Spotted Towhee (7¹/₂") is common, if often overlooked. The male is black above with white spotting on the back and wings. The head is black. The flanks are rufous. The belly is white. The females are drabber than the male. The tail is long. The eyes are usually red.

Male Spotted Towhee

© Tom Ulrich

Feeding: This species splits its diet between insects and vegetable matter, with a slight majority going to the animal portion. The insect portion of the diet comes from beetles, insect larvae, and other invertebrates found on the ground. As winter approaches, this species switches to a mostly vegetarian diet. It forages on the ground while scratching the litter for food.

Habits: Very secretive and will stay well within dense vegetation, only occasionally singing from an exposed perch.

Nest: The singing of the male defends the nesting territory. The female builds a cup of grass, weeds, rootlets, and other plant matter under a shrub or small tree. The nest is lined with grass and hair. She incubates the 3-4 brown-spotted off-white eggs for 12-13. The male rarely visits the nest during the incubation period. After hatching, both parents feed the nestlings for 10-12 days.

Voice: The song of this species is a trill. The distinct call is a *"chewink"*. The call is a weak, harsh *"meew"*.

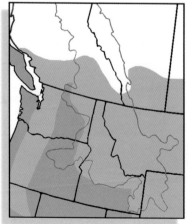

Primary Habitat Characteristics: Dense, shrubby deciduous growth is indicative of suitable Spotted Towhee habitat.

Other Habitats: The Spotted Towhee also inhabits sagebrush shrublands and some open riparian areas that contain willows.

Conservation: Once it was considered the same species as the Eastern Towhee under the of Rufous-sided Towhee. The two have subtle differences in plumages and voice. The Spotted Towhee is common in appropriate habitat.

225

Dry Conifer Forest

*Clad in thick bark like a warrior in mail, it extends its bright ranks
over all the high ranges of the wild side of the continent:
Flourishes in the drenching fog and rain of the northern coast
at the level of the sea, in the snow laden blasts of the mountains,
and the white glaring sunshine of the interior plateaus and plains,
on the borders of mirage haunted deserts, volcanoes, and lava beds,
waving its bright plumes in the hot winds undaunted,
blooming every year for centuries, and tossing big ripe cones
among the cinders and ashes of nature's hearths.*

–JOHN MUIR

Ever take a good long whiff of a ponderosa pine? I know it sounds completely off the wall, but do yourself a favor and do it. You will be treated to a wonderful vanilla aroma. This is just one of the many surprises in the dry conifer forest.

Dry conifer forests are found throughout the Northern Rockies. They are dominated by ponderosa pine and Douglas-fir, with ponderosa pine more prevalent in the driest sites. Where temperatures become too cold during the winter for the ponderosa pine, Douglas-fir is the dominant conifer species in these forests.

The ponderosa pine forests are found on dry sites, and these conifer stands are usually the first habitat zone above grasslands. Immediately above the pure stands of ponderosa pine, Douglas-fir becomes co-dominant with the pine. On the east side of the Continental Divide, pure stands Douglas-fir comprise the dry conifer forest type, although ponderosa pine is also present east of the Divide.

The ponderosa pine is adapted for warm, dry conditions that are found on west and south-facing slopes. They have very open canopies (10%-60% coverage), and, often, these open forests can be described as "ponderosa pine savannas". The understory is usually composed of grasses (pinegrass and Idaho fescue) and various forbs. Occasionally shrubs such as ninebark and common snowberry can be found in dense understory patches. Grand fir can also be a part of the understory.

The mixed Douglas-fir/ponderosa pine dry conifer forests are found in slightly cooler, wetter areas than the pure ponderosa pine stands. Ponderosa, Douglas-fir, and grand fir are the dominant species in these forests. They are found on west- and south-facing slopes. The canopy closure is slightly greater than that of the pure ponderosa pine forest. The vegetation of the understory is very similar to that of the ponderosa pine forest.

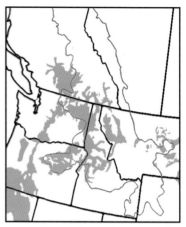

Range of ponderosa pine

The dry Douglas-fir forests found in the east side of the Continental Divide occupy the coldest sites where the dry conifer forest habitat type exists. These locations are too cold for ponderosa pine and too dry for lodgepole pine. They are not only found on the west- and south-facing, but on the lower-elevation north-facing slopes as well.

The understory of the dry Douglas-fir forests is typically dominated by pinegrass. Bunchgrasses such as bluebunch wheatgrass and Idaho fescue are also relatively common.

Forest fires play a significant role in the nature of the dry conifer forest. Historically, fires occur every 5-25 years. These fires are normally of a low intensity. This promotes the elimination of smaller trees; however, the large trees are clad in thick, fire-resistant bark. Lightning starts most of these fires, but, historically, Native Americans set some of these fires. They did this so the forest understory would remain open, and, therefore, improved for hunting. Since fire suppression started in earnest in the first half of the previous century, the understories of the dry conifer have become thick with saplings, and the stands became more multi-storied. The shrubs and grasses of the understory have been remarkably reduced.

After a forest fire, a specialized conifer takes roots. The lodgepole pine is a seral species that thrives after forest fires. It has two specialized cones; one that is sealed tight until the heat of fire opens it up and another that spreads seeds every 1-3 years. The seeds of the lodgepole sprout upon the ashy earth. The stands of lodgepole pine can grow thick, earning the nickname "doghair forest". As these forests age, the lodgepole pines are gradually replaced by the climax

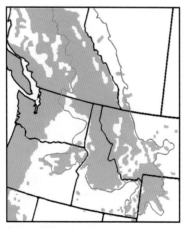

Range of Douglas-fir

species, such as ponderosa pine and Douglas-fir.

The birds that live in the dry conifer forest habitat are usually associated with older, more open stands.

A few birds can be thought of as obligates to ponderosa pine forests. These include the White-headed Woodpecker, Flammulated Owl, and Pygmy Nuthatch. All of these species have evolved along with ponderosa pine and the habitat it helps to create.

The Flammulated Owl is a ponderosa pine specialist that until recently was thought to be extremely rare in the Northern Rockies. This tiny owl is the only small owl in the region that has black eyes. It arrives in the spring when insects begin to fly about the boughs of the forest. Flammulated Owls swoop down upon these invertebrates from hunting perches. This creature's small size and treetop lifestyle keep it below the radar of managers. As more people have begun to look for owls and other birdlife, the Flammulated Owl has started to show up in some surprising places. They have been found in the ponderosa pine forests around Missoula and Helena, Montana. The bulk of their range extends westward from eastern Washington and Oregon and southward from Idaho-Nevada border. The Flammulated Owl's secretive nature makes it hard to find, but there is a reward in hearing the unique hoot and maybe, just maybe, catching a glimpse of those large black eyes full of character.

Within the dry conifer forest, birds tend to forage at specific locations within the vertical structure of the forest. Red Crossbills cruise from one treetop to the next, and the Blue Grouse forages on the forest floor. Mountain Chickadees hang on the lower branches, while the Red-breasted Nuthatch crawls up and down along the entire trunk.

Ah, vanilla. Who would have thought of standing next to a tree and experiencing the smell of your grandmother's baking? It is just one of the many pleasant surprises of the ponderosa pine forest.

Relative foraging heights of select dry conifer forest birds

Sharp-shinned Hawk
Accipiter striatus

J F M A M J J A S O N D

B/R

Description: Sweeping through the forest, the Sharp-shinned Hawk (10-14") has evolved for a life of hunting other birds in the trees. The wings are short and broad, which is advantageous to twisting, turning flight. The upperparts are grayish-brown. The underparts are rufous and finely barred. The eyes are a varying shade of red. In flight, the tail appears to be squared-off and the neck seems short. The legs are long. Like the other *Accipiters,* the female is considerably larger than the male.

Feeding: Often using an inconspicuous perch, the Sharp-shinned Hawk waits for an unsuspecting bird to pass by. It will burst into flight, overtake the prey, and capture it. It will also take birds on limbs or the ground using a stealthy flight.

The small Sharp-shinned Hawk

Habits: Migratory individuals fly southward along the ridges of the high mountains during the autumn. Prey are cleaned at a plucking post 150-300 feet from the nest. Sharp-shinned Hawks can be a terror to songbirds at a feeder.

Nest: The Sharp-shinned Hawk will do an undulating display flight during court-ship. The nest, a platform of sticks lined with bark chips, is built in a mature tree 20-60 feet off the ground. The female incubates the 4 brown-blotched bluish eggs for about 30 days. Both parents care for the nestlings for 3 weeks, when they leave the nest. The parental care continues for 8 more weeks.

Voice: The alarm call of this hawk is a sharp repeated series of *"kik-kik-kik"*.

Primary Habitat Characteristics: Prefers open forests. It was often found near openings, streams, or lakes.

Other Habitats: The Sharp-shinned Hawk also lives in open riparian habitats, cottonwood bottom forests, open conifer forests, and shelterbelts.

Conservation: Like many raptor species, the Sharp-shinned Hawk is recovering from declines caused by DDT and other pesticides. Now, it is a fairly common species.

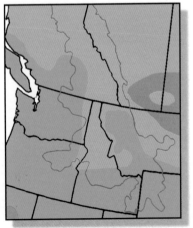

Cooper's Hawk

J F M A M J J A S O N D

Accipiter cooperii

B/R

Bird-hunting Cooper's Hawk

© Peter LaTourrette

Description: On average, the Cooper's Hawk (14-20") is larger than the Sharp-shinned Hawk, though there is some overlap. The back is dark brown. The dark crown contrasts with the lighter nape. The base of the bill (cere) is yellow. The rufous underparts are finely barred. The yellow legs are long. In flight, the tail appears to be long and rounded.

Feeding: Most of the prey (more than 50%) taken by the Cooper's Hawk is birds. The hawk will wait on a concealed perch or silently cruise through the forest. Upon flushing prey, it rapidly overtakes the bird and grasps it with the talons. Small mammals are the remaining diet.

Habits: The Cooper's Hawk aggressively defends the nesting territory by giving a preemptive alarm *"kek-kek-kek"*. Like the Sharpie, it uses a plucking post within 150-200 feet of the nest. It does not defecate around the nest.

Nest: During courtship, the male will slowly fly over the nest territory with exaggerated wingbeats. He will also bring the female fully or partially plucked birds. The nest is a platform of sticks lined with bark chips placed on the major limb near the trunk of a mature tree. The nest is usually close to nests from previous years. The female incubates the 4 blue-tinted white eggs for 30-35 days. Both parents feed the nestlings for 4 weeks in the nest. After leaving the nest, the parents continue to care for the fledglings for another 4 weeks.

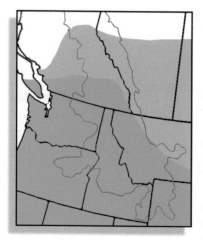

Voice: Both sexes give a *"kek-kek-kek"* call when threatened or when dueting.

Primary Habitat Characteristics: Open stands near water and surrounded by a matrix of habitat are keys to good Cooper's Hawk habitat.

Other Habitats: Shelterbelts and cottonwood bottom forests are also used by this species. They be can be found in any forested habitat.

Conservation: Overall populations are stable. However, as a top predator the Cooper's Hawk should be monitored carefully.

231

Merlin

J F M A M J J A S O N D

Falco columbarius

B/R

Description: Seen with greater regularity during the winter, the Merlin (10-14") is slightly larger than the American Kestrel. The overall coloration is dark, though the males are brighter. The wings and back are slate blue. The head is dark with lighter facial markings including a darkening of the cheeks. He has broad black bands across his tail. The underparts are rufous with fine streaking. The females are uniformly brown with streaking on the underparts. The wings are long and pointed.

The agile Merlin

Feeding: The Merlin is a masterful hunter of other birds. It captures and consumes birds as large as Rock Doves, although smaller species are more often taken. It will fly quick and low over the ground until it meets its intended prey. Sometimes, they are seen to stealthily follow their prey for some distance before overtaking the victims. This bird also eats insects and small mammals.

Habits: The number of Merlins overwintering in the Northern Rockies is related to the abundance of small flocking birds as Common Redpoll or Bohemian Waxwings.

Nest: During courtship, the female begs for food and the male performs aerial displays. They build no nest; instead the Merlin uses an abandoned nest of the *Corvids*. Cliff ledges and natural cavities are also known to be Merlin nest sites. The female incubates the 5-6 heavily purple-spotted buff eggs for 31-34 days. Both parents care for the nestlings, which fledge at 40-44 days.

Voice: A loud high-pitched *"klee-klee-klee"*.

Primary Habitat Characteristics: The Merlin prefers broken forest with nearby open areas for feeding.

Other Habitats: During the winter, they can be found in greater numbers in urban areas. During migration, it can be found in grasslands and marshes as well.

Conservation: Overall Merlin numbers have been stable, if not increasing slightly since the 1960's.

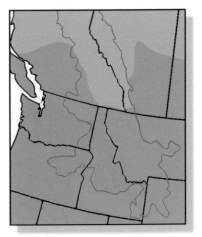

Blue Grouse

JFMAMJJASOND

Dendragapus obscurus

R

Description: The Blue Grouse (18") walks slowly as it feeds in the open forest. The male is bluish-gray overall with orange-yellow eye-combs. On the sides of the neck there are white feathers that encircle a bare patch of reddish skin. These air sacs are inflated during courtship. The fanned tail is all black (there is a gray tail band in birds south of Yellowstone). The female is a camouflaging mottled brown above. Her underparts are pale gray, and her tail is all black as well.

© Milo Burcham

Male Blue Grouse

Feeding: The diet of the Blue Grouse is slightly more varied than that of the closely related Spruce Grouse. During the summer, it eats leaves, buds, flowers, berries, and conifer needles. Conifer needles are almost the only item consumed during the winter. This species feeds on the ground.

Habits: Like the Spruce Grouse, this species is bafflingly tame.

Nest: The male uses a deep call to attract a female. He will also engages in short, noisy flights. He may display in front of her with his tail spread and his air sacs exposed. The female lines a simple scrape that has overhead cover with leaves, needles, twigs, and feathers. She incubates the 5-10 brown-marked buff-colored eggs for 25-28 days. The female is a fierce protector of her young, which leave the nest soon after hatching. They take their first flights at 8-9 days.

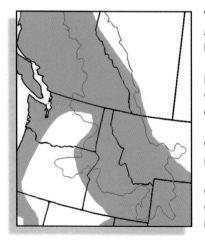

Voice: The male gives low-pitched hoots that are more felt than heard. The inflated air sacs help to amplify the sound.

Primary Habitat Characteristics: The Blue Grouse prefers areas where open forest meets open country such as sage shrubland.

Other Habitats: It is found breeding in aspen parklands and other open coniferous forests.

Conservation: Relatively common, the Blue Grouse is one of few species that benefits from regenerating clear and seed-tree cuts.

233

The small Flammulated Owl

© Judy Hoy

Description: The region's only small owl with black eyes, the Flammulated Owl (7") is incredibly shy and retiring in old-growth ponderosa pine stands. In the Northern Rockies, lives the gray color phase, which has a mottled gray back with unique rufous shoulder markings that extend across the side of the wing. The facial disc is a light gray and the head is adorned with small, yet conspicuous, ear tufts. The bill is normally bluish-gray. The underparts are quite mottled with dark-brown and black streaks on top of a gray underwash.

Feeding: This little owl consumes mostly insects (moths, beetles, and grasshoppers) and other arthropods (mainly spiders). Small vertebrates (mammals, reptiles, and amphibians) are a small portion of the diet. Most of the hunting takes place at night when this owl swoops down on prey, or it may grab insects out of the air.

Habits: The Flammulated Owl is the most migratory of the owls present in the Northern Rockies. It winters in Central Mexico and Central America.

Nest: The nest site is usually an old woodpecker hole or another type of natural cavity in a tree. The female incubates the 2-4 eggs for 21-24 days. During this time, the male feeds her. The newly hatched young are cared for by both parents for 21-25 days until they fledge. After fledging, they are still fed by their parents for a couple more weeks.

Voice: The song is a single or double hoot given every several seconds.

Primary Habitat Characteristics: The Flammulated Owl is generally associated with mature to old-growth dry conifer forests with brushy understory.

Other Habitats: Aspen stands are occasionally used.

Conservation: The removal of large snags for firewood is a concern for the relatively stable Flammulated Owl.

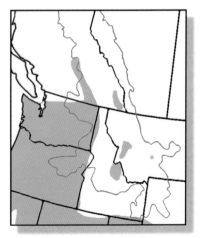

B/R

Description: This little owl has a large head in proportion to the body; the Northern Saw-whet Owl (8") is normally seen in its day roost on a conifer limb. The head has no ear tufts and it is finely streaked in the crown. The white above the eyes and bill forms a V. The bill is black. The overall body coloration is a cinnamon or red. The back is speckled with large white spots.

Feeding: A nocturnal hunter blessed with excellent eyesight and hearing, the Northern Saw-whet Owl eats almost exclusively small mammals, especially deer mice and meadow voles. They will swoop down from a perch and grasp the prey with the talons. They carry the prey to a perch where they can feed upon their prize in peace. They will occasionally eat small birds and insects.

The tame Northern Saw-whet Owl

Habits: The Northern Saw-whet Owl is very tame and will allow close approach. The perches used for day roosts are often quite low to the ground, as little as 5 feet. It is not uncommon to spy this little owl looking at you at eye level.

Nest: Northern Flicker holes are the favored nesting cavity for this small owl. The 5-6 eggs are incubated for 26-29 days. The young fledge in 27-34 days. Both parents care for young. The female usually abandons her brood at around 20 days, leaving the male alone in their care.

Voice: Completely silent outside of the breeding season, it gives a *"hoo"* during the four months of active courting and breeding.

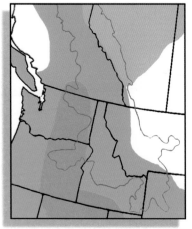

Primary Habitat Characteristics: Northern Saw-whet Owls tend to be found in mature forest that are not unbroken and have a dense deciduous understory.

Other Habitats: During the winter, they will use lower elevation habitats like cottonwoods.

Conservation: Loss of nesting sites is one of the conservation concerns for this small owl.

B/R

Flycatching Lewis's Woodpecker

© Peter LaTourrette

Description: Often seen bursting from its perch in pursuit of a flying insect, the Lewis's Woodpecker (10³/₄") is one of our drabber woodpeckers. The upperparts are very dark green as is the head. The light gray extends from the breast to the collar and joins on the back. The face is crimson and the rest of the underparts are a grayish-pink.

Feeding: They begin bark gleaning at the base of the tree and work their way up and out onto larger branches. The insects they glean are the wood-boring species, but those on the surface of the bark. They will flycatch flying insects as well. This behavior is nearly unique among the region's woodpeckers. They eat a small amount of nuts and fruit.

Habits: The Lewis's Woodpecker has many different flight patterns than the typical woodpecker flap and glide. It is gregarious.

Nest: During the courtship, the male gives many displays including a circling flight, drumming, and chattering calls. They excavate a nest in the large tree 20-65 feet above ground. At the bottom of the nest there is a layer of wood chips. Both sexes incubate the 5-9 white eggs (the male does the nighttime incubation alone) for 12-16 days. Both care for the young during the day, and the male continues his solo parenting during the night. The young fledge at 26-28 days and remain close to the nest for another 10 days.

Voice and Drumming: The call of the Lewis's Woodpecker is short series of harsh *"chr"*. The drumming pattern is short and weak volley, and followed by several taps.

Primary Habitat Characteristics: They prefer forests with very open canopies with a deciduous understory and snags.

Other Habitats: The Lewis's Woodpecker will occur in cottonwood bottom and post-fire forests. They breed in a variety of open forests.

Conservation: Sensitive to habitat fragmentation and loss, the Lewis's Woodpecker has declined by 50% over the past few decades.

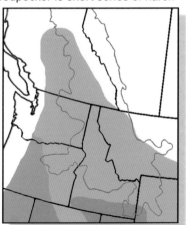

White-headed Woodpecker

Picoides albolarvatus

J F M A M J J A S O N D

R

Description: Associated more closely with ponderosa pine forest than any of the other woodpeckers, the White-headed Woodpecker (9¹/₂") possesses a wonderful contrasting plumage. The body is black. The wings have white wing patches. The head is black from the crown back and the rest is white. The male has a bright red patch on the back of the head. The female lacks this marking.

Feeding: The White-headed Woodpecker uses its bill to chip and flick away bark in search of a variety of insects, both adult and larvae. It will, like the Lewis's Woodpecker, occasionally take flying insects out of midair.

Habits: It flies with an undulating flap and glide flight pattern.

Ponderosa pine specialist White-headed Woodpecker

© Tom Ulrich

Nest: Both sexes engage in a variety of displays, which serve to cement the relationship both before and during the nesting period. The nest is excavated in a large snag (greater than 22" in diameter) 3-25 feet above the ground. They build a new cavity each year; however, these nest sites are often in the same tree. Both sexes incubate the 4-5 white eggs for 2 weeks. The young fledge in around 26 days. Both parents continue to care for them for some time after fledging.

Voice: The call is a sharp *"pee-dink"*. The drumming of this woodpecker is at a medium pace and long.

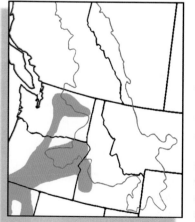

Primary Habitat Characteristics: The White-headed Woodpecker prefers open canopies of large mature to old-growth ponderosa pine forests and an abundance of snags for feeding and nesting. The canopy density ranges from 40 to 75%.

Other Habitats: It will occur in mixed-species conifer stands.

Conservation: Although numbers are stable, the White-headed Woodpecker's reliance on older forests makes it vulnerable to habitat alteration through commercial logging.

Eyebrowed Mountain Chickadee

Description: Whether mobbing a Northern Saw-whet Owl or spying on a hiker, the Mountain Chickadee (6") is a cheerful forest denizen. The upperparts are gray. The crown and nape are sooty black. There is a white superciliary stripe and a black eye-stripe. The white superciliary stripe can become worn and indistinct. The bib is a sooty black. An olive wash adorns the flanks. The underparts are a grayish-white.

Feeding: The Mountain Chickadee feeds upon many different insects. It will use its bill to pick eggs and pupae from the crevices of bark. They glean from the trunk, branches, and leaves. They are often seen hanging upside down as they forage with abandon. The diet is completed with some seeds and berries as well.

Habits: They form winter-feeding flocks that in many instances include nuthatches, Brown Creepers, Downy Woodpeckers, kinglets, and other chickadee species.

Nest: Although it can excavate its own nests, the Mountain Chickadee prefers to use a natural cavity or old woodpecker hole. The cavity is lined with moss, bark, fur, feathers, and bark stripes. The female incubates the 5-12 red-marked glossy white eggs for 14 days. The male feeds her during the incubation period. The male continues bring the female food as he begins to feed the nestlings as well. The nestlings fledge in 19-21 days.

Voice: The song of the Mountain Chickadee is a 3 or 4 note phrase, like *"fee bee bay"*. The call is a harsh *"chickadee-deedee"*.

Primary Habitat Characteristics: They reach their greatest abundance above 5,000 feet.

Other Habitats: The Mountain Chickadee also lives in a variety of other conifer and mixed forests, including spruce-fir and cedar-hemlock.

Conservation: Most hikers in the Northern Rockies are accustomed to the company of Mountain Chickadees.

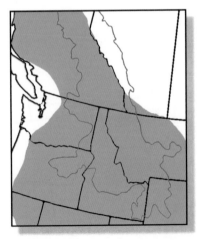

Red-breasted Nuthatch   *Sitta canadensis*

J F M A M J J A S O N D

R

Description: The laughter of the Red-breasted Nuthatch (4¹/₂") is one of the most often heard sounds in the forests of the Northern Rockies. The upperparts are gray. The heads have a black cap and a distinct white eyebrow. Below the eyebrow and extending back from the bill, there is a black eye-stripe. The chin and throat are grayish-white. The bill is black. The underparts are a rusty-red as are the undertail coverts. Females differ from the males with a more faded plumage.

The harlequin Red-breasted Nuthatch

Feeding: It is seen climbing up and down the trunks and crawling out on the branches of trees in search of insects and other invertebrates, especially spiders. It uses its bill to probe into cracks and crevices. During the winter, it will eat many pine nuts.

Habits: Irruptions can occur during winters when the cone crop fails.

Nest: Courtship takes place high in the trees and, therefore, it is difficult to observe. Both sexes excavate the nest cavity in the dead, rotten limb around 15 feet above the ground. The nest itself is made of grass, rootlets, and moss, and lined with shreds of bark, fur, and feathers. They smear some pitch at the entrance of the nest cavity. The sap smearing behavior may help to deter certain nest predators. The female incubates the 5-6 rufous-speckled white eggs for about 12 days. Both parents care for and feed the nestlings for 18-21 days. After they have fledged the young stay in the company of their parents.

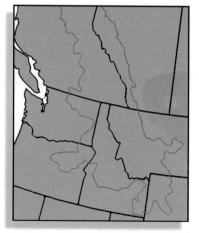

Voice: The nasal, high-pitched *"ank-ank-ank"* is the Red-breasted Nuthatch's call.

Primary Habitat Characteristics: The Red-breasted Nuthatch favors mature forests with a matrix of openings.

Other Habitats: They also inhabit other conifer forests, mixed deciduous-conifer stands, and aspen parklands.

Conservation: Very common and widespread.

Pygmy Nuthatch

Sitta pygmaea

J F M A M J J A S O N D

R

Description: Small bands of Pygmy Nuthatches (4¹/₄") move from treetop to treetop. They live up to their name by being the smallest nuthatch in the Northern Rockies. The upperparts are gray with a dull white spot barely visible on the nape. The cap is grayish-brown. The throat is white and the rest of the underparts are cream-colored. The dark bill is short and sharp, perfect for probing into the crevices of bark.

Foraging Pygmy Nuthatch

Feeding: The Pygmy Nuthatch specializes in foraging among the highest and most distal branches of tall conifers. During the summer, it feasts upon insects such as beetles and caterpillars. Pine nuts are a major component of the winter diet. The Pygmy Nutnatch will cache excess food in crevices of the bark.

Habits: Most frequently seen in small, roaming flocks. It tends to stay higher in the canopy than the nuthatch species.

Nest: Pygmy Nuthatch pairs are usually aided by 2-3 of the previous year's offspring in the defense of territory and rearing. The adults excavate a cavity in rotten wood usually 20 feet above ground. The nest in the cavity is made of a variety of plant fibers. The female incubates the 6-8 red-spotted white eggs for 15-16 days. The helpers in the feeding of the nestlings join the parents. They take their first flights in 20-22 days.

Voice: The song has a *"peedee"* note and given at in a rapid series. Rarely, the *"peedee"* is heard at irregular intervals.

Primary Habitat Characteristics: They tend use pure stands of ponderosa pine that are very open and savanna-like.

Other Habitats: Very rarely, the Pygmy Nuthatch can be found foraging in juniper-limber pine stands.

Conservation: The Pygmy Nuthatch is common in habitat, even if difficult to locate.

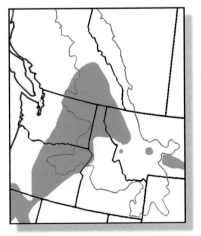

Description: The less common of the two bluebirds in the Northern Rockies, the Western Bluebird (7") is more colorful than the Mountain Bluebird. The upperparts are grayish-blue. The chin, throat, wings, and tail are a wonderful azure blue. Across the chest, a chestnut-red wash is present. This wash is also found on the flanks and shoulders. The females are less colorful than males with grayish-brown upperparts and head. The blue is more subdued. The underparts are grayish-white, save for the rusty washed breast.

Feeding: When present in the Northern Rockies, the Western Bluebird is primarily a consumer of insects. It will consume a small amount of berries and other fruits, especially during the winter. The favored feeding tactic of this species is to swoop down onto an insect from a low perch. It will also flycatch and hover-pounce for invertebrate prey.

Male Western Bluebird

© Milo Burcham

Habits: This cavity nester has benefited greatly from the profusion of the bluebird boxes across the West. It will give calls while in flight.

Nest: The female selects a nest site in a natural cavity, old woodpecker hole, or a nest box. She places grass and weeds in the cavity. She incubates the 4-6 pale blue eggs for 13-14 days. The nestlings fledge in 19-22 days; however, both parents continue to care for them for several more weeks.

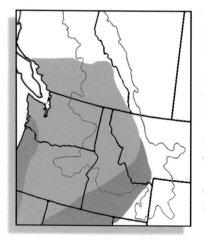

Voice: The song of the Western Bluebird is not often heard, except at dawn. It is a series of notes. A whistled *"pew pew pew"* is a call.

Primary Habitat Characteristics: They prefer very open stands, in particular ponderosa pine savanna.

Other Habitats: They will inhabit open habitats with scattered trees.

Conservation: Its affinity for nest boxes has benefited the Western Bluebird greatly.

Western Tanager

Piranga ludoviciana

J F M A M J J A S O N D

B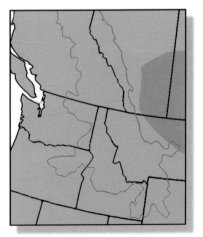

Male (l) and female (r) Western Tanager

Description: The color of flames, the Western Tanager (7") is a burst of fiery plumage in the dry conifer forest. The male has a black back, wings, and tail. His head is yellow with a bright red face. The underparts are yellow. The wings are adorned with 2 wingbars. The female comes in two color morphs. The greenish morph is mostly greenish yellow with a gray back. The grayish morph is gray overall and the head and undertail coverts are yellow.

© Ross Knapper (l)

Feeding: Moving from among the treetops, the Western Tanager gleans insects from the heights. The insects consumed include ants, bees, and beetles. It will occasionally flycatch for flying insects. The insects account for roughly 80% of the total diet. This species rounds out its diet with berries and other fruits.

Habits: It will join mixed-species foraging flocks on occasion.

Nest: The male uses his song to establish a nesting territory. The female makes a saucer-shaped nest of grass, twigs, and rootlets, and lines it with fur and rootlets. She places it in the fork of a branch 15-65 feet above ground. She incubates the 3-5 brown-blotched pale eggs for 13-15 days. Both sexes are involved in the feeding and rearing of the young. The nestlings take their first flights at about 2 weeks of age. They remain in the vicinity of their parents for some time after fledging.

Voice: The song of the Western Tanager is reminiscent of that of the American Robin, although the tanager's song has 4-5 notes. The song can occasionally be 6 notes long.

Primary Habitat Characteristics: The Western Tanager favors forests with open canopies at a variety of the elevations.

Other Habitats: They also inhabit open canopy conifer and mixed deciduous-conifer forests.

Conservation: The Western Tanager is stable and widespread across the Northern Rockies.

242

Chipping Sparrow

Spizella passerina

J F M A M J J A S O N D

B

Description: The Chipping Sparrow (5") is a creature of dry, open forests. The upperparts are mottled brown. The rump is pale gray. The crown is bright red. A black eye-stripe goes through the eye with a white eyebrow above. The underparts are unmarked gray. The tail is long and notched.

Sunlit Chipping Sparrow

Feeding: During its time in the Northern Rockies, the Chipping Sparrow eats primarily insects. These invertebrates are taken by gleaning them from the ground and, less often, in the lower reaches of the trees. At other times of the year when they are not present in the Northern Rockies, they eat many different types of seeds and grains.

Habits: The males sing almost constantly from an exposed perch in a tree. They are rather fast, direct flyers.

Nest: The male Chipping Sparrow is known to mate with multiple females. The female constructs a cup of grass, forbs, and rootlets lined with grass and hair. She places this nest low in a conifer, usually 3-10 feet above the ground. The female incubates the 3-4 colorfully marked blue-green eggs for 11-14 days. Once the eggs hatch, both parents feed the young, which leave the nest after 9-12 days. It is a common Brown-headed Cowbird host.

Voice: The song of the Chipping Sparrow is a dry, rapid trill that lasts several seconds. This vocalization is similar to the Dark-eyed Junco's, though the junco's trill is more musical in tone.

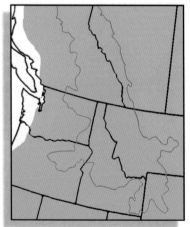

Primary Habitat Characteristics: The Chipping Sparrow favors forests that are very open and have adjacent open areas. The understory is usually only herbaceous growth.

Other Habitats: This species can be found living on the edges of coniferous forests and riparian corridors that have a conifer element.

Conservation: Common and widespread. It has adapted well to humans and their alterations of the landscape.

Cassin's Finch

Carpodacus cassinii

J F M A M J J A S O N D

R

Red-crowned Cassin's Finch

© Tom Ulrich

Description: The Cassin's Finch (6") is most often seen during the winter when it descends to lower elevations of the Northern Rockies. The male has brown upperparts and a bright red crown. The crest is often raised. The belly is white without streaking. The female is streaked brown above and streaked white on the underparts. Her head is faintly patterned with a brown ear patch and a light eyebrow. The bill is long and conical. The tail is notched.

Feeding: This species forages amongst the trees, where it eats many different kinds of seeds. It also savors the buds and berries. During the short summer, they consume some amount of insects.

Habits: The Cassin's Finch will readily come to seed feeders, especially during the winter. They are very nomadic and tend to nest in different locations each year.

Nest: The male displays by raising his crest and fluttering with rapid wingbeats. They nest in loose colonies. The female builds a nest of twigs, weeds, and plant fibers lined with grass and hair. She incubates 4-5 black- and purple-spotted blue-green eggs for 12-14 days. The nestlings are cared for by both parents for 14 days.

Voice: The song is extensive warble that often contains learned portions of other birds' songs. The flight call is *"teeyup"*.

Primary Habitat Characteristics: The Cassin's Finch prefers ponderosa pine forests that open to semi-open canopies. Dry Douglas-fir forests are used for breeding to a lesser extent. These Douglas-fir forests also have open canopies.

Other Habitats: They will live in spruce-fir and other conifer forests. The Cassin's Finch can also be found in extensive numbers in post-fire forests. During the winter, it moves into shrublands and coniferous riparian areas.

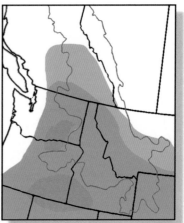

Conservation: Populations are very stable.

Red Crossbill

Loxia curvirostra

R

Description: The members of a noisy flock of Red Crossbills (6") will all descend on the single tree and begin foraging. The overall coloration of the male varies from red to orange-yellow. His wings are black as is his tail. The female is generally grayish with an olive wash. The most unique is the crossed bill, which is an adaptation for feeding on conifer cones.

Foraging Red Crossbill

Feeding: The bill of the Red Crossbill is well suited to prying apart the scales of cones and removing the seeds within. Crossbills forage in flocks that key in on conifers. They will occasionally glean other seeds, berries, and insects. They will come to seed feeders, particularly during irruptive winters.

Habits: In common with many of its finch kin, the Red Crossbill is very nomadic. It will irrupt southward during winters when the cone crop fails.

Nest: The Red Crossbill has the curious habit of nesting at anytime of year depending on the cone crop. The female constructs a nest of twigs, grass, and plant fibers lined with grass, moss, lichens, and hair. The nest is placed on a branch of a conifer 10-40 feet above the ground. She incubates the 3-4 purple- and black-spotted bluish white eggs for 12-15 days. The nestlings leave the nest after 18-20 days.

Voice: The Red Crossbill's song is a rapid warble. The flight call is a clear *"jip jip jip"*.

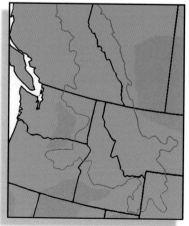

Primary Habitat Characteristics: The Red Crossbill prefers coniferous forests that do not have a tall deciduous component and lower-density canopy covers.

Other Habitats: They also inhabit other conifer forests such spruce-fir and Douglas-fir. Their nomadic ways find them in a variety of habitats.

Conservation: There are several types of Red Crossbill, which have different bill sizes and shapes, and calls. These types may actually be unique species that each require management.

Pine Siskin

Carduelis pinus

J F M A M J J A S O N D

R

Description: Often seen at seed feeders in the towns of the Northern Rockies during the winter, the small Pine Siskin (5") is subdued in patterning. The upperparts are streaked brown. The underparts are light brown and streaked with dark brown. The wings and tail have distinctive yellow markings. The bill is dark and conical, though it is thinner than the bills of other finches.

Acrobatic Pine Siskin

Feeding: The Pine Siskin acrobatically forages in trees and shrubs, often hanging upside down much like a chickadee. It often forages in flocks, and eats mostly seeds and other vegetative parts. It will also consume a small amount of the insects to round out their diet.

Habits: It will irrupt during harsh winters. It will join mixed-species feeding flocks including American Goldfinches and chickadees. These flocks rove over the landscape in search of feeding opportunities.

Nest: The male will fly in tight circles above the female during courtship. He will occasionally feed her during this time as well. The female builds a cup of twigs, grass, and plant fibers lined with moss, hair, and feathers. The nest is placed on a branch 10-35 feet above the ground. The female incubates the 3-4 brown- and purple-spotted green-blue eggs for 14-15 days. Both parents care for the young in the nest. They fledge after 14-15 days.

Voice: The buzzy *"zreeeee"* call of the Pine Siskin is quite distinctive. The song is a rich mixture of warbles and trills.

Primary Habitat Characteristics: Pine Siskins tend to favor the edges of the forest, or when found in the interior, they favor lower density canopy covers.

Other Habitats: They also live in other conifer and mixed deciduous-conifer forests.

Conservation: Populations are very widespread and secure.

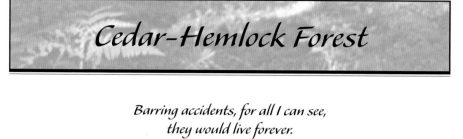

Cedar-Hemlock Forest

Barring accidents, for all I can see,
they would live forever.
– JOHN MUIR

Under the dark shadows of the almost completely closed canopy of towering western red cedars, there is almost no understory growth. Walking through this forest is relatively easy, save for the occasional tangle of decaying fallen timber or crossing a channel of the braided stream. Turning my eyes skyward, I peer out of darkness at the sunlit canopy. Dropping my gaze, I see the forest floor dotted with shade-loving fungi, mushrooms and creeping slime molds. Suddenly from high above, the haunting whistle of a Varied Thrush slices the humid air. This strange metallic note sounds as if it is composed of simultaneously off-tone delivered notes. The Western red cedar forest feels like the primordial forest of ages gone by.

Western red cedar grows from the Pacific coast (northern California to Southwestern Alaska) inland to humid regions to the west of the Continental Divide. It thrives in the cool, moist areas of the Northern Rockies, where it covers roughly 5 million acres. It grows in pure stands and, more commonly, in mixed-species stands with western hemlock, Engelmann spruce, Douglas-fir, and western larch. This tree can reach heights of more than 120 feet and the massive trunks can be upwards of 10 feet in diameter. The leaves grow in scale fashion with one overlapping the next.

Western hemlock is present in the moister stands, and it is occasionally co-dominant with western red cedar. They grow to great heights of more than 150 feet with trunks more slender than those of western red cedar. The hemlock tree can look rather feather-like when seen from a distance. The leaves of the western hemlock are yellowish-green, blunt needles.

Both of these species are very shade tolerant. They thrive in the moist, cool, and wet north-facing draws of the west side of the Northern Rockies where annual precipitation exceeds 30 inches of moisture. Cedar-hemlock forests are generally found from 1,500 to 6,000 feet in elevation. Shade- and moisture-tolerant shrubs like yew and twinberry grow in the understory.

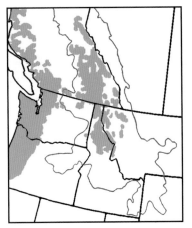

Range of western red cedar

Western red cedar is a tree with many uses to both animals and people. The sloughing bark of a dying giant cedar can be home to roosting silver-haired bats and the nest sites for the diminutive Brown Creeper. The fibrous bark was twisted and woven into clothing and baskets by Native Americans. The wood of the western red cedar is prized for home building, and giants have been heavily logged. Many of these harvested stands have not been replanted, therefore, the western red cedar has disappeared from many places. The dense branches of the cedar provide good cover for nesting birds, such as the Golden-crowned Kinglet.

The climate of the western red cedar-western hemlock forest has long, warm summers interrupted by cool, wet winters. The snowpack from the previous winter tends to melt quite slowly in the inky shadows of the closed canopies. These climatic conditions exist west of the Continental Divide in western Montana, northern Idaho, northeastern Washington, and southeastern British Columbia on western slopes. This type of forest is the most productive forest in the Northern Rockies.

Under the giants, a most unique shrub grows. The devil's club is a shrub that thrives in cool, wet areas that have nitrogen-rich soils. It has very large maple-like leaves and long stems adorned with many sharp thorns. These thorns easily puncture the skin and sink deep, often causing an infection if left untreated.

Pacific yew also grows in the cedar-hemlock forest. This amazing tree is the source for a powerful anticancer drug called Taxol. Many yews were once harvested for this chemical; however, it has been synthesized, much to the yew's benefit. This is just another example of native vegetation coming to the aid of humans.

Across the Northern Rockies, an invader is becoming increasingly more common. It has come from the East, and it is descending down the spine of the Rockies. The Barred Owl was once considered rather rare in the Northern Rockies; however, in recent decades this large owl has invaded the Northern Rockies. This owl is primarily a hunter of small rodents, vole species

Devils Club

in particular, which are captured by swooping down upon them from an elevated hunting perch. It will occasionally take another bird or small vertebrate. The Barred Owl can be thought of as an indictor species for old-growth cedar-hemlock forest. An indicator species is one that can be used to estimate the health of an ecosystem or habitat by its presence or absence. The Barred Owl requires an old-growth component for nesting and without this element of habitat, the Barred Owl will probably not establish a breeding territory.

The recent range expansions of the Barred Owl in the West have caused problems for one of its closest relatives, the Spotted Owl. Where the ranges of these two cousins overlap, they can possibly hybridize. The beleaguered populations of Spotted Owl cannot absorb the introduction of these new genes and maintain as a species. It is hoped that the breeding behavior of the two can keep their genes separate and conservation efforts can fortify the numbers of the Spotted Owls.

This gray owl is a perfect emblem for the cedar-hemlock forest, a beautifully effective predator that weaves its way through dense old-growth forest as it hunts. The way it uses the broken tops of dead giants to bring new life into the forest indicates the value of renewal in even the most ancient of forests.

Bohemian Waxwing

Barred Owl

J F M A M J J A S O N D

Strix varia

R

Description: Invading from the East, the Barred Owl (17-24") is increasing in the Northern Rockies. The chest, head, and upperparts are grayish with strong dark brown barring. The head lacks ear tufts and the eyes are dark. The dark brown back is spotted with white. The facial disc is gray with 4-5 brownish concentric circles.

Feeding: Swooping down from its hunting perch, the Barred Owl has enough power to overtake most of the available prey. This species has a remarkably wide range of animals it will hunt and eat. The bulk of the total prey consumed comes from small mammals, mainly rodents. The rest of the diet is birds, reptiles, amphibians, insectivores, insects, mollusks and, even, fish.

The invading Barred Owl

© Milo Burcham

Habits: It hybridizes with and out-competes the closely related Spotted Owl in the Cascades and Coastal Ranges. This hybridization situation is of concern to Spotted Owl managers.

Nest: During courtship, the Barred Owl pair will do a duet call. The male may also feed the female during the courtship. Mating for life, the Barred Owl selects the hollow of a large snag for a nest site. This nest site is normally over 25 feet above the ground. They may use large raptor nests, as well. The female incubates the clutch of 2-3 white eggs for 28-33 days. Both parents care for the young for as long as 4 months, well after they have fledged.

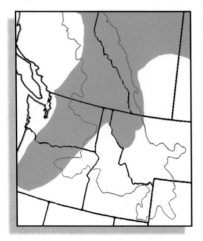

Voice: The Barred Owl gives *"you cooks for you, who cooks for you all"* as a territorial call.

Primary Habitat Characteristics: The Barred Owl prefers thick, mature woods with nearby openings for hunting. Large snags (greater than 20" in diameter) are required for nesting.

Other Habitats: It can be found in other dense, moist forests. These forests can be mixed deciduous-conifer and deciduous.

Conservation: Its range in the Northern Rockies has been expanding.

Aerial foraging Vaux's Swift

© Mike Danzenbaker

Description: Seen cruising swiftly over the treetops, Vaux's Swift (4³/₄") is the smallest swift in North America. It is generally dark overall with swept, pointed wings. The throat and chest are paler gray than the rest of the body. The tail is short and squared-off at the end.

Feeding: An aerial forager, the Vaux's Swift captures and consumes its insect prey on the wing. The flying insects are pursued in flight or, rarely, hover-gleaned from the surface of vegetation. Feeding takes place over areas of insect concentration, such as lakes.

Habits: The Vaux's Swift will tend to be loosely colonial. It flies with stiff, rapid wingbeats.

Nest: Nesting in small, loose colonies, the Vaux's Swift does many ritual pursuits of mates during courtship. The nest site is the hollow located at the top of a broken-top snag or an abandoned woodpecker hole. The nest inside the cavity is made of twigs gathered by both sexes and cemented in place using saliva. Both adults incubate the 6 white eggs for 18-19 days. The nestlings fledge after 28-36 days of care by both parents and, possibly, one or more helper birds.

Voice: In flight, one will hear the rapid *"chitter-chitter-chitter"* and the *"chip"* calls.

Primary Habitat Characteristics: They use the old-growth cedar-hemlock forest for nesting and they require broken-top snags for nest sites. The heartwood of these nest sites has rotted out, leaving the hollow that is used for nesting.

Other Habitats: The Vaux's Swift will feed low over water and above the treetops. Other conifer and mixed conifer-deciduous forests are known nesting habitats.

Conservation: Populations are declining. This decline may be tied to the reduction of the old-growth forests or the removal of broken-top snags for firewood and safety reasons.

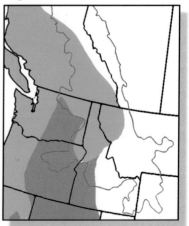

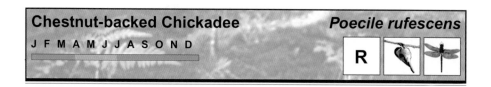
Description: Foraging among the shadows of towering cedars and hemlocks, the Chestnut-backed Chickadee (4³/₄") is the most colorful chickadee in the Northern Rockies. Upperparts are a deep chestnut and the cap is a dirty brown. The cheeks are white and the bib is black.

Feeding: It will glean-forage from the ground to the treetops. They will cling upside down while feeding at times. It will often deftly pick a meal from the crevices in the bark. Its favored food is insects. It consumes a small amount of berries and pinecone seeds.

Habits: During the winter, these chickadees form feeding flocks. Brown Creepers, kinglets, and nuthatches will join these flocks.

© Peter LaTourrette

The colorful Chestnut-backed Chickadee

Nest: The Chestnut-backed Chickadee excavates its own nesting cavity in rotten and dead wood 2-20 feet over the forest floor. They use existing cavities and nest boxes as well. These nest sites may be used for multiple years. Within the cavity, they build a cup of moss, ferns, grass, hair, and feathers. It is lined with fur and feathers, and placed on top of a mat of moss. The female alone incubates the 6-7 dull white eggs for 11-12 days. The young fledge after 3 weeks of parental care.

Voice: The voice of the Chestnut-backed Chickadee is higher pitched than those of the other chickadees. The hoarse, fast *"chick-zee-zee"* and *"cheq cheq"* are the two most often heard calls.

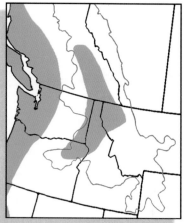

Primary Habitat Characteristics: The Chestnut-backed Chickadee prefers the edges of the cedar/hemlock forest at streams or adjacent deciduous woods. They also require snags with rotten wood for nesting.

Other Habitats: They can occur in other moist coniferous forests and riparian habitats (especially if willows are dominant).

Conservation: Thought to be expanding its range eastward and to the south, it remains uncommon in the Northern Rockies.

Brown Creeper

Certhia americana

J F M A M J J A S O N D

R

Description: Spiraling up the trunk of a tree, the Brown Creeper (5¼") uses its long, decurved bill to probe for insects and their larvae in the crevices of the bark. The upperparts are streaked mottled brown for camouflage against the bark background. The underparts are white. The tail feathers are long and pointed.

Feeding: The Brown Creeper uses its bill to pick out many different species of insects and their eggs from the cracks in the bark. It forages by crawling up the trunk of a tree and out onto its limbs. Upon reaching the top of the tree, it flies down to the base of another nearby tree and begins its ascent anew. It will also consume a small amount of seeds.

The tree-climbing Brown Creeper

Habits: Unlike nuthatches, the Brown Creeper never crawls down headfirst. When it feels threatened, it flattens against the tree and remains motionless. It uses its tail to brace itself as it climbs upward.

Nest: The male chases the female during courtship. His song is used to defend the nesting territory. The female constructs a small cup of twigs, leaves, moss, and bark fibers lined with soft fibers. She places this nest behind a loose slab of bark. She incubates the 5-6 red-spotted white eggs for 14-17 days. Both adults feed the young while they are in the nest. The nestlings fledge at 13-16 days.

Voice: The song of the Brown Creeper is high-pitched series of whistles like *"see wee see u wee"*. The thin call is a *"tseee"*.

Primary Habitat Characteristics: The Brown Creeper prefers mature to old-growth forests with many large-diameter trees. Many of these trees are dead with sluffing bark, which provides nest sites.

Other Habitats: They also inhabit other mature coniferous and mixed conifer-deciduous forests.

Conservation: The reduction of mature and old-growth forests has almost undoubtedly led to reductions in Brown Creeper numbers.

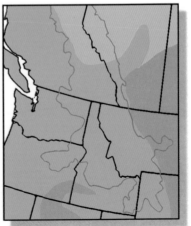

Winter Wren
Troglodytes troglodytes

J F M A M J J A S O N D

R

Description: Stalking among the dense tangle under the closed canopy, the Winter Wren (4") is the only wren that typically remains in the Northern Rockies over the winter. The body shape of this little wren is stubby. The upperparts are dark brown with some mottling. Tail is very short. The underparts are buffy brown, and the belly is barred.

Winter Wren in the understory

Feeding: The Winter Wren forages for insects in the dense undergrowth. It feeds on the ground as well as in lower vegetation, mostly on insects and other invertebrates.

Habits: In its dense habitat, the Winter Wren tends to be rather secretive and elusive, only its song giving away its locations. When perched on a low branch or shrub, it bobs the head up and down.

Nest: The male displays in front of the female by swaying side to side while singing. The nest site is a small cavity usually less than 6 feet high. Both sexes build a nest of grass, forbs, and moss lined with hair and feathers in the cavity. The female incubates the 5-6 sometimes reddish-spotted white eggs for 14-16 days. Both parents feed the nestlings. They fledge at 19 days of age. The young disperse within their parents' territory.

Voice: The wonderful song is series of trills and musical notes. The call is a sharp *"chip-chip"*.

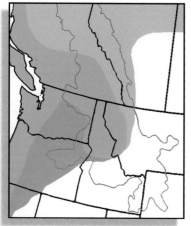

Primary Habitat Characteristics: The Winter Wren inhabits moist forest with a dense understory near water. These areas are typically cool and dark.

Other Habitats: The Winter Wren resides in spruce-fir forests near or adjacent to streams. It also lives in dense riparian thickets and cottonwood stands.

Conservation: The Winter Wren has stable populations across the Northern Rockies, and its habitat seems to be secure.

Varied Thrush

Ixoreus naevius

J F M A M J J A S O N D

B/R

Male Varied Thrush

Description: The haunting, metallic whistled song of the Varied Thrush (9$\frac{1}{2}$") is associated with cedar/hemlock forests in the Northern Rockies. The male has slate-gray upperparts. He has an orange eyebrow and wingbars. Black extends from the bill through the eyes. His underparts are orange with a prominent black chest band. The female is drabber with upperparts an olive color.

Feeding: Underneath the dense canopy, the Varied Thrush forages mostly on the ground. It will scatter litter in search of food. In the summer, its diet is mostly insects and other invertebrates. As the fall approaches, it switches to more fruits and nuts. It will occasionally glean in the low branches.

Habits: More often heard than seen, the Varied Thrush is a very shy, retiring species. When flushed it flies onto a low branch.

Nest: The male's singing probably serves as a territorial defense and establishment behavior. The female builds the nest near the trunk of a small conifer. The nest is a bulky cup of twigs, leaves, weeds, and other plant material packed into mud. It is lined with grass. She incubates the 2-5 blue eggs for 2 weeks. Both parents feed and care for the young until they fledge. Time of fledging is not accurately known at the present.

Voice: The song of Varied Thrush is probably the most unique of the songbirds in the Northern Rockies. It is a series of off-pitch, metallic whistles with each phrase given at a different pitch. One of its calls is a *"chyup"*.

Primary Habitat Characteristics: The Varied Thrush truly favors wet, dark mature forest, often near water and with a dense understory.

Other Habitats: It can be found in moist Douglas-fir and spruce-fir forests.

Conservation: Populations are apparently stable.

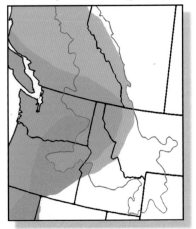

Description: Usually appearing in great numbers during the winter, the Bohemian Waxwing (8¼") is a resident in the northwest portion of the Northern Rockies. The upperparts are grayish-brown. The darker wings have yellow and white spots. The head is crested and has a black eye stripe. The undertail coverts are rich red. The tail has a bright yellow terminal band.

Feeding: Feeding in flocks, the Bohemian Waxwing consumes mostly insects during the summer. These invertebrates are captured in flycatcher fashion. As winter arrives, they switch to a diet rich in berries, especially those of the mountain-ash. These fruits are plucked from the tree while the bird is perched or hovering.

Feeding Bohemian Waxwing

Habits: This species is almost always found in large flocks. They are irruptive during harsher winters.

Nest: Bohemian Waxwings perch next to one another and pass a piece of food between them. Both sexes construct a nest of twig, grass, and moss lined with grass and feathers. The nest is located on a branch 6-20 feet above the ground. The female incubates the 4-6 black-spotted bluish eggs for 14-15 days. Both parents feed the young insects. The nestlings leave the nest after 14-18 days.

Voice: The call of the Bohemian Waxwing is a high-pitched buzzy trill.

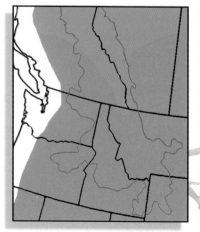

Primary Habitat Characteristics: Bohemian Waxwings tend toward the edges of dense forest or where the trees are very tall with a deciduous understory.

Other Habitats: During the winter, they descend upon towns and riparian corridors where there are abundant food sources, namely the berries of mountain ash and juniper.

Conservation: Use of the urban habitat during the winter has probably lead to increased winter survival, and, therefore, slightly higher populations overall.

Male Townsend's Warbler

Description: From the tops of the trees, the Townsend's Warbler (5") is a splash of brightness in the otherwise dark surroundings. The most striking feature of the male is its head patterning of yellow and black. The upperparts are greenish-yellow with heavy black streaking. The breast is bright yellow. The underparts and sides are bright yellow.

Feeding: The Townsend's Warbler gleans insects from the crowns of the conifers. It will hover-glean and even flycatch occasionally. During migration, it is known to visit suet feeders.

Habits: This warbler feeds high up in the treetops. It will join mixed species feeding flocks, especially in the winter. When gathering nest material it will hover. They are slow migrants, taking their time to the Pacific coast or, in greater number, Mexico.

Nest: Throughout courtship and nesting, a resident male is highly aggressive toward other intruding males. The nest is placed on a major limb high up in a conifer tree. These nests have been recorded as high as 100 feet above the ground. They are shallow cups of arboreal lichens, feathers, bark fibers, and twigs woven together and lined with moss, soft plant fibers, and fur. The female incubates the 3-5 brown-spotted white eggs for 11-14 days. The young are fed by both parents for 8-11 days. After fledging, the young gradually move away from the nest.

Voice: The Townsend's Warbler's song is a series of high-pitched, buzzy notes, *"zee zee zee weezit"*. The flight call is a sharp *"see"*. Another call is a clear, high-pitched *"tsik"*.

Primary Habitat Characteristics: The Townsend's Warbler prefers shady, wet mature forests with towering trees.

Other Habitats: Douglas-fir and spruce-fir forests are also the home of the Townsend's Warbler.

Conservation: There is scant information on the conservation status and concerns for this species.

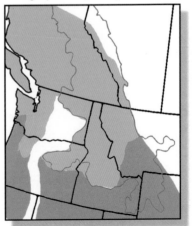

Post-fire Forest

*We hold a species monopoly over fire. With fire we claim
a unique ecological niche: this is what we do that no other
creature does. Our possession is so fundamental to our understanding
of the world that we cannot imagine a world without fire in our hands.
Or to restate that point in more evolutionary terms,
we cannot imagine another creature possessing it.*

—STEPHEN J. PYNE

Forest fires are a very natural and necessary component of the ecosystem. Forest fires alter and create habitats; they not destroy them. All forests in the Northern Rockies have evolved along with fire, and each has it own reactions and adaptations to fire. The effect of a fire on a forest ecosystem depends on its intensity. Hotter, longer lasting fires have more extensive effects than cooler, short-lived fires.

After a light to moderate intensity fire, seeds and roots will re-vegetate rapidly, sending up new shoots. Plant nutrients in the form of ash are put back into the soil, resulting in rich new plant growth. Shrubs and trees with deep roots or thick bark are less likely to be damaged by moderately intense fires and will renew quickly.

If a low to moderate intensity fire does not burn too long in an area, it can return nutrients to the soil. Frequent low intensity fires help prevent a build-up of fuel. Hotter fires generate high soil temperatures that destroy most plant life as well as many soil microorganisms and invertebrates. Accumulated fuels result in intense fires. It takes many years for soil and vegetation to recover from an intense fire.

In severely burned sites, plants and roots are destroyed. New growth depends on unburned seeds buried in the organic soil layer or seeds brought in by animals or the wind. A high mineral concentration in severely burned soils provides good seed beds for germination.

Fires may not burn an entire area, particularly under wet conditions. They may burn in a patchwork pattern, leaving islands of unburned vegetation. This creates a mosaic of plants in different stages of succession, which supports a wide diversity of wildlife species.

Forest ecosystems are always changing. Plants grow using soil nutrients and eventually die, returning nutrients to the soil. Animals feed on plants and leave waste. Bacteria, fungi, and insects thrive on decaying plants, animals, and animal waste, breaking down these materials and replacing soil nutrients. These interactions of plants, animals, bacteria, fungi, and insects constantly occur in ecosystems.

Succession is a change in plants and animals that occurs periodically in all communities. An open space or meadow will eventually be overgrown by a forest that in turn will grow to a climax forest. The length of time and kinds of plants involved in each successional change depends on many factors. The most common natural disturbance that affects succession is fire started by lightning. This has occurred throughout time and is a natural part of forest ecosystems. Regardless of the existing successional stage, forests provide essential elements of habitat: food, water, shelter, and space. In any ecosystem, the diversity of plants and their spatial structures influence the diversity of animals utilizing available habitat. The plants and animals in an ecosystem change with each successional stage.

While some creatures are unfortunately killed by wildfires (particularly bird nestlings and other young), most native animals have evolved to deal with fires. Long-toed salamanders and rubber boas will retreat into the moist interiors of rotting logs or burrows. Those with wings or four legs will simply move away from the fire.

When a fire burns through an area, it leaves standing snags. These snags attract many insects, including metallic wood-boring beetles, which use the snags for food and to lay their eggs in. These insects, in turn, bring in a particular group of birds, the woodpeckers. The two woodpeckers that truly need fire to create habitat are the Northern three-toed and Black-backed Woodpeckers. The Black-backed woodpecker even evolved the black back that helps the bird camouflage itself against the blackened spire of the snags. In addition to food, these snags provide nesting sites for the woodpeckers. Woodpeckers are known as primary cavity nesters, this means they actually excavate the holes in the snags. After the woodpeckers have created nesting cavities for a couple of years, a second group of birds, the secondary cavity nesters, move into these burned areas. The secondary cavity nesters include such birds as Mountain Chickadee, nuthatches, and Mountain Bluebirds, and they are joined by northern flying squirrels.

The flush of herb and grass growth after a fire attracts many of the grazing species. Elk and mule deer thrive on the early successional grasses and shrubs, particularly ceanothus, whose fire-resistant seeds can lie dormant for up to 200 years before a fire stimulates them to germinate. These grazers are, in turn, prey species for large carnivores, such as wolves.

Wildfires always have been a component of forest and they will continue to be so long into the future. The fires rejuvenate habitat and provide opportunities to the species that have evolved to benefit from conflagration.

Past Significant Wildfires in the Northern Rockies

	Year	State(s)	Acres	Outcome
1910 Fire	1910	Idaho and Montana	3,000,000	85 Deaths, many acres burned
Tillamook	1933	Oregon	311,000	1 Death
Mann Gulch	1949	Montana	4,339	13 Smokejumpers Killed
Yellowstone	1988	Montana and Idaho	1,585,000	Many acres burned
Canyon Creek	1988	Montana	250,000	Many acres burned
Foothills Fire	1992	Idaho	257,000	1 Death
Idaho City Complex	1994	Idaho	154,000	1 Death
Cox Wells	1996	Idaho	219,000	Many acres burned

Three-toed Woodpecker

Picoides tridactylus

J F M A M J J A S O N D

R

Description: One of two woodpeckers that have only three toes (the other is the Black-backed Woodpecker), the Three-toed Woodpecker (8³/₄") is rather unassuming. The back is barred black and white. The wings are mostly black with some white. The head is striped with black and white. The males have bright yellow crown patches. The flanks are heavily barred with black and white. The underparts are white.

Feeding: These woodpeckers specialize in foraging for wood-boring insect species. They uncover these food items by scaling the bark away from the trunk or limb. Sometimes entire dead trees are completely denuded of their bark. This species will also visit sapsucker wells.

Feeding Three-toed Woodpecker

Habits: This species can be quite tame, particularly around the nest site.

Nest: The nest site is a cavity on a conifer snag 5-15 feet high. Both sexes incubate the 3-4 white eggs for 12-14 days. They continue their care of the nestlings for 22-26 days until they fledge. The juveniles remain in the company of their parents for another 4 weeks.

Voice and Drumming: The Three-toe's call is an accented *"teek"*. The drumming pattern is a short, rapid burst of taps.

Primary Habitat Characteristics: The favorite foraging habitat of the Three-toed Woodpecker is post-fire forest, several years after the fire. During this interval, many species of wood-boring insects infest the blackened forest. These stands were usually mature to old-growth forests before the inferno.

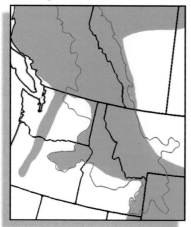

Other Habitats: They also live in other coniferous forest, especially spruce-fir. Large areas of insect-killed or otherwise disturbed stands also provide foraging habitat.

Conservation: The Three-toed Woodpecker numbers are apparently stable, which may be due habitat adaptability.

Black-backed Woodpecker
Picoides arcticus

J F M A M J J A S O N D

R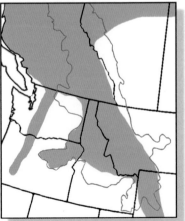

© Milo Burcham

Black-backed Woodpecker

Description: Almost never seen away from the blackened spires of a post-fire forest, the Black-backed Woodpecker (9¹/₂") has evolved to exploit this unique habitat. The upperparts are completely flat black. The head is patterned with black and white. The male has a yellow crown patch. The sides are barred with black and white. Like the Three-toed, this species has three toes on each foot instead of the four of other woodpeckers.

Feeding: The larvae of wood-boring and bark beetles are the preferred food of the Black-backed Woodpecker. These morsels are obtained by flicking away the bark of a dead tree. This species will meticulously work an entire tree.

Habits: Like the Three-toed Woodpecker, this species is very docile around the nest site.

Nest: They aggressively defend their nesting territory against other woodpeckers, in particular the Three-toed Woodpecker. The nest site is a cavity on a conifer snag 2-15 feet high. The male does most of the excavation work. The bark is removed from the immediate area around the entrance. Both sexes incubate the 4-5 white eggs for 12-14 days. They continue their care of the nestlings for 24-27 days, at which time they fledge.

Voice and Drumming: The drumming pattern is a series of several long volleys. The call is a sharp *"kek"*.

Primary Habitat Characteristics: No other bird in the Northern Rockies is so tied to the post-fire forest habitat. They can be found entering a burned forest as it still smolders and smokes.

Other Habitats: They will also inhabit insect infested forest and, rarely, undamaged conifer forests, especially spruce-fir.

Conservation: With the return to natural fire regimes gaining acceptance, the Black-backed Woodpecker population will, in all likelihood, expand.

264

Description: Singing from the elevated perch of large Douglas-fir snag, the Olive-sided Flycatcher (7¹/₂") sounds like it is ordering a beer. The upper-parts are olive-brown, while the sides are the same color but streaked. There are two white tufts above the rump that are visible in perched birds. The head appears to be block-shaped and the black bill is long. The white of the throat extends down the breast to the belly in a distinct line. The rest of the upperparts are light gray.

Feeding: From its perch, the Olive-sided Fly-catcher sallies out to snatch flying insects. After the capture, it almost always returns to its original perch. The diet of the Olive-sided Flycatcher is almost exclusive flying insects.

Quick Three Beers

Habits: This flycatcher uses the flycatching tactic more often than the other flycatchers. The flight is direct and swift with agile twists and turns.

Nest: The courting male will chase after the female, who selects a nest site that is usually on a branch well out from the trunk. She builds a loose cup of twigs, root-lets, and lichens. The majority of these nests are in coniferous trees; however, nests have been noted in aspen and willow trees. She incubates the 3 brown-spotted pale rose eggs for 15-19 days. The male brings her food during this time. Both parents care for the young once they hatch. The duration of their care is 21-23 days.

Voice: The song of the Olive-sided Flycatcher is the catchy *"quick three beers"*. The call is a sharp *"pip-pip"*.

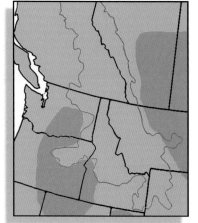

Primary Habitat Characteristics: The Olive-sided Flycatcher prefers early successional stage forests (mostly post-fire) with standing dead trees. These snags serve as feeding and singing perches. The stands where the Olive-sided Flycatcher lives have low canopy cover.

Other Habitats: The edges of streams, lakes, and wetlands provide dead trees for perching.

Conservation: The destruction of their Andean winter range has led to some decreases.

Description: The first bluebird is a sure sign that spring has sprung. The male Mountain Bluebird (7¼") is powder blue above. His underparts are paler, and the belly is white. The female is generally grayish-brown with a white belly. Her wings are blue. The bill is black.

Feeding: Insects are the bulk of the summertime diet. The species consumes grasshoppers, ants, flies, and many larvae of various species. This species will occasionally eat berries and other fruit during the summer. The fruit portion of the diet becomes very important during the winter, which is spent to the south.

*Mountain Bluebird male (l)
and female (r)*

Habits: A few rare, hardy individuals have been known to overwinter in the Rockies.

Nest: A cavity nester, the Mountain Bluebird uses natural cavities, old woodpecker holes, or nest boxes for nesting. The female selects the nest site. Both sexes construct a nest of stems, grass, twigs, and conifer needles lined with fur and feathers. The female incubates the 5-6 light blue eggs for 13-17 days. Both parents feed the nestling a protein-rich insect diet. The nestlings leave the nest after 17-23 days, and the parents continue their care for another 4 weeks.

Voice: The Mountain Bluebird's song is series of *"tru"* notes and rattles. The call is a song note repeated twice.

Primary Habitat Characteristics: Originally and to a lesser extent today, the Mountain Bluebird nests in post-fire forests where woodpeckers have created cavities in snags, and the denuded trees are great feeding perches.

Other Habitats: They can be found in the edges of conifer forests. Where there are nest boxes, this species can be found in abundance.

Conservation: The abundance of nest boxes has led the Mountain Bluebird increasing and come into new habitats, such as agricultural and grass lands.

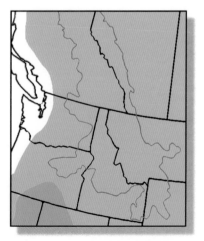

© Ross Knapper

Description: Often seen alone, the Townsend's Solitaire (8½") stays in the Northern Rockies throughout the winter. This slender-looking thrush is gray overall. It has a white eye-ring. The long tail has white outer tail feathers. In flight, note the buff-colored wing patches.

Feeding: They eat many insects during the summer. Many of these invertebrates are captured using a flycatching tactic. This bird will also hover-glean or swoop down on its prey. Berries, especially juniper berries, are the majority of the winter diet.

Habits: Townsend's Solitaire will move to lower elevations during the winter. It can be territorial on wintering grounds.

Townsend's Solitaire

Nest: From a conspicuous perch, the male sings proudly during the breeding season. The nest is a ground depression hidden under a ledge or some other protecting structure. The nest is a cup of twigs, grass, stems and conifer needles lined with grass. The 4 gray- and brown-blotched blue eggs are incubated for around a couple of weeks. Both sexes feed the nestlings, which leave the nest after 2 weeks.

Voice: The song is a series of musical notes at seemingly random pitches. The call is heard year around and is a high-pitched *"eek"*.

Primary Habitat Characteristics: The post-fire forest provides the exposed rocky slopes or dirt banks that the Townsend's Solitaire uses for nesting. This species is

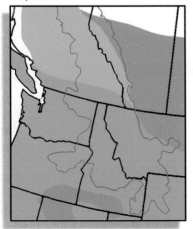

one of a handful of birds that will be present in a post-fire forest almost immediately after the fire.

Other Habitats: The Townsend's Solitaire will inhabit open coniferous forests or montane shrubland. They prefer juniper-limber pine stands, where they feed heavily upon juniper berries, and steep-walled canyons with patches of shrubs or small trees during the winter. In general, the Townsend's Soltaire is quite tolerant of a variety of forested habitats.

Conservation: The population of Townsend's Solitaire appears to be stable.

After the Inferno: Birds and Fire

Walking into the black moonscape of what was once a mature Douglas-fir forest, I have the almost knee-jerk human reaction to forest fires, "My God, it's all been destroyed." Upon further contemplation, I soon realize that this view is mistaken. Fire is an essential element of the life in the Northern Rockies. The blackened limbless spires stand atop a bed of newly rejuvenated fertile soil. Even though fire swept through a mere eight months ago, wildflowers are already bringing color to the blackened landscape. Within a few years, the evidence of the wildfire will be all but wiped from this forest.

Wildfire is an essential component of the forest's health. And each type of forest has its own unique fire regime.

The fire regime of the dry conifer forest varies greatly. It depends on the climatic conditions of the forest, which tree species dominate, and the past fire history. The general pattern is a combination of low-intensity surface fires and stand-replacement fires. When Douglas-fir is the dominant tree in a stand, a wildfire is more likely crown out, which means that it reaches the canopy and races with incredible speeds. These crown fires are often stand-replacing events. ponderosa pine is more fire-tolerant than Douglas-fir, and it can survive most low intensity burns. It has thick fire-resistant bark, and the frequent fires of the ponderosa pine forest result in a very open stand structure.

Moist Douglas-fir forest tends to have less frequent and less intense fire than those experienced by the drier Douglas-fir stands. This is due to the local climatic condi-

Fire Characteristics in specific forests

Ponderosa pine	Frequent, low-intensity burns
Dry Douglas-fir	Frequent, stand-replacing fires
Cedar-hemlock	Burns with variable frequency and intensity
Moist Douglas-fir	Infrequent, varying intensity burns
Lodgepole pine	High-intensity, stand-replacing fires
Spruce-fir	Infrequent, stand-replacing fires
Whitebark pine	Fires of varying intensity and frequency

tions of the moist Douglas-fir forest (more moist and cool).

Spruce-fir forest has a fire regime that is characterized by low frequency, high intensity fires that tend to replace the stand. Forests that are dominated by Engelmann spruce and subalpine fir burn only every 200 years. The structure of the subalpine fir, the branches reaching low to the ground and being tightly packed, aids the fire in reaching the canopy. This results in the classic stand-replacing inferno.

Other forests such as the cedar-hemlock and whitebark pine also experience infrequent burns with varying degrees of intensity.

Since "Bambi", there has been an embedded impression that wildfires kill many creatures.

The images of the deer and bluebirds fleeing the flames are branded into our collective memories. However, this notation is very inaccurate. Wildfires actually kill very few animals, and those killed tend to be those that have limited mobility, such as nestlings and other young. The level of fire-caused mortalities in birds is highly dependent on the timing of the wildfire. Early season fires are much more likely to destroy nests than late-season fires. So, the majority of birds killed in wildfires are nestlings and fledglings. Lower intensity fires tend to harm more ground nesting birds than those that nest in the trees. High intensity fires are much more destructive to birds of all natural histories.

How do birds avoid being injured or killed during a wildfire? Simple: they can fly away to avoid the flames and smoke. Birds will leave the area and immigrate to a secondary area of appropriate habitat. So with the initial burn there is a mass exodus of birds.

After the fire, many birds begin to immigrate in to the burn. The Black-backed and Three-toed Woodpeckers feast upon the wood-boring beetles that infest the standing dead trees. Many other cavity nesting and bark gleaning birds also move into the post-fire habitat. On occasion, predatory and scavenging birds are attracted to the post-fire habitat soon after the flames have died down. Here they feed upon the unfortunate few that were left dead and dying following the fire.

Post-fire Forest Succession
and Avian Communities

Immediately after fire
Plenty of ash cover and blackened snags.

- Clark's Nutcracker
- Cassin's Finch
- Red Crossbill
- Pine Siskin

Up to 25 years post-fire
Mostly shrub cover with snags and young trees.

- Black-backed Woodpecker
- Western Wood-pewee
- Cordilleran Flycatcher
- Western Bluebird
- Mountain Bluebird
- American Robin
- Olive-sided Flycatcher
- American Kestrel
- Northern Flicker
- Hairy Woodpecker
- Lewis's Woodpecker
- Three-toed Woodpecker

25-150 years post-fire
The forest is composed of maturing trees with extensive patches of shrubs.

- Orange-crowned Warbler
- Nashville Warbler
- MacGillivray's Warbler
- Lazuli Bunting
- Dark-eyed Junco
- Spotted Towhee

More than 150 years post-fire
The forest is composed of a mixture of large trees and younger vegetation.

- Calliope Hummingbird
- Rufous Hummingbird
- Williamson's Sapsucker
- Northern Flicker
- Dusky Flycatcher
- Steller's Jay
- Red-breasted Nuthatch
- Plumbeous Vireo
- Warbling Vireo
- Black-headed Grosbeak

More than 300 years post-fire
The forest has matured into large trees in even stands.

- Pileated Woodpecker
- Hammond's Flycatcher
- Brown Creeper
- Winter Wren
- Golden-crowned Kinglet
- Swainson's Thrush
- Hermit Thrush
- Varied Thrush
- Townsend's Warbler

Lodgepole Sapling

Moist Douglas-Fir

There is no final ecological truth. All knowledge is a current approximation, and each addition to that knowledge is but a small, incremental step toward understanding.

−JACK WARD THOMAS

The morning air hangs thick with humidity under the dense canopy. Overhead, giants stretch towards the energy-laden rays of the sun. Ferns grow in the carpet on the forest floor, and arboreal lichen dangles off the massive limbs of the Douglas-fir. This is as near to a rain forest that you can get in the Northern Rockies. As I slip under a leaning tree, a loud *"kik-kik-kik-kik"* pierces the stagnant air. I have accidentally ventured under the nest of a Northern Goshawk. These birds are infamous for the their fierce protection of the nest from any would-be egg and nestling thief. I remember the full-brimmed helmet of the Goshawk researcher in the Panhandle of Idaho. It was covered with the scars of the black talons of the angry Goshawk. She had many stories of dive-bombing raptors and the damage they can inflict on the unprotected body. With as much speed as I can muster, I head uphill, away from the nest, and out of danger. Pausing on a downed log, my legs burn with builtup lactic acid. As the pounding of my heart slows, a symphony of sweet sounds fills the air. Cassin's Vireos and Hammond's Flycatchers sing from the treetops and the drumming of a lone Pileated Woodpecker resonates throughout the forest. There is a certain harmony of sound and ecology in the moist Douglas-fir forest.

The moist Douglas-fir forest usually occurs above the cedar-hemlock forest, which tends to stay in the sheltered, wet draws. The upper limit for this type of habitat is the spruce-fir zone of the higher altitudes. The moist Douglas-fir forest is located on the east and north-facing slopes that receive more precipitation than the surrounding forests.

The Douglas-fir is an amazing species. It has the ability of thrive in an incredibly wide variety of climatic conditions. This tree is found in almost every forest in the Northern Rockies, the ultimate adapter among the conifers of the West.

The Douglas-fir in the moist

habitat can grow to more than 200 feet with a diameter of 5 or more feet at the base. Its bark is thick enough to withstand low intensity fires, but not the intense heat of an all out wildfire. The seeds are consumed by a variety of mammals and birds, including the Red and White-winged Crossbills. The high branches of the tall Douglas-fir provide nesting cover for songbirds and the Northern Goshawk.

Dwarf mistletoe is a parasitic plant that uses conifers as hosts. These parasites drill into the branches of the tree and live off the nutrients that flow within. The parasitic relationship can end in the death of the host; however, this can take thousands of mistletoe generations. A tree infected with mistletoe will develop dense, deformed branches called "witches' brooms". This growth is an adaptation to the mistletoe infection. Often these brooms break off and lie upon the ground, where they provide excellent cover for Ruffed Grouse and other ground-dwelling birds.

The Pileated Woodpecker is a giant woodpecker, the same size as a crow, that lives among the giants of old-growth forests. Its flaming red crest is reminiscent of Woody Woodpecker, but this is no cartoon character. This bird is one of the more old-growth dependent species. They are usually found in late successional forests amid trees with large diameters. It tends to roost in old-growth forests that have not experienced the impact of logging. The roost site is usually a natural hollow or a vacated nest hole. They spend the nights in these roosts trees, which have up to 16 different entrance holes.

When the Pileated Woodpecker excavates its nesting cavity, it does so in a large diameter tree. The entrance to the nesting cavity is a unique rectangular hole. In many of the largest snags in the moist Douglas-fir forest, you will find many such holes.

Both sexes construct these nests; however, the male does the lion's share of the labor. The woodpecker drives its massive bill into the wood with a spray of wood chips. Once the cavity is large enough, the Pileated Woodpecker brings out the chips by the bill-full. They discard up to 40 bill-fulls of the wood chips during nest excavation.

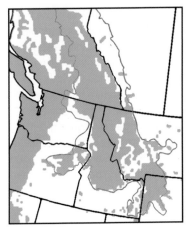

Range of Douglas-fir

Once the nest is completed, the female lays usually 4 white eggs. The female incubates these eggs during the day, and the male takes over incubation duties during the night. After 18 days, the eggs hatch and the next phase of parental care begins.

Both parents feed and care for the nestlings as they mature toward fledging. The young give a very loud raspy feeding cry. The parents feed the chicks by regurgitating insect meals for them. These insects are retrieved from the rotting snags of ancient Douglas-firs. The young fledge after 24-28 days of parental care.

The old-growth moist Douglas-fir forest dictates the entire life history of the Pileated Woodpecker. The bird and the habitat seem to shape and mold one another. For the rest of the day, I listen to the drumming of the Pileated Woodpecker as it defends its territory and attracts a mate, and the sun casts swinging shadows across the verdant forest floor.

Northern Goshawk

Accipiter genilis

R

The largest Accipiter

Description: With a wild twisting flight, the Northern Goshawk (21-26") maneuvers through the dense forest to hunt other birds. The female is larger than the male. It is dark gray above and the underparts are lighter gray with very fine, dense barring. The head is dark with a dark stripe over the eye that flares out toward the back. In flight, the short, broad wings are flapped with deep, powerful strokes. This wing arrangement is designed for high wing loading, which allows the Northern Goshawk to change direction in flight quickly and easily. The tail is long, which also helps the bird stabilize in flight.

Feeding: Like the other *Accipiter* hawks, the Northern Goshawk is a specialized hunter of mostly birds. From its perch, the raptor will scans for prey through the trees. It launches into a sprint to overtake the prey and capture it with the talons. It is also known eat small mammals.

Habits: This large hawk's body has evolved for life in the forest with short, broad wings and a long tail. During some winters, the Northern Goshawk will invade the southern portions of its winter range.

Nest: Over the nesting territories, the birds glide in circles. At the juncture of a large limb with the trunk, the female builds a nest out of sticks lined with leaves and plants. She incubates the 3-4 bluish eggs for 36-38. The male feeds her throughout the incubation period. The young are tended by the female at the nest, and the male brings the family food. The juveniles leave the nest in 6 weeks. If you are to approach a goshawk nest, the female may very well slash your head with her talons.

Voice: When mates meet, they give a series of *"kek kek kek"*.

Primary Habitat Characteristics: Northern Goshawk habitat tends to have a deciduous component in the nesting territory and large diameter trees for nesting.

Other Habitats: The edges of the forest.

Conservation: Numbers may be declining.

Williamson's Sapsucker
Sphyrapicus thyroideus

J F M A M J J A S O N D

B

Description: The Williamson's Sapsucker (9") is one of the more secretive of the woodpeckers. The male is black above with a white rump. The wings are also black with a large white patch in each wing. The dark head has a white stripe extending back from the eye and another drawing out from the base of the bill. The chin area is red. The belly is lemon yellow, while the breast is black. The female appears entirely different. She is heavily barred with brown and white on the back, sides, and wings. Her head is brown as well, though it lacks the barring. She has a white rump patch like the male's.

Male Williamson's Sapsucker

©Tom Ulrich

Feeding: As it climbs along the trunks and limbs, the Williamson's Sapsucker uses its bill to remove bark, and its long tongue to capture a variety of insects. It will also create small, square wells where sap will run. The sap is a sweet, tasty treat for the sapsucker.

Habits: The Williamson's Sapsucker often goes unnoticed with its shy, retiring attitude. When entering the nest, it lands above the hole and climbs down to it.

Nest: The Williamson's Sapsucker will make a new nest cavity every year. These nest holes are often in the same tree. The nest is 5-60 feet above the ground. The male excavates the cavity. The 5-6 white eggs are incubated by both sexes for about 2 weeks. They feed the young 3-4 weeks at which time they leave.

Voice and Drumming: The voice of the Williamson's Sapsucker is series of *"cherr"* notes. The drumming pattern is a rapid burst followed by irregularly timed taps.

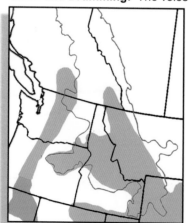

Primary Habitat Characteristics: Unlike other sapsuckers, the Williamson's Sapsucker seems to prefer unbroken forests with trees infected with heart-rot fungus.

Other Habitats: It can also be found in spruce/fir and aspen stands.

Conservation: Little is known about the current conservation status of the Williamson's Sapsucker.

R

The crested Pileated Woodpecker

Description: The largest of the woodpeckers in the Northern Rockies, the Pileated Woodpecker (18") leaves its rectangular holes in the large snags. The overall coloration of both sexes is black. The head is braced with a flaming red crest and white stripes. The chin is white. The males have red malar stripes and their red crowns are larger. In flight, there is white marking on each of the black wings. The Pileated Woodpecker flies with deep, slow wing-beats when compared to the other woodpeckers.

Feeding: The larvae of wood-boring beetles and carpenter ants are among this species' favorite foods. It feeds by using its specialized bill and head, which has features that allow it to absorb the pounding, to chip away and pry apart rotten and dead wood. The long tongue then enters the crevices to snare its food. The Pileated Woodpecker will feed on both standing dead and fallen trees. It will also consume a small amount of fruits.

Habits: It can become quite habituated to human presence.

Nest: This species uses its drumming to defend its territory. The nest is an excavated cavity that has a rectangular entrance. Both sexes incubate the 3-5 white eggs for 15-18 days. The nestlings are fed regurgitated insects for 26-28 days. The fledged young remain in close proximity to the parents for another 3 months.

Voice and Drumming: During the breeding season, it gives a series of *"wioka"* notes that fade at the end. The drumming pattern is like the sound of a diving board, fast and loud at first and then slowing down.

Primary Habitat Characteristics: Strongly associated with mature to old-growth forests.

Other Habitats: The Pileated Woodpecker also inhabits cottonwood bottom forests, Douglas-fir, and other mature conifer forests.

Conservation: With its ability to habituate to human presence, the Pileated Woodpecker has stable populations.

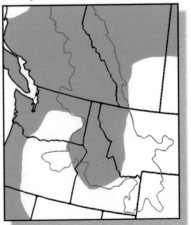

Hammond's Flycatcher

Empidonax hammondii

J F M A M J J A S O N D

B

Description: Almost identical looking to the Dusky Flycatcher, the Hammond's Flycatcher (5¹/₂") differs in habitat preference (wetter) and voice. The upperparts are olive-brown and the head is grayish-brown. The underparts are white with a grayish wash. The eye-ring is white and bold. The bill is diminutive and black. The tail appears to be shorter than the Dusky Flycatcher's. The wings have rather subdued wingbars that are easily noticed.

© Tom Ulrich

The hard to identify Hammond's Flycatcher

Feeding: Flying insects comprise the majority of the Hammond's Flycatcher's diet. They are captured midair as the bird bursts from its perch. These perches can be at varied heights in conifers. This species also gleans insects and caterpillars from the surface of vegetation.

Habits: While perched high in the trees, it flicks its tail and wings.

Nest: The male displays to the female by giving the trilled song and flicking his wings. The female builds a cup of grass, forbs, bark strips, and other plant material on a branch 10-100 feet high. Like many of the flycatchers, it incorporates spider webs into its nest. The female incubates 4 creamy-white eggs for 12-16 days. The nestlings fledge after 16-18 days, and the parents continue to care for them for another week afterward.

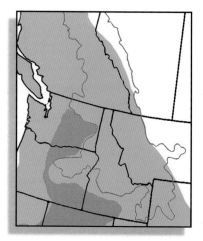

Voice: The song is a series like *"chibek brrk breet"*. The call is sharp *"peent"*.

Primary Habitat Characteristics: This flycatcher usually lives in cool, moist coniferous forests.

Other Habitats: The Hammond's Flycatcher can be found foraging in spruce-fir forest and aspen stands.

Conservation: Its dependence on mature conifer forests makes the Hammond's Flycatcher vulnerable to habitat alteration.

Cassin's Vireo
Vireo cassinii

J F M A M J J A S O N D

B

A solitary Cassin's Vireo

© Peter LaTourrette

Description: The white spectacles of the Cassin's Vireo (5") are its most distinguishing feature. The throat is white as well. The upperparts are olive, and the hood is bluish-gray. The wings have conspicuous white wing bars. The sides and flanks are bright yellow. The breast and belly are off-white.

Feeding: Feeding among the stems and leaves, the Cassin's Vireo is a gleaner of insects from the foliage. It will occasionally sally for flying insects.

Habits: It will build multiple nests and use only one.

Nest: During courtship, the male exposes his yellow flank feathers to the female while he bows and sings. He selects the nest site at the fork of a low branch in a small tree. The nest is suspended by the rim and is made of grass, plant material, and spider silk. It is lined with fur and grass and often encrusted with arboreal lichens. Both sexes incubate the 3-5 lightly brown and black-spotted white eggs for 15 days. Upon hatching, the young are cared for by both parents. The young normally fledge in two weeks time.

Voice: The song is higher-pitched than that of the Plumbeous Vireo and is a series of slurred notes like *"see you, cheerio, be seein you, so-long, seeya"*. The call is a harsh descending *"shep shep shep "*.

Primary Habitat Characteristics: They favor mature, open-canopy forests with a strong deciduous understory component.

Other Habitats: The Cassin's Vireo can occur in other coniferous forests and along streamside riparian thickets.

Conservation: Once it was lumped with Plumbeous and Blue-headed Vireos as the Solitary Vireo. The split of the Solitary Vireo was prompted by subtle differences and DNA sequencing. It is the most westerly of the three species.

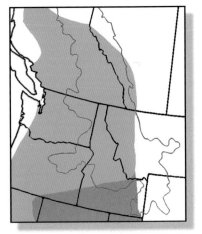

Plumbeous Vireo

Vireo plumbeus

J F M A M J J A S O N D

B

Description: Like the Cassin's Vireo, the white spectacles are the Plumbeous Vireo's (5") most distinguishing feature. The throat is white as well. The upperparts are gray, and the hood is bluish-gray. The wings have conspicuous white wing bars. The sides and flanks are bright yellow. The breast and belly are off-white. The bill appears to be more robust than that of the Cassin's Vireo.

Plumbeous Vireo

© Mike Danzenbaker

Feeding: Feeding among the stems and leaves, the Cassin's Vireo is a gleaner of insects from the foliage. It will occasionally sally for flying insects.

Habits: It will build multiple nests and use only one.

Nest: During courtship, the male exposes his yellow flank feathers to the female while he bows and sings. He selects the nest site at the fork of a low branch in a small tree. The nest is suspended by the rim and is made of grass, plant material, and spider silk. It is lined with fur and grass and often encrusted with arboreal lichens. Both sexes incubate the 3-5 lightly brown- and black-spotted white eggs for 15 days. Upon hatching, the young are cared for by both parents. The young normally fledge in two weeks.

Voice: The song is lower-pitched than the Cassin's Vireo's and it is a series of slurred notes like *"see you, cheerio, be seein you, so-long, seeya"*. The call is a harsh descending *"shep shep shep "*.

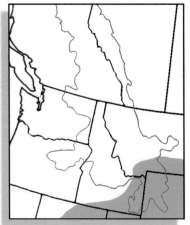

Primary Habitat Characteristics: They favor mature, open-canopy forests with a strong deciduous understory component.

Other Habitats: The Plumbeous Vireo can occur in other coniferous forests and along streamside riparian thickets.

Conservation: Once it was lumped with Cassin's and Blue-headed Vireos as the Solitary Vireo. The advent of DNA technology aided in the split. It is the most southerly of the three.

Spruce-Fir Forest

A raven, the bird that helpeth the gods,
In my right hand I hold: A hawk, to flutter in thine
evil face In my left hand I thrust forward.
—AN INSCRIPTION FROM A BABYLONIAN TABLET

The spruce-fir forest of the Northern Rockies brings a bit of the northern taiga to the mountainous regions of the West. From a distance spruce-fir looks dark green with the skinny crowns of the tallest trees reaching above the rest of the forest. As you stand below the spires of subalpine fir, a cool breeze causes the trees to sway back and forth with gentle ease. These forests are dark and moist, and under the canopy of the higher reaches snow hangs in well into the short summer. There is a special kind of silence in the spruce-fir forest that is interrupted only by shocking loud wing claps of a courting male Spruce Grouse. Many of the birds that live in the spruce-fir forest tend to stay up high in the canopy, foraging from spruce to fir. The thin wisp of a song from the Golden-crowned Kinglet is barely audible on the forest floor. These forests are remote and difficult to access, but the effort to reach them exposes you to an entirely unique suite of species.

Engelmann spruce and subalpine fir have adapted well to the harsh conditions found at the altitudes where the spruce-fir forest dominates. These trees are able to grow well in cold, humid, and shady conditions that exclude most of the other species of conifer in the Northern Rockies. Both of these species of conifer have needles that are borne singly, in contrast to the pines that have needles borne in bundles. The subalpine fir has smooth bark, and its cones stand upright upon the branches. The bark of the Engelmann spruce is rough and scales off easily with a swipe of the hand. Its cones hang down like pendulums of grandfather clocks. The narrow spire-like builds of the Engelmann spruce and subalpine fir are adaptations to the powerful winds of the subalpine regions. The narrow shape allows the wind to easily pass around the tree, protecting it from being blown down because these trees have shallow root systems that do not lend a great deal of support when compared to the roots of hardwoods. The shallow

roots are further hindered by the extremely shallow soils of these forests. This shape may also help keep heavy snow off of the trees.

The spines of boreal-like forest were deposited in the Northern Rockies during the last Ice Age. As the glaciers pushed their way south, the boreal forest spread before them. As the ice retreated, the spruce and fir were left isolated in the higher mountains that provide proper climatic conditions.

The spruce-fir forest can be thought of as subalpine forest, reaching up the treeline and descending down to the upper reaches of moist Douglas-fir and lodgepole forests. The lodgepole pine will, in fact, be occasionally present within the larger spruce-fir forest with its distinguishable yellowish-green crowns. Most of the moisture that falls on the spruce-fir forest comes in the form of snow. The understory of the forest is usually littered with many fallen spruce and fir, which remain for a long period of time due a fire regime with longer intervals. Due to their remoteness, spruce-fir forests have been spared, for the most part, from industrial logging and other human practices.

Most of the birds found within the spruce-fir forest also live in the vast spruce forests of the taiga that stretches across the northern tier of the continent below of the arctic treeline. The Northern Hawk-Owl is one such species that is linked to the spruce-fir forest. This incredible owl appears, like its name, to be a combination of a typical owl and *Accipiter* hawk. It is present in the Northern Rockies only from the region of northern Glacier National Park northward toward the muskeg forests of Canada. This not often seen species (in the Northern Rockies) is usually located perched atop a dead or dying tree on a bare, exposed branch. As perhaps the most unusual owl in the Northern Rockies, the Northern Hawk-Owl does not give the stereotypical hoot or whistle that is associated with most owls. It, instead, emits a bubbly, trilled series of whistled notes that can last as long as 15 seconds.

The hunting style of the Northern Hawk-Owl is also unique among the owls of the Northern Rockies. It swoops down from a perch when it determines a prey item. The unusual part comes from this owl's ability to hover over prey, and when it is not successful, it glides in low toward a perch and then it swings up steeply to the perch. Most of the prey items taken by this owl

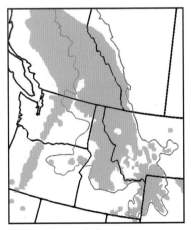

Range of spruce-fir forests

are birds, including White-tailed Ptarmigan, and small mammals, such as voles and even weasels. When the prey is captured, the hawk-owl will mantle over its meal. Mantling is when the bird stands over the prey and surrounds it with its wings. This behavior is probably a response to other owls and raptors that might attempt to steal the meal if they knew of its existence.

During the winter, the Northern Hawk-Owl can stage irruptions to the south of its normal breeding range. This is a common theme among many of the birds that breed in the spruce-fir forest. Birds such as the White-winged Crossbill, Evening Grosbeak, and Pine Grosbeak all breed within spruce-fir forests. However, over most the Northern Rockies, they are considered to be winter irruptive species.

Many of the alpine and whitebark pine associated birds will pass through the spruce-fir forest during the spring and, again, the autumn. The Gray-crowned Rosy-finch and Clark's Nutcracker can be seen flying over the spires of the spruce-fir forest.

The range of one spruce-fir associated bird is expanding in the Northern Rockies. No, its numbers are not increasing, nor has it been displaced from somewhere else. It is simply being noticed. The Boreal Owl was long been thought to be rare in the Northern Rockies; however, recently this unassuming small owl has been found in a variety of locations in the region. Owl enthusiasts have ventured out in the cold winter nights on cross-country skis and snowshoes. The playback of a Boreal Owl call has caused the actual owl to respond and confirm its presence in the Northern Rockies. This is an instance where the amateurs have aided science and managers in a large way.

The upper reaches of forest in the Northern Rockies are home to the Engelmann spruce and subalpine fir. These conifers create a habitat like that of the northern forests, and the bird species found within them reflect this similarity.

Spruce Grouse · *Falcipennis canadensis*

J F M A M J J A S O N D

R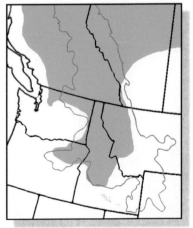

Male Spruce Grouse

Description: Often letting one approach to within mere feet before it walks away, the Spruce Grouse (15") is camoflauged. The birds in the Northern Rockies belong to the subspecies once called the Franklin's Grouse. The male is mottled brown with an all-dark tail. The upper breast and throat are black with white borders. Above the eyes, there are bright red eye-combs. The females have a camouflaging brown plumage and the all-dark tail with white tips.

Feeding: Primarily a ground forager below the spruce-fir forest canopy, the Spruce Grouse eats what most of us would find distasteful, conifer needles. It has special adaptations for digesting these seemingly inedible items. During the summer, it will also consume fresh shoots, berries, and invertebrates. In winter, they almost exclusively feed upon needles in the trees.

Habits: This grouse is known as the "Fool Hen", the Spruce Grouse is very tame and unassuming. During the winter, they will gather into small, loose flocks.

Nest: When it does the territorial display, the male flutters up and produces a loud drumming with its clapping wings. The female scrapes out a depression that is lined with pine needles. She incubates the 4-8 brown-blotched rosy eggs for 20-24 days. The young are able to feed themselves soon after hatching. They stay in the company of their mother for up 12 weeks.

Voice: The muted wing drumming and the shocking loud clap of the wings are the most often heard sounds of the Spruce Grouse.

Primary Habitat Characteristics: This species lives under dense, closed canopies with nearby clearings.

Other Habitats: Other moist coniferous forests are also the haunts of the Spruce Grouse.

Conservation: The local populations of Spruce Grouse are cyclical in nature.

Northern Hawk-Owl

Sturnia ulula

J F M A M J J A S O N D

R

Northern Hawk-Owl with a menacing glance

Description: The Northern Hawk-Owl's (16") shape is more like that of a falcon than a typical owl. The upperparts are dark brown with white spots on the upper wings and the crown is spotted. A black strip borders each side of the light gray facial disc. The bill is a dull yellow and the eyes are bright yellow. The tail is long and rounded. The underparts are white with heavy dark barring. The legs are completely feathered.

Feeding: The Northern Hawk-Owl is a swooping hunter. During the summer, its diet is mostly small mammals, especially rodents. With the onset of winter, though, the diet usually switches to a majority of avian prey. Some of these birds are captured in midair. The Northern Hawk-Owl has been observed hovering in midair.

Habits: The Northern Hawk-Owl is active during the day and quite tame. Its hearing is probably not as well developed as other owls'. Adults will occasionally eat their own young. The flight is low and fast.

Nest: The pair will duet during courtship. A cavity nester, the Northern Hawk-Owl uses enlarged Pileated Woodpecker or Northern Flicker holes as nesting sites in addition to broken top hollows and abandoned *Corvid* nests. The female incubates the 3-10 white eggs for 25-30 days. The young fledge at 25-35 days. The family will remain together until the next spring.

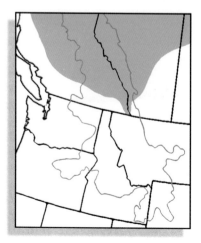

Voice: The slurred *"chip"* note is repeated in a rapid series. The distinctive *"chimp"* call can also be heard on a frequent basis.

Primary Habitat Characteristics: Favors stands that are not all that dense with broken top snags and open areas.

Other Habitats: During the winter, the Northern Hawk-Owl will move out into open clearings or even grasslands.

Conservation: With its isolated habitat, the Northern Hawk-Owl has stable populations.

Boreal Owl

Aegolius funereus

J F M A M J J A S O N D

R

Description: Once thought to be rare, the Boreal Owl (10") is now known to be more common. The upperparts are dark brown with large white spotting. The ear-less head is heavily spotted. The facial disc is white with a dark brown border. The underparts are streaked brown on white. The feet are fully feathered.

Feeding: Voles and deer mice make up the bulk (75%) of the Boreal Owl's diet. It will also consume other small mammals, birds, and insects. Most of its hunting comes in the form of swooping from a perch. It will cache some food when prey is abundant.

© Caleb Putnam

Reclusive Boreal Owl

Habits: Males tend to remain on their territories throughout the year, while juveniles and females will move to more hospitable locations at lower elevations during the winter.

Nest: The male ritually feeds the female during courtship. It prefers to use the old holes of Pileated Woodpecker and Northern Flicker as nesting sites. These nest sites are usually 10-25 feet above the ground. The 3-6 white eggs are incubated for 25-32 days. The female alone does the incubation. They fledge in another 4-5 weeks of parental care by both sexes. The parents continue their care for another 2 weeks after fledging.

Voice: The Boreal Owl gives 5-10 whistled *"hoo's"* in a rapid staccato fashion. This vocalization is heard during the nights of late winter until early spring.

Primary Habitat Characteristics: In the Northern Rockies, they occur with greatest regularity above 5,000 feet.

Other Habitats: They can be found in subalpine forests like subalpine fir and whitebark pine. During the winter, the females and juveniles will descend in altitude.

Conservation: The known range has been expanding as we find more breeding populations and locations. Increased abundance during the late winter is due to active calling by the males.

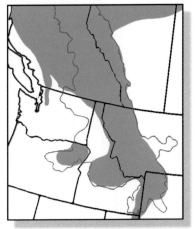

R

Description: The Camp Robber or Whiskey Jack are but a couple of the colloquial names for the Gray Jay (11$\frac{1}{2}$"). It is chubby appearing, and it has a long tail. The upperparts are slate gray. The nape is a charcoal gray and the crown is very light gray. The throat is white and the rest of the underparts are white. The stubby bill is black.

Feeding: An opportunistic feeder, the Gray Jay will consume berries, pine nuts, insects, other invertebrates, small mammals, birds' eggs, and carrion. With such a wide range in food preference, this species will employ an accordingly wide breadth of foraging strategies. It will use special mucus-like saliva to form balls of berries and seeds. These balls are stuck to crevices in bark for later use.

Gray Jay enduring winter

Habits: Living up to its nickname, the Camp Robber, it can become a nuisance at camps, both in the backcountry and in developed areas. It will move into lower elevations in small flocks, during particularly harsh winters.

Nest: Staying together throughout the year as a pair, the Gray Jays begin nesting usually when there is still snow in the ground. Both sexes build the nest of twigs, lichens, moss, and bark strips. It is lined with feathers and fur. The female incubates the 3-4 variable-spotted greenish-white eggs for 16-22 days. Both parents tend to their brood. The nestlings fledge in 15 days and they remain with their parents for another 4 weeks.

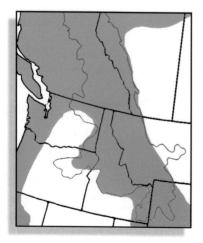

Voice: It is the most silent of the Northern Rockies *Corvids*, although it gives a raspy *"churr"* alarm call. A variety of other calls are also given in specific situations.

Primary Habitat Characteristics: They show a preference for spruce-fir forests.

Other Habitats: This bird also inhabits higher-elevation aspen stands and moist Douglas-fir.

Conservation: Very common, and populations seem to be steady.

Steller's Jay

J F M A M J J A S O N D

Cyanocitta stelleri

R

The camp-robbing Stellar's Jay

Description: With its dark blue matching the shadows, the Steller's Jay (11½") is always a joy to behold. Overall coloration is dark, deep blue with black touches, especially on the wings. The head has a prominent crest, and it is darker than the rest of the body. The forehead may be streaked with lighter blue. The throat has some indistinct white streaking. The long tail has black barring.

Feeding: Similar to many of its *Corvid* cousins, the Steller's Jay is an opportunistic omnivore. It will consume pine nuts, seeds, berries, insects, other invertebrates, small mammals, birds' eggs, and carrion. It is known to come to suet feeders at remote mountain cabins.

Habits: Where its range overlaps with the Blue Jay, especially along the Front Range in Colorado, the Steller's Jay will hybridize with its cousin. They can occur in large numbers around adequate food sources. The Stellar's Jay when in small flocks will fly in single file.

Nest: Ritual feeding is part of the courtship. He will also circle around her as a display. Both sexes construct a cup of twigs, stems, grass, and other material in a tree 8-40 feet above the ground. The nest is lined with grass, rootlets, and pine needles. The female incubates the 4 olive-spotted blue-green eggs for 16-18 days. The nestlings fledge after several weeks of parental care at the nest. The juveniles will remain with their parents throughout their first winter.

Voice: The most often heard call is repeated *"shaack-shaack-shaack"*.

Primary Habitat Characteristics: In the Northern Rockies, the Steller's Jay seems to favor moister conditions in its breeding habitat. It also has a preference for forests with openings over unbroken forest.

Other Habitats: When not breeding, it will live in a variety of forest types.

Conservation: It is very secure and stable.

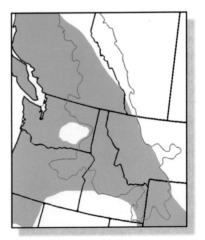

290

Common Raven

Corvus corax

J F M A M J J A S O N D

R

Description: Soaring like a raptor, scavenging like a vulture, the Common Raven (24") is the largest songbird in North America and perhaps, one of the most intelligent. The overall coloration is flat black. The bill is long and heavy, perfect for a bird with an omnivore's diet. The tail is wedge-shaped and this shape is useful to tell it apart from the American Crow. When soaring, the large wings appear to have "fingers".

The adaptable Common Raven

Feeding: One the most adaptable birds in the Northern Rockies, the Common Raven will eat almost anything: insects, berries, nuts, small mammals, birds' eggs, other vertebrates, and carrion. Breeding couples hunt in pairs with one bird flushing out the prey and the other capturing it. They track the movements of large predators such as wolves and eat from their kills after the predators are through with them. They are often seen on roadsides consuming road kill.

Habits: During the fall and winter, they form large communal roosts of non-breeding individuals. Breeding pairs stay on their territory throughout the year.

Nest: During courtship, the male does a variety of aerial displays, such as rolls and dives. The nest is large bulky cup of sticks that is lined with grass, bark fibers, moss, and fur. The female incubates the 4-6 brown-blotched blue to green eggs for 18-21 days. Both parents tend to their brood, which fledge at 38-44 days.

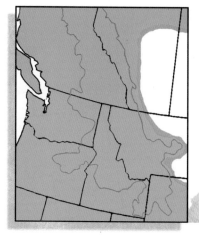

Voice: The Common Raven's call is gravelly, low *"gronwk"*.

Primary Habitat Characteristics: The Common Raven tends to use forests that are not unbroken and dense.

Other Habitats: It also inhabits other forests, shrublands and the grasslands if nest sites are available.

Conservation: The bird is one of the region's most common species, and is seen in a variety of situations. It is among the smartest of birds.

Boreal Chickadee

Poecile hudsonicus

J F M A M J J A S O N D

R

Subdued Boreal Chickadee

Description: The least often seen of the chickadees in the Rockies, the Boreal Chickadee (5¹/₂") is also the least colorful. When perched or feeding, it appears to be quite plump. It is grayish-brown above including the cap. The cheeks are dirty white. Like the other chickadees, it has a black bib. The sides and flanks are olive-brown. The underparts are white.

Feeding: Moving from one tree to the next, it gleans mostly insects for the surface of the branches, trunks, and needles. The insects on the menu include beetles, moths, and, particularly in winter, the eggs and pupae of insects. It will also consume a small amount of seeds and fruit.

Habits: Of the four chickadee species in the Northern Rockies, the Boreal Chickadee is most shy and retiring. It forms winter foraging flocks. It will irrupt during some winters, moving southward.

Nest: Like its relatives, the Boreal Chickadee is a cavity nester. It will use natural cavities, old woodpecker holes, or excavate its own. The nest site is 1-10 feet above the ground. The nest itself is a clump moss, fur, bark fibers, and feathers, lined with hair. The female incubates the 5-8 rufous-spotted white eggs for 11-16 days. Both parents care for the nestlings, which leave the nest after 18 days.

Voice: The song, *"tseek-a-day-day"*, of the Boreal Chickadee is more nasal than the Black-capped Chickadee's.

Primary Habitat Characteristics: Found high in the mountains, this chickadee favors humid spruce-fir forest. It also requires trees with heart-rot for nest excavation.

Other Habitats: Rarely a Boreal Chickadee will turn up in another type of moist conifer forest, especially cedar/hemlock and moist Douglas-fir forests.

Conservation: Due to their isolation, the Boreal Chickadee has not been markedly affected by habitat alteration.

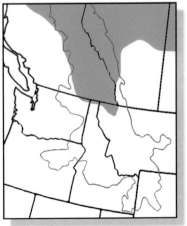

Ruby-crowned Kinglet

Regulus calendula

J F M A M J J A S O N D

B

Description: Its thin, wispy song coming from the treetops is more often heard than the small Ruby-crowned Kinglet is seen (4¼"). The upperparts are grayish-brown. The wings have 2 white wingbars. The head has bold white eye-rings. The male possesses the bright red crown patch; however, it is concealed under grayish-brown feathers except for when displaying to the female or an intruder in his territory.

© Peter LaTourrette

The tiny Ruby-crowned Kinglet

Feeding: A connoisseur of insects, the Ruby-crowned Kinglet gleans its prey from the foliage and branches. It hover-gleans and flycatches as well. The insects consumed include flies, hoppers, beetles, and ants. During the winter, it will join mixed-species flocks that include chickadees and Golden-crowned Kinglets.

Habits: It tends to stay high in the trees making observation difficult. On occasion, when feeding, one will appear in the lower levels of the canopy. When they move about, they make a chattering noise.

Nest: The male raises the namesake ruby crown when he is displaying in front of the female. The nest of lichens, moss, plant fibers, needles, and spider silk is built by the female and attached to a small branch. The nest is high in the canopy, usually 15-30 feet up. The female incubates the 7-8 occasionally brown-spotted white to buff eggs for 13-14 days. The nestlings fledge after 12-16 days.

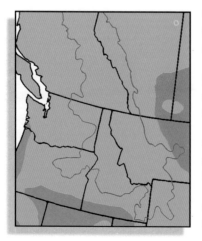

Voice: The song of the Ruby-crowned Kinglet is a very high-pitched *"see-see-see you-you-you look-at-me, look-at-me, look-at-me"*

Primary Habitat Characteristics: It favors older forests, as these stands have grown tall enough for treetop life.

Other Habitats: The Ruby-crowned Kinglet also inhabits Douglas-fir and pine forests during the breeding season.

Conservation: This tiny songbird is widespread and common.

Golden-crowned Kinglet

Regulus satrapa

J F M A M J J A S O N D

R

The bright crown of the Golden-crowned Kinglet

Description: Unlike its cousin, the Ruby-crowned Kinglet, the diminutive Golden-crowned Kinglet (3¹/₂") stays in the Northern Rockies throughout the entire year. The overall coloration is light brown. The cap is black with a golden crown in the middle. It has a white eyebrow and two white wingbars.

Feeding: Any insects found in the surface of a conifer can be considered a food item. The Golden-crowned Kinglet is extremely active while feeding, hopping from one branch to another. It will even hang upside down from the thinnest twigs. It will also employ hover-glean and flycatching feeding tactics.

Habits: As it hops from one limb to the next, it flicks its wings. During the winter, it is often seen in mixed-species feeding flocks with chickadees and nuthatches.

Nest: As he defends his territory during the nesting season, the male Golden-crowned Kinglet will raise his crown in a threat display. The female builds a delicate cup of lichens, moss, bark fibers, and spider webs lined with feathers and other fine materials. She hangs this nest from twigs near the trunk and normally 4-60 feet high. The female incubates the 8-9 gray- and brown-spotted white eggs for 2 weeks. The male feeds her during the incubation period. Both adults care for the nestlings. They fledge in 14-19 days.

Voice: The song is a remarkably high-pitched *"see-see-see"*.

Primary Habitat Characteristics: It seeks denser stands, which may provide greater thermal cover than more open stands.

Other Habitats: This bird also lives in other conifer forests including Douglas-fir and lodgepole pine. During the winter, it can be found in mixed deciduous-conifer stands.

Conservation: The Golden-crowned Kinglet is a common forest species.

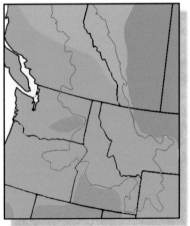

Description: From a high perch above its thick habitat, the Hermit Thrush (6³/₄") sings with joyful abandon. The upperparts are a tad variable in color ranging from olive to grayish-brown. The tail is rusty red. The thin eye-ring is bright white. The underparts are buff with spots.

Hermit Thrush

Feeding: The Hermit Thrush feeds mostly on the ground and will turn over leaves. It eats mostly insects and other invertebrates. It gleans from the lower branches as well. Berries and fruits round out the diet.

Habits: The Hermit Thrush sings from a high, exposed perch at dawn and dusk. It is constantly flicking its wings. The tail is bobbed when the Hermit Thrush becomes threatened.

Nest: The male will chase the female around the nesting territory during courtship. The female builds the nest in a tree 1-8 feet above the ground or, rarely, on the ground. The nest itself is a thick-walled cup of twigs, grass, moss, and ferns that is lined with pine needles and other plant material. The female incubates the 3-6 light blue eggs for 12-13 days. The male feeds her throughout the incubation period. Both parents care for the young for 10-12 days at which time they leave the nest.

Voice: The song the Hermit Thrush opens with a long, clear note that transitions into a series of flute-like notes. The *"chup"* and the harsh *"wee-er"* are two commonly heard calls.

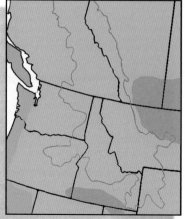

Primary Habitat Characteristics: The Hermit Thrush tends to favor moist, mature spruce/fir forests in the Northern Rockies. These tracts of forest are dense and undisturbed.

Other Habitats: They will reside in other coniferous forests and streamside thickets, with medium to high percentage of cover.

Conservation: The populations are steady, although they seem to be less tolerant of habitat disturbances than was once thought.

Yellow-rumped Warbler male (l) and female (r)

Description: A warbler that occasionally turns up during winter counts, the Yellow-rumped Warbler (5¹/₂") is the first to arrive and the last to leave. The male is dark blue-gray overall. He has yellow patches in the crown, rump, and throat (white in the Myrtle's race). There is some white on the wings. The female is browner overall. She has faint yellow markings on the crown and throat. Her yellow rump is prominent.

Feeding: The Yellow-rumped Warbler is an insect's worst nightmare. It consumes all manner of insects and other invertebrates, especially spiders. It feeds using several different tactics. It gleans insects from the foliage and on the ground. This species hover-gleans, picking prey from the tips of branches. It will flycatch with some regularity. During the winter, it will consume many different types of berries. The male Yellow-rumped Warbler tends to forage higher in the trees.

Habits: It is rather active and is seen flicking its tail. The Yellow-rumped Warbler will join mixed-species feeding flocks in the winter months.

Nest: During courtship, the male displays his crown feathers and raises his wings. The female constructs a nest of forbs, bark stripes, and rootlets lined with feathers and hair. The nest is placed on a branch toward the distal end 4-50 feet above the ground. She incubates the 4-5 gray-marked light buff eggs for 12-13 days. The adults feed the nestlings and they fledge after 10-12 days.

Voice: A two-part trill with the second phrase changing pitch. The call is a loud *"chwit"*.

Primary Habitat Characteristics: They prefer the edges of the forest with clearings, or forests with open structure.

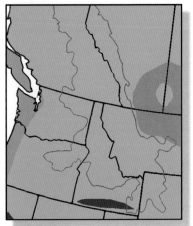

Other Habitats: They also live in other conifer forests.

Conservation: The Yellow-rumped is one of the most abundant warblers in the Northern Rockies, and likely to seen in any conifer forest.

Description: With its large, robust bill, the Pine Grosbeak (9") does not strike one as a member of the finch family. The males are grayish overall with black wings that have 2 white wing bars. The back, head, and chest are rose-red. This coloration can be variable with a russet variation being somewhat common. The female is grayish overall with black wings. She has yellowish green coloration on the head and rump. The bill is robust and black. The tail is long and notched.

Feeding: With its adapted bill, the Pine Grosbeak eats many seeds from cones and deciduous buds (alder and Rocky Mountain maple). They will also consume seeds, grass, and forbs. When feeding in the trees, it moves from one branch to the next. It tends to work the entire limb before moving on.

Wintering Pine Grosbeak

Habits: Pine Grosbeaks are some of the tamer finches, allowing for close approach. Food is transported to the nestling in a special sublingual pouch. During the winter, they will form feeding flocks with up to 30 individuals. These flocks may include Bohemian Waxwings.

Nest: The male sings from the perch during the nesting season. The nest is a cup of forbs, twigs, and rootlets lined with grass, lichens, and moss. It is placed on a branch 5-25 feet high. The female incubates the 2-5 black- and purple-spotted blue-green eggs for 13-15 days. The nestlings leave the nest after 2 or 3 weeks for parental care by both sexes.

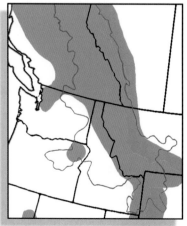

Voice: Its song is a lovely musical warble. The flight call is a whistled *"pui pui pui"*.

Primary Habitat Characteristics: The Pine Grosbeak is found at higher elevations.

Other Habitats: During the winter, it can be located in deciduous stands in the valleys.

Conservation: Though it uncommon, the overall numbers of Pine Grosbeak are secure and steady.

Nomadic White-winged Crossbill

© Jim Zipp

Description: Always moving from one area to another, the White-winged Crossbills (6¹/₂") are the nomads of the spruce-fir forest. The males are pinkish-red overall. The wings are black with two large white wingbars. The female is grayish overall with olive washing on the head and back. The breast and rump are greenish-yellow. She also has the black wings with 2 white wingbars. The bill is large and the tips cross.

Feeding: The White-winged Crossbill feeds mostly by going from branch to branch in search of cones. It possesses one of the most specialized bills in the Northern Rockies. The crossed tips of the bill are used to pry apart conifer cones and exposed the seeds within.

Habits: It has the habit of irrupting during some winters, to the joy of many birders.

Nest: Unlike almost all of the other songbirds, the White-winged Crossbill will nest at any time of the year. Their nesting is dependent on the localized cone crop. The males have been observed chasing the females during courtship. The female builds a nest of stems, grass, twigs, and bark fibers lined with lichens, rootlets, moss, and other fibers. It is placed on a branch 10-15 above the ground. She incubates the 2-4 purple and brown-spotted blue eggs for 12-14 days. Both adults will care for and feed the nestlings.

Voice: The White-winged Crossbill gives a rapid warble with interrupting rattles for a song. The flight call is a *"chif-chif"*.

Primary Habitat Characteristics: Breeding tends to center around stands of spruce.

Other Habitats: It will feed in other conifer forests.

Conservation: The population of White-winged Crossbills fluctuates with the cycles of the cone crop.

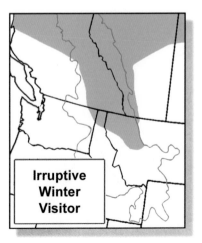

Irruptive Winter Visitor

Evening Grosbeak

Coccothraustes vespertinus

J F M A M J J A S O N D

B

Male Evening Grosbeak

© Peter LaTourrette

Description: What a wonderful burst of color on the white background of winter! The Evening Grosbeak (8") is a nomad exploiting ephemeral food sources. The stocky body of the male begins brown at the head and fades to yellow by the tail. He has a bright yellow forehead and eyebrow. The female is a subtle grayish-brown. The tails of both are black and notched. In flight, the wings have obvious white patches. With the arrival of spring, the large bill changes color from yellow to light green.

Feeding: In noisy flocks, Evening Grosbeaks feed in the trees and, rarely, on the ground. They crack and gulp every seed they find. This species is particularly fond of the buds of deciduous trees. During the summer, is adds a small amount of insects to its diet.

Habits: In common with many of the finches, the Evening Grosbeak is irruptive during the winter.

Nest: The male will feed the female during courtship. The female constructs a nest of small sticks lined with grass, moss, and conifer needles. The nest is located on a branch 20-60 feet above the ground. She incubates the 3-4 variable color-blotched pale blue to greenish-blue eggs for 11-14 days. The nestlings fledge after 13-14 days of care by both adults.

Voice: The song is a choppy warble. The call is loud, bell-like *"peerp"*.

Primary Habitat Characteristics: A shrubby understory or a strong deciduous component is important to Evening Grosbeak foraging.

Other Habitats: They will inhabit other conifer and mixed deciduous-conifer forests. In the winter, they will come into urban areas where they visit seed feeders.

Conservation: This species is stable in the West and has been its range eastward.

Wolf-Bird
Ravens and Wolves

The raven and the wolf are both beasts of prey.
The raven can see better in the daylight than in the darkness.
The wolf said, "Daylight, don't come, daylight, don't come."
It would be able to hunt the caribou
better if daylight didn't come.
The caribou stays in one place when it is dark.
— INUIT TALE, "ORIGIN OF LIGHT"

Driving through the milky dawn twilight, the hills and forest of the Lamar Valley in Yellowstone National Park begin to gradually materialize with the ever-increasing light. The air flowing over the vehicle seems to almost crackle with the intense cold of a Yellowstone winter. It is roughly 20 degrees below zero outside of the metal and glass frame, and the temperature is somewhat warmer inside. I had started this drive in the pitch-black darkness of 3 a.m. I have come to this place in search of one of the spectacles of the Northern Rockies, to see the gray wolf roaming wild and free in an essential unaltered environment. Just a few years ago, it was impossible to see the gray wolf in the Rockies.

Pulling into a turnout at the Specimen Ridge trailhead, I get out of the vehicle to face to brute force of the winter for the first time. It is the type of cold that burns your nose and sucks the wind out of your lungs. The frigid air slices through the wool and synthetic fibers of my clothing with the ease of a needle through cloth. Almost immediately my ears and nose sting with intensity that clouds the mind with ideas of a warm bed and hot chocolate. This cold does not seem to affect the wolves and ravens. They, in fact, thrive in these harsh conditions. These creatures are perfectly suited for

the climate of the Northern Range of Yellowstone National Park.

With a semi-frozen ear, I hear the mournful howl of a distant wolf cascade over the sparsely vegetated rolling hills. It is a liquid sound that seems to flow with an incessant momentum. The howl of a wolf brings up many primordial feelings for some

people. The fear of the un-
known and the dread of being
in the presence of a skilled and
cunning predator. The sense of
wilderness and kinship arises
for others, creating a conflict in
the human heart and mind. I
also felt the former was more
true than the latter. The wolf is
the very essence of wildness
to many of us humans.

Another sound quickly accom-
panies the howl of the far off wolf, the hoarse call of the Common Raven.

The raven and the wolf seem to coexist with a certain sense of harmony and understanding. The predator provides scavenging opportunities for the bird, and the bird
may be welcome company on the coldest of nights.

The relationship between the wolf and raven has become the stuff of myths and
legends for the Native Americans and other groups around the world. Both raven
and wolf were important to these cultures.

Among the Norse to see a wolf and raven together was a good omen for success
in an upcoming battle.

The Cree use the relationship between the wolves and ravens to explain the creation
of the earth.

"When all the land was covered with water, the trickster Wisagatcak pulled up some
trees and made a raft. On it, he collected many kinds of animals swimming in the waters. The Raven left the raft, flying for a whole day, and saw no land, so Wisagatcak
called Wolf to help. Wolf ran around and around the raft with a ball of moss in his
mouth. The moss grew, and earth formed on it. It spread on the raft and kept on
growing until it made the whole world. This is how the Earth was created."

As native cultures told stories about wolf and raven for thousands of years, residents
and visitors in the Northern Rockies have had an opportunity to see how wolf and
raven interact since the reintroduction of the former.

The wolves have killed an elk during the night, and the half eaten carcass is lying in
the gully. Where the cow had crashed through the snowdrift, there are three sets of
wolf tracks alongside. They dragged her down by the haunches, and delivered the
deathblow by ripping her throat. The predators then feasted on the warm flesh as the
elk's body heat steamed in the moonlit night. They ate until their bellies were full, and
distant sun began to lighten the eastern horizon. The wolves had retreated into the
nearby timber, and we occasionally caught a glimpse of one of the small, black,
young wolves.

Standing atop the carcass, a large raven picks chunks of meat from the rapidly freezing body. It soon is joined by other ravens and Black-billed Magpies. These scavengers have sought out this kill from some distance away. Watching the ravens, I wonder if the black birds witnessed the hunt that took place the previous night. Did a silhouetted raven against the moon maintain a watch on the life and death struggle, and hope for death?

A shy coyote has joined the mob at the carcass. It acts like a scolded child as it smells the wolves at the kill. It quickly rips off a mouthful and retreats to a safe distance. For the small dog knows if the nearby wolves catch it at their kill, it will mean a quick, violent death from the crushing jaws of its cousins.

By the late afternoon, the light is fading and the wolves are rising. On an exposed hillside, the pack begins to stir. They are making ready for another night's hunt. A couple of the younger wolves come down to the carcass for a snack. As they approach, the magpies flush in a cacophony of harsh calls. Ravens launch up into the air, and they circle around. Except for one, which has perched on the exposed limb of a dead Douglas-fir. It watches intently as the pair rips bits of frozen muscle from the elk's body. The bird seems to be almost studying the wolves, trying to learn more about their habits.

The pair of wolves turn and lope up the sage-covered hill to rejoin the pack. With a series of howls and other vocalizations, the entire pack trot off for the night's hunt. The raven takes flight, and follows the pack's path. The companions are together again for the hunt.

Aspen Parklands

*Called quaking aspen for the trembling of its leaves, it is anything
but timorous or fragile. It is unfathomably ancient and enduring,
approaching what has been called "theoretical immortality."
It is a lifeform persisting over time without offspring,
in suspended animation, waiting patiently through the
dark passage of millennia for something we can only guess at.*

–DAVID LUJAS

A stiff August breeze circulates heat around the white trunks and through the parched tops of late summer grass. Each pulse of wind sends waves through the understory. Walking in the heart of this giant, you feel the presence of an ancient life. This organism is among the largest on the face of this small blue planet, it is an aspen stand. This mass of life can reach up to 100 acres in size. Each individual "tree" is in actuality a sucker of large organism that is present underneath the soil and grass, which is part of the large, shallow root system.

The aspen stand is the ultimate survivor. When a catastrophic event like a fire or avalanche comes and removes all of the standing aspens, the extensive root system kicks into overdrive. New suckers almost immediately sprout from the earth and be-

gin transforming the sunlight into energy for the aspen stand. The stand grows quickly and reaches maturity long before other types of forest. They can reach maturity in 30 years. The trade-off for being able to grow quickly in disturbed sites is a lack of longevity. The aspen only survives for a relatively short period of time, on average only about 50 years. Soon, after reaching maturity, other types of forest will begin to crown out the aspens. In very rare situations, the aspen stand may survive for a thousand years or more.

Where aspen stands are near larger streams, they are the preferred dam-building material and food for the beaver. They gnaw through the trunk of the tree, so the tree falls earthward. It takes the smaller branches and sticks them in the mud of the pond behind the dam.

The larger limbs are carefully added to the dam in order to re-enforce it.

Aspen stand provide birds with two things: cover for nesting and roosting, and feeding opportunities. Under the open canopy of the aspen stand, many small trees and shrubs thrive in the filtered sunlight that makes its way through the golden leaves. These plants and the aspens themselves are used for nesting. The Ruffed Grouse often lays its eggs in the ground depression under the cover of one of these shrubs. The Western Wood-Pewee weaves its cup of grass on the branch of an aspen. The Red-naped Sapsucker excavates its nest in the rotten heartwood of a dead aspen.

This same dead aspen harbors many wood-boring insects that the sapsucker feasts upon, and by drilling sap wells into the bark of living aspen, which run with the ooze of sweet sap, the bird is treated to a succulent dessert. The open ground cover enables the ground grouse to forage with ease on young sprouts and insects. The insects that fly about the canopy are pursued by the pewee.

The aspens grow, mature, and die; their fallen comrades litter the forest floor. These logs are important to the breeding biology of the Ruffed Grouse. The male grouse uses the largest logs in defined locations as drumming logs. He will perch atop the log and rapidly beat his wings against his chest. This produces a low-pitched drum roll that carries well through the forest. He does this both to attract females and to define his territorial boundaries to other males in the area.

Aspen stands tend to have multiple layers in their canopies. The lower levels are

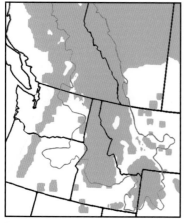

Range of aspen

made up of shrubs and saplings that find spots of sunlight in which to grow. Many songbirds that are associated with riparian and montane shrublands will build their nests in this layer of aspen. The taller aspens form an upper canopy, which is the preferred location for the Western Wood-Pewee. This small flycatcher will hunt for flying insects from an exposed perch. After it has flown out and caught an insect with its bill, the wood-pewee will return to its perch just to start hunting again.

Of the birds found in the aspen stand, the Red-naped Sapsucker lives the most tightly associated with the aspen. The Red-naped Sapsucker is a woodpecker that has evolved an interesting

habit of harvesting the sap of aspen. The sap is rather sweet and packed with calories. The sapsucker drills wells into the bark of the aspen from which the sap will flow. These wells will be in lines along the trunk of an otherwise healthy aspen. The sapsucker will visit these wells and lap up the tasty treat. These wells also attract other birds, particularly hummingbirds, and insects that crave the sweet sap as well.

Red-naped Sapsuckers also take the insect portion of their diet from the aspen. They excavate wood-boring insects from softer, rotten wood and glean crawling insects from the bark's surface.

The Red-naped Sapsucker not only uses the aspen stand as a food source, it also builds its nest in the aspen snags that are located within the older portions of the stand. The aspen even plays a role in the breeding biology of the sapsucker. When the breeding season approaches, the sapsucker will begin to drum on an aspen.

Aspen stands have been able to survive and thrive in the Northern Rockies. One of the largest organisms on Earth, it deceives the eye as it sends up thousands of stems that seem like individual trees.

Foraging Ruffed Grouse

Description: Blending in perfectly with its habitat, the Ruffed Grouse (17") survives by camouflage. The overall coloration is mottled, camouflage brown. The tail when fanned shows a black terminal band. This terminal band is usually broken in the females. The head has a small crest. The black feathers on the neck are usually concealed, except during courtship.

Feeding: The diet of the Ruffed Grouse seems to change with each season to take advantage of the situation. During the spring, fresh shoots and buds are consumed. Insects are taken during the heat of the summer. With autumn approaching, berries and other fruits become important. During the winter, the bird switches back to the tree buds. Most of their foraging takes place on the ground; however, they will ascend into the trees as well.

Habits: They, like many other grouse species, are rather tame. The female will even aggressively charge a potential threat to her brood.

Nest: From the top of a downed log, the male drums during courtship. This drumming is produced by stronge wingbeats against his chest. The female lines a ground depression with leaves, grass, and conifer needles. She incubates the 9-12 cream to ivory eggs for 23-25 days. The chicks are able to feed themselves soon after hatching. The female leads them to food sources and protects them from predators until they become independent in several weeks.

Voice: Near the nest, the sharp *"chee chee"* is heard.

Primary Habitat Characteristics: The Ruffed Grouse prefers aspen stands that have nearby or adjacent conifer forest for cover.

Other Habitats: It also inhabits other deciduous and mixed deciduous-conifer forests. It avoids pure conifer forest.

Conservation: Our most common and widespread grouse species.

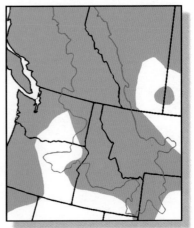

B

Description: Looking at the bark of an aspen, if you see rows of sap wells drilled into it, you know you are in the habitat of the Red-naped Sapsucker (8¹/₂"). The upperparts are black with a white rump patch. The black wings have an extensive white patch as well. The head is striped black and white with a bright red forehead. The males have an entirely red throat and females have a variable red throat and a white chin. There is a black bib below the red throat patch. The underparts are washed yellow.

Male (l) & fenale (r) Red-naped Sapsucker

Feeding: Eats many different insects that are bark-gleaned. This feeding behavior is consistent with other woodpeckers. The most visible feeding behavior of this species is the creation of the rows of wells that they drill into aspen, birch, or coniferous trees. They lap the sap, which is carbohydrate rich, from these oozing wounds.

Habits: The Red-naped Sapsucker will hybridize with Yellow-bellied and Red-breasted Sapsuckers where their ranges overlap.

Nest: Both males and females drum during courtship. The nest site is an excavated cavity in a dead, sometimes rotten tree. This cavity is lined with wood chips. Both sexes incubate the 4-6 white eggs for 12-13 days. They continue to feed the nestlings for 35 days. Nestlings fledge after 25-29 days.

Voice and Drumming: The series of *"cherr"* is a common call. The drumming pattern is a short burst following by off-timed taps.

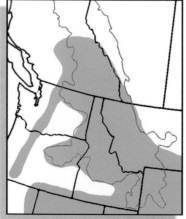

Primary Habitat Characteristics: The Red-naped Sapsucker favors aspen stands that have some amount of standing dead tree with heart-rot for nesting.

Other Habitats: They also live in other deciduous and mixed deciduous-conifer stands.

Conservation: It is very common in aspen stands in the Northern Rockies. It was once considered the same species as the Yellow-bellied Sapsucker.

Western Wood-Pewee

J F M A M J J A S O N D

Contopus sordidulus

B

Adult Western Wood-pewee

Description: During summer days, the Western Wood-Pewee (6¹/₄") perches atop a deciduous tree or shrub, and hawks for flying insects. The upperparts are grayish-olive. The head is peaked. The dark wings have 2 wingbars. The throat is white and the rest of the underparts are light gray. The bill is dark with the upper mandible being black. There is normally some orange at the base of the lower mandible.

Feeding: Insects, insects, and more insects are the diet of the Western Wood-Pewee. Waiting on an exposed perch, the bird will burst into flight and snatch the insect from the air. It will then return to its perch. This species also hover-gleans insects from the foliage.

Habits: It gives the dawn song that is a rapid version of the regular song. The Western Wood-Pewee is often seen perched on a bare branch that extends above the leaved branches of the crown.

Nest: The males will chase the females during courtship. The female constructs an open cup of grass and plant fibers lined with moss, lichens, and leaves. The nest is placed on a branch away from the trunk. She incubates the 3 reddish-brown-blotched pale yellow eggs for 12-13 days. Both adults feed the young in the nest and they fledge after 14-18 days.

Voice: The song is a *"twsee-tee-breet"* and the call is buzzy *"peeer"*.

Primary Habitat Characteristics: The Western Wood-Pewee favors open stands of aspen.

Other Habitats: It also lives in deciduous riparian habitats and cottonwood bottom forests. The Western Wood-Pewee can be seen on montane shrublands, both in the foothills area and within coniferous forests.

Conservation: The Western Wood-Pewee is very abundant.

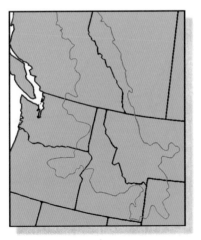

Whitebark Pine Forest

*I saw today a Bird of the woodpecker kind which fed
on Pine burs its bill and tale white the wings black
every other part of a light brown, and about the size of a robin.*
—WILLIAM CLARK OF THE CORPS OF DISCOVERY DESCRIBING THE
CLARK'S NUTCRACKER FOR THE FIRST TIME

They stand twisted and gnarled, shaped by the unrelenting wind and cold of the higher altitudes. In these extreme conditions they are able to produce a bounty of fatty seeds that are so important to a host of creatures that live here. Each tree is a testament to the ability of life to survive and thrive in variety of conditions and locations. From one tree to another, small flocks of noisy gray birds, Clark's Nutcrackers, feed greedily in the seeds of the pines. They stuff the excess seeds into specialized pouches in the mouth. These seeds are then transported to cache sites on west and south-facing slopes. Some of these seeds are not consumed, and they germinated into a whitebark pine seedling. This is the relation-ship between the whitebark pine and Clark's Nutcracker has existed for thousands of years. It is an ancient arrangement between an ancient-looking bird and the ancient trees of the treeline.

Growing in the harsh subalpine and alpine reaches of the Northern Rockies, the whitebark pine can be counted as one of the hardiest plant species in the Northern Rockies region. It is very cold tolerant, and usually it is found alone, without competition. They are long-lived with ages of 500 years or more not uncommon.

The whitebark pine looks very much similar to the limber pine of lower elevations. The three-sided needles grow in bundles of 5. The bark is light gray and becomes cracked as the tree ages and matures. The cones of the whitebark pine are small and oblong.

At the lower reaches of their range, whitebark pines can be found in stands along with subalpine fir, Engelmann spruce, and lodgepole pine. The trees in these stands

have wide trunks and full, broad crowns. In the highest whitebark pine stands, they found in isolated "islands" of trees that are shaped and twisted by crushing snow-packs and brutal winds. This growth form is known as Krummholz.

There are two forms of Krummholz. Erect trees that reach only heights of 6-12 feet characterize flagged krummholz. At these heights, the tops of these trees will protrude above the winter snowpack. Therefore, they are subjected to battering abrading winds that shape the trees. The branches of these trees grow only on the leeward side of the stem, and the windward side is often polished by the wind and ice. The portion of the tree that remains below the snowpack grows in a thick cushion fashion. As the stand matures, most of the low cushion-type growth survives, while relatively few of the stems that remain above the snowpack survive. This condition creates a stand that is generally low in structure with a few prominent flag-shaped stems scattered within.

Cushion krummholz occurs when conditions are so severe that no stems that pro-trude above the snowpack survive, and only the thick cushion growth lives to matu-rity. Cushion krummholz occurs only on the coldest and windiest reaches of the mountains in the Northern Rockies.

Much like the spruce-fir forests, the whitebark pine forest's isolation has kept it from the ravages of logging and other human disturbances. Fires are infrequent due to the moist soil conditions and climate of the treeline.

With such harsh conditions, why would birds and mammals ever be found in whitebark pine forest? One thing draws these creatures in, whitebark pine seeds. The seeds of the whitebark pine are high in fat content, and, thereby, an important food source. Clark's Nut-crackers and red squirrels are the chief harvest-ers of the whitebark pine cones. The nutcrackers pry the seeds out of the cones and place them in caches. The squirrels build large "middens", which are basically large caches of cones. These caches are important to both grizzly and black bears, which raid them in the fall for the valuable whitebark pine seeds. They are an im-portant calorie-rich food that pack on the pounds needed for the long winter's slumber.

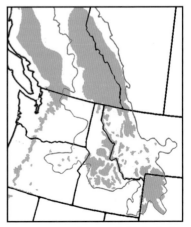

Range of whitebark pine

Unfortunately, whitebark pine has been declining drastically over the past several decades. Their numbers have been reduced as much as 60% or more in several areas of the Northern Rockies. In fact, it is functionally extinct in up to one-third of its former range. The primary reason for these declines is a fungus, the pine blister rust. Blister rust was imported to the New World in the 20th century. It kills many trees, which severely reduces the ability of the forest to produce adequate cone crops needed for stand regeneration. Two lesser culprits are the mountain pine beetle and dwarf mistletoe.

Other than Clark's Nutcracker, many other species make forays in the whitebark pine forest to feed on the seeds. Steller's Jays, Common Ravens, Hairy Woodpeckers, Mountain Chickadees, Cassin's Finches, Red-breasted Nuthatches, Red Crossbills, and Pine Grosbeaks are all known to feed on whitebark pine seeds, although they are not nearly as dependent on them as the Clark's Nutcracker.

Even if only one bird is so strongly associated with the whitebark pine forest, it is important to other creatures as a food source. Instead of merely surviving at the extremes of treeline, the whitebark pine thrives in that climate.

Clark's Nutcracker   *Nucifraga columbiana*

J F M A M J J A S O N D

R

Description: Calling loudly as it flies overhead, the Clark's Nutcracker (12") has evolved a mutually beneficial relationship with the whitebark pine. The bird is generally gray with black wings that have white patches. The tail has black central feathers and white outer tail feathers. The bill is long and black. It flies with deep, slow wingbeats.

The pine nut storing Clark's Nutcracker

Feeding: Like most *Corvids,* Clark's Nutcrackers are omnivores that forage both on the ground and in the trees. They will eat seeds, berries, insects, birds' eggs, nestlings, and carrion. Their favorite food, however, is the nuts of whitebark pine. They collect these nuts by breaking open the cones. These nuts are very rich in protein and fat. The pine nuts are stored in a specialized sublingual pouch and transported to a cache. They will have hundreds of caches (up to 33,000 seeds total) and remember their positions during the winter. They can become nuisances at campgrounds.

Habits: When cone crops fail, this species will irrupt eastward and southward.

Nest: Males will follow the female for long distances at the start of courtship, which begins in the late winter. Both sexes build a nest of small sticks lined with grass, bark fibers, and conifer needles. The nest is placed in a tree 9-150 feet above the ground. Both adults incubate the 2-3 brown- and gray-spotted green eggs for 16-18 days. The nestlings fledge after 18-21 of parental care at the nest.

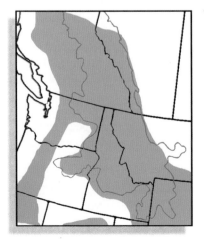

Voice: The voice of the Clark's Nutcracker is a harsh *"kraaa"*.

Primary Habitat Characteristics: The open structured whitebark pine forest is favored.

Other Habitats: It will also be found in other conifer forests and juniper-limber pine shrublands. During the summer, it is not uncommon to find it at or above treeline.

Conservation: A common bird in the Northern Rockies, the outbreak of blister rust in whitebark pine may be of some concern.

Symbiosis

Most of us think of interactions between two organisms as the typical predator-prey scenario. Every night on the Discovery Channel, we see a predator chasing down and dispatching some hapless victim. One organism benefiting at the misfortune of another. However, not all interactions between life forms necessarily result in the demise of one of the participants. Some interactions are to the benefit of one and have no ill effects to the other, or both partners gain an advantage from the other. These kinds of interactions are known as mutualisms.

Mutualisms are relationships in which both partners are living in close association called symbiotic. The classic examples of symbiotic mutualism are lichens. Lichens are those multicolored crusts on many of the rocks you see. Lichens are not a single organism, but rather a partnership between algae and fungi. Both the fungus and algae are benefiting from the presence of the other. The fungus structure offers protection to the algae from damaging sunrays and drying out. The alga leaks important metabolic products, which are used by the fungus.

Another example of a co-evolved symbiotic mutualism is between plants, their roots to be more specific, and nitrogen-fixing fungi known as mycorrhizae. The fungi infect the plant roots from the surrounding soil. The mycorrhizae then extend through the soil from the plant roots, where they aid in decomposition of the organic matter in the soil. As the fungi go about their business, they draw nitrogen and phosphorus into the root tissues, thus benefiting the plant. These sub-terrainian plant-fungi relationships are indispensable in nutrient-poor soils such as many of those found in the Northern Rockies.

A whole other class of mutualistic relations is known as facultative mutualisms. They are diffuse relationships involving entire groups of species rather than specific individuals. These facultative mutualisms result in activities such as seed dispersal and plant pollination.

An example of facultative mutualism, which results in seed dispersal, is the relationship between the Clark's Nutcracker and whitebark pine. The Clark's Nutcracker is unmistakable with its ghostly gray body contrasted by black wings and tail. The white outer tail feathers flash like plane beacons in flight. If you were to draw a cartoon combining a crow with a woodpecker, you would have the Clark's Nutcracker. It is a member of the family *Corvidae*, which includes jays, crows, and ravens. In the past, though, it has been considered to belong to many different families. It was first discovered by Western science during the Lewis and Clark Expedition. Clark described it as "some form of woodpecker." This bird of integrated traits has been called Clark's woodpecker, camp robber, Clark's crow, woodpecker crow, meat bird, and meat hawk at different times and places.

Clark's Nutcrackers generally live in high mountain whitebark pine forests, often near the treeline. They seem to prefer forests that are open or, at least, patchy with frequent openings. They seem to prefer these high elevation habitats. Clark's Nutcrackers can be found in a variety of forested habitats. Considered permanent residents, they move throughout the environment. These complex and variable movements may be due to failure of cone crops in the mountains.

Regardless of its physical traits, the Clark's Nutcracker exhibits a range of behaviors that are unique. Its feeding behaviors and food selections are highly specialized and varied. Much of the diet is pine seeds and the remainder is composed of nuts, berries, insects, eggs and young of other birds, and in the winter carrion. The problem with liv-

ing on pine seeds is that the seeds are tucked away in the protective cone. How to get the fatty seeds? In comes the nutcracker's bill and head. The bird will pluck some of the scales off the cone and hold it steady on the ground or limb with its foot. The bill is then smashed into the cone repeatedly until the seeds are accessible. There are modifications to the bones of the jaw that allow the bill and head to go undamaged during the pounding. Some of the seeds are consumed immediately, and the rest are stored. In late summer and fall, the nutcracker will begin to store its seeds in caches located on exposed slopes. As many as 90 extracted seeds are placed in a special throat pouch and then flown to the caches. On the open slope, the bird buries the seeds in the soil. A single Clark's Nutcracker may cache upwards of 30,000 seeds each year, and there may be

as many as 1,000 separate caches. In the winter, they will use these food stores to see them through the season of poverty. How in the world does a bird remember the exact position of these caches? The Clark's Nutcracker, like many of its family, is incredibly intelligent.

This creature, however, does not solely rely on its food stores. The varied diet is obtained through a variety of specialized feeding techniques. They forage in the trees and on the ground. The Clark's Nutcracker does an adequate imitation of a flycatcher, snatching insects out of midair in flight. Occasionally, this *Corvid* becomes a woodpecker using its specialized jaw structure and bill to pound and probe dead wood for insects. It will peck scrapes off the bones of winterkills like its cousin the Common Raven.

Most of us know the gray ghost from picnics and camping trips. As we finish our meals and start to wash the dishes, the gray ghost swoops in behind us to clear the area of any scrapes that were left behind. Some of them will eye the sandwich in your hand and make attack dives on your chips. There is a gray ghost in the woods, and he is able to survive through intelligence and flexibility of habits. Whitebark and the closely related limber pine produce seeds that are large and wingless. Only animals can transport these seeds. The nutrious seeds are eaten and hoarded by chipmunks, grizzly bears, and by Steller's Jays and Clark's Nutcrackers. Only the nutcracker possesses the behavior appropriate to disperse the seed constantly and far enough away from the parent tree. The Clark's Nutcracker caches them deep enough in the soil to greatly reduce the problem of rodents finding and consuming the caches. A single Clark's Nutcracker can cache as many as 33,000 seeds in a single year. The bird will inevitably fail to retrieve a certain percentage. The unused seeds that survive have established seedlings. Although the cost is extremely high, whitebark pine is virtually dependent on the bird for its seed dispersal.

Not only has the Clark's Nutcracker evolved to take advantage of the whitebark pine, the tree has evolved to use the bird. The whitebark pine has evolved several cone and seed characteristics that maximizes the Clark's Nutcracker efficiency in dispersing the seeds. The cones that breakaway scales and seed-retaining cores. The seeds are wingless which causes them to more available to the nutcracker.

The next example of facultative mutualism is pollination. The goal of pollination is to carry genetic information from one plant to another, and that is accomplished through a variety of methods. Some plants simply use the wind. This method only works well when the plant grows in large homogeneous stands, such as grasses and pine trees. However, wind dispersal is unreliable when plants occur in scattered populations and locations. This is where these plants have only the animals to disperse their pollen. A good example of animal-dependent pollination is between many of the tubular flowers and hummingbirds. The hummingbirds do not visit the flower with the thought of aiding in pollination. They come because they receive a food reward, nectar, at each flower. As the hummingbird plunges its long bill into the tubular flower, its face is brushing against the stamens of the flower. From this contact, pollen adheres to the feathers and bill of the hummingbird. As the bird visits a subsequent flower, the pollen on the bill and face rub against the pistils of that flower. The hummingbird will visit many hundreds of flowers each day, always picking up and dropping off pollen.

Another unique relationship that is very indirectly mutualistic has been observed between the American badger and the coyote. Both live to hunt and consume ground squirrels, the snack food of the animal kingdom. As both hunt for the ground squirrels, they may actually benefit one another. The badger rips through the burrows, ground squirrels flush above ground. Here, the coyote may capture a few individuals and push the remainder back into the burrows, into the waiting jaws of the badger. Both the coyote and badger use the other's presence to their own gain.

So, the next time you observe two animals interacting with one another, ask yourself whether it is a Discovery Channel relationship, or one that is beneficial to both. A gray ghost glides silently through the tangle of forest and across the canyon to the open south-facing slope. As it alights on a juniper, a number of its own kind appear out of the mist. Raucous greetings grate over the winter-shrouded box canyon. They comb the hillside, probing the ground with black sabers. The gray ghost is none other than the Clark's Nutcracker.

Meadows

Crossing a meadow in the morning, the dew soaks through boots and pants as it makes its way to the skin. The grass stands knee high. Underfoot, water seeps up from the saturated soil. I've come to this meadow in Glacier National Park to find one of the most difficult to locate sparrows in the Northern Rockies, the Le Conte's Sparrow. This well camou-flaged passerine is very difficult to see. Its song is the only giveaway of its presence in the meadow. I follow the high-pitched buzzy *"tika-zzzz-tzt"* to one spot, only to hear it coming from another. This game of cat and mouse with the Le Conte's Sparrow goes on through the morning, and I never lay eyes upon my quarry. This meadow is thick with sedge and other water-loving plants as the water table is just inches below the ground's surface. Turning to leave the meadow with the waterlogged sound of soaked shoes, I hear the Le Conte's song one last time as the sun warms my shoulders and back.

Meadows can be formed in a number of ways: an ancient glacier that has melted in a basin, soils that drain poorly next to bodies of water, or well drained soils that receive heavy seasonal moisture. They can also be created when an event such as a forest fire clears a suitable patch of forest in which the meadow will grow. No matter how they are created, a meadow can be described as either wet and dry.

Dry meadows resemble small pockets of grassland. The suite of birds found within these meadows can be rather similar to that of nearby expanses of grassland. These dry meadows are commonly located on ridges, south-facing slopes, or within the ma-trix of a ponderosa pine savanna. The dry meadows tend to flush with wildflowers in the spring as snow melts. They usually have well-drained soils, so they become dry quickly. When summer reaches its peak, the dry meadow is filled with tinder-dry grasses and forbs. These climatic extremes generally prohibit trees and shrubs from gaining footholds in the dry meadow, although a few hardy trees may take hold where microclimate allows, such as a shallow gully that hold water longer.

The subtlest wetland can be the wet meadow. Wet meadows retain their water throughout the year, while dry meadows become devoid of water in the summer. The sedge, rushes, grasses, and shrubs that grow in meadows are tolerant of soggy and low oxygen soils. They form a thick mat of vegetation that provide cover for vast numbers of meadow voles, deer mice, and northern pocket gophers. These rodents, in turn, attract raptors, such as Red-tailed Hawk and Northern Harrier, and mammal carnivores like the red fox. Deer and elk forage on the abundance of grasses and sedges that thrive in a meadow.

Another wetland/meadow is the sphagnum bog, created when an impeded stream or stagnant pool of water allows the growth of sphagnum moss. This moss has incredible ability to act as its own water reservoir, holding tremendous amounts of water. The surface of a bog may look dry, but as you attempt to walk across, the water will squish up and your feet slip below the surface. In the Northern Rockies, most sphagnum bogs are isolated high in the mountains. One curious resident is the northern bog lemming, a colonial vole-like rodent that thrives on the bog's sedges and grasses. They are remnants of the last Ice Age. Naturally creatures of the colder latitudes, northern bog lemmings were pushed southward by the glaciers. Once the glaciers receded, several pockets of Northern Bog Lemmings were left on isolated alpine sphagnum bogs. They are still there today.

What would be the strangest owl that one can imagine? How about one that is diurnal and the size of a songbird. Sounds a tad farfetched, but there is such an owl in the Northern Rockies. The Northern Pygmy-Owl is small, only seven inches in length. This diminutive stature hides the fact that the Northern Pygmy-Owl is a voracious predator that captures and kills a wide range of prey, including birds larger than itself. It hunts mainly during the day by staying on a perch and waiting for prey to make itself available. The little owl swoops off the perch and captures its victim with the sharp talons of its small feet.

So, how does one find such a small elusive creature? The Northern Pygmy-Owl's prey will help you find it. When chickadees discover that there is a Northern Pygmy-Owl in their midst, they begin to harass the owl, all the while calling with much passion. The little songbirds are relentless as they generally pester the owl until it becomes so frustrated that it leaves the chickadees' territory.

From the small end of the owl size scale to one of the largest owls, the Great Gray Owl, meadows have it all. The Great Gray is truly impressive with its camouflaging plumage that obscures it within the timber. There is nothing quite as impressive as watching this giant owl cruise silently over a meadow as it scans below for rodent prey. The Great Gray's hearing is unbelievable. This bird has the auditory ability to hear a rodent moving underneath the blanket of snow. Upon locating its prey, the Great Gray Owl will plunge talons-first into snow, grasping the rodent in a deadly embrace.

Meadows have always been magical places for people. One feels a certain kind of relief as you leave the thick, dark forest and arrive in the light and space of the meadow. I am sure the birds of the meadow feel the same way.

Great Gray Owl

Strix nebulosa

J F M A M J J A S O N D

R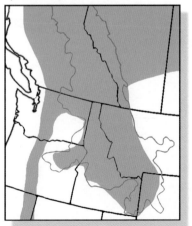

Gray ghost, the Great Gray Owl

© Milo Burcham

Description: A gray ghost that flies silently through the forest and over the meadow, the Great Gray Owl (24-33") is the largest owl in North America. The back is grayish-brown with dark mottling. The large head does not have ear tufts. The facial disc is light gray with dark gray concentric circles. The borders of the facials are dark becoming white at the edges. Both the eyes and bill are yellow, although the eyes are much brighter. The underparts are light gray with dark brown streaking.

Feeding: Small rodents are up to 90% of the Great Gray's diet. The rest of the diet is rabbits, weasels, and birds. It hunts at night from a perch and swoops down on prey. Its hearing is so acute that it can locate prey under the snow, and it will plunge in to capture its victim.

Habits: Quite tame and allows close approach. When the Great Gray Owl is perched, it remains perfectly still and sits near the trunk.

Nest: While it does not build its own nest, the Great Gray Owl uses an abandoned raptor or Common Raven nest, or the hollow of a broken top snag. The female incubates the 3-5 white eggs for 28-36 days. The male feeds her during the incubation period. The young fledge before 55 days; however, they remain close to the nest, and the adults continue their care for an additional 4-8 weeks.

Voice: The song is a slow-paced series of evenly spaced hoots, *"whoo whoo"*.

Primary Habitat Characteristics: Great Gray Owls prefer an edge where dense coniferous forest meets open meadow. Nesting seems to be concentrated around meadows at 6,000-7,000 feet.

Other Habitats: They will roost within dense coniferous forests. These areas provide them with thermal cover.

Conservation: With low population densities, the Great Gray Owl can be affected by habitat alteration.

Northern Pygmy-Owl

Glaucidium gnoma

J F M A M J J A S O N D

R

Description: Most often seen during the day, the Northern Pygmy-Owl (7") is the region's only small owl that is predomiantly diurnal. The upperparts are grayish-brown. Its unique features are the two large "eye spots" in the nape of the neck. The head lacks ear tufts and is spotted. The eyes are lemon yellow and the bill is very drab yellow. The tail is long and dark brown. The underparts are somewhat lighter than the back.

The diurnal Northern Pygmy-Owl

Feeding: The Northern Pygmy-Owl is an aggressive daylight hunter that chases, captures, and consumes small mammals, birds, and insects. It will sometimes take reptiles and amphibians. This owl swoops out of a tree onto its intended prey.

Habits: The Northern Pygmy-Owl is diurnal and quite tame. It can be located by following the harassing call of chickadees, which routinely mob these owls. The Northern Pygmy-Owl remains on its breeding territory throughout the year.

Nest: The male feeds his mate during courtship. The nest site is a cavity, either natural or an old woodpecker hole, 8-25 feet above the ground. The female incubates the 4-6 white eggs for 4 weeks. Both adults feed the nestlings, which take their first flights in about 4 weeks. The young remain with their parents for another 20-30 days after fledging.

Voice: The Northern Pygmy-Owl gives a repeated, clear *"too"* as a call.

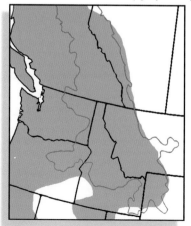

Primary Habitat Characteristics: The Northern Pygmy-Owl favors the edges where forest meets with meadow.

Other Habitats: It can be found in the forest surrounding a meadow, recent burn, or some other opening. The Northern Pygmy-Owl avoids unbroken, dense forest.

Conservation: Always very common, and increasing due to nesting success associated with boxes. This species may split due to DNA differences with the Southwest birds.

Broad-tailed Hummingbird   *Selaphorus platycercus*

J F M A M J J A S O N D

B

Description: The least seen of the hummingbirds in the Northern Rockies, the Broad-tailed Humming-bird (4") loves to feed on the flowers of the meadow. The male is bright green above. The underparts are white, save for the tan washed flanks. His gorget is a solid bright red. The female is also green above and white below. However, her flanks and sides are washed with a rufous shade. The long bill is straight.

Female Broad-tailed Hummingbird

© Chris Gamel

Feeding: Like other hummers, the Broad-tailed Hummingbirds are consumers of mostly nectar from a variety of flowers. They feed while hovering in an open meadow. They will also eat insects, which are taken using gleaning and flycatching tactics. They will visit the sap wells created by sapsuckers.

Habits: This species is quite noisy and more often heard than seen. Very docile and usually dominated by other hummingbird species.

Nest: The male does a dive display for the female. He ascends 35-75 feet and then dives. The trill sound is produced at the bottom of the U-shaped dive. The nest is a tiny cup of plant fibers and hair bounded together by spider silk. The nest is placed at the bottom of the canopy. The female incubates the 2 white eggs for 14-19 days. She alone feeds the nestlings, which leave the nest after 21-26 days.

Voice: The male's wings produce what has been called a "silvery trill". *"Tschip"* is the commonly heard call of the Broad-tailed Hummingbird.

Primary Habitat Characteristics: Meadows with an abundance of nectar-producing flowers are great for feeding.

Other Habitats: Aspen stands, riparian thickets, the edges of coniferous forests, and some montane shrublands are other habitats where this species will live.

Conservation: Very common in the appropriate habitat.

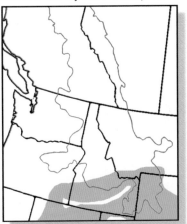

Description: Inconspicuous and retiring, the Le Conte's Sparrow (5") is found in the wetter meadows. The crown is dark with a white central stripe. The eyebrow is orange. The ear patch is gray. The upper breast and flanks are buff with dark streaking. The upperparts are streaked (reddish streaks on the nape and straw streaks on the back).

© Tom Ulrich

Meadow-dwelling Le Conte's Sparrow

Feeding: It is thought to be chiefly a consumer of insects during its time in the Northern Rockies. It feeds on the ground, often obscured from view by dense grass cover. These invertebrates tend to be those found on the ground or in the grass. They will also consume some seeds of grass and forbs.

Habits: When threatened, the Le Conte's Sparrow runs through the grass in lieu of flying. This species sings both day and night.

Nest: The male displays to the female by singing while he raises his wings. Attached to grass stems several inches above the ground, the nest is constructed by the female. It is a cup of grass and sedges lined with grass. It is interwoven into the surrounding grass stalks. She incubates the 3-5 heavily brown-spotted white eggs for 12-13 days. Both parents probably feed the nestlings.

Voice: The song of this bird is a high-pitched buzzy *"tika-zzzz-tzt"*.

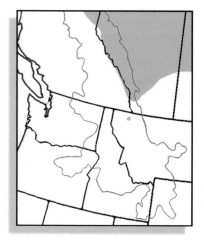

Primary Habitat Characteristics: It favors meadows that are wet and may even have some standing water and are dominated by sedges and water-tolerant grasses.

Other Habitats: The Le Conte's Sparrow will also live at the edges of wetlands. It has been reported in alfalfa fields.

Conservation: Although it remains elusive, the Le Conte's Sparrow can be fairly common in its habitat. It is being watched closely due to fluctuations caused by the droughts, which affect its wet meadow habitat.

Alpine

Truly it may be said that the outside of a
mountain is good for the inside of a man.

−GEORGE WHERRY

The alpine tundra of the North Rockies is the coldest, most inhospitable habitat in the region. Winter comes in September or early October, and it hangs in until June or July. The temperatures drop to -50 or more degrees below zero. The snow pack can be come thick and dense as the snow accumulates through the winter. The summers are brief and cool. There is scant favorable growing weather for the hardy plants that cling to existence here above the treeline.

Very few birds live in the harsh realms of the alpine tundra. Most of these species like the American Pipit and White-crowned Sparrow actually leave the lofty heights before winter's crushing onslaught. Only the White-tailed Ptarmigan stays in this habitat during the winter, although even it will move somewhat lower on the mountain. This tough little grouse spends the winter plucking up willow and alder buds and leaves that remain above the snow.

In the Northern Rockies, there is one group of birds that visits the alpine reaches during the late summer and early fall. Raptors use the favorable winds and updrafts for their southward migration. To visit these birds and view this spectacular display, one has to be willing to exert considerable energy.

Through sweat-stung eyes, I assess the final staircase of stone that leads to the spine of the Bridger Mountains. After nearly an hour and a half of slugging twenty pounds of camera gear, binoculars, and myself up the switch-backing cat track carved along the face of Bridger Bowl, I have almost reached a vantage point for

this spectacle like no other in the West.

Every fall the Bridger Range is the corridor for the largest known migration of Golden Eagles in North America. They ride uplifting thermals and favorable southbound winds during their autumn sojourn to warmer climes. Along with the Golden Eagles, a whole host of other western birds of prey cruise southward along the craggy peaks. Swainson's Hawks bound for the pampas of South America, Rough-legged Hawks that came from the arctic to settle for the winter in our valley.

Young White-crowned Sparrow

Picking my way through the rocky obstacles of the ridge, I reach an observation platform where two people have already set up for a day of hawk-watching. Their binoculars are scanning the distant ridges for the familiar silhouettes of flying raptors with their outstretched wings catching invisible currents of solar-heated air. They offer me some water, "No thanks, got my own," and some caramel popcorn; I did not want to impose. When I take the backpack off, a breeze against my sweaty back causes an instant chill. As I unload my camera and tripod, the altitude-intensified sun pushes down on me, and young White-crowned Sparrows forage among the rocks. The two hawk-watchers introduce themselves as Ryan and Tracy of HawkWatch.

Clark's Nutcrackers alight on some gnarled, stunted trees about thirty yards down the slope from us. Their eyes dart back and forth across the sky; I guess they are Hawk-watchers also, but for an entirely different reason. With a raucous crescendo of cries, the birds flush from their perches. In the midst of this blur of flight is a lone Steller's Jay, standing out like a sapphire set in gray metal. For a long while the only sound is the ever-present wind whistling across the knife-edge of the ridge.

Pika, a common resident of the alpine habitat

"Golden eagle," Ryan calls out.
"Where?" asks Tracy.
"Over forested ridge number five," he replies.

Our binoculars swing across to the horizon, scanning for the eagle's form. She — I assumed the eagle was a female for no other reason than my own intuition — comes quickly out of the

One of disappearing glaciers of Glacier National Park

north along the west side of the ridge. Silently she cruises below us, and it is interesting sight to see an eagle from above. Passing the platform, she tips a wing like a fighter pilot, seeming to acknowledge our presence. As soon she passes, the eagle fades into the distance and out of mind.

Ryan settles onto his unrolled pad and Tracy leans back into her chair, the usual routine for them, while I pace nervously back and forth along the spine anxiously waiting for the next raptor to come down the ridge in front of the advancing winter. Tracy tells me that sometimes they see up to forty birds per hour and other times they are lucky if they see only one, solitary bird in sixty minutes. This unpredictability, however frustrating, is the very reason why hawk-watching is so addictive — each bird an unexpected treat sent from the north.

Our continued vigil yields a lone Cooper's Hawk, which is similar to the closely related Sharp-shinned Hawk. We scrutinize the shape of the tail (rounded corners suggest a Cooper's) and look for a strongly contrasting crown compared with the back. The rest of morning yields only a few eagles and hawks, including a Sharp-shinned Hawk. With my time fading, there are always other obligations, I pack my gear and shoulder the load. Ryan and Tracy say good-bye and I begin the trudge down off the ridge.

The alpine spines of the Northern Rockies are difficult to access, and hard hiking is usually the price of admission of the lofty reaches. However, the effort is worth it. The sight of an American Pipit or a clutch of White-tailed Ptarmigan chicks is the reward for the adventurous birder.

White-tailed Ptarmigan

Lagopus leucurus

J F M A M J J A S O N D

R

Description: The master of camouflage that inhabits the barren heights of the Northern Rockies, the White-tailed Ptarmigan (13") wears many coats through the year. During the fall and spring, this grouse is mostly white mottled brown patches on the head and back. The summer male has white underparts and mottled brown above. The female is mottled brown above and barred below. The winter plumage is entirely white with a red eye-comb. All plumages have fully feathered legs and the black bills.

Feeding: White-tailed Ptarmigans use their bills to deftly pick buds and leaves off of vegetation while walking along. They focus on willows for foraging, with birch, alder and other shrubs being secondary to the diet. They feed in small flocks.

© Milo Burcham

Winter plumaged White-tailed Ptarmigan

Habits: The heavily feathered feet may actually act like snowshoes allowing this bird walk on top of the snow. The White-tailed Ptarmigan forms feeding flocks during the winter.

Nest: The males put on quite a show during courtship, strutting in front of the females with spread tails and raised eye-combs. The female lines a shallow depression with various materials. She incubates the 4-8 brown-spotted buff eggs for 22-24 days. The male leaves her soon after the nestlings have hatched. She continues to care for the young as they grow. They fledge at 10-12 weeks.

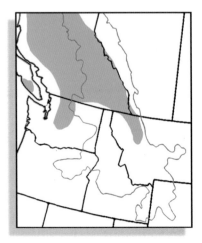

Voice: This species gives a variety of chicken-like clucks and a low-pitched, soft hooting.

Primary Habitat Characteristics: The only year-long resident of the alpine areas. They tend to key on areas with willows, which are a favored food source.

Other Habitats: During the winter, the White-tailed Ptarmigan will descend into whitebark pine and taller willows/alders.

Conservation: Living high above humans, this species has avoided most disturbances.

331

American Pipit

J F M A M J J A S O N D

Anthus rubescens

B

Breeding American Pipit

Description: Often seen flying high while singing, the American Pipit (6¹/₂") is filled with joy. With a drab plumage, it is gray-brown above and light below with fine streaking. The breast and belly are washed with buff. The cheeks are dark and there is a buff eyebrow. The legs are black or dark brown. In flight, notice the white outer tail feathers.

Feeding: As picks it way along the ground, it gleans many insects (beetles, larvae of various species, moths, and bugs). They will occasionally consume the seeds of grass and forbs.

Habits: Bobs its tail while it feeds. The American Pipit is usually seen in pairs or small flocks.

Nest: The singing flight of the male American Pipit is characterized by the bird launching from the ground to heights of 100 feet and then parachuting down with open wings. He sings throughout this flight. The female constructs a cup of grass and other plants lined with grass, feathers, and hair under a clump of grass or an overhanging ledge. She incubates the 4-6 brown-spotted grayish eggs for 13-15 days. The male feeds her during the incubation period. The nestlings are fed by both adults. They leave the nest at 2 weeks. The young will remain in a family group with their parents until migration.

Voice: The song of American Pipit is a repeating series of *"chwee,chwee"*. The flight call is the ringing *"pi-pit"*.

Primary Habitat Characteristics: This species has a propensity toward areas of low growth such as dwarf willow and grass. Its alpine habitat usually has many such features. Southern exposures are preferred for nesting as they become snow-free early

Other Habitats: During migration, the American Pipit regularly shows up on agricultural fields, grasslands, and mudflats.

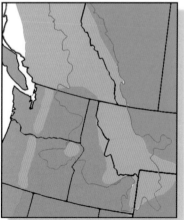

Conservation: It is very common in its habitat.

White-crowned Sparrow

J F M A M J J A S O N D

Zonotrichia lecophrys

B

Description: Perched on top of a wind-stunted whitebark pine, the White-crowned Sparrow (7") is the songster of the alpine tundra. The upperparts are mottled brown and gray. The head is patterned by bold white and stripes. The nape is light gray, and the throat is whitish. The rest of the underparts are unmarked light gray. The bill is pink-orange.

Nesting White-crowned Sparrow

Feeding: As they hop along the ground and between the boulders, White-crowned Sparrows consume mostly seeds. During the summer, they supplement their diet with a variety of insects. They will visit seed feeders during the winter.

Habits: This sparrow forms small winter foraging-flocks (10-20 individuals) that slowly roam throughout the lean months. It migrates at night.

Nest: During courtship, the male sings from exposed perches. The female builds a nest of grass, stems, twigs, and bark fibers lined with grass, feathers and fur (especially mountain goat). She places the nest at the base of the small shrub or clump of grass. The female incubates the 4-5 chestnut-spotted pale blue to greenish-blue eggs for 11-14 days. She is joined by the male in feeding duties after the nestlings have hatched. The young fledge after 7-12 days, and they remain with their parent, particularly the male, for some time.

Voice: The song is a series of whistled notes followed by a trill. The call is an abrupt, high-pitched *"pink"*.

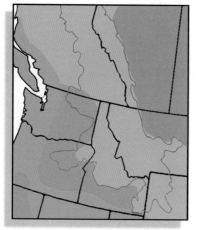

Primary Habitat Characteristics: The White-crowned Sparrow favors areas where low shrub patches meet alpine tundra.

Other Habitats: It also inhabits some montane shrublands, particularly those at higher elevations. During the migration, it will turn up in almost every type of habitat.

Conservation: This species is common in the Northern Rockies. Its winter survivability has increased with use of seed feeders.

Gray-crowned Rosy-Finch

Leucisticte tephrocotis

J F M A M J J A S O N D

R/W

The Gray-crowned Rosy-Finch winters in the valleys

© Tom Ulrich

Description: Spending the summers high above the treeline, the Gray-crowned Rosy-Finch (5³/₄") is seen in the valleys during the winter. The male is mostly streaked brown above. The rear half of the crown is light gray. The underparts are a rosy red. The female is brown overall with a gray hindcrown. The bill is yellow during the winter, and it changes to black with the spring.

Feeding: The diet of the Gray-crowned Rosy-Finch is primarily seeds. It forages in flocks that literally cover the ground. It will eat buds, insects, and vegetative parts during the brief alpine summer.

Habits: The population balance is skewed toward the males. The Gray-crowned Rosy-Finch forms huge winter foraging-flocks that can number in the thousands. They will come to seed feeders.

Nest: The female constructs a nest of grass, lichens, and moss lined with grass, feathers, and hair. This nest is placed between two boulders or under an overhanging rock. She incubates the 4-5 white eggs for 12-14 days. Both adults feed the young while they are in the nest. The nestlings remain in the nest for 14-18 days.

Voice: The harsh *"chew-chew-chew-chew"* song descends. The call is a high-pitched *"chip"*.

Primary Habitat Characteristics: Gray-crowned Rosy-Finches seem perfectly at home on rocky alpine tundra where snowfields may persist through the summer.

Other Habitats: During the winter, they descend onto the open valleys, grasslands, and urban areas. Many a seed feeder is blessed with their presence during the harsh winter.

Conservation: Populations are apparently stable due, in part, to the inaccessibility of their alpine habitat and their ability to use agricultural fields during the winter.

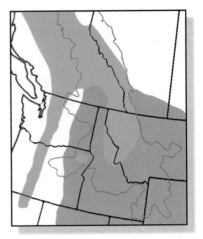

Black Rosy-Finch
Leucosticte atrata

J F M A M J J A S O N D

© Tom Ulrich

Description: Living high among the barren peaks and spires of ranges like the Beartooths and Wind River, the Black Rosy-Finch (6") is among the hardiest of songbirds. The male is blackish brown overall. The nape is light gray. The wings and rump are the namesake rosy color. The female is very subdued with dark brown as the principal coloration. She has very little gray on the nape.

Feeding: The diet of Black Rosy-Finches is primarily seeds. They forage in flocks that cover the ground. They will eat buds, insects, and vegetative parts during the brief alpine summer. They pick out dead insects that are entombed in snowbanks. The young are fed insects. With the onset of winter, the diet of the Black Rosy-Finch becomes almost entirely made up of seeds.

Habits: This species has habits similar to those of the Gray-crowned Rosy-Finch. They form large winter feeding-flocks. Males outnumber females.

Nest: The female constructs a nest of grass, lichens, and moss lined with grass, feathers, and hair. This nest is placed between two boulders or under an overhanging rock. She incubates the 4-5 white eggs for 12-14 days. Both adults feed the young while they are in the nest. The nestlings remain in the nest for 20 days.

Voice: The harsh song is very similar to that of the Gray-crowned Rosy-Finch, *"chew-chew-chew-chew"*. The call is the same sharp *"chip"*.

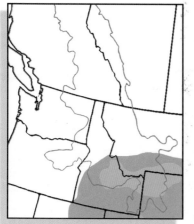

Primary Habitat Characteristics: This rugged species is found on the most inhospitable rocky peaks and permanent snowfields. During the breeding season, it is normally from 9,000 and 11,000 feet above sea level.

Other Habitats: Like the Gray-crowned Rosy-Finch, it comes into lower valleys and towns during the winter months.

Conservation: It is uncommon. With its entire breeding population isolated in such a small geographic area, it warrants close monitoring.

Cliffs and Rock Fields

Looking up the seemingly endless stretch of solid stone, I see a small black streak cross the sky into the path of the sun. Soon several other flying Black Swifts join it. These small birds have been described as "cigars with wings", and this description is perfectly apt. Besides being one of the fastest flyers in the Northern Rockies, the Black Swift also has one of the most unusual natural histories of any bird in the region. As these birds fly about the cliff, the noise from the waterfall is deafening. The water cascades from 200 feet above and crashes with a steady roar. Studying the Black Swifts closely, it seems as if they are crashing into the waterfall. The Black Swifts are nesting right alongside the waterfall; in fact, some of the nests are located behind a veil of misty white water. These little birds are able to build their nests on the saturated ledges. The nest is a saucer of mud and moss, and the parents produce a single offspring each year.

Why nest on a cliff face? It seems that the danger of an egg falling into oblivion would be too much for the birds to take the risk. What does the cliff or rock field offer the nesting bird? The cliff affords the nest a measure of protection from would-be predators. Most mammal and reptile predators can access nests placed high on cliffs. As for the avian egg predators, the parents fend them off. In general, nesting on a ledge is safer than nesting in a tree or on the ground.

Of the birds that are typically associated with cliffs, the Peregrine Falcon is the most impressive, to my mind. The highly efficient hunter of other birds can reach speeds approaching 200 miles per hour in a steep dive. The fleeing bird is hit from above as the hallux digs into the body. The bird dies quickly, often hitting the earth already dead. The sight of a hunting Peregrine had always been uncommon, but by the 1960's it was almost unheard of in the West.

The Peregrine Falcon was one of the most widely spread raptors in North America. As commercial insecticides became introduced into the environment, the numbers of Peregrines crashed. The population west of the Mississippi had been cut by as much as 90% by the end of the 1960's. The known population had dropped to 39 pairs of breeding Peregrine Falcons. The federal government, state governments, and non-profit organizations began a

Counts of Peregrine Falcon on Breeding Bird Survey routes in the Northern Rockies.

massive recovery effort. They bred Peregrines in captivity and release the resulting young at strategic hack sites in remote locations across the continent. The population began to gradually increase, and in 1999, the Peregrine Falcon was formally removed from the Endangered Species list.

Did you ever think that people create cliffs? Our buildings are to some cliff-nesting species perfect nesting habitat. Cliff Swallows are likely to be encountered as they nest under the eaves of buildings. Their mud flasks cling to where eave meet outer wall. Peregrine Falcons have also adapted to the urban cliffs. The ledges of the tallest buildings are very well suited to the nests of this falcon, and there is a plentiful food supply for these predators in the city. The urban Peregrine Falcon can feast upon the introduced, city-loving Rock Dove or Pigeon.

The cliffs and rock fields of the Northern Rockies provide a home to a unique suite of birds that uses Earth's vertical features to their advantage. Cliffs provide protection from predators and long views of approaching danger.

Peregrine Falcon

J F M A M J J A S O N D

Falco peregrinus

B/R

Description: Cruising at high speeds, the Peregrine Falcon (17-21") is the embodiment of all that is wild and free. The cap and nape are black, and the cap extends down below to the eye to form "sideburns". As with many of the *Falco* species, the Peregrine Falcon has variable plumage, and these variations can be grouped along subspecies lines.

The ultimate hunter — the Peregrine Falcon

Feeding: This falcon begins most of its hunts from patrolling high above. When it spots potential avian prey, it folds its wings in and plummets in a spectacular dive. Once on the prey, it rips the hallux talon into the back of unfortunate bird. Smaller birds are grabbed midair, and larger ones allowed to tumble earthward and consumed on the ground. It will eat a few small mammals and, on very rare occasions, carrion.

Habits: Among the fastest birds in the world, the Peregrine Falcon's dives can reach speeds up to 200 miles per hour. Falconers have used it for centuries.

Nest: Males court females by circling them and engaging in high dives and chases. The nest is placed on the protected edge of a cliff. No materials are added to the nest. The 3-4 heavily brown-marked cream eggs are simply laid in the scrape on the ledge. The male feeds the female for the 29-35 days while she incubates their clutch. Both parents take great care the young until they fledge at 35-42 days.

Voice: The voice is a harsh, rapid series of *"ki ki ki ki"*.

Primary Habitat Characteristics: Peregrine Falcons are normally found in great expanses of open country with cliffs for nesting nearby. These cliffs are commonly located near water.

Other Habitats: They can be found hunting for waterfowl and shorebirds over lakes and marshes.

Conservation: The use of DDT had utterly decimated the Peregrine Falcon. Following the ban of that pesticide and a massive recovery effort, it is once again ruling the sky.

339

The Chukar thrives in rocky areas

© Tom Ulrich

Description: A southern Asian import, the Chukar (14") is a common gamebird in the appropriate habitat. It is generally variable grayish brown above. A black stripe goes through the eye and continues to outline the off-white throat. The bill and legs are rather dark red. The gray breast abruptly abuts the buff underbelly. The flanks are heavily barred. The sexes are very similar, although the males have small leg spurs.

Feeding: The Chukar is mainly a consumer of seeds and other vegetative matter. Many of its preferred plants are, like the Chukar, transplants from the Old World. These species include Russian thistle and cheatgrass. It eats many insects during the summer. While feeding, the members of the covey will give a muted *"chuka"* call to maintain group cohesion.

Habits: They gather in 20-40 member coveys during the autumn.

Nest: During courtship, both will give mock mutual feeding displays. Underneath an overhang or shrub, the nest placed in a ground scrape. The depression is lined with feathers, twigs, and grass. The female incubates the 9-16 brown-spotted pale yellow eggs for 22-24 days. Upon hatching, the young will leave the nest, and are usually cared for by the female. The young find most of their food by themselves, and they are fully independent in about 2 months.

Voice: It gives a call that is very much like its name, *"chuck chuck"* in a rapid series.

Primary Habitat Characteristics: South-facing rock outcrops and cliffs are important during the winter. It is here where snow can melt more quickly.

Other Habitats: Patchy grasslands interspersed with sagebrush.

Conservation: Introduced from Asia, the Chukar is doing well in arid, rocky habitats across the West.

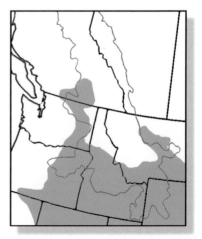

Description: Sickle-winged acrobatic missiles, the Black Swift (7¼") descends out of the mountains each dawn and dusk to feed on flying insects. The Black Swift is the largest and most nondescript swift in Northern Rockies. It is generally black overall with lighter wing primaries. The tail is somewhat forked.

The Black Swift nests near waterfalls

© Tom Ulrich

Feeding: With its mouth held agape, the Black Swift snaps up a plethora of flying insects, including bees, caddis flies, flying ants. It will forage very high in the air and never lands during foraging bouts.

Habits: This species flies higher than the other swift species. It is the only swift associated with waterfalls.

Nest: After a courtship that includes aerial chases of the female by the male and the pair copulating in flight, both sexes select a most unusual nest site. Black Swifts nest in small colonies of a few pairs. The nest is placed on a protected ledge or crevice, which is most often behind or beside a waterfall. The nest is a saucer of mud, moss, scraped algae, and other nearby plant material. They lay but one white egg that is incubated for 24-27 days. They feed the single offspring for 45-50 days, when the young Black Swift makes its first leap from its cliff home.

Voice: The Black Swift is generally silent, both in flight and at the nest.

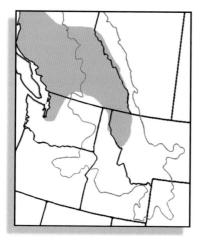

Primary Habitat Characteristics: Strongly associated with cliffs that have waterfalls and seeps. These cliffs are damp and dark.

Other Habitats: It feeds over an incredible variety of habitats that are within flying distance of nesting and roosting sites.

Conservation: Its association with cliffs that have waterfalls has probably served to keep the Black Swift localized and generally uncommon. Often seen in the company of Vaux's Swifts while feeding. Rock climbers must take considerable care not to disturb this incredible bird.

341

White-throated Swift

Aeronautes saxatalis

J F M A M J J A S O N D

B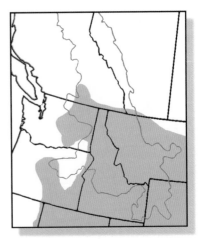

The fast flying White-throated Swift

© Tom Ulrich

Description: During the warmest summer nights, this swift can be seen foraging overhead. By far the most common of the Northern Rocky Mountain swifts, the White-throated Swift (6½") is a fast flyer in its aerial sorties overhead. Blessed with a tuxedo-like appearance, it has black upperparts and a white throat, which extends into a white belly stripe. Along the flanks there are large white patches. The long, thin wings are dark with lighter gray wing primaries. The tail is deeply forked. Wingbeats are rapid and stiff.

Feeding: The White-throated Swift is quite adept at snaring flying insects out of midair as it zooms back and forth over a feeding area. Unlike the Black Swift, it will forage low over lakes, streams, and treetops.

Habits: Its fast flight allows the White-throated Swift to forage many miles from nesting and roosting sites. It is not an uncommon sight it over lakes on the valley floor. This species stops flying only to nest and occasionally roost. When roosting, the birds can be in groups of up to 200 individuals.

Nest: The White-throated Swift nests in small colonies of up to 12 pairs. A saucer of feathers and plant fibers is placed in the crack of a high cliff. The nest is held together with a White-throated Swift's adhesive saliva. This fluid also holds the nest in place. The female lays 4 white eggs.

Voice: The call is descending, shrill *"skee"*.

Primary Habitat Characteristics: The White-throated Swift requires cliffs that have vertical cracks and crevices.

Other Habitats: It forages over an amazing variety of habitats including lakes, streams, forests, and grasslands.

Conservation: The most common of the swifts present in the Rockies, the White-throated Swift has declined in BBS surveys.

Description: Approaching a Cliff Swallow nesting colony often results in hundreds of Cliff Swallows (5¹/₂") exploding from their nests to swarm around the intruder. The crown is black with a white forehead patch. The throat is reddish-brown. The rest of the underparts are white. The back is generally dark with variable white streaking and a buff rump patch that is seen in flight. The tail is short and squared off at the end.

Cliff Swallows nesting under an eave

Feeding: Feeds heavily upon flying insects, which are captured and consumed in flight. The Cliff Swallow generally forages in large feeding flocks that may include other swallow species.

Habits: The Cliff Swallow has developed the habit of using building eaves as nesting sites, so the bird has become quite common around dwellings, where they dive-bomb the inhabitants.

Nest: The nesting colonies of the Cliff Swallow usually have synchronized breeding. The nest is the overhang of a cliff or eave of a building where the pairs construct flask-shaped nests out of mud pellets. The interior of the nest may be lightly lined with grass and feathers. Both parents incubate the 4-5 brown- and gray-spotted white eggs for 14-16 days. They continue their care of the young for about 3 weeks, at which time they take their first flight.

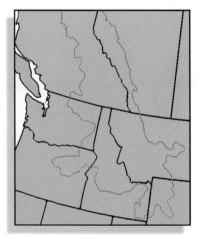

Voice: When disturbed, the Cliff Swallow emits a nasal *"nyew"* call.

Primary Habitat Characteristics: Cliffs with overhangs are important to nesting success. These cliffs are near open water.

Other Habitats: Occasionally seen foraging over agricultural fields, and it has been observed nesting in gravel pits.

Conservation: Use of building eaves as nest sites has led to an increase of Cliff Swallow populations over historical norms.

Rock Wren

The rock-hopping Rock Wren

Description: Bouncing among the talus and boulders, the Rock Wren (5¹/₂") is extremely active in its pursuit of prey. The palest of the Rocky Mountain wrens, the Rock Wren is dull brown above with fine small spots. The breast and belly are pale gray. In flight, take notice of the cinnamon rump patch and buffy corners on the tail. The bill is slender and long, perfect for probing into cracks and crevices.

Feeding: Hopping about the rock field, the Rock Wren eats many species of insects and other small invertebrates. Its long, decurved bill comes in handy when probing in cracks and fissures.

Habits: The Rock Wren bobs up and down when it is alarmed. It will sometimes construct a "sidewalk" of small rocks in front of the nest.

Nest: The male Rock Wren sings in order to claim a nesting territory. Both sexes build a cup of grass and forbs in the crevice between two rocks or some other protected place. The nest is lined with fur and other fine material. They have the unusual habit of placing small rocks at the "walkway" to the nest. The female alone incubates the 4-8 brown-spotted white eggs for at least a couple of weeks. After hatching, the male takes on half of the parental duties.

Voice: The song of the Rock Wren is a 3 to 6 time repeated *"tarlee"*. The male can acumulate a library of varied songs, up to 100 or so. It will give a variety of trilled calls.

Primary Habitat Characteristics: Rock Wrens prefer rocky areas that have crevices or other nooks and crannies for nesting. These rocky habitats are normally found in arid and semi-arid areas, and they can be found quite some distance from water.

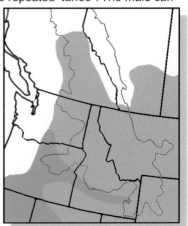

Other Habitats: Rock Wrens will occasionally be found in agricultural areas.

Conservation: Very common and stable.

344

R

Description: The lovely song of the Canyon Wren (5³/₄") is heard more than the bird is seen in the Northern Rockies. The back is brown with small white and black spots. The tail is finely barred. The crown of the head is a dark gray. The throat is paper white and the belly is rich reddish brown. The black bill is very long and slightly decurved. The body is slightly laterally compressed, which aids in slipping between rocks.

© Donald Jones

Canyon Wren with a millipede

Feeding: Using its long, curved bill to pick and probe into cracks and crevices between rocks, the Canyon Wren is an enthusiastic consumer of a variety of ground-bound insects such as crickets and ants. It is often seen alone hopping from one crevice to another.

Habits: Very secretive among the steep rock faces that are home. Canyon Wrens pump their rears up and down.

Nest: The rich song of the Canyon Wren is used to establish the nesting territory. In a crevice, both sexes build a cup of moss, grass, and other plant materials that is lined with fur, feathers, grass, and other fine fibers, and placed on a base of twigs. The female incubates the 5 red-spotted white eggs for 12-18 days. Both parents feed the nestlings until they fledge at 2 weeks. The juveniles remain near their parents for a short while after fledging.

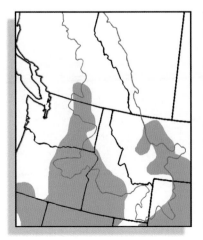

Voice: The song of the Canyon Wren is a luxurious series of silvery whistles that are slurred.

Primary Habitat Characteristics: The Canyon Wren is found in steep rocky areas with plenty of crevices and other features, often near water.

Other Habitats: During the winter, the Canyon Wren may use stream riparian thickets as foraging habitat.

Conservation: Although elusive, the Canyon Wren is apparently common, and numbers may be declining slighty.

345

Forest Generalists

*My ample opportunities of fully observing these interesting birds
in captivity as well as in a state of freedom, and indeed all that
I have seen of them. Their magnificent bearing; their objection to carrion,
and strictly carnivorous tastes would make me rank these winged
tigers among the most pronounced and savage of the birds of prey.*
—ERNEST T. SETON ON THE GREAT HORNED OWL

Jacks-of-all-trades. Creatures that can adjust and adapt to a variety of situations. The generalists make full use of the entire ecosystem. They can be used in almost every habitat. This is a small group of ultimate survivors; the Great Horned Owl, Dark-eyed Junco, and American Robin.

All three of these species remain residents in the Northern Rockies during the winter, although the American Robin will be present in very low numbers and the Dark-eyed Junco can nearly be considered irruptive during the winter.

This group thrives by doing a multitude of things well, not by specializing so that they do one thing excellently. The physical characteristics of these birds allow them to be generalist in behavior and habitat preference.

Among the Forest Generalists, the Dark-eyed Junco shows the most visible variation. The plumage of this sparrow is quite different from one region of the Northern Rockies to the next.

The Dark-eyed Junco of the northwestern Montana, the northern half of Idaho, Washington, Oregon, and the Rockies of Canada is known as the Oregon Dark-eyed Junco. The males are chestnut-brown above with a characteristic dark hood that covers the head and descends down as bib on the chest. The females are somewhat duller with grayer hood. This Dark-eyed Junco tends towards open coniferous forests.

In central and southwestern Montana, northwestern Wyoming, and eastern Idaho, the Dark-eyed Junco is of the Pink-sided form. The Pink-sided Dark-eyed Junco has a gray hood and breast, and along the flanks there is a wash of pinkish brown. The Pink-sided Dark-eyed Junco is a bird of the edges of the forests, whether these are coniferous or deciduous.

During the winter, this race will commonly descend upon feeders in towns and rural areas.

During the winter, the Slate-colored Dark-eyed Junco can be found throughout the Northern Rockies, especially during irruptive years when they are pushed southward by harsh weather. They tend to be restricted to dense stands of pine, especially lodgepole pine.

Each race or subspecies, depending on your view those matters, of Dark-eyed Junco has evolved to its local environs. This results in generalists across the species' entire range.

Of the owls in the Northern Rockies, the Great Horned Owl is the fiercest. This bird will usurp the nests of other raptors, including hawks and eagles, for itself. It is such a generalist that it is not picky about what it hunts and eats. The Great Horned Owl will hunt and kill skunks. Imagine how you would feel with a face full of that stink. It has been known to eat even fish and almost every other medium-sized to small vertebrate in the Northern Rockies.

The American Robin can be found everywhere. They can be found nesting on the upper reaches of the treeline to the middle of large metropolitan areas in yards and parks. In fact, it takes quite a bit of effort to rid yourself of the company of the robin during the summer. Although it is thought of as the bringer of spring, this thrush is present, albeit in low numbers, throughout the Northern Rockies during the long, cold winter.

What a strategy to be a generalist! It is the path of having the best of all worlds. I think that we as humans have special kinship with this suite of species for, you see, we are generalists as well. Doing a lot of things, not specializing in any one area of expertise.

Great Horned Owl

Bubo virginianus

J F M A M J J A S O N D

R

Description: Throughout the Northern Rocky Mountains, the very large Great Horned Owl (22") is the owl we think of when we dream of the dreary night. The ear tufts or "horns" of this owl are its most visible feature. It is the only large species of owl to have ear tufts. The facial disc is outlined with black. The eyes are lemon yellow and the throat is white.

Feeding: An indiscriminate hunter of all sorts of animal prey; however, small mammals tend to make up the bulk of the diet. Great Horned Owls are known to eat other birds, reptiles, amphibians, invertebrates, and fish. The Great Horned Owl is one of the few predators that will kill and consume skunks on a regular basis. It normally hunts at night and it swoops down from its perch to capture its prey with the massive talons.

The fierce Great Horned Owl

Habits: Very aggressive, the Great Horned Owl will generally dominate all other birds of prey in its territory. *Corvids* and chickadees will actively harass and mob this owl; follow these sounds and you might meet it up close. There is documented siblicide among nest mates.

Nest: Great Horned Owls begin to nest in the late winter. They will typically take over the nest of another large bird such a Red-tailed Hawk or Common Raven. They add very little new material to these nests. The female incubates the 2-3 white eggs for four to five weeks. After hatching both parents care for the nestlings. The young begin to "branch" in 5 weeks and they fully fledge in about 9 weeks.

Voice: Heard in every horror film, the resonant *"hoo-a-hoo, hoo-hoo"* of the Great Horned Owl familiar to almost everyone in the West.

Primary Habitat Characteristics: The Great Horned Owl is found in or above every habitat that exists in the Northern Rockies. They are miraculous adapters, and both their food and habitat preferences (or lack thereof) accurately represent this.

Conservation: One of the most common and widespread birds in the West.

349

The ubiquitous American Robin

Description: Commonly thought of as a bringer of springtime weather, the American Robin (10") is seen in about every habitat in the Northern Rockies. Slate gray above, this bird is more known for its bright red breast and upper belly. The lower belly is white. The eye is surrounded by a bold, broken eye-ring. The bill is a pale yellow. Females are somewhat more drab than males.

Feeding: For many of us our first image of a bird is the American Robin hopping around the yard in pursuit of earthworms. However, the majority of the diet is composed of insects and other invertebrates. This prey is taken while running about and seeming to look down at the ground with one eye by tilting the head. In the colder months, berries and fruits become an all-important portion of the diet.

Habits: Very adaptable, the American Robin has been able take advantage of habitat created by humans. In the autumn and winter, it gathers in large feeding flocks.

Nest: The male American Robin uses its song to establish and defend a nesting territory. On a horizontal branch, the female builds a thick-walled cup of grass and sticks held together with mud. The nest is then lined with grass. The female incubates the 4 "robin's-egg" blue eggs for two weeks. Both sexes care for and feed the young. The nestlings fledge in two weeks after hatching. The American Robin may brood twice if environmental conditions allow.

Voice: The familiar song of the American Robin is a series of resonant whistles that sound like *"cheeryup"*.

Primary Habitat Characteristics: It has adapted to almost every habitat that provides trees for nesting and water. These include urban areas, all forests, riparian areas, cottonwood bottom forest, and many types of grassland.

Conservation: The American Robin is among the most abundant bird species in the Rockies. It is ubiquitous, to say the least.

Dark-eyed Junco

Junco hyemalis

J F M A M J J A S O N D

R

Description: From the understory of a conifer, small flocks of Dark-eyed Juncos (6¼") roam throughout the woods. They are commonly encountered when hiking as they flush from their concealed nests beside the trail. They are variable in plumage, and the birds of the Northern Rockies generally fall into two groups; Pink-sided and Oregon. The Pink-sided variety is dull brown above. The breast is gray as well. There is a pinkish wash along the flanks. The Oregon type has an all-dark head and a rusty-brown back. The female Oregon Dark-eyed Junco is somewhat paler than the male. The underparts of both types are white, as are the outer tail feathers. Juveniles are generally streaked brown above and whitish below.

Pink-sided Dark-eyed Junco

Feeding: With the warmth of spring and summer, the Dark-eyed Junco consumes a great deal of insect matter in addition to the seeds and grains that make up the bulk of total food intake. It feeds mostly on the ground, where they hop their way around the understory.

Habits: They form large flocks containing up to 30 individuals in the winter, which visit feeders when the chance arrives.

Nest: The nest of the Dark-eyed Junco is well hidden within a tussock of grass, under a log, or in a small cavity in the ground. It is a cup of fine grass that is constructed by the female. She incubates the 3-5 variable colored eggs for 12-13 days. Once they hatch, both parents feed the young for 10-13 days. Dark-eyed Juncos will commonly double brood.

Voice: The song of Dark-eyed Junco is a trill that is similar to that of the Chipping Sparrow, although it is more melodic in the junco. The call note, *"dit"*, is common among the flocks.

Primary Habitat Characteristics: The Dark-eyed Junco prefers conifer or mixed forest that is not dense.

Other Habitats: It will occur in towns in winter.

Conservation: Very common.

> *The care of the Earth is our most ancient and most worthy,*
> *and after all our most pleasing responsibility. To cherish*
> *what remains of it and to foster its renewal is our only hope.*
> — *WENDELL BERRY*

The lone cowboy on the range is emblematic of the popular Western mythology. It is the scene burned into the association of the West in the minds of many people across the country.

Agriculture came to the Northern Rockies relatively late in terms of overall human history, spreading considerably in the latter decades of the 19th century when the Europeans began to arrive in substantial numbers. They brought with them a collection of land-use practices that had their origins in the distant past of the Old World. When the railroads snaked their way through the West, agricultural was not far behind.

The European settlers had first came to the Northern Rockies were trappers, and these folks were soon followed by the cattle rancher. The cattlemen use the expanse of grassland to their livestock's benefits. In order to make room for the cattle, bison had to be removed from the landscape. Cattle are, unlike the native bison, sedentary in nature. This has caused many problems with damage to riparian areas and increased Brown-headed Cowbird parasitism of songbirds.

The next wave of agriculture came in the form of farming. The European farmers brought with them a host of crops native to Eurasia. These include wheat, barley, rye, and oats. They also increased the production of corn and other crops native to North America. These farmers also brought foreign livestock with them. Pigs and chickens were spread across the West.

The farmer transformed the landscape from a varied and robust assemblage of plants and animals into vast monoculture plots that came to dominate the grasslands of the West. Most high-intensity farming has occurred on grasslands where the soil is the most fertile. These soils are high in organic matter and nutrients such as nitrogen and phosphorus, as compared to those of the forests.

Along with the introduction of non-native crops, agricultural also brought in a variety of unintentional weeds. Among the most troublesome of these weeds are the spotted knapweed and leafy spurge.

Spotted knapweed is a native plant of Eurasia that has choked out many native plants across the West. This weed was first documented in British Columbia in 1883. The rate at which the spotted knapweed has spread is unbelievable, from 20 counties in the Northwest in 1960 to 326 counties in the West including every county in Washington, Idaho, Montana, and Wyoming. This weed reduces the amount of forage for ungulates and it disrupts native grasslands.

Western Kingbird taking advantage of a utility pole

The spotted knapweed crowds out other plants by a process called allopathy, which means that this poisons the soil around itself so that native plants cannot take hold. The spread of spotted knapweed has been aided by transportation, which rapidly spreads the seeds from one disturbed site to another.

Leafy spurge is another Eurasian import that has spread across the North American continent. It has been estimated that it infested nearly 3 million acres in 29 states. Much like the spotted knapweed, the leafy spurge crowds out native vegetation and disrupts native habitats.

Another type of intruder also can be associated with the spread of agricultural, the non-native bird. A couple of introduced species, the Ringed-neck Pheasant and Gray Partridge, were brought to the New World from Eurasia. They were and are game birds for the hunter. These birds had adapted to the agricultural lands of the Old World, and they maintained this relationship as they spread in the Northern Rockies. These two birds also use native grasslands to a lesser extent. Three other imports, the Rock Dove,

House Sparrow, and European Starling, are normally associated with the urban areas of the Northern Rockies, but they make use of the agricultural areas. They mainly thrive on the waste grains of the fields and storage buildings of farms.

Some native birds have also adapted well to the farms and ranches of the Northern Rockies. The American Crow and Brown-headed Cowbird use farms and ranches as areas in which to forage. The crow finds a wide range of food items on the ranch and farm, while the Brown-headed Cowbird uses the sluggish movements of cattle to scare up insects. The Barn Owl uses farm buildings for nesting and the fields for nighttime foraging.

Male Ringed-necked Pheasant

Description: A gamebird introduced from Asia in the 1850's, the male Ring-necked Pheasant (33") is a brilliant splash of color in the fall. He is beautiful bronze mottled with green, black, and brown overall. The head is purplish-green with inflamed red wattles around the eyes and ear plumes. Below the head, the neck is ringed with white. The elegant tail is very long. As the male has evolved for sex appeal, the female (21") is designed for hiding. She is a mute and mottled brown overall. Her tail is shorter.

Feeding: The Ring-necked Pheasant is quite omnivorous in feeding habits. It will consume many seeds, grains, shoots, nuts, insects, snails, slugs, and worms. As it feeds on the ground, it will use its feet to scratch at the soil to reveal food.

Habits: Males are very territorial, especially in the spring, and they may mate with multiple females within their territory.

Nest: The male proclaims his territory by giving his crowing call from an elevated perch. In a shallow ground depression, the female constructs a nest of grass, stems, and leaves. She lays as many as 15 eggs, although the norm is 10-12 olive-brown eggs. She incubates the eggs for 23-25 days. Upon hatching, the young are very percocious, feeding themselves while mother acts as a protector. They become fully independent in approximately 3 months.

Voice: The male gives a crowing *"skwacock"*, which is a territorial defense.

Primary Habitat Characteristics: Close water is a good attribute of suitable Ring-necked Pheasant habitat. Pheasants can be especially plentiful in stubblefields.

Other Habitats: They can found in the shelterbelts of many farms and old homesteads. Marsh edges are favored when adjacent.

Conservation: Management as gamebirds has led to local increases in numbers.

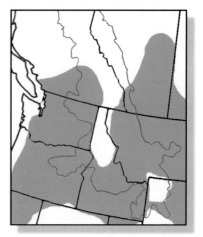

Gray Partridge

Perdix perdix

J F M A M J J A S O N D

R

Description: A gamebird introduced from Asia by bird hunters in the 19th century, the Gray Partridge (13") is normally seen in flocks or pairs. The overall plumage is mottled gray. The face and throat are chestnut. The flanks are heavily barred with brown. The underparts are gray, except for the male's brown belly patch. The tail feathers are chestnut. Its overall plumage conceals it well.

Feeding: As it walks along, the Gray Partridge uses its specialized bill to pick up different kinds of seeds, including those of grass and forbs. During the summer, they eat a small amount of insects.

Habits: Forms wintering coveys of 10-20 birds during the fall. These coveys roost together during the night in tight huddles. They remain hidden until one approaches closely, then they burst into a rapid flight.

Nest: During courtship, the male Gray Partridge will show the female his dark brown belly. The female scrapes a shallow depression that is lined with grass and leaves. She incubates a large clutch of 9-20 olive to brown eggs for 21-26 days. Both parents tend to the young, which leave the nest very soon after hatching. The young fledge in 13-15 days. They will remain with their parents until fall, and some-times they even join the same wintering covey as the adults.

Voice: The male gives a *"kee-ahk"*, which may attract a female.

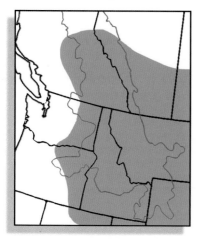

Primary Habitat Characteristics: This Asian import prefers fields that have shelterbelts or some trees nearby.

Other Habitats: It will also live in grasslands that have short vegetative structure.

Conservation: Managed as gamebirds over its entire range, although it seems to be declining somewhat. It can one of the most abundant birds on many ranches and farms in the Northern Rockies.

Barn Owl

Tyto alba

J F M A M J J A S O N D

R

Heart-shaped face of the Barn Owl

Description: When entering an old barn the harsh hissing of the Barn Owl (16") is startling, to say the least. This owl is slim with long legs. The back is reddish-brown with lighter spots. The underside is light (ranging in color from white to pinkish) and is very lightly spotted with black. The facial disc is heart-shaped and pure white. The dark eyes stand out against the face.

Feeding: Hunting at night, the Barn Owl swoops down from a low patrolling flight to capture a variety of small mammals; including mice, voles, shrews, young rabbits, and gophers. It will also hunt reptiles, amphibians, and other bird species. It will occasionally adopt a swooping attack from a perch.

Habits: The hearing of the Barn Owl may be the most highly developed of the region's owls. Its hearing is so accurate that it can pinpoint and capture small rodents in complete darkness.

Nest: The male engages in display flights for the female, in which he claps his wings loudly. They do not place a true nest. They tend to place the 3-8 white eggs in a variety of concealed locations such caves, rafters, and under bridges. The female incubates her clutch for 30-34 days. Once the eggs hatch, the male brings food to the female, who in turn feeds the young. She joins her mate in hunting after 2 weeks. The juveniles leave the nest in approximately 60 days. They tend to hang around the nest site several weeks after fledging.

Voice: They give a raspy screeching or hissing. When disturbed they will click their bills.

Primary Habitat Characteristics: They prefer open habitat with adequate rodent numbers, and agricultural lands fit the bill.

Other Habitats: They are also found in grasslands, marshes, and suburban areas.

Conservation: It appears to be stable in its range that includes the far western and southern portions of the Northern Rocky Mountains.

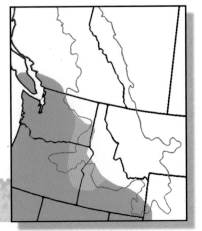

American Crow

Corvus brachyrhynchos

Description: Once shot for mere sport or some perceived infraction, the American Crow (17½") has not only survived but flourished. A large glossy black bird, the American Crow can be separated from the Common Raven by two features; the bill is considerably less robust and the tail is fan-shaped.

Adapted to agriculture

Feeding: The American Crow is not picky about what it eats. It will eat insects, invertebrates, carrion, seeds, berries, small mammals, eggs, and garbage. Mostly feeds while walking about. It occasionally gleans in low trees and shrubs.

Habits: They form large roosting flocks in the evening, especially during the fall and winter. It has adapted to humans, both in urban areas and farms.

Nest: The male's bow-display with fluffed feathers and partially spread wings serves to entice the female. Together they build a nest of sticks, stems, and mud lined with grass, bark, and moss. This nest is placed in a tree 5-70 feet above the ground. The female incubates the 4-6 brown-speckled blue to greenish-blue eggs for 18 days. The feeding of the young falls upon both sexes. The juveniles leave the nest after 4-5 weeks of care. Offspring from the previous year sometime serve as "assistants" when it comes to feeding the young and defended the nesting territory.

Voice: The drawn out *"caw"* of the American Crow is familiar in the fields of the Northern Rockies.

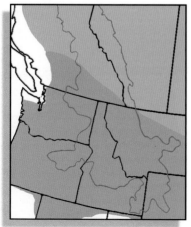

Primary Habitat Characteristics: Nearby trees are required for nesting and the farm/ranch must provide enough food.

Other Habitats: It can be found in many habitats, including urban areas, grasslands, shrublands, and along roadsides that provide bountiful carcasses.

Conservation: As the American Crow comes into our cities and towns, its numbers are increasing. The American Crow is a good example of adaptation to man's activity.

Brown-headed Cowbird — *Molothrus ater*

J F M A M J J A S O N D

B

Female Brown-headed Cowbird

Description: Once only found mostly in the presence of bison herds that roamed across the prairie, the Brown-headed Cowbird (7¹/₂") has spread with the emergence of cattle ranching in the West. The male has a shiny greenish black back and a dark brown head. The underparts are slightly lighter than the upperparts. The female is paler than the male and lacks the brown head. The breast is subtly streaked and the throat is whitish.

Feeding: When the Brown-headed Cowbird is present in the Northern Rockies, it splits its diet between seeds (from forbs and grains from grasses) and insects such as grasshoppers and beetles. They consume slightly more vegetative than animal matter. They feed while walking along the ground. They forage often in the company of large ungulates, which help to scare up insects.

Habits: Very gregarious. When Europeans brought agriculture to the West, the Brown-headed Cowbird benefited greatly as cows replaced bison of the prairie.

Nest: A true nest parasite, the Brown-headed Cowbird builds no nest of its own. The female places 1-7 of her white eggs into the nest of another songbird. She can lay 1 to 3 eggs a day for period of several weeks. These eggs hatch in short order, giving the young a jump-start on its "siblings". The nestling Brown-headed Cowbird grows more quickly than its nest mates and garners a lion's share of the food provided by its adoptive parents.

Voice: Brown-headed Cowbirds give a fluid *"bubblebubblesee"* as a song. *"Ptseeee"* and *"ch-ch-ch"* are two oft-heard calls.

Primary Habitat Characteristics: They use open country during the summer.

Other Habitats: Brown-headed Cowbirds also occur in grasslands, riparian, and shrublands.

Conservation: The population seems stable. Their habit of nest parasitism serves them well.

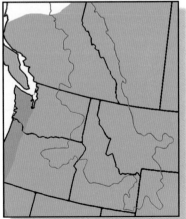

The Trouble with Cowbirds

Imagine a parasite creeping into your home, laying its eggs in your nest, and, then, your taking care its young as your own offspring starve and wither. That is exactly what the Brown-headed Cowbird does to its hosts.

The Brown-headed Cowbird is the most widespread brood parasite in North America. This bird does not build its own nest; instead it lays its eggs in the nests of other birds. It has been documented to parasitize the nests of the 220 species of birds in North America. The species range from small songbirds such as Red-eyed Vireos to at the large end of the scale with the Blue-winged Teal.

The Brown-headed Cowbird was historically restricted to the Great Plains in the heart of North America. Here they followed the vast herds of bison roaming over the prairie. The pounding and shuffling of countless hooves stir up thousands of insects that the Brown-headed Cowbirds feasted upon. The Brown-headed Cowbird's parasitic nesting habits were a result of the bison's nomadic life-style. As the bison roamed, the cowbird had to follow, which limited their ability to maintain their own nest. The habit of nest parasitism is a response. As they followed the herds of bison, the Brown-headed Cowbirds would parasitize very few nests in any given locale before they moved on. The relationship between bison and the Brown-headed Cowbird lasted for thousands of years, only to be broken when Europeans removed the great beasts from the Great Plains and almost from existence. It would have seemed that the Brown-headed Cowbird was left with no means for finding food, but an adequate replacement was soon on the way. Cattle and sheep replaced the bison on the grasslands of the West. The Brown-headed Cowbird population exploded after they switched associations to domesticated livestock. They could now remain in a single location throughout the breeding season. This has resulted in many more songbird nests falling victim to the Brown-headed Cowbird. The species has reached almost to the Arctic Circle and across the entirety of the North America. Wherever there is livestock, the Brown-headed Cowbird is almost assuredly present.

Many songbird species of the Great Plains have evolved along with the Brown-headed Cowbird. They had coping strategies for brood parasitism, such as the ability to identify foreign eggs and eject them from the nest. With their range expansion, the Brown-headed Cowbird came into contact with species that had never evolved the coping strategies of the Great Plains songbirds. These birds have experienced drastic population declines as they raise the Brown-headed Cowbird chicks instead of their own progeny. The Brown-headed Cowbird is not solely responsible for these declines but it is a contributing factor.

Brown-headed Cowbird parasitism can be incredibly high among certain species of songbirds. Erick Greene of the University of Montana has found that upwards of 50% of the Lazuli Bunting nests he studied had been parasitized by the cowbird. However, the nesting success between parasitized nests and those that are not is not dramatically different in this particular species.

Other species have learned to deal with Brown-head Cowbird parasitism. The Yellow Warbler can recognize the Brown-headed Cowbird egg, and though they are not able to eject the egg, they will build a new nest atop the old one. This destroys the cowbird as well their own first brood. Yellow Warbler nests have been documented with up to 7 such nesting layers in response the Brown-headed Cowbird parasitism.

The Brown-headed Cowbird today favors areas where agricultural fields and grasslands meet with open deciduous stands. This edge puts them in contact with foraging opportunities and nesting songbirds. The rates of Brown-headed Cowbird parasitism are higher in areas with greater amounts of edge. They tend to avoid unbroken expanses of conifer forest. Other than these expanses of forest, Brown-headed Cowbird parasitism can occur in almost every habitat type. This species has been able to make full advantage of the human manipulation of the environment.

Brown-headed Cowbirds can lay more eggs than any other bird in the Northern Rockies. A single female can deposit upwards of 40 eggs during the breeding season (May-July). That means as many as 40 nests can be parasitized during a single breeding season.

Warbling Vireo feeding a Brown-headed Cowbird chick

The female Brown-headed Cowbird will wait for the host female to leave the nest, and then she quickly lays her eggs in that nest. Studies have shown that she will 60-70% of the time eject one the host eggs as well. Once the host begins to incubate her clutch, the Brown-headed Cowbird eggs develop much more quickly than the host eggs. The parasitic egg hatches in 11-12 days, much shorter than the average incubation timing of most of the songbirds in the Northern Rockies. Once they are out of their shells, the Brown-headed Cowbird chicks are larger than their nest mates, and they develop more rapidly. The larger cowbird's gaping mouth towers above that of the host's genetic offspring. Birds appear to be hard-wired to feed the tallest mouth, and, therefore, the

Brown-headed Cowbird chick garners the lion's share of the food that is delivered by the host parents. Many of the host's genetic offspring die due to starvation during the nesting period while in the company of the Brown-headed Cowbird.

With many songbird populations declining, the Brown-headed Cowbird has been fingered as the factor in these decreases. How do we deal with a native bird that has become a problem due to our activities? We have to decrease the Brown-headed Cowbird population without harming other birds. Trapping, poisoning, and shooting are all inefficient and costly. The most effective tactic to limit the Brown-headed Cow-bird is to limit the human activities that lead to favorable conditions for the parasite. Within forested habitats, efforts should be taken to limit the size and number of openings people create. These include both industrial and recreational sites.

The parasite has reached the Northern Rockies in great numbers, and the fates of many songbirds hang in the balance. The future could be bleak; however, if we learn to adapt our activities in order to limit the Brown-headed Cowbird, the battle can be won.

Urban

Across the Northern Rockies they are spreading. Stretching their tentacles out into the surrounding countryside, turning what was once farmland or native habitat into suburbia and shopping centers. Urban areas are growing across the West as the population continues to climb upward. The conservation of native habitat to more humane surroundings crowds out many native birds that cannot adapt to the changes. However, several imports and one native bird have made urban areas their most used habitat in the Northern Rockies. Several other native species have adapted to take advantage of urban areas during particular times of the year.

To think of towns and cities as habitat is a leap for many conservationists and birdwatchers. It is important to remember that habitat that appears unusable for one species can be essential to the existence of another species.

The House Sparrow, European Starling, and Rock Dove are all imports coming from the Old World. The European Starling is the embodiment of a bird that adapted very well to the activities of man. The Starling is native to Eurasia, where it thrives in and around the dwellings of humans. It came to North America when someone decided to bring a little of their European home to New York City. The year was 1890 when the release of 100 European Starlings into Central Park established the North American foothold for the species. This was not the first attempted introduction of the Starlings to North

America. There had been at least two previous introductions into New York City. This small flock soon began to flourish amongst the tall buildings of Gotham. Starlings have been noted as thriving with the presence of people since the earliest records. Aristotle mentioned tamed Starlings as mimicking human speech. Starlings probably began their relationship with mankind with the advent of agriculture. The birds are making a living off the waste grains, insects that are considered agricultural pests, and the crops themselves.

The European Starling has been detrimental to the population of native secondary cavity nesters. The more aggressive Starlings will take over a nesting cavity and exclude the native bird from it. The native birds affected include bluebirds and nuthatches.

From the original 100 birds in New York City, the European Starling undertook a rapid westward expansion. The flood of Starlings inundated the towns and farms of the Midwest where they solidified their reputation as agricultural pests. The massive flocks of Starlings can come into a farm and literally eat the farmer out of house and home. The Starlings continued their march to the Pacific throughout the first half of 20th century. The rapid spread of the European Starling was due in part to their ability to take of advantage of the foods provided by man, double brooding, earlier breeding of young adults. The European Starling was solidly entrenched in the Northern Rockies by the 1940's, and they arrived at the western terminus of the Pacific Ocean by 1950.

One native bird has made urban areas its preferred home, the House Finch. The House Finch has adapted to take advantage of towns for both nesting and feeding opportunities.

Other native birds have learned to visit the seed feeders provided by people. These species include chickadees and Pine Siskins. These seedeaters attract Sharp-shinned Hawks and Merlins into the towns and cities. The raptors can be seen perched menacingly on a nearby fence, eyeing the action of the small songbirds at your feeder.

Rock Dove

Columba livia

J F M A M J J A S O N D

R

Description: Pigeons. Who can think of a city park without imagining a flock of Rock Doves (13") eating breadcrumbs? This dove is quite variable in plumages; however, the most seen plumage is generally gray overall with a darker head. The rump is white and the tail ends with black band. The other birds range from all-white to individuals that have rufous coloration.

The Rock Dove or Pigeon

Feeding: Walking along the ground, the Rock Dove consumes mostly seeds. In urban areas, it has become accustomed to being fed bread or other human foods.

Habits: Very tolerant of humans, perhaps even dependent on them, the Rock Dove is usually found not far from people. It is very gregarious, feeding, roosting, and nesting in flocks.

Nest: During courtship, the males perform a wing-clapping flight where the wings are clapped loudly together and the bird descends with the wings held in a deep V. In a ledge, the female builds a loose saucer of sticks and grass. They both incubate the 2 unmarked white eggs for 16-19 days. Like all doves, the Rock Dove produces a "milk" in its digestive system, which is given to the offspring. The young fledge in 25-26 days. The Rock Dove can have several broods each year if conditions are favorable. It has been noted that the Rock Dove may nest year-round.

Voice: The *"coo"* of the Rock Dove is just as common as the honk of a car horn or someone answering a cell phone in our cities and towns.

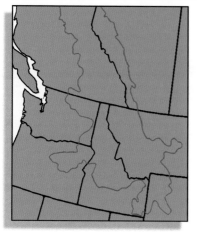

Primary Habitat Characteristics: Buildings are advantageous to Rock Dove nesting success. The Rock Dove will nest on top of buildings or on the ledges.

Other Habitats: Some populations of Rock Dove have regained their wild heritage. They nest on cliff faces often far from towns.

Conservation: Populations are apparently stable and generally abundant.

Fall and breeding (inset) plumage European Starling

Description: In an attempt to bring a little of England to the New World, the European Starling (8¹/₂") was introduced into New York City in 1890. This species comes into three unique plumages each year. In the breeding plumage, it is purplish-black with a yellow bill. The head is solid-colored and rest of the body has small light spots. After breeding, it molts into a fall plumage where the black feathers are all prominently tipped with white. During this time the bill is brownish. As the feathers wear, the white speckles become less and less noticeable. Juveniles are brown with a brown bill.

Feeding: European Starlings' diet changes throughout the year. During the warm months, they feed heavily upon all manner of insects and other invertebrates. With the onset of the chill of winter, they switch their diet to seeds and fruits. They forage in the ground and may even use their long, sharp bill to probe into softer soil.

Habits: They gather into truly spectacular flocks in the fall. These flocks can be seen undulating across the skyline. They will mimic other birds, especially raptors.

Nest: The unusual song of the male attracts the female. They are cavity nesters (old woodpecker holes or other crevices). The male starts the construction of the nest, which is a layer of stems, grass, and other materials placed in the bottom of the cavity, and the female finishes the building. The 4-7 pale blue eggs are incubated by both sexes for 12-14 days. The young fledge after 3 weeks of care.

Voice: The song of the European Starling, if you can call it a song, is a jumbled series of squawks, whistles, and the poorly imitated calls of other birds.

Primary Habitat Characteristics: Suburban areas provide many nest sites.

Other Habitats: European Starlings are abundant in agricultural fields during the autumn and even around garbage dumps.

Conservation: Extremely common.

House Finch   *Carpodacus mexicanus*

J F M A M J J A S O N D

R

Description: A native bird, the House Finch (6") has adapted well to the presence of man and his dwellings. The male has a red forehead and upper breast. The back is brown, save for the red rump patch. The belly is streaked. The red coloration can vary to orange to yellow. The female is a streaked brown overall. The undertail coverts of both sexes are streaked white.

Feeding: Seeds are the majority of the House Finch's diet, with berries and some vegetation making up the remainder. They feed mainly while on the ground; however, they do spend more time than the House Sparrow in the lower limbs.

Male House Finch

Habits: Easily adapts to humans and their buildings. Readily comes to feed, especially during the winter when it forms large foraging flocks.

Nest: The House Finch pairs while in its winter flocks. The males court by singing while in flight. The female builds a cup of twigs and grass lined with soft materials such as feathers or plant down. The nest is placed in a wide range of locations. She will incubate the 4-5 sometimes spotted pale blue eggs for 14 days. After they hatch, both sexes of the House Finch care for the young for about another two weeks. The House Finch will usually have multiple broods per year.

Voice: Song of the House Finch is a warbled series of three-note phrases that ends with a slurred *"zjeeer"*. The most common call note is a sharp *"wheat"*.

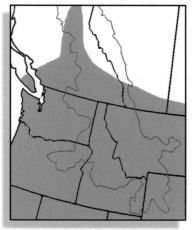

Primary Habitat Characteristics: Although the native habitat for the House Finch is shrublands, this bird is now more commonly associated with suburban areas.

Other Habitats: In agricultural areas with buildings, the House Finch does well with the abundance of waste grains to feed on.

Conservation: The House Finch's ability to utilize human-created habitats and accidental introductions has led to its range expansion across the Northern Rockies.

369

R

Male (l) and female (r) House Sparrow

Description: Since coming to this continent in the mid-1850's with an introduction into New York City, the House Sparrow (6¼") has done extraordinarily well. The male has a rich reddish-brown nape and a black bib and bill. The crown is gray. The underparts are gray and the rest of back is brown. The female has a buff eye-stripe and streaked back.

Feeding: The House Sparrow consumes mostly seeds from various plants and waste grains. It does most of its foraging while hopping along the ground; however, it will occasionally ascend the stalks of larger weeds for their seeds. It will eat a small amount of insects in addition to the seeds.

Habits: As the name implies, the House Sparrow is very much at home among people and their dwellings. They can be quite aggressive at feeders, pushing other birds aside.

Nest: During courtship, the male bounces in front of the female while puffing his chest out. The House Sparrow is a member of the Weaver Finch family, which is known for creating intricate pendulum nests. This species lacks this ability, however. Both sexes build the crude jumble of grass stalks and stems in a cavity or crevice. They both incubate the 3-6 gray-spotted white eggs for 10-13 days. The young leave the nest after another two weeks of parental care.

Voice: The song of the House Sparrow is a repeated series of *"chirdik"*.

Primary Habitat Characteristics: It is always found in and around buildings.

Other Habitats: It can occur in agricultural areas near buildings. It will feed heavily upon waste grains in these farms.

Conservation: Since its introduction to New York in the mid-1850's, the House Sparrow has colonized the entire contiguous United States and the southern tier of Canada.

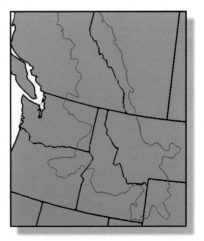

Of Birds and Men:
A Short History of Humans & Birds

People have always been fascinated with a bird in flight, the freedom they must experience while gliding effortlessly on unseen columns of rising air. They can travel, in a matter of minutes, distances that would take a man hours or days to cover.

As the earliest forms of humans walk upon the African plains, it is very likely that they spent much of their time scavenging. The protein from of this behavior allowed for the larger brain capacity. Vultures circling over a carcass may have alerted the hominids to the presence of the meat-rich meal. Our ancestors also probably hunted for the eggs of nesting birds, which is a meal that provides great nutrition at relatively little energy cost.

Birds must have been particularly interesting to early people who had not figured out the physics of flight. They must have seemed to be magical beasts with the abilities of wizardry. Many legends developed about the flying creatures.

As civilization gained its foothold along the banks of the Nile River, the importance of birds to the early Egyptian religion was reflected in their creation myth. They believed that at the beginning of time everything was devoid of light, a concept called Nun. From this darkness, the creator god, Atum, emerged in the form of a heron called Bennu. Bennu flew to the future site of the ancient city of Heliopolis, which is near modern-day Cairo. He alighted upon a stone that received the first-ever rays of sunlight. Atop this structure, Bennu built a nest of aromatic plants and spices. The nest burst into flames and consumed Bennu. Bennu then sprang back to life. Bennu was the phoenix of ancient Egypt.

The people of the New World developed many myths and traditions centered around birds and their meanings to people. They used birds in their folklore to explain the world around them and to teach moral lessons. Traditions were developed in which family or clans were associated with particular animals, including birds.

The Inuit of the Arctic believe that the raven is responsible for the creation of the world. It was the time when there were no people on the face of the earth. For four

days the first man lay in the pod of a beach pea. On the fifth, he burst forth, falling to the ground, and stood up, a full-frown man. Feeling unpleasant, he stooped and drank from a pool of water, then felt better. Looking up, he saw a dark object approaching with a waving motion until it stopped just in front of him. It was a raven. Raven stared intently at man, raised one wing, and pushed up his beak, like a mask, to the top of his head, and changed immediately into a man. Still staring and cocking his head from side to side for a better view, Raven said at last: "What are you? Whence did you come? I have never seen the likes of you." And Raven looked at man, surprised to see that this stranger was so much like himself in shape. This story comes from E.W. Nelson in 1899.

Birds also had a utilitarian value to people throughout history. The most obvious of these values is the use of birds for meat and eggs. Birds were among the earliest animals to become domesticated. Among the species tamed by man were peafowl, chickens, and pigeons.

Another group of birds that become domesticated were the raptors. Domesticated may not be the right word, but they learned to work in partnership with man. Falconry has a history that dates back to earliest written recordings. Falconry is represented on bas-reliefs from the Assyrians of the seventh century B.C. It is known that the early Emperors of China from 200 B.C. enjoyed falconry as a leisure activity. The sport probably originated in the region of Persia and Arabia.

As trade increased from Europe and the Far East, the sport of falconry was carried to the far reaches of the known world. It is believed to have reached Europe by about 400 A.D. The sport reached its zenith from 500 to 1600 A.D. It was once considered the sport of wealth and royalty, but with the march of time it became a past time enjoyed by people of all socio-economic classes. It was even considered a fashionable fad in Medieval Europe. The clergy was one class that took a particular interest in the hunting of birds with falcons. Pope Leo X was an avid falconer as were many of his bishops and priests. It became so entrenched into the culture of Europe that there were laws stating

which class could use which raptor for hunting. The following list comes from The Boke of St. Albans, written by Dame Juliana Barnes.

- Emperor — Golden Eagle, Vulture, & Merlin
- King — Gyrfalcon (male & female)
- Prince — Female Peregrine
- Duke — Rock Falcon (subspecies of the Peregrine)
- Earl — Peregrine
- Baron — Male peregrine
- Knight — Saker
- Squire — Lanner Falcon
- Lady — Female Merlin
- Yeoman — Goshawk or Hobby
- Priest — Female Sparrowhawk
- Holywater clerk — Male Sparrowhawk
- Knaves, Servants, Children — Old World Kestrel

At the end of the 16th century, falconry declined greatly in popularity. A new pastime centered on the birds began to take over. The first prominent example of a birdwatcher was a man named John James Audubon.

He was born in 1785 on the island of Hispaniola. Audubon was quite talented in illustrating the natural world. His seminal work *Birds of America* was the benchmark for illustrations of birds in North America. Audubon explored North America in an effort to observe as many of the continent's birds as possible. His interests also included the mammals of North America, which were chronicled in *The Quadrupeds of America.*

Since Audubon's passing in 1851, the popularity of the pastime of birdwatching has continued to increase, and passion for birding similarly increased. What's the difference between a birdwatcher and birder? The birdwatcher is someone who appreciates birds and enjoys their company, the birder is a fanatic who lives and breathes birds in all aspects of their lives. Basically, birders are obsessed, and birdwatchers are somewhat normal. Birding has been one of the fastest growing outdoor activities in North America over the past few decades, and as more people become involved in birding, the greater the number of voices speaking for preserving habitat and conserving wild bird population.

Pectoral Sandpiper

Transients and Rarities

American Black Duck
American Golden-Plover
American Woodcock
Ancient Murrelet
Anna's Hummingbird
Arctic Tern
Ash-throated Flycatcher
Baltimore Oriole
Band-tailed Pigeon
Bay-breasted Warbler
Bewick's Wren
Black Scoter
Black-and-white Warbler
Black-bellied Plover
Black-legged Kittiwake
Black-throated Blue Warbler
Black-throated Gray Warbler
Black-throated Green Warbler
Black-throated Sparrow
Blackburnian Warbler
Blue Grosbeak
Canada Warbler
Cape May Warbler
Cassin's Kingbird
Cattle Egret
Chestnut-sided Warbler
Chimney Swift
Common Moorhen
Connecticut Warbler
Costa's Hummingbird
Curlew Sandpiper
Dickcissel
Dunlin
Eastern Bluebird
Eastern Phoebe
Eastern Wood-Pewee
Eurasian Collared-Dove
Eurasian Wigeon
Garganey

Glaucous Gull
Glaucous-winged Gull
Golden-winged Warbler
Gray Flycatcher
Gray-cheeked Thrush
Great Crested Flycatcher
Greater Scaup
Green Heron
Harris's Sparrow
Hooded Oriole
Hooded Warbler
Hudsonian Godwit
Iceland Gull
Indigo Bunting
Interior Least Tern
Ivory Gull
Kentucky Warbler
Laughing Gull
Least Bittern
Lesser Goldfinch
Little Blue Heron
Little Gull
Long-tailed Duck
Long-tailed Jaeger
Marbled Murrelet
Mew Gull
Mississippi Kite
Mourning Warbler
Mute Swan
Nelson's Sharp-tailed Sparrow
Northern Bobwhite
Northern Cardinal
Northern Mockingbird
Northern Parula
Orchard Oriole
Pacific Loon
Painted Redstart
Palm Warbler
Parasitic Jaeger

Philadelphia Vireo
Pine Warbler
Piping Plover
Pomarine Jaeger
Prairie Warbler
Prothonotary Warbler
Purple Martin
Red Knot
Red Phalarope
Red-bellied Woodpecker
Red-shouldered Hawk
Red-throated Loon
Rose-breasted Grosbeak
Ruby-throated Hummingbird
Ruddy Turnstone
Rusty Blackbird
Sabine's Gull
Sanderling
Scarlet Tanager
Scissor-tailed Flycatcher
Sedge Wren
Semipalmated Plover
Sharp-tailed Sandpiper
Short-billed Dowitcher
Smith's Longspur
Snowy Plover
Stilt Sandpiper
Summer Tanager
Surf Scoter
Swamp Sparrow
Thayer's Gull
Tufted Duck
Western Scrub-Jay
Whimbrel
Whip-poor-will
White-rumped Sandpiper
White-throated Sparrow
White-winged Dove
White-winged Scoter
Wood Stork
Wood Thrush
Yellow Rail
Yellow-bellied Flycatcher
Yellow-bellied Sapsucker
Yellow-billed Cuckoo
Yellow-billed Loon
Yellow-crowned Night-Heron
Yellow-throated Warbler

Organizations helping birdlife in the Rockies

Greater Yellowstone Coalition
P.O. Box 1874
Bozeman, MT 59771
http://www.greateryellowstone.org

Montana Audubon
P.O. Box 595
Helena, MT 59624
http://www.mtaudubon.org

Montana Raptor Conservation Center
P.O. Box 4061
Bozeman, MT 59772
http://btc.montana.edu/bsw/

Ninepipes Wildlife Research Center
P.O. Box 39
Charlo, MT 59824
http://www.owlinstitute.org

Raptors of the Rockies
P.O. Box 250
Florence, MT 59833
http://www.raptorsoftherockies.org

Wyoming Audubon
400 East 1st Street
Casper, WY 82601

Common Name Index